Conservatism

International Library of Sociology

Founded by Karl Mannheim

Editor: John Rex, University of
Aston in Birmingham

Arbor Scientiae
Arbor Vitae

A catalogue of the books available in the **International Library of Sociology** and
other series of Social Science books published by Routledge & Kegan Paul will be
found at the end of this volume.

Conservatism

A Contribution to the Sociology of Knowledge

by

Karl Mannheim

Edited and introduced by
David Kettler, Volker Meja and Nico Stehr

Translated by
David Kettler and Volker Meja
from a first draft by Elizabeth R. King

Routledge & Kegan Paul
London and New York

First published in 1986
by Routledge & Kegan Paul plc

11 New Fetter Lane, London EC4P 4EE

Published in the USA by
Routledge & Kegan Paul Inc.
in association with Methuen Inc.
29 West 35th Street, New York, NY 10001

Set in 10 on 11 point Times
by Fontwise
and printed in Great Britain
by Thetford Press Ltd,
Thetford, Norfolk

Library of Congress Cataloging in Publication Data

Mannheim, Karl, 1893–1947.
Conservatism.

(International library of sociology)
Bibliography: p.
Includes index.
1. Knowledge, Sociology of. 2. Conservatism.
I. Kettler, David. II. Meja, Volker. III. Stehr, Nico.
IV. Title. V. Series.
BD175.M31513   1986   306'.42   85–19354

British Library CIP data also available

ISBN 0–7102–0338–1

Contents

Acknowledgements

The present edition of *Conservatism* rests on a typescript of the text found among the papers, after his death in 1980, of Paul Kecskemeti, who played an important role in the posthumous publication of several works of Mannheim. We are grateful to Kurt H. Wolff (Brandeis University) and to Martin Rein (M.I.T.) for gaining us access to Kecskemeti's papers. The unedited German typescript has been deposited, together with other papers left by Kecskemeti, at the Brandeis University Library in Waltham, Massachusetts. The original text has been published by the present editors in German, under the title *Konservatismus: Ein Beitrag zur Soziologie des Wissens* (Frankfurt: Suhrkamp, 1984).

The editorial and translation work on this book as well as the research on our introduction was financially supported by the Memorial University of Newfoundland, Trent University, the University of Alberta and the Social Sciences and Humanities Research Council of Canada. We have benefited from the help of Juan E. Corradi (New York), Joseph Gabel (Paris), Éva Gábor (Budapest), Ingrid Gilcher (Heidelberg), M. Rainer Lepsius (Heidelberg), A. P. Simonds (Boston), and Henk Woldring (Amsterdam). We are, as always, very grateful to Laura C. Hargrave for her efforts in readying the manuscript for publication.

David Kettler
Trent University

Volker Meja
Memorial University of Newfoundland

Nico Stehr
University of Alberta

David Kettler, Volker Meja and Nico Stehr
Introduction: The design of *Conservatism*[1]

The historian of science, Thomas S. Kuhn, has argued that new developments in science are more decisively influenced by exemplary empirical studies than they are by exclusively theoretical reflections. If Karl Mannheim's *Ideology and Utopia*[2] and *Structures of Thinking*[3] represent his important theoretical exercises, the essay on 'Conservative Thought'[4] has more commonly been taken as paradigmatic for a strictly empirical sociology of knowledge. Many social scientists and historians, who are not wholly satisfied with Mannheim's attempts to work out the theoretical presuppositions and the implications of the discipline he helped to initiate, acknowledge Mannheim's inquiry into conservatism as a decisive influence in the scientific enterprise of showing the social roots of complex intellectual structures.

The text which has had such influence represents little more than one-half of the work which led to Mannheim's *Habilitationsschrift* in Heidelberg in 1925. Considerably more than half of the original was omitted when 'Das konservative Denken' was published two years later in the *Archiv für Sozialwissenschaft und Sozialpolitik*. But Mannheim showed that he continued to value more of it when he sought to incorporate additional parts of the manuscript while preparing the text for English publication late in his life. This project, like so many others, was interrupted by his premature death and completed by his executors. The full text, only recently discovered, clarifies the relationship between Mannheim's study of conservatism and the rest of his achievement, because it helps to explain the considerations which led Mannheim to pursue the parallel lines of sociological explorations, as empirically sound as he could make them, and philosophical reflections, speculatively probing such claims as the one which

1

represents sociology of knowledge as the 'organon for politics as a science'.

The shortened published versions bring out one of the levels of the complex study, as Mannheim quite probably wanted them to do. As the essay has appeared in the past, in English as well as in German, it has quite reasonably been taken as an empirical study of the social factors underlying the formation and development of a certain pattern of political belief. And the model of inquiry abstracted from this example has since been considerably refined, both with regard to the ways in which the patterns to be explained are delineated and with regard to the specification and substantiation of the sociological imputations involved. But as the work was written, it also manifests Mannheim's preoccupation with the nature of political *knowledge*, not belief alone, and his continuing hope that modes of scientific inquiry can serve as the way to such knowledge without sacrificing scientific devotion to evidence or disinterestedness. What is at issue in the new reading made possible by the discovery of the complete text is not a falsification of accepted interpretations, but the recognition of an additional dimension, more problematical and philosophically ambitious, and indicative of the uneasiness with which Mannheim subjected himself to that scientific asceticism which Weber promulgated.

Mannheim's empirical turn

The idea behind Mannheim's study of conservative thought is that the enduring distinction between natural and historical sciences as well as the most influential approaches contesting the second of these domains have their historical progenitors in the conservative movement of nineteenth-century Germany. In his analysis here, he proceeds in three stages: the first is based on the social history of ideas, the second on a morphological explication, and the third involves an historical interweaving of textual and sociological interpretations.

First, then, Mannheim tries to account for the central place which political ideology, as a distinctive kind of cultural formation, comes to assume in the spiritual ordering of human experience during the eighteenth and nineteenth centuries. On this basis, he considers how it happened that a world-view centered on the political ideas of conservatives gained prominence after the French Revolution. In making the clash of political convictions central to the organisation of world-views, Mannheim changes the more idealistic theory he had earlier developed on the basis of reflections on art history, adding consideration of conflict and structural changes. The explanation for the new ideological world and for the place of conservatism within it emphasises the effects of the dual process of state formation and comprehensive rationalisation. Conservatism crystallises out of the psychological attitude of traditionalism among social actors (and some observers) who experience these new developments as harmful, but cannot ignore them or simply respond in private, individual ways. Ideologies comprise the orienting mode appropriate to the newly rationalised state-centred societies, displacing traditional and religious ways of assigning meanings to the experienced world. Conservatism appears, in Mannheim's first account of it, as a way of thinking about 'man and society', which gives weight to certain spiritual as well as material interests damaged by rationalisation but provides a practical orientation with a measure of effectiveness in the newly politicised and rationalised world. It thus clearly belongs to the new time, like its opponents.

Mannheim's second characterisation of conservatism seeks to explicate an inner structure common to the diverse and changing manifestations of this ideology. Such a 'morphology', Mannheim stresses, must not confuse what he himself calls a 'style of thought' with either a theoretical system or a political program. The structural analysis to be done requires a distinctive method, adequate to this distinctive kind of object. This method uncovers a characteristic formative attitude towards human experience in conservative thought, as it exists prior to any theoretical elaboration, a rootedness in concrete experience and in particular locales, as well as a special sense of continuities in time. At a more theoretical level, then, conservative thought stands against all constructions of human relationships which take them as governed by rationalistic universal norms, such as is found in Enlightenment doctrines of natural law. Although Mannheim briefly contrasts liberal and conservative concepts of property and freedom, he is much less interested in the conservative political creed than he is in the thematic emphases and methods of thinking which he considers constitutive of the conservative 'style'.

Mannheim's third and most ambitious level of analysis traces a part of the formative history of conservatism, with the aim of distinguishing decisive stages and variations in its development and showing empirically how the sociological and morphological attributes uncovered in the first two treatments interact to shape an historical style and movement. In an introductory overview, Mannheim projects eight stages for this development, but he only writes about two in any detail. In the more finished of the completed sections, he draws on the writings of Justus Möser (1720–1794) and Adam Müller (1779–1829) to present a form of conservatism in which the political perspective of 'estates' hostile to the modern bureaucratic or liberal state acts upon the Romantic thinking which originated among the preachers' sons who form the new post-Enlightenment intelligentsia. The second historical analysis deals with Savigny (1779–1861), foremost exponent of historical jurisprudence, whose work is explained as embodying the fastidiousness with which an officialdom having aristocratic connections reacted against schemes of universal codes or universal rights. The ingenuity with which Mannheim works out this analysis, without reductionism of the ideas or arbitrary sociological imputations, has led many sociologists to consider the work on conservative thought as his outstanding achievement, as a paradigm for empirical research into the social genealogy of political beliefs.

All of Mannheim's subjects are jurists, but legal issues as such do not interest him here any more than in his other writings. His concern is rather with contrasting conceptions and methods of knowledge, with intellectual strategies alternative to the abstract logical systematisations Mannheim identifies with natural science, capitalism, state-formation, and other aspects of the pervasive process of rationalisation.

While the social and political sources and uses of these strategies help to specify and to map them, these aspects do not in Mannheim's judgment exhaust their significance. And the study constantly comes back to this wider significance, and especially to its bearing on an interpretation of the intellectual situation in his own time. In this connection, then, it is remarkable and regrettable that Mannheim abruptly ended the text after the account of the second historical stage, since so much of the discussion looks ahead to the undone section of Hegel, whom Mannheim presents as representative of a conservative standpoint with particularly telling ramifications, including recent adaptations in socialist thought by such followers of Marx as Georg Lukács. Mannheim nevertheless says enough to make clear his belief that conservative thinking somehow enters into the most recent manifestations of opposition to the predominance of natural science models in intellectual life and liberal-capitalist rationalisations in social knowledge. Yet *Conservatism* does not elaborate this wider suggestion. On its face, the work asks its readers to take it above all as a disinterested study integrating sociological and morphological approaches for the limited purpose of presenting conservatism as a structure of thinking.

Mannheim's study of conservatism is in fact unique among his works. Modest in its explicit theoretical claims, it presents itself as a monographic product of the sociology of knowledge, a new academic specialty. None of his other investigations concentrates so exclusively on materials from the past or attends so discriminatingly to the ideas of particular thinkers. In the introductory remarks on method, moreover, Mannheim treats the great methodological controversies of the time, which he subjects elsewhere to controversial handling, with diplomatic tact. If anything, he inclines here towards an empirical and explanatory approach, stressing the need for the new discipline to uncover causal linkages between cognitive and social phenomena and warning against the propensity to rest content with interpretive elucidations of congruencies among meanings. These characteristics of the study, given special prominence in the shortened versions published by Mannheim and his later editors, have led numerous commentators who are otherwise critical of Mannheim's design for a sociology of knowledge, to single out the essay on 'Conservative Thought' as a sociological contribution unspoiled by what they take to be misleading philosophical pretensions in some of his other writings.[5]

It is surprising that Mannheim should have composed such a work at this point in his intellectual development. The manuscript was submitted under the title *Altkonservatismus* to the Heidelberg Faculty of Philosophy in December 1925, in the midst of a period of great productivity, which also saw the completion of such major published essays as those on 'Historicism'[6] and 'The Problem of a Sociology of Knowledge', as well as the ambitious 'A Sociological Theory of Culture and its Knowability (Conjunctive and Communicative Thinking)', written in 1924. In all of these studies, empirical and explanatory inquiries are subordinate to an overarching search for a philosophy of history. In all of them, moreover, Mannheim admires Georg Lukács' *History and Class-Consciousness*,[7] and finds in Lukács' Hegelian reading of Marxism important directions for his own intellectual course. While Mannheim never accepted Lukács' Communist political teachings or the Marxist projection of socialist revolution as the culmination of class struggle, he was intrigued by Lukács' notion of theorising as integral to practical intervention in the social world, serving to undermine the reifications inhibiting social development by exposing their sources and functions within a complex totality, helping to constitute the social actors destined to carry development further, and thus contributing to the 'next step'. The sociological interpretation of the understandings which collective social actors take to be social knowledge belongs, according to Mannheim, to this class of theoretical activity and leads to the theoretical understanding of the historical totality, in Lukács' sense. But how can a monograph intending to deal dispassionately with German conservatism in the first half of the nineteenth century fit into such a scheme?

A 'value-free' treatment of the ideas, in any case, would appear to abandon the critical implications in this 'historicism', as Mannheim was conceiving it in his other writings of the time. The question of assessing the validity of the social knowledge cannot, on this view, be separated from the work of historical interpretation itself. If the ultimate reality of things is comprehended by the philosophy of history and if a sociological reading of knowledge claims enables us to specify their localised connectedness with that historical reality, to show the range and limits of their comprehension, critical judgment inheres in sociology of knowledge. There may be some work for philosophy in explicating the logic applied in such assessments, but there could be no distinctive process of autonomous evaluation because there is no autonomous domain of validity within which it could operate. In *Conservatism*, Mannheim reverted to the position he took in his doctoral dissertation on epistemology, which he first wrote in Hungarian in 1917 but published in German'[8] and in 'The Distinctive Character of Cultural Sociological Knowledge',[9] written in 1921. There he had argued quite the opposite case, contending that an account of the social genesis of any cultural entity cannot logically imply judgments concerning its validity because such judgments must meet the cultural product on its own terms. But the thoroughness with which Mannheim had put these earlier views aside during the years of *Conservatism* can be epitomised by noting a terminological shift he made when adapting a section of his 1921 methodological study for publication in 1926. The section on '*Immanent* and Genetic Interpretations', which is followed in the older work by an exposé of the genetic fallacy in Marx's formulation of the relationship between material base and ideological superstructure,[10] appears revised in the later one as 'The *Ideological* and the Sociological Interpretation of Intellectual Phenomena',[11] with the term 'ideological' being employed with quite the Marxist critical connotation. The finality of this change, despite some equivocations in the text, must make us wonder about a major work prepared at the same time which claims to leave questions concerning the evaluation of the thought it is interpreting to a different kind of discourse.

Establishing a career

To account for such puzzling features of Mannheim's study,[12] it may be useful to begin with his situation at the time of composition. Mannheim was a Jew, an Hungarian, and a political refugee, having fled Budapest at the collapse of the Béla Kun Soviet regime. With this study, he was seeking to fulfil the crucial requirement for certification as a teacher at the University of Heidelberg, where he had been in residence as a private scholar since 1921. Those records of the deliberations on his application which have been preserved, indicate attitudes which could not have been unknown to him and which may well have influenced him to be rather cautious about stating all of his views in this text.

The written work itself was quickly endorsed by the Faculty, on the enthusiastic recommendations of the sociologists Emil Lederer and Alfred Weber. But the Inner Senate of the University, upon receiving the Faculty's favourable recommendation, queried whether Mannheim should not be first required to secure German citizenship. In the reply to the Inner Senate, the Faculty stated that Mannheim's extensive publications had all appeared in German, that his mother had been a *Reichsdeutsche* and had relatives serving as German 'officials, judges, and officers', and that Mannheim himself was well known even outside his own faculty. The letter continues:

> The representatives of the discipline have repeatedly and at length given the Faculty altogether reassuring accounts of the personality of Dr. Mannheim, as a man who has never exposed himself politically in the past and who will not, to judge by his entire attitude and all his inclinations, ever do so in the future. Mr. Lederer and Mr. Weber have personally vouched for this last point in particular, in protocolled statements.[13]

Several points must have been awkward. Contrary to the statement of the Faculty, Mannheim had indeed begun to establish himself as a publicist in his native Hungarian.[14] His writings even include two literary letters characterising the narrowness of Heidelberg,[15] and he had uncharacteristically claimed as late as 1924 to be a genuine political exile from Hungary, and had proudly argued that there is a marked difference between those forced to stay away because of their perhaps thoughtless involvement in the revolutionary Kun regime and those like himself who stay away in principled protest against the oppressive Horty regime. Voluntary exile like his own, he had observed, 'has an important national purpose: it saves and keeps alive the free spirit of the Hungarian mind, and it awakens the conscience of the Hungarian people'.[16]

These details indicate that Mannheim must have subjected himself to self-denial in several respects in order to make good the guarantees of political attitude given by his sponsors. In the event, their efforts on his behalf succeeded, and the Inner Senate, by a narrow vote of six to four, approved his licensing as *Privatdozent* in May of 1926. The naturalisation, on the other hand, dragged on for years; and the records of the time cite instructive objections from ministries in Württemberg and Bavaria, opposing the grant of citizenship to such 'foreign bodies', 'alien in culture'.[17]

The character of the interplay between Mannheim and his sponsors while he was writing on conservatism can of course only be matter for conjecture and inference from later events. One interesting indication concerns Alfred Weber. He had high regard for Mannheim, welcoming him to his seminar and encouraging him in many ways. But the transcript of the discussion following Mannheim's well-received presentation at the 1928 Congress of German Sociologists shows that Weber was quick to attack Mannheim in public when he thought that Mannheim had strayed too close to Marxism. And the transcript also shows that Lederer was equally quick to leap to Mannheim's defense, and to lead him to disavowals on this score.[18] Mannheim's students admired his courage because he began his career as *Privatdozent* at the University of Heidelberg with a year-long seminar on Georg Lukács' Marxist writings, but there is nevertheless reason to suppose that as applicant for that certificate he distanced himself from those preoccupations, constrained to caution by his own ambition as well as out of consideration for his supporters. A few years later, Mannheim emphasised the intimate connections between conservatism and the German univerisities.[19] His study of conservatism, in its methods and contents as well as tactful omissions, appears to respect that relationship.

Intellectual experiments

Despite the undoubted relevance of these circumstances to an understanding of *Conservatism*, a reduction of Mannheim's design to a piece of biography would give a narrow and misleading reading of it. Mannheim himself, as interpreter, confronts a similar problem about the interrelationships between motives inferrable from external circumstances and the characteristics of serious writing when he discusses the incentives inclining Adam Müller to give a polemical anti-liberal emphasis to the lectures he delivered to the court of Sachsen-Weimar. Mannheim maintains that the evidence about Müller's probable motives adds empirical weight to judgments about intellectual and social affinities between Müller and the anti-liberal aristocracy which are evident in the intellectual structure of the text itself, and he implies that the meaning and effect of those affinities must be sought by explicating the thought and not simply by researching motivating interests.

Similarly, it is important to inquire into Mannheim's affinities with the world to which he was seeking admission. When he first arrived in Heidelberg, he stated a contrast which helps to explain the commitment to the university which made him dependent on its approval: 'On one side is the university, on the other the boundless literary world'.[20] To understand what Mannheim was seeking within the university and the academic discipline of sociology and how conservative thinking relates to this search, it is necessary to look at the work more carefully and to place it less crudely in the context of his larger intellectual undertaking.

Mannheim's earliest writings lay out a project which he never relinquished. The task for his generation, he claims, is to acknowledge the findings of the preceding one, that cultural and social history are constitutive of social experience and social knowledge, and then to transform that acknowledgement itself into the starting point for a way beyond the reductionism and relativism bound up with 'historicism'.[21] In the philosophical language of the time, he speaks of the need for an ontology to transcend the cultural and social crisis attending historical deconstruction of the certainties guaranteed by the old epistemology. Apart from incidental enthusiasms for Dostoyevsky and German mystics, he is attracted to two alternative ways towards such an accomplishment. One involves some method for factoring out the social dimensions in the constitution of the relationships between the knower and the known, along lines suggested to philosophically minded publics by Husserl and Heidegger. This is the possibility Mannheim explores in the writings which distinguish sharply between social analysis and immanent assessment of cultural objects, but at the same time present the former as necessary prolegomenon to the latter. The other way counts upon the possibility of uncovering a philosophy of history that can ground a dynamic understanding of what is becoming and must be, and how it can be known. This is the promise Mannheim saw in his admired mentor, Georg Lukács, both before and after Lukács' turn to the source Mannheim often referred to as 'Hegel-Marx'.[22] Although it is the second of these possibilities that seems most attractive to him around the time of *Conservatism*, there are several considerations which lead him to keep the other way open, and, indeed, to remain alert to additional possibilities.

Mannheim consistently professed to value such openness in itself. This commitment is implicit in his rationales for publishing collections of essays rather than systematic works. In 1928, for example, Mannheim arranged the publication of his two essays on

'Historicism' and 'The Problem of a Sociology of Knowledge' together with a new essay on Max Weber in book form.[23] When the publisher, Paul Siebeck, asks Mannheim to rework the two previously published essays, so as to make a more novel and integrated whole, Mannheim replies:

> As for the reworking of the two other essays, this could not be radical in any case, if only because these works represent a searching, experimenting penetration of the contemporary intellectual condition; and the author's changes in position, his intellectual adventures, must not be covered over.[24]

In both the German and the English versions of *Ideology and Utopia*, Mannheim insists that the constituent essays must be accepted as distinct and overlapping experiments. In a letter to Wirth, indignantly refuting the critical review of *Ideology and Utopia* by Alexander von Schelting in the *American Sociological Review*, Mannheim protests that von Schelting

> suppresses the fact that the author expressly says that he is on the search, that a number of systems are at work in a single human being, and that therefore he himself – relying on the new method of 'experimental thinking' – does not cover over the inconsistencies that arise.[25]

Curiously enough, openness also provides the main theme for a dramatic effort by Mannheim, written in German in 1920. At the denouement of the one-act play, *Die Dame aus Biarritz*, it turns out that the main protagonist, an artist, has been paradoxically deceiving his wife by *not* deceiving her during his annual visits to a beloved supposed to be in Biarritz. Amid suffocating clouds of earnest pipe-smoke and Nietzscheian declamation, the hero insists that his story of a distant beloved was necessary in order to preserve the distance between himself and his wife and within himself, which is required to keep possibilities open:[26]

> 'I have discovered the puzzle, posed the question: Man is only one of his own possibilities; the others lie buried in us. I want to dismantle it all in myself; one must destroy and not cling to the self-enclosed day.
> The way leads far behind us, and away from the fixed forms.'

Taken by itself, such vitalist pathos reveals little. Put together with Mannheim's lifelong insistence that his work must be allowed to explore incompatible possibilities, however, it indicates a profound conviction, or at least a deeply rooted fantasy.

Finally, between the text and the notes to the manuscript of *Conservatism*, as it appears to have been submitted to the Faculty,

Mannheim introduces a page which repeats a similar theme: 'The present work is only part of a still incomplete book; many an unevenness in exposition and treatment may be excused by this fact.'[27]

As this record indicates, Mannheim had a strong sense of his intellectual activity as a continuing and unfinished series of experiments, but he sought to put the rhetorical antinomianism of the play behind him, and to establish the legitimacy, rigour and internal coherence of each of the subsequent experiments. Mannheim consequently attached special importance to the constraining framework of the university and its academic disciplines. He accepted the challenge of pursuing his large quest by way of an exercise within set limits and attempted to establish the matters vital to him in a manner acceptable to the judgment at Heidelberg. In one respect, as will become clear, there was a breakdown; but the design is both interesting and clear.

Social roots: explanation and justification

Mannheim's other writings at the time of *Conservatism* claim that historicism, in the sense of philosophy of history, is the way in which his contemporaries are working their way through the crisis in thought and culture. But this historicism is also intellectually suspect, in the light of its popularisation by Spengler[28] and others of his kind and of its association with Marxism. *Conservatism* sets forth several vital connections between this historicism and the old conservative style of thought and undertakes to show that conservatism has its roots in strata hostile to capitalist and liberal rationalism. The account is not cast as an exposé of ideology, in the manner of Marxist criticism or of Mannheim's own emphasis elsewhere on the relativising effects of such interpretations. It is better taken as showing the groundedness of historicism, providing a conservative legitimation for even such varieties of 'dynamic' thinking as the Marxism of Lukács. Phenomena treated by conservative critics as rootless and disruptive are presented by Mannheim as heirs of German conservatism, with a claim to legitimacy. Although value-neutral in the sight of Weberian social science, Mannheim's treatment gives substantial support to the phenomena whose genealogy it uncovers, when viewed with conservative eyes. This form of irony is a recurrent feature in Mannheim's writings of the time: his studies of methods in the sociology of culture[29] both announce that they have been employing the methods being studied to constitute the studies, and his essay on the problem of a sociology of knowledge[30] confidently lays claim to the same reflective move.

Mannheim's awareness of the positive sense attached to a showing of social roots in conservative thought and his own experimenting with that sense are expressed very dramatically in one terminological choice, involving a concept central to his whole subsequent approach. Throughout his work on sociology of knowledge, Mannheim uses two similar terms, usually interchangeably, to stand for the quality common to all the thought he subjects to sociological interpretation. In German, he speaks of '*Seinsgebundenheit*' and '*Seinsverbundenheit*'. These have been difficult for commentators and translators, especially in connection with one passage in a later methodological discussion, where Mannheim differentiates between them without adequate explanation.[31] Before discussing Mannheim's significant special use of the second of these terms in *Conservatism*, its general place in his writings should be clarified. *Seinsgebundenheit*, then, refers to an objective and comparatively strict linkage between the conditions under which thought exists in the world and the makeup of the thought itself; *Seinsverbundenheit* also expresses such linkage, but takes it more nearly as a function of the subjective commitments and identifications of those who bear the thought in society, and accordingly as less firmly fixed. This suggestion takes up distinctions between secondary connotations of the two terms, with the former approaching to causal determination in one of its senses and the latter being used more often for spiritual connections and family ties. Another way of putting the contrast, close to Mannheim's thinking at the time, would consider the more binding tie, *Seinsgebundenheit*, as a reified form of the connectedness comprehended by *Seinsverbundenheit*. That formulation helps most with the passage, first published in 1931, in which Mannheim plays the terms off against one another:

> The direction of research in the sociology of knowledge may be guided in such a way that it does not lead to an absolutising of the connectedness to existence (*Seinsverbundenheit*) but that precisely in the discovery of the existential connectedness of present insights, a first step towards the resolution of existential bondedness (*Seinsgebundenheit*) is seen.[32]

In any case, the terms are ordinarily very close in Mannheim. Both refer to that intimate tie between the social qualities of thinkers and the characteristics of thought which the sociology of knowledge is to explicate, while avoiding a specification of the exact logical status of the connection.

In *Conservatism*, Mannheim introduces the expression '*seins-*

verbundenes Denken' in his discussion of the conservative jurist, Savigny, to designate the more conservative of two types of legal thinking. The distinction between these two types assumes special importance because it follows so closely the distinction between 'communicative' and 'conjunctive' thinking which Mannheim had made central to his own most ambitious earlier attempts to explain cultural sociology.[33] Here, Mannheim is ascribing it to Savigny's legal thought. One type of thinking, then, is called 'abstract thinking, detached from the organic' and is said to operate with rigorous definitions and to be restricted to mere elaborations of form. The distinguishing characteristic of the other is, 'that the knowing subject must be existentially rooted in the community in which the living, always changing law is to be found'.[34]

Mannheim thus establishes a terminological association between the ultimate origination of modern historicism in the conservative movement against rationalisation and the type of thinking integral to the life of a community, honorifically characterised. Both are conceived as displaying the quality of being rooted in concrete existence, in contrast to strictly definable, logically systematised formal abstractions. The same design is evident in the connotation which Mannheim attaches to the notion of 'socially unattached intellectuals' (*sozial freischwebende Intelligenz*) in *Conservatism*. The best known uses of this expression occur in the essay on politics as a science which is at the theoretical core of *Ideology and Utopia*; and there it characterises a social stratum said to have a decisive role, by virtue of its unique capabilities for openness and choice, in generating a synthesis out of incompatible ideologies and thus making possible an effective practical way out of crisis. In the present work, however, the qualities associated with this social position appear more ambiguous. The difference is shaped through nuances and amounts to a far more ironic view of intellectuals.

Mannheim introduces the expression 'socially unattached intellectuals' in *Conservatism* to identify the proponents of romanticism, but quickly notes that the same social formation had also promulgated Enlightenment thought and then goes on to claim that such intellectuals have continuously been caretakers of the world of the spirit since the eighteenth century. As long as they stayed with the Enlightenment, he maintains, they kept up a connection with the bourgeois class from which most of them sprang, but when they reacted against rationalism, impelled by ideal reasons alone, it seems, they found themselves in 'sociological as well as metaphysical alienation and isolation'.[35] Only then did the intellectuals display the full mix of qualities essential to this social entity, above all 'an extraordinary sensitivity combined with moral unsteadiness, a constant readiness for adventure and obscurantism'.[36] 'These unattached intellectuals,' Mannheim also observes, 'are the archetypical apologists, "ideologists" who are masters at providing a basis and backing for the political designs whose service they enter, whatever these may be.'[37]

On the other hand, according to Mannheim, this stratum is also the locus of phiolosophical reflection on history and comprehensive reading of the times, initiating in its romantic phase the line of thinking which carries forward through Hegel, Treitschke, and Marx to the German sociology of Mannheim's own time. 'This is certainly the positive side of their activity,' he writes, 'for there must and should always be people who are not so bound by their immediate ties that they care only for the "next step".'[38] But this productive achievement comes about, in his view, when 'socially unattached intellectuals, with their inherent sense of system and totality, bind themselves to the designs of social forces which are concretely manifest'.[39] There must be, in other words, a tie to a social reality more effective than their spiritual state, if the socially unattached intellectuals are to perform their larger spiritual tasks. With this extension of the notion of social connectedness, however, it becomes evident that Mannheim is doing more than merely assimilating historicism to the historical conservative movement by providing it with authentic social roots. In the discussion of Savigny cited earlier, in fact, the designation of organically rooted thinking as 'seinsverbunden' proves to be only provisional and gives way to a characterisation as 'the thought of fellowship-associations or thought bound to community'. This represents a shift in the concept in a direction diametrically opposite to the shift which Mannheim makes when he speaks of the quite distanced connectedness between intellectuals and primary social forces. Recognising this difference does not negate the initial insight into the most obviously conservative aspect of Mannheim's experimental design, but it requires consideration of additional levels of the work.

Conservative ways of thinking

We have found that Mannheim's own treatment of conservatism can be seen, when viewed from a conservative point of view, to exemplify a conservative way of thinking about things, establishing meaning by identifying social roots and ramifications. But Mannheim actually takes this to be only one of three conservative ways of understanding and organising the functions of thinking. A review of all three will at the same time suggest the supplementary intellectual strategies which Mannheim also deployed in his own study. He applies conservative thinking to conservatism in order to show how a thinking which was originally conservative rises above that political association to perform decisive new functions in contemporary society. Mannheim, in other words, cannot be taken as simply accommodating himself to the conservatism he finds prevalent in the university and in its disciplines. He means to show that this disposition has meanings and implies tasks which conservatives do not recognise. He hopes to achieve changes, as he puts it in his essay on historicism, simply by showing the present its own true face. This design explains why Mannheim is so little interested in the political substance of conservatism and concentrates so heavily on aspects and phases of its style of thought.

The first of the three conservative ways of thinking which Mannheim identifies, then, is the one we have encountered. He identifies the *seinsverbundenes*, *gemeinschaftsgebundenes* kind of thinking he finds displayed and elevated in Savigny with the function of elucidation (*Klären*). If the thought is integral to a community to which the thinker is deeply committed 'with his total personality' then his elaborated thinking simply clarifies and explicates what is already in the deepest sense inarticulately known by those to whom he addresses his thoughts. This conception, which Mannheim traces back from Savigny to Justus Möser, is very similar to the 'conjunctive' thinking which Mannheim had made paradigmatic for cultural sociology, in his earlier theoretical treatise on this subject. In *Conservatism*, too, Mannheim extrapolates from Savigny to the undertakings typical of cultural sociology in his own day. This fixes one aspect of his own work.

The conservative paradigm for a second conception of the function of thinking, Mannheim finds in Adam Müller. Mannheim calls this conception 'mediation'. Its main characteristics are, first, that it takes things to be in mutual oppositions, and second, that it equates thinking with the active judgment of practitioners expounding an efficacious solution to a given conflict, which they somehow derive from following along the course of the oppositions involved. Mannheim considers this way of thinking an important alternative to the 'rational-progressive' conception of understanding, which he characterises as depending exclusively on the systematic subsumption of particulars under general laws, and he stresses its practical character. Its effectiveness depends not only on its insight into the contesting forces and its partial accommodation to both, but also on an aesthetic sense of the fitness of a given judgment to a given state of the oppositions to which it is applied. Such judgment solves the practical problem but it does

15

not thereby eliminate the oppositions or subject them to logical systematisation. Müller himself, Mannheim notes, tended to be schematically fanciful in his account of the oppositions in things, inclining towards forced impositions of the male-female polarity, and he first romanticised and then – once in Austrian employ – reified the locus of mediation. Despite Müller's corruption of the design, Mannheim considers the conception fruitful. It contributes to the subsequent development of what he calls dynamic thinking and proves able to handle irreducible antinomies in a purposive way.

Mannheim uses the term 'synthesis' to refer to the judgments constituting this way of thinking, but he stresses that the character of each synthesis depends on the standpoint from which it originates, or, more actively, on the design which it implements. There is movement towards accommodation and incorporation of opposites, but no reintegration into a comprehensive new totality eradicating the old oppositions, as is supposed to happen in full dialectical thinking. In the intellectual field of his own time, Mannheim finds this impulse to mediation most evident in a curiously introverted form. *Lebensphilosophie*, he believes, tends to absolutise the twofold experience of moving through a world of opposites and of making vital judgments, so that it has little to propose about the reality itself. It nevertheless displays its breeding, so to speak, by its opposition to liberal rationalism in all its forms.

Such vitalism plays some continuing part in Mannheim's willingness to put out unfinished work, justified as an authentic record of ongoing growth. But his indebtedness to this conception of 'mediation' in the organisation of his own thinking derives more importantly from its earlier forms. He presents the history of conservatism as a succession of points of concentration (*Knotenpunkte*), each of which represents a synthesis of the partial, partisan type he associates with Müller. The oppositions between liberal rationalism and conservative impulses and traditions enter into each characteristic combination, in accordance with the achieved stage of development and other historical circumstances, with the conservative elements predominating. Mannheim does indicate a plan for treating later stages, when conservatism increasingly fails to comprehend the movement of things, but his survey stops far short of these. In the interpretations of his own time scattered throughout the text, conservatism appears either as an integral protagonist in a political-intellectual field which also contains liberal and socialist partisans or as an ensemble of elements in 'the contemporary state of thinking'. In either case, Mannheim depicts a confrontation among seemingly irreconcilable opposites but not, as in *Ideology and Utopia* a few years later, a crisis. Different possible combinations strive for supremacy, but the contestants are constrained within a common field, and matters continue to move along. There is no impasse. The insistence that liberal and conservative elements, although opposed, can never be wholly divorced from one another lies in the very conception of conservatism as a way of rationalising traditionalist impulses with which the study begins.[40] And a striking feature of Mannheim's contemporary references is the confidence with which he repeatedly returns to similarities and affinities between socialist and conservative thinking, despite social and political antagonism between them.

Every actual turn of things – in short, the practical movement through time – appears as a product of mediation in Müller's sense, as outcome of judgments which severally gain enough support to be provisionally effective without denying their partisan starting points or presuming to eliminate or absorb oppositions. It may be little more than an historical oddity that this projection of conservatism as an element in various combinations was written in the year that Paul von Hindenburg was elected President and the conservative *Deutschnationale Volkspartei* first took full part in a coalition government under the Weimar constitution. In any case, this view of things in Mannheim's work will be recast a few years later in *Ideology and Utopia* as the operation of *Realdialektik* ('empirical dialectics' probably captures it best), but there the process will have to cope with what appears to Mannheim as the emergence of crisis and immobilisation, as well as a more urgent theoretical demand for higher unification of opposites through drastic recontextualisation of the totality. The contrast with this later work brings the comparative modesty and sceptical moderation of *Conservatism* into clearer focus. In some contexts, perhaps, one might be justified in speaking of a sober optimism.

As with the aspect of conservative thinking abstracted by him from the account of Savigny, Mannheim manages to convey a politically and even metaphysically interesting message to conservative readers through his adaptation of Müller's mode of mediation, without manifestly abandoning his frequently repeated undertaking to write in this work only about the facts of conservative thinking, in a scientific manner which eschews valuation. That at least appears to be the design.

Mediation in this sense also governs much of the inner organisation of *Conservatism*. The elements of morphological explication and sociological explanation are juxtaposed and then combined in an historical account. But that account does not render the treatment wholly socio-historical, since many features

17

of conservatism, like the ways of thinking now under review, are taken as structural entities having significance in historical contexts quite different from those which account for their emergence. The rise of conservatism itself has paradigmatic importance for grasping the present. Mannheim was aware of this complementarity in his method, even later on, when he was more determined to overcome it. According to the minutes of a seminar held jointly by Mannheim and Alfred Weber in February 1929, Mannheim concluded the seminar by conceding that 'morphology' also 'has its justification' alongside of the functionalist historical explanations of thought he was defending and which Weber had stigmatised as 'intellectualism'. 'As complementary aspects of things', he is reported to have said, 'morphology and intellectualism have joint justification.'[41] The occasion on which this statement was made, however, – a joint appearance with Alfred Weber on the subject of Georg Lukács – must remind us of our initial questions about the importance of prudence and tact in the shaping of Mannheim's *Conservatism*.

Mannheim between Hegel and Weber

These questions can only be answered after considering the place in the work of the third type of thinking which Mannheim traces to conservatism. The partial and provisional syntheses characteristic of Müller's way of thinking do not represent, according to Mannheim, the limit of what has appeared possible to conservative thought. Nor does Mannheim accept them as the final term of his own methodological aspirations. The study of conservatism keeps looking ahead to Hegel, and Mannheim repeatedly anticipates the discussion of dialectics as a third mode of thinking rooted in conservative precedent. Dialectical thinking, in this account, grows out of the awareness of opposition and movement represented by Müller, but it conceives the synthesis as comprehensive and ontologically grounded in the dynamics of reality. Mannheim asserts that dialectical thinking successfully managed to rationalise what romantic and Enlightenment thought had achieved, integrating it into a single comprehensive theory of development under conservative auspices, and that this discovery was subsequently transmuted by Marx into an organon for the thought of a class better placed to counter capitalist-liberal rationalisation.

This projection of the development of conservatism represents the most audacious aspect of Mannheim's study, because it proposes a relationship between conservatism and the new historicism which wholly supercedes the other two aspects of conservative thinking and altogether submerges the historical political contents of conservatism. From this point of view, embodied also in Mannheim's other writings during those years, the analysis of conservatism would ultimately pivot around the concept of *Funktionswandel* (change in function). The conservative contributions would be seen at last as elements in a given originating historical context whose functions change radically and indeed paradoxically in the course of subsequent development. The point of the study would be to establish the historical obsolescence of conservatism and to ground its socialist successor's claims upon the dialectical reversal of conservatism's crowning intellectual achievement.

Something like this is projected and anticipated in a few programmatic passages, if not quite so boldly, but no such treatment ever materialises. As mentioned above, the section on Hegel, which is introduced by the last sentence of the manuscript, was never written. In fact, the culminating importance Mannheim attaches to Hegel's dialectics in his discussions of philosophical themes appears casually denied by the inclusion of Hegel in a list of six other topics, some of them having only the most narrowly historical interest, left to later investigations. Yet this implicit denial cannot be credited, in the light of the remaining evidence, and Mannheim's failure to fulfil the many promises he connected with Hegel and the dialectical integration of his work must be investigated.

The obvious explanation is once more suggested by the biographical and historical circumstances. If Mannheim was convinced that his account of the conservative contribution to contemporary historicism would lead to an understanding of the present similar to that put forward by Lukács, as dialectical continuator of Hegel and Marx, might it not be politically and professionally prudent to stop with two lines of analysis which do after all give conservative reasons for paying respectful attention to contemporary historicism, while remaining convinced that the Marxist mode of analysis would in the end prevail? Would it not be needlessly provocative to spell out the full, politically explosive and professionally destructive message? This line of explanation, though plausible and surely not irrelevant, however, fails to do justice to Mannheim's consciousness as well as his perplexity.

Mannheim consistently accepted Lukács' argument that the socialist form of dialectical thinking depends upon a commitment to the modern industrial proletariat as the concrete social force destined to take the next step in history. This was a commitment, however, which Mannheim never would make. Mannheim's problem, if he was to follow through with the projections arising from his philosophical reflections, was to find an alternative way of earning the right to the kind of dialectical integration which Hegel had grounded on conservative commitments and metaphysical reasonings, and Marx on socialist commitments and economic analysis. He could not accept either. In the absence of such a way, dialectics remained an uncompleted sketch for him, an aspiration.

His real move, proudly accepted, was to the suspended judgment inherent in academic discipline. This is worked out programmatically in the discussion of the school for politics in the essay on politics as a science written later (1929). But the most moving formulation, because addressed to the Communist son of Mannheim's liberal mentor, Oscar Jászi, and because written two weeks before Hitler's designation as Chancellor, appears in a letter:

> What we can offer you is a rather intensive study group, close contact with the lecturers, but little dogmatic commitment. We do not think of ourselves as a political party but must act as if we had a lot of time and could calmly discuss the pros and cons of every matter. In addition, I think it is very important not merely to continually discuss dialectics but to look at things, to carefully observe individual problems and aspects of social reality rather than merely talking about them.[42]

Mannheim's well-founded failure to settle accounts with Hegel has as counterpart a failure to finish with Max Weber. In his 'Letter from Heidelberg'[43] written in 1921, Mannheim speaks of the sociologists there as followers of Max Weber and took them as representatives for the university as a whole, in polar opposition to the literary circle dedicated to Stefan George.[44] Mannheim's own choice of sociology as disciplinary setting for his work, then, opened a question about his relationship to the dead Max Weber more basic than the questions arising out of his living relationships with the brother, Alfred. There are critical assessments of different aspects of Weber's cultural sociology in Mannheim's earlier writings, and various later attempts to specify the ways in which he has continued but also transmuted Weber's undertaking in sociology. The very title of the well-known chapter in *Ideologie und Utopie*, 'Ist Politik als Wissenschaft möglich?' (Is a Science of Politics Possible?) refers to Weber's two best-known essays in a challenging way, as witness also the concluding references to him; and the central theme of Mannheim's *Man and Society in an Age of Reconstruction*[45] concerns Weber's concepts of rationality. Although it is thus possible to add up Mannheim's changing judgments on many of Weber's ideas, the central place which Mannheim assigned to him in the constitution of the discipline and in the symbolic representation of the university makes it all the more noticeable that he never fulfilled a long-standing promise to write on Weber at length. He had already proposed Max Weber as one of three possible topics for his inaugural lecture as *Privatdozent* at Heidelberg. Between 1928 and 1932, he kept Paul Siebeck, the publisher for J.C.B. Mohr, waiting, first for an essay on Weber and then for a whole book. But there has never been any trace of such a work. Mannheim's comments on Weber remain scattered, episodic, and inconsistent.

Mannheim brings Weber into *Conservatism* in a curious and striking way, and he differentiates himself from him in a way equally revealing. In analysing Savigny's reliance on certain irrational forces as ultimate guarantors of social meaning, Mannheim goes back to the writings of an earlier German jurist, Gustav Hugo (1764–1844). Hugo's thought, in turn, he characterises as representative of a certain kind of hard, hopeless acceptance of a world of facts in which all principles are relative and all developments ultimately fortuitous. Mannheim accounts for such bitter toughmindedness by reference to a situation in which two competing social strata are evenly balanced and the observer uses the insights of each to discredit the other: 'Here value-freedom, the absence of utopia, become, as it were, the test of objectivity and proximity to reality.'[46] He calls this state of mind *Desillusionrealismus*, and he finds its exact parallel pervading German thinking in Max Weber's time. In its modern form, this realism acknowledges socialist exposures of liberal illusions, but then turns the method of disillusioning against socialist utopianism as well. Max Weber, according to Mannheim, is the most important representative of this style of thinking, and his conceptions of reality and scientific method are deeply marked by this fundamental attitude.

Mannheim does not expressly extend the parallelism to himself, but it is deeply interesting to see how he accounts for Savigny's movement beyond the realism of Hugo:

> Between Hugo's and Savigny's ways of reasoning we have the defeat at Jena, foreign rule, and the wars of liberation, which transformed theoretical discussion into real discussion and a national uprising . . . into reality.[47]

The difference rests on 'a generational distinction'. This side of the case, Mannheim says, also has contemporary application, and on this matter he attaches his deepest concerns and convictions to generational destiny:

> In periods like ours, in which self-reflectiveness and a many-

sided relativism are reducing themselves to absurdity, as it were, a fear grows up instinctively about where all this will lead. How can relativism be overcome in history? If we can learn from the example [of Savigny], the answer would have to be: not by way of immanent theory but by way of collective fate – not by a refusal to think relativistically, but by throwing new light on new, emerging contents. Here the fact of the generational growth of culture is of immense significance. Although considerable individual latitude is possible, it can be phenomenologically ascertained that the newly arising faith has quite a different character in the most recent generation than it has in those who, coming from an earlier generation, do not take part in this upsurge.[48]

Such a vitalist principle of distinction between his own generation and that of Weber, although it echoes a theme already present in Mannheim's earliest major essay, could not be a satisfactory clarification of his relationship to Weber. And it could especially not suffice since its full realisation would have required, once again, that commitment to the socialist movement to the proletariat which Mannheim, unlike Weber's one-time protégé Georg Lukács, would not make.

The problem of generations is, then, the subject of Mannheim's next major investigation; and problems of utopia, disillusionment, and the mutual discrediting of social knowledge and ideals occupy the succeeding years. No one familiar with these complex, painstaking, and ultimately unfinished works can doubt that Mannheim's struggles to overcome the pessimism he found in Weber's empirical discipline were not lightened by dialectical leaps or generational upsurges. The state, form, and matter of *Conservatism* testify to the seriousness and difficulty of his enterprise. Its academic reserve has this last explanation.

Mannheim himself bitterly recalled the promise of generation, itself ironically a leitmotif in the supposed rejuvenation of Germany in 1933, in a letter to Oscar Jászi, smuggled out of Germany by Socialist party courier in April, 1933:

It is a pity that everything is in shambles here; a progressive generation that could have, acting within the German nation, channeled history in a different direction, was successfully brought together. But it was too late. This is the second time that I am living through something like this, but I always have strength to start anew, unbroken.[49]

Mannheim was to get another chance in England, in a land which first exasperated and then delighted him by its conservatism.

The aggressive sociologism of his last years presupposed an audience deeply moved by traditional resistance to modernist rationalisations. It is part of the tragedy of the forced intellectual emigration of the 30s that the emigrants were too often compelled to choose between accepting a role as alien and esoteric prophets, granted at most a 'heuristic' value for the ongoing scholarly enterprises in their host countries, or recasting their thought into modes whose capacities for subtlety they could not easily master. Theodor W. Adorno, a witness well-qualified to speak, who opted for each of the alternatives in turn, wrote:

> Every émigré intellectual, without exception, is damaged. And he better admit it, if he does not want to have the harsh lesson brought home to him behind the tightly closed doors of his self-esteem. He lives in surroundings that must remain incomprehensible to him, however well he may find his way among labor organisations or in traffic. He constantly dwells in confusion. . . . His language has been expropriated, and the historical dimension, that nourished his knowledge, has been sapped.[50]

The costs of emigration were also great for Karl Mannheim, and they are manifested in the state of his English writings, as well as in the translations of his earlier work. The works which he and his dutiful executors attempted to render strictly 'empirical', to adjust them to the requirements of scientific relevance in the new setting, are less subtle and less interesting than the thinking which underlay them, especially since the attempted adjustments never succeeded in more than part. That is most dramatically exemplified in the English version of *Ideologie und Utopie*.[51] On the other hand, the interest in empirical methods and in Weberian reflections on social science embodied in his German-language work is obscured. The historical recovery of Mannheim's original work in its full complexity serves, paradoxically enough, to take the achievement out of the museum and to make it usable for present scientific purposes.

Notes

1 An earlier version of this introduction was published under the title 'Karl Mannheim and Conservatism: The Ancestry of Historical Thinking' in the *American Sociological Review* (February 1984) 49,1: 71–85.
2 Karl Mannheim, *Ideology and Utopia*, transl. Louis Wirth and Edward Shils, London: Routledge & Kegan Paul, 1936. [*Ideologie und Utopie*, Bonn: Cohen, 1929].

3 Karl Mannheim, *Structures of Thinking*, ed. and intr. David Kettler, Volker Meja and Nico Stehr, transl. Jeremy J. Shapiro and Shierry Weber Nicholsen, London: Routledge & Kegan Paul, 1982. [Strukturen des Denkens, ed. David Kettler, Volker Meja and Nico Stehr, Frankfurt am Main: Suhrkamp, 1980.]

4 Karl Mannheim, 'Conservative Thought', in *Essays on Sociology and Social Psychology*, ed. Paul Kecskemeti, London: Routledge & Kegan Paul, 1953, pp. 74–164. ['Das konservative Denken. Soziologische Beiträge zum Werden des politisch-historischen Denkens in Deutschland', *Archiv für Sozialwissenschaft und Sozialpolitik* (1927) 57: 68–142, 470–95.]

5 Cf. Robert Merton, 'Karl Mannheim and the sociology of knowledge', in *Social Theory and Social Structure* [1941], Glencoe, Ill.: Free Press, 1957, pp. 497 ff.; Lewis A. Coser, *Masters of Sociological Thought*. New York: Harcourt, Brace, Jovanovich, 1977, pp. 436 ff.

6 Karl Mannheim, 'Historicism', in *Essays on the Sociology of Knowledge*. ['Historicism', *Archiv für Sozialwissenschaft und Sozialpolitik* (1924) 52: 1–60.]

7 Georg Lukács, *History and Class Consciousness: Studies in Marxist Dialectics*, Cambridge, MA: MIT Press, 1971. [*Geschichte und Klassenbewusstsein. Studien über marxistische Dialektik*, Berlin: Malik, 1923.]

8 Karl Mannheim, 'Structural Analysis of Epistemology', *Essays on Sociology and Social Psychology* (London: Routledge & Kegan Paul, 1953), pp. 15–73. ['Die Strukturanalyse der Erkenntnistheorie', *Kant Studien*, Supplement 57 (Berlin: Reuther & Reichard, 1922).]

9 Part one of *Structures of Thinking* ['Über die Eigenart kultursoziologischer Erkenntnis', *Strukturen des Denkens*.]

10 *Ibid.*, pp. 77–80, [*Ibid.*, pp. 85–8.]

11 Karl Mannheim, 'The Ideological and the Sociological Interpretation of Intellectual Phenomena,' in Kurt H. Wolff, ed., *From Karl Mannheim*, London: Oxford University Press, 1971, pp. 116–131. ['Ideologische und soziologische Interpretation der geistigen Gebilde,' *Jahrbuch für Soziologie* (1926) 2: 424–40.]

12 Among these puzzling features is, for example, the curious contrast between Mannheim's relatively sympathetic treatment of conservatism and the almost pejorative use of 'conservatism' in 'The Problem of a Sociology of Knowledge', p. 185 [1925, p. 645].

13 Report of the Faculty of Philosophy at the University of Heidelberg to the 'Inner Senate' (April 8, 1926), in Mannheim's *Habilitationsakten*, University of Heidelberg Archives.

14 Karl Mannheim, 'Az ismeretelmélet szerkezeti elemzése', *Athenaeum* (1918): 233–47; 'Lélek és kultura', Budapest: Benkö Gyula, 1918.

15 'Heidelbergi levél I', *Tüz* (1921): 46–50; 'Heidelbergi levelek II', *Tüz* (1922): 91–5.

16 'Levelek az emigrációból I', *Diogenes* (January 5, 1924): 13–15.

17 See the article in *Deutsche Zukunft* (June 5, 1929) on the conflict between the interior ministries of Baden and of Württemberg. On the opposition of the Bavarian government to Mannheim's naturalisation see the papers on Mannheim in *Badisches Generallandesarchiv* in

Karlsruhe.

18 *Verhandlungen* des Sechsten Deutschen Soziologentages, 1928, Tübingen: J.C.B. Mohr (Paul Siebeck], 1929, pp. 88–92, 106–7. Reprinted in Volker Meja and Nico Stehr, eds., *Der Streit um die Wissensoziologie*, Frankfurt am Main: Suhrkamp, two volumes, pp. 371–6, 383–5).

19 *Ideology and Utopia*, p. 106 [*Ideologie und Utopie*, p. 125].

20 'Heidelbergi levél I', p. 50; David Kettler, Volker Meja and Nico Stehr, 'Karl Mannheim's early writings on cultural sociology', in *Structures of Thinking*, p. 12.

21 'Lélek és kultura', p. 6; Karl Mannheim, 'Seele und Kultur', in *Wissensoziologie*, ed. Kurt H. Wolff, Berlin and Neuwied: Luchterhand, 1964, pp. 72 ff.

22 Karl Mannheim, 'Karl Mannheim's Letters to Georg Lukács', *The New Hungarian Quarterly* (1975) 16: 93–105; 'Besprechung von Georg Lukács, *Die Theorie des Romans*', *Logos* (1920–21) 9: 298–302; 'A Review of Georg Lukács' *Theory of the Novel*', in *From Karl Mannheim*, ed. Kurt H. Wolff, New York: Oxford University Press, 1971, pp. 3–7.

23 Mannheim failed to deliver the manuscript of the book and it was therefore never published. The originally proposed title, *Wissenssoziologische Analysen zur gegenwärtigen Denkweise. Drei Essays über M. Weber, Troeltsch und Scheler*, was later changed by Mannheim to *Analysen zur gegenwärtigen Denklage. Drei Untersuchungen über M. Weber, Troeltsch, und Scheler*. Cp. Mannheim's letter to Paul Siebeck of October 12, 1928, Siebeck's letter to Mannheim of May 28, 1929, both in the Archives of J.C.B. Mohr (Paul Siebeck) Verlag, Tübingen, and the first edition of *Ideologie und Utopie*, Bonn: Cohen, 1929, p. 215.

24 Mannheim to Siebeck, October 1, 1928.

25 Mannheim to Louis Wirth (December 28, 1936), University of Chicago, Joseph Regenstein Library, Archives, Louis Wirth Papers.

26 'Die Dame aus Biarritz. Ein Spiel in vier Szenen', Typescript 1920, Magyar Tudoman Akademia Kezirattara, Budapest.

27 In this volume, p. 188, below.

28 Cf. Mannheim's characterisation of Troeltsch in 'Historismus', and the special anti-Spengler issue of *Logos* 9, 2, (1920–21), which illustrates the mobilisation of academic specialisms against Spengler, notwithstanding the general character of the journal as an organon of the search for comprehensive systematisation and its emblem of Heraclitus.

29 *Structures of Thinking* [*Strukturen des Denkens*].

30 'The Problem of a Sociology of Knowledge' ['Das Problem einer Soziologie des Wissens'].

31 The English version of *Ideology and Utopia* omits the distinction between Seins*verbundenheit* and Seins*gebundenheit* altogether, rendering them both as 'situational determination'. See A. P. Simonds, *Karl Mannheim's Sociology of Knowledge*, Oxford: Clarendon Press, 1978, p. 27; Volker Meja, 'The Sociology of Knowledge and the Critique of Ideology', *Cultural Hermeneutics* (1975), 3: 67n.

32 'The Sociology of Knowledge', *Ideology and Utopia*, p. 271. ['Wissen-soziologie', *Ideologie und Utopie*, 3rd ed., Frankfurt: Schulte-Bulmke, 1952, p. 259.] This article, included in the English translation of *Ideology and Utopia* and the 3rd to 5th German editions as a concluding chapter, was originally published under the title 'Wissen-soziologie', in the *Handwörterbuch der Soziologie*, ed. Alfred Vierkandt, Stuttgart: Enke, 1931, pp. 659–80. Our retranslation.

33 'A Sociological Theory of Culture and Its Knowability', *Structures of Thinking* ['Eine soziologische Theorie der Kultur und ihrer Erkenn-barkeit', *Strukturen des Denkens*].

34 In this volume, p. 159, below.

35 In this volume, p. 117, below. This is one of the few interpretations which Mannheim changed when he published a portion of the text in German (1927). The purely 'immanent' sources of the development from Enlightenment to romanticism are now presented as responses to social and political developments. The difference is quite important, not least because the question of spiritual and intellectual creativity is a touchstone for his mentor Alfred Weber.

36 In this volume, p. 118, below.

37 In this volume, p. 118, below.

38 In this volume, p. 118, below.

39 In this volume, p. 213, below (note 149).

40 Ernst Troeltsch, whose thought Mannheim treats very respectfully in 'Historicism,' had called for the infusion of more 'natural-law' thinking of the liberal type into German historicist jurisprudence in a lecture given in 1922 and cited in Mannheim's earlier work. Cf. his *Naturrecht und Humanität in der Weltpolitik* [1923], Berlin: Verlag für Politik und Wissenschaft, 1957.

41 'Protokoll der Sitzung der vereinigten Seminare von Prof. A. Weber und Dr. Mannheim' (February 21, 1929), p. 7 (typescript).

42 Letter to Gyuri Jászi (April 16, 1933), Columbia University Libraries, Rare Book and Manuscript Library.

43 'Heidelbergi levél I'.

44 David Kettler, Volker Meja and Nico Stehr, 'Karl Mannheim's early writings on cultural sociology', *Structures of Thinking*, p. 12.

45 Karl Mannheim, *Man and Society in an Age of Reconstruction: Studies in Modern Social Structure*. (Based on *Mensch und Gesellschaft im Zeitalter des Umbaus*, Leiden: A. W. Sijthoff, 1935). Revised and enlarged by the author, transl. Edward Shils, London: Routledge & Kegan Paul, 1940.

46 In this volume, p. 175, below.

47 In this volume, p. 179, below.

48 In this volume, p. 180, below.

49 Letter to Oscar Jászi (April 25, 1933), Columbia University Libraries, Rare Book and Manuscript Library.

50 Theodor W. Adorno, *Minima Moralia. Reflexionen aus dem beschädigten Leben*, Frankfurt am Main: Suhrkamp, 1951, p. 32.

51 Cf. David Kettler, Volker Meja, and Nico Stehr, *Karl Mannheim* London: Tavistock; Chichester: Ellis Horwood, 1984.

Conservatism:
A Contribution to the Sociology of
Knowledge

Contents

romanticism and anti-capitalist tendencies. The irrational element in the dialectic.

Part II Conservatism: its concept and its nature

1 Traditionalism and conservatism
The concepts of objective and historical-dynamic structural contexture. 'Traditionalist' as a formal-psychological category; 'conservative' as historical-sociological category. On the history of the term 'conservative'.

2 Historical note on the concept of political conservatism
J. Fr. Stahl: revolution and conservatism as political systems. Stahl's ahistorical approach and intellectualism. Constantin Frantz's formal definition of conservatism. Gustav Radbruch's investigations into world-views as context for political ideologies.

3 The sociological background of conservatism
The functionalisation of the traditionalist attitude to life. State and society. The dynamicisation of historical social complexes.

4 Morphology of conservative thought
(a) **The fundamental design of conservative thought**
The tendency of progressive thought towards system and of conservative thought towards the individual case. Conservative experience and the conservative concept of property. The conservative concept of liberty. Conservative experience and thinking at the level of reflection.
(b) **The theoretical core of conservative thought**
The sociological pre-history of natural law. Natural-law thinking in the eighteenth century. The conservative attack on natural-law thinking.

Part III Early conservatism in Germany

1 The first conservative position: romanticism and the estates
Historical analysis of the estate-oriented romantic position. Sociological analysis of the strata behind the estate-oriented romantic opposition. The sociological meaning of romanticism and its social bearers. Adam Müller, Edmund Burke and Justus Möser. Bureaucratic and bourgeois rationalism. The concept of mediation in Müller and in Catholic thinking. Theory and practice in estate-oriented romantic thought. Dynamic experi-

ence and thinking in Hegel and Marx. Concepts of reality in anti-bourgeois thinking.

2 **The position of the 'historical school'**
The function of cognition in liberal thought, in Hegel, and in the historical school. The two forms of knowledge in Savigny. Rationality and irrationality in liberal Enlightenment thinking. The 'unconscious' in Schelling and Savigny. The generational difference between Hugo and Savigny. Hugo's relativism, technique of thinking and conception of reality. Conservative historicism. Savigny and Müller: their ways of thinking and conceptions of knowledge.

Part I   General problems

1 Statement of the problems[1]

We want to anticipate the most essential point at the very outset: the aim of the investigations below is to show, in a limited section of the historical domain, that thinking is bound to existence. We shall not be talking about thinking and knowing *in general*, but about determinate thinking and knowing within a determinate life space. The specific theme of this work is to establish the fact that in the first half of the nineteenth century in Germany, a cohesive tendency of thought, which can be called 'Early Conservatism (*Altkonservatismus*)', took form, borne by determinate social strata – a thinking which has a distinctive constitution and which can be imputed to its sociological source in a clearly comprehensible way.

It will be the narrowly circumscribed task of the present monographic inquiry to explicate this distinctive make-up through phenomenological description and typological classification, and to establish the material sociological roots of this tendency of thinking. In this introduction, however, it is appropriate to say something as well about our position on the more general problem of inquiry, in order to prepare for a proper understanding of the subsequent monographic work.

2 German conservatism and the problem of history

The central problem for all sociology of knowledge and research into ideology is the linkage between thinking and knowing on the one hand, and existence on the other (*Seinsgebundenheit allen Denkens und Erkennens*). While the philosophical disciplines and the history of ideas examine thinking in what may be called its immanence, disregarding the historical-sociological genesis of the history of ideas, the sociology of knowledge has it as its distinctive task to trace the assembled intellectual materials back to the historical-sociological constellation from which they have severally in fact arisen, and to understand their emergence on the basis of the total process.

>*Thinking and knowing may become the objects of various scientific lines of inquiry, and before we turn to the problem of the sociology of thinking that concerns us here, we ought at least to point out the essential differences between the lines of inquiry pursued in relation to thinking by philosophy, the history of ideas, and sociology. What philosophy and the history of ideas have in common is that both start out from the premise that the product of thinking is always separable from its psychological or sociological genesis, and their plans of inquiry therefore always set out from the level of immanent entities, independent of their genesis. While the philosophical disciplines investigate the structures or contents of these detached theoretical entities with a view to their justification and validity, the history of ideas attempts an historical reconstruction of the developmental interconnections in time, but detached from the sequence of concrete events (e.g., the gradual unfolding of one group of ideas from another, or their joint emergence). Greatly as these two disciplines may differ from each other in general, the thing they nevertheless have in common is their failure to take into account the total socio-historical process which lies behind the individual theoretical constructs, as the historical place of their origination.
>
> But it is precisely this genesis of thought and of forms of thinking out of the total socio-historical process, disregarded by philosophy and the history of ideas, which the sociology of knowledge makes into its field of inquiry. Since the sociologist's focus of interest in the study of contextures of thought is so completely different from that of the philosopher and the historian of ideas, we need not concern ourselves here with the purely philosophical question as to how the different findings ultimately relate to one another. At this point it will be enough to say that the systematic relevance attached to genetic observations will generally be dependent upon the particular philosophical viewpoint from which this antinomy is approached. This latter decision, even if it should prove to be completely negative concerning the philosophical relevance of socio-genetic findings, can be considered immaterial to the present investigation, since even the most thoroughly systematic

---

* *Editors' note:* In the original German manuscript, the excursus above is contained in a footnote. Like several other important excursuses it has been brought into the main body of the text (indented in the manner of quotes and enclosed by asterisks), since it offers an immediate and valuable supplement to the principal text.

philosophical attitude cannot reject as a purely empirical question the legitimacy of the question about the social genesis of intellectual entities. And the present work concerns itself exclusively with such *questions of fact.**

A second essential difference between philosophical and sociological inquiries into thinking and knowing consists in the fact that philosophy tends to ground itself upon a timeless and unchanging reason, or at least to presuppose the unchangeability of the formal determinants of reason (especially of the categories). The sociology of knowledge,[2] as an empirical specialised science, is not allowed to accept such a postulate as binding upon itself. These problems are questions for its factual inquiries. If empirical investigation should reveal that the forms of thinking themselves vary with the historical and social process, the sociology of knowledge will simply register this fact as a finding of empirical science.

Although the postulates of philosophy thus cannot in principle disturb the investigations of the empirical specialised sciences, it is nevertheless the case that the philosophical doctrine of the self-identity and timelessness of the formal determinants of reason does in fact serve to inhibit historical and sociological investigations into transformations in the forms of thinking. Under the reign of the philosophical doctrine of a timeless reason, there prevailed an aversion to problems of this sort, an aversion which prevented the problem of the rootedness of forms of thinking in the overall social process from being raised.

But it has been precisely this inhibition, working unconsciously as well as consciously, which has been the reason for our failure until now to penetrate deeply into an especially interesting problem, the nature of historical and political ways of thinking. Nowhere else is it as clearly the case that the objects of knowledge are constituted by everyday experience, as well as by the historical cultural sciences with their historically changing and socially differentiated categorical apparatus, and that both the questions they ask and the objects they bring into focus are closely connected with the particular historical and social grounds out of which these ways of thinking arise.

Since Rickert,[3] working at a philosophical and methodological level, established the distinction between the natural sciences and the historical cultural sciences, there have been attempts from various sides to deepen and to ground it. But the distinction was not only important at the level of inquiries in methodology and the systematic theory of science. It also served as the starting point for a new historical inquiry into the development of ideas. A historical

33

research programme got under way at just about the same time as the systematic one.[4]

The question is not only, as in philosophical inquiry, how history as science may be possible, but also how modern historiography arose, and how long we have had (or, at least, have seen as problematic) a *disjunction between 'nature' and 'history'*.

This more general concern brings us to our particular problem. Since we too want to know about the origins of this disjunction between nature and history, so formative for the present state of thinking, we are led, in our pursuit of the historical, to the point where the opposition is first radically stated and given expression, namely to the political and ideological struggles at the time of the French Revolution. In searching for the beginnings of this disjunction – leaving Vico and Herder aside for now – one comes to the French traditionalists, on the one hand, and, on the other, to Burke, and then to German romanticism, the historical school, and so forth – in short, to the historical figures and constellations that constitute the subject-matter in our present investigation.

When we began, our investigation also simply addressed itself to the history of ideas. But it took on its distinctive character as sociology of thinking when we ceased to be satisfied with detailed examinations of the immanent intellectual origins of the disjunction between nature and history and asked ourselves *from which general sociological constellation this disjunction arose* and *which social forces promoted it and brought it to its gradual unfolding*. Why did this line of inquiry arise at just that particular point in history? Or at least: why did this disjunction obtain its modern character at that particular time? And why was it specifically in Germany that the formation arose that we generally call 'historicism'?

Once posed in this manner, such questions converted the original problem in the history of ideas into a problem in the sociology of thinking. With the shift in the emphasis of the questions being asked, there followed a comparable change in their purport. *The distinction between nature and history revealed itself as the outpost of an even more radical antithesis between two fundamentally different ways of thinking rooted in two fundamentally different world-views.*

It was inevitable that the whole inquiry would take on new form once we stopped considering the emergence of this distinction within the development of thought and world-view purely in the context of immanent problem-sequences in thought; when we broadened our range of vision in the manner of the sociology of thinking by asking also about the historical situation in which the issue arose, and above all, when we set about understanding the

34

differences in styles of thinking and world-view, so far as possible and proper, on the basis of the contestations among active social forces.

Such research is no longer concerned with the disjunction between nature and history, as it might arise in a history of intellectual problems, but with a contradiction between two world-views and ways of thinking, borne by social forces: *the disjunction between liberal and conservative thinking* which arose at the turn of the nineteenth century in direct connection with the concrete political and philosophically self-reflective debate about the French Revolution.

If the first sociological step was thus to establish the social and political split as the source of the division observable in the spiritual current, the further task was to look at the subsequent course of this divergence as well as later attempts at synthesis of the two styles of thought[5] in conjunction with the general course of society. If the constitutive role played by the social and political constellation at the origins of the cleavage between the two modes of thought had been quite evident, it seems at least probable that sociological forces will similarly continue to be at work in achieving syntheses between them. But this supposition can naturally be no more than a possibility, since it is always a question which can only be empirically decided from case to case whether, on the one hand, a determinate sociological situation is important only *at the origins* of the new ideological elements – with these ideological elements, once originated, then developing according to their immanent logic, quite independent of the social process – or whether, on the other hand, the ideological development unfolds in *constant contact with the material sociological context*. In our case, the second possibility applies. It is not only that 'historical thinking' was unquestionably brought into action by conservative social elements against 'generalising', 'natural law' and 'revolutionary' thought, but also that this division of roles continued to play its part (with certain exceptions, to be discussed in detail) in the further course of development. It lasted approximately until the 1840s; and it is only at this point, where the social and political organism of Germany undergoes significant restructuring, that the spiritual domain also reveals new constellations, whose study poses an altogether different task for the sociology of knowledge.

To state our thesis provisionally in simplified points: a differentiation of styles of thought emerged in Germany during the first half of the nineteenth century, parallel to the social and political differentiation of the times; and it has by and large continued to exist, albeit with many modifications. Only on this basis can we gain a genetic understanding of the distinction between natural-scientific and historical thinking which prevails today in the sphere of methodology.

That is how the problem which we want to explore in its full complexity appears in crude outline, in a first approximation. A subtler exploration of these matters, however, requires us to make many distinctions, in both the specification of the problems for inquiry as well as in the execution of the historical-sociological research. So long as the sociology of knowledge limits itself to formularised observation, it cannot investigate the very complex web of connections in the real world through which the inter-actions between 'base' and 'superstructure' occur; and so long as the interconnections are limited to the schematic kind, its observations will not be raised to the level at which scientific dispute can reach authoritative conclusions. Detailed work is necessary, carried out step by step, which will progressively modify the first statement of the thesis and give it ever more complex form. If we nevertheless place this provisional simplified formulation at the beginning of our account, it is only because it is necessary to cling to such a formulation, as to the leitmotif of a piece of research, in order to avoid losing ourselves in the whirl of individual facts.

The first thing required to refine the inquiry was a more precise characterisation of the distinctive properties of the styles of thinking which were initially so schematically juxtaposed. This could be done with the necessary rigour only if we succeeded in showing in detail, first of all, that what we called 'historical thinking' was a tendency of thinking coherent in its constituent parts, standing in contrast to 'universalising', 'liberal' thinking. The way to show this consists in drawing out of the works of the various authors, wherever possible, all the fundamental concepts that distinguish this type of thinking, while, at the same time, observing and exhibiting the effect on them of the *fundamental design (Grundintention)* underlying this style of thought. That is to say, we find, as we follow up in detail the fundamental concepts upon which this style of thinking rests, that we are dealing with the gradual formation of a distinctive 'logic', which has such inner consistency that it even undertakes to redirect concepts taken over from elsewhere into its own course. The concepts of 'spirit of the people (*Volksgeist*)' and 'freedom', to cite only the most import-ant examples, have different meaning according to whether they are found in thinkers still oriented to 'natural law' or in 'historical thinkers', and even within the latter category they take on additional different shades of meaning insofar as they are taken up by different tendencies of historical thought. The first thing, then, is to *grasp the unity of the style of thought in its formative principle*, for which the *analysis of meanings* offers a firm handhold, not as end in itself but as a resource for both investigation and proof.[6]

Were we to engage in the analysis of meaning only in the immanent sense of the history of ideas, and in this manner try to establish the 'stylistic unity' of the tendency of thought in question, it would be obvious, even at this stage, that we are dealing with the development and elaboration of a specific 'logic' which came into being as a counter, so to speak, to the thinking grounded in natural law – as noted above. The possibility of something like this, that two opposing styles of thought share the same historical life-space, is made more comprehensible by the circumstances, evident upon a reading of the authors of the time, that in fighting against the ideas of 1789, the 'counter-revolution' very deliberately sought not only to confront the substantive theses of the liberal opponent with counter-theses, but also to advance a counter-logic against the 'Jacobin', natural-law-grounded way of thinking.

The ideological campaign of the 'counter-revolution' exhibits two stages (as will be shown in detail below), not necessarily identical with its chronological sequence:

At the first stage, they attempt to beat the opponent on his own premises, at the level of reasoning at which he confronts them. Theses and antitheses are pitted against one another, but the formal assumptions are the same as those of the opponent, as when, for example, they went along with natural-law premises, but drew different conclusions from them.

The second stage of the ideological campaign is discernible where the determination is reached, often quite consciously and expressly, to tear out what is 'revolutionary' root and branch and, accordingly, not only to attempt to demolish the doctrinal contents of 'Jacobin thinking', but also to set a different method or way of thinking against the 'wrong method of thinking' capable of yielding such revolutionary results.

This account alone already reveals that, while historical thinking may have been a creation or discovery of the conservative tendency, the obverse of the thesis is by no means accurate. Not all conservative thinking is historical thinking – quite the contrary. Here where we set out to trace the conservative style of thought of the first half of the nineteenth century in its totality and to describe its chief stages, it is also necessary to emphasise those currents in the conservative stream which remain ahistorical and grounded in natural law. Due to this qualification, the original thesis loses its clear-cut profile. But it is much more important to acknowledge the complexity of things than to distort historical reality for the sake of clear-cut lines. Although the thesis remains valid that the historical thinking of the period that interests us here has conservative origins, the obverse thesis, according to which all conservative thinking is historical, is by no means correct. But precisely this qualification arising from the historical materials holds new problems for the sociology of knowledge. That is to say, as we differentiate the conservative pattern of thinking according to its different tendencies, as is required, we are immediately faced by another problem: which currents within conservative thinking became historical during the critical decades around the French Revolution? And further, which social strata 'bear' the currents in which the historical element emerged, and which ones retain thinking grounded in natural law?

The results of our research may give an answer to this question, insofar as it is at all answerable. But this point brings us close to the limits of the inquiries appropriate to the sociology of knowledge. Even if it can be shown that the most *fundamental ideological changes can be imputed to shifts in the social structure*, this does not by any means suggest that there must be a change in the social base to correspond to every change on the ideological surface.

We must always take into account the logical immanence which brings forth new figurations from a given starting-point in thinking, on its own initiative, as it were. Moreover, we must also respect the range of free play within which the achievement which is altogether a matter of personal creativity enters in. But this must not, on the other hand, stand in the way of letting sociological analysis penetrate as deeply as possible into achievements of the spirit, in order to be able to impute to social factors everything in those achievements that is in fact, on the strength of historical evidence, rightly imputable to them. The essentially sociological task thus consists in carrying out *sociological imputations*, and to account for these imputations in such a way that the intellectual achievements of the knowing subject are not turned into the speculative constructions of the sociologist, but that they are, rather, reconstructed.

If it is claimed, for instance, that historical thinking is simply a creation of the conservative movement, it is not enough, for example, to establish the contemporaneousness of the rise of the two movements (intellectual and social), or to cite plausible analogies. It is rather necessary to demonstrate, wherever possible, the conservative political origins of the individual component parts of this thinking, while expounding them.

This involves, then, a thorough scrutiny of currents and elements of thinking (concepts and forms of thinking), which must establish case by case the political and social tendencies to which each of these elements are to be imputed.

*Establishing an adequate *sociological imputation* can be carried out in two stages: (a) by showing that the imputation has correspondence on the level of meaning, (b) by showing that the imputation is adequate on the level of empirical causality.[7]

An imputation is adequate on the level of meaning, for example, if we can demonstrate by reference to the meaning expressed by a concept – as used in an epoch or by a certain author – that it has grown out of the fundamental conservative design. Some illustrations of this, to be considered later, are when conservative thinking enlists a 'qualitative' concept of freedom against the 'liberal' concept of freedom, or when a specifically apologetic feature is built into the concept of 'tradition', or when the category of 'concreteness' is given positive normative emphasis and contrasted to the emptiness of the 'abstract'.

Showing an imputation to be adequate on the level of meaning is the first stage in establishing the accuracy of the imputation in question. However, this is by no means sufficient, because it is too easily possible that there might be a sense of evidentness which confirms the adequacy of the imputation of a concept at the level of meaning to conservative thinking, for example, when in fact – i.e., historically – the rise or use of the concept does not derive from the conservative fundamental current in any way. Proof is only complete if we can also establish a material-causal imputation. Such proof is commonly achieved when we succeed in finding historical evidence of the way in which the concept in question, having been given the *meaning in question* by conservative authors, arose in the course of political and ideological conflict. The maximally possible proof that can be provided would be supplied if the correctness of the imputation's adequacy on the level of meaning as well as its causal adequacy could be shown. Such absolute proof is possible only in happy exceptions – if only because there is not always evidence at hand to show the causal adequacy of the imputation, since the formation of new concepts and categories does not always occur in written works. New meanings may emerge in active life, in spoken discourse, and it may no longer be possible to reconstruct their direct material-causal origin due to the lack of written evidence. There is nevertheless a help for such cases, and this is the method of indirect proof. If we have not only delivered an imputation adequate on the level of meaning but also proved its causal adequacy for several of the fundamental concepts which form, so to speak, the cornerstones of a style of thinking – to stay with our example of conservative thinking, then, the concepts in question would include the conservative concepts of freedom and tradition, as well as the 'abstract-concrete' dichotomy – it is always possible to decipher in them the conservative fundamental design (*Grundintention*), the principle of formation in conservative thinking, with such clarity that, should the correctness of the imputation for this fundamental design also be shown, we can consider as equally 'conservative' all the concepts formed by this design, but for which imputability on the level of causal adequacy can no longer directly be shown. The two-phased total proof, in short, is only required for the 'cornerstones' of a style of thinking. Once these are secured, it will be sufficient to show adequacy on the level of meaning for the remaining elements.

If the problem of sociological imputation contains imponderables, left to careful estimates by the sociological-historical instincts of researchers and readers, this remainder is no greater than with any other kind of study. The false path to arbitrary or 'merely plausible' constructions is blocked by the fact that every imputation achieved must be justified for each case. The point of the double imputation is to supply criteria to the sociology of knowledge and thereby to render its discussion subject to controls.

All of cultural sociology rests upon the problem of imputation. This problem forms its methodological axis. Imputations are doubtless constructions, but every other historical science is a construction as well, since it reconstructs the past from surviving documents, and is thus forced to reconstruct what was once coming into being on the basis of what has now come to be. The decisive question can only be whether the construction that has been arrived at is grounded in the substance of the matter. A reconstruction which rests upon correspondence of meanings alone runs the risk of becoming nothing but construction – of not rising above the level on which the philosophy of history moved.

The sociology of culture does not become a positive science until it undergirds interpretations adequate on the level of meaning with historical causation, and until it keeps the fact in view that mere adequacy of meanings (inner logicality) can serve as nothing more than starting point for historical-sociological conclusions.

The greatest danger of imputations which are nothing more than adequate on the level of meaning consists of over-generalising intuitively meaningful interpretations. It would be easy to be misled into asserting a constant correlation between historicism and conservatism, to return to our example, because inherent plausibility speaks for the proposition that history-mindedness and emphasis on historicity flow out of a conservative fundamental impulse. But nothing could be further from the truth. The conservative conception of history – which appears, so to speak, 'self-evident' to us – is the product of a specific sociological constellation, the after-effects of which continue to the present day. The best counter-evidence is provided by the fact that the revolutionary Enlightenment also displayed an intense interest in history.[8] This Enlightenment concept of history, however, is completely different from the traditionalist and historicist one; and this is a difference which we cannot deduce *a priori* but which can only be deciphered from the historical matter, from the sociological embeddedness of this concept, by analysis of the meanings involved.

Another guarantee against over-generalisations of imputations resting on self-evidence of meanings is familiarity with intellectual history, because this allows us to trace down the point at which the meaning of a concept received the specific form in which it became imputable in a certain way. In order to be able to make correct claims, it is necessary, in sum, to refine one's approach as much as possible and to begin by tracing the unique interconnections within the overall development of an historical life-space.

If there is danger on the one side from a generalising superficiality, which constructs necessary connections out of mere plausibilities of meaning, there is also a contrary danger arising from exaggerated methodological scrupulousness about what can be proved. To the extent that this relies exclusively upon material proofs (*Realbeweise*), it succumbs to agnosticism. In view of the actual course of historical events, it would be utterly wrong to put all the weight on the material-causal proofs of an imputation, and so, for example, to impute to conservative thinking only those concepts for which the political place of origin can be demonstrated. The utopian aim of such a research-mentality would involve producing statistics of the concepts used by conservative authors, and the attempt to make imputations on the basis of such statistics. Such rigour, if at all feasible, would nevertheless be misconceived, since it would, for its part, neglect the significance of the imputations based on correspondence of meanings. The question in imputation is not, after all, 'how often' a concept is used by conservative authors, but 'how' it is used. The fundamental design (*Grundintention*), the inclination of the intellectual project (*Denkwollen*), the stylistic principle are the determining factors – the inclination, in short, which finds latent expression in the constitution of the concept. The fact to which this consideration points is so weighty that a concept will even retain its conservative makeup when it is incidentally used by liberal authors. It is therefore essential to stress this inclination and the fundamental principle upon which it can be shown to rest.

Freedom governs the spheres of thought and mind: logically speaking, the individual may well deliberately take a political stance entirely different from that dictated by his actual habits of thinking. It seems that it is by and large only in *collective movements* that the designs and styles of thinking hang together. But precisely because the individual taken alone possesses the capacity for unconstrained choice in any particular case, it is wrong by the standards of real history to seek the sole criterion of imputability in the actual carriers of the thought.

Imputation by reference to sociological factors in itself is even more uncertain than imputation on grounds of adequacy of meanings. When we look more closely and disregard the obvious limiting cases, it is frequently not at all clear whether an individual is to be taken as conservative, for example, or as progressive. That an individual's own professions are not always correct, needs hardly to be emphasised. Illusion and lack of ability to grasp the actual character of one's own existence often block the way to accurate self-assessment. Whether to classify someone as 'conservative' or 'progressive', then, depends upon considerations which themselves involve adequacy on the level of meaning. The problem of adequacy in respect to meanings thus comes back at the stage of causal imputation (*Zurechnung*). Where the political and social classification (*Zurechnung*)[†] of a historical personage is uncertain, the

---

[†]Mannheim takes surprising advantage here of a terminological ambiguity. He has been using the term '*Zurechnung*' to cover the claims made by the two kinds of analysis which together form, in his view, sociology of knowledge and, more broadly, sociology of culture. They are claims about correspondence of meanings between some analysed occurrence and another, presumably more comprehensive or systematic structure, and claims about empirical linkages between concrete intellectual phenomena and unit(s) of analysis constituted by sociological and/or historical study. At the present point, however, in order to further his argument about the interdependence between the two types of analysis, he shifts to a use of the term which has very little to do with interpretive or explanatory statements of relationships (which 'impute' some result to the logical or empirical operations of an antecedent entity). Problems of classification, interesting and real as they may be, are not identical with problems of imputation. To translate '*Zurechnung*' as 'imputation' would be misleading here, but failure to indicate the linguistic connection would obscure the pattern of Mannheim's argument at this point. *Trs.*

42

analysis of its way of thinking, its style of thinking, can be decisive.

Clearly in such cases we assume that the socio-political characteristics of the concepts and modes of thinking for that time have been ascertained on the basis of other sources. An immediate objection to this may be that we are moving around in a circle, because on one occasion we establish, for example, the imputation of a style of thinking from the real bearers of the style; and, on another, we explain the imputation of a specific bearer by his style of thinking. This circularity does in fact exist, but it also exists in the other cultural sciences, as for example in art history. A methodologist in art history has written:

> At the outset we determine the classification of an undated work by tracing certain characteristics of style to a particular period of art; whereupon our knowledge of the style of this period will be enhanced on other points by this specific piece of work.[9]

But the situation takes on such hopeless form only when stating the problems in abstraction. While actually engaged in research and moving through the concrete subject matter under study, it is precisely this reciprocal illumination which brings about the most complete penetration of the materials.*

Once we have established to which social and political currents we can impute the most important basic concepts and other fundamental forms of thinking, observation of their subsequent fate is within our reach, because it is always possible to relate the perceivable changes in meaning to the political and social fate of the 'bearing' strata. The hypothesis that change is related to change in the social and political constellation can be established fairly easily with regard to elements in the contents of thinking. The ideologies of conservative strata (their objectives, political beliefs, etc.) change in line with the total constellation in which these ideologies have to assert themselves. Further, all changes that can be traced back to the fact that new strata are pushed into a conservative position, always find some ideological expression. Conservatism assumes different forms in accordance with the changing composition of the 'bearing' strata. Properly speaking, the conservatism of the aristocracy, small estates, bureaucracy and monarchy vary. They change individually and conjointly according to the forms of their interrelationships and according to the relationship between their conservatism and that of the church.

Ideological shifts will also take place when new strata come to conservatism, as when the bourgeoisie, having 'arrived', assume conservative positions. Such changes, of course, rather than

43

coming about in leaps come about only gradually, and always in closest contact with the elements of thought earlier contained within the tradition.

Our present interest is by no means principally directed towards the aspects we have just lightly sketched, concerning the *contents* of conservatism, but towards the *formal* determinations of this way of thinking. The problem here is whether this 'counter-logic', once arisen, is to be regarded as a *unity* undergoing change in the further course of events, or whether it quickly dissolves and is to be seen as a short-lived product of a unique situation. The question is, accordingly, whether it is only the contents of conservative thinking that are sociologically conditioned and which transform themselves in their development in accordance with their bonds to existence (*seinsgebunden*), or whether this manner of transformation applies to the whole way of thinking and its corresponding forms of thinking. We believe that this dimension too – the social bondedness of forms of thought, during the epoch we are investigating – can be established.

We have made German conservatism the particular object of such an analysis since what is creative, in our view, in this thinking is that it has achieved the '*counter-revolutionising*' of the forms of thought. It is for this reason that the basic tendencies of this thinking can be grasped here, as it were, in its pure state.

That it is precisely Germany which until the middle of the nineteenth century exhibits this marked division between two kinds of 'logic', has causes which can be ascertained by way of sociological analysis. These causes include, to begin with, the supra-sociological factor that the German spirit possesses a distinctive philosophical and logical aptitude and that disturbances in the existential foundation will therefore make themselves felt even in the spheres of philosophy and logic. A comparison of the various types of romanticism clearly demonstrates this.

The romantic experience is a general European phenomenon which emerged at approximately the same time in all European countries. It arose partly as a genuine reaction to identical problems presented by a rationalised capitalist world, and partly as a result of secondary ideological influences. While its basic cause – the general similarity of the total situation throughout the modern Western world – is thus everywhere the same, the way in which this common historical factor works itself out in different countries varies with the distinctive social and cultural characteristics of the different nations. And it is already striking, in a comparison of the romanticisms of different countries, that, for example, while romanticism articulated itself in France through the medium of poetry, in Germany it obtained its special expression in philosophy. Not romantic poetry, but the unique phenomenon of German romantic thought characterises German romanticism. This is merely noted as a symptom of the fact that in Germany reactions to changes in the social and intellectual substructure are far more intense on the philosophical level than in other countries. Since Marx,[10] it has practically become the inevitable starting point for every interpretation of modern development to accept that Germany experienced the French Revolution on the plane of philosophy.

While this is indeed by and large the case for German idealism, the opposite thesis can lay claim to even greater validity: that in Germany the counter-revolution, or the 'opposite of the revolution' (to use a French traditionalist term),[11] developed the logical and philosophical part of its intellectual universe more thoroughly than was the case elsewhere. As France played the role of providing the most radical elaboration of all the enlightened and rationalistic elements in consciousness, and thus became the acknowledged bearer of 'abstract thought', Germany can be said to have played a complementary role, since she turned conservative organic and historical thought into a spiritual weapon, giving it at the same time an inner consistency and logic of its own.

Even this ideological difference among countries has its socio-historical components.[12] It is usual to consider England as the archetype home of evolutionary development, and the romantics especially have impressed on us the conservative turn that may be given to this evolutionism, by simultaneously presenting England as both evolutionary and conservative. This is doubtlessly correct to some extent – especially if England is contrasted with France, which is in fact the archetypical radical revolutionary country of the new era. But if we shift our attention to Germany we can see that these evolutionary features are also characteristic of her modern development. Until now there have been no revolutions in Germany (in the radical French sense), but at most internal growing pains and temporary disturbances. But while evolution-ism in England is based on the fact that the conservative strata displayed an extraordinary elasticity and adaptability to new circumstances, and could therefore always preserve their power amid constant change, the evolutionary character of German development rested upon the strong pressure of the ruling groups on those below, preventing revolution. The existence of this strong barrier against internal disturbances is almost certainly connected with the fact that the military stratum constituted the nucleus of German society. (This in its turn is connected with the geographi-cal situation, especially of Prussia between two enemy countries, which led to the formation of a military state.)[13] And this meant a strong backing for both the conservative movement and its emotional and intellectual world.

Summing up the comparison, then, it can be said that English evolutionism rests upon the flexible mentality of the conservative strata, epitomised by the fact that England's aristocracy never became a caste,[14] while the continuity of German development is grounded upon the relatively strong exclusivity and domination which characterises German conservatism. Although development did not proceed by sudden eruptions in either country, the different ways in which they were evolutionary was bound to affect the form and structure of their respective ideologies. This is most clearly reflected in the political contrasts as we may find them at the beginning of the period with which we are concerned.

For a very long time liberalism in Germany was unable to affect conservatism and influenced it very little. We have to wait until Stahl before we can detect the first traces of any liberal influence on conservatism. Accordingly, liberalism and conservatism stood sharply opposed to each other – it is tempting to say, like thesis and antithesis. By contrast, the relations between Whigs and Tories in England up to 1790 were such that it is not at all possible to grasp them adequately by means of the German political terminology. In particular, Whiggism does not correspond to what was called liberalism in Germany.[15]

The fact that the fundamental conservative design could assert itself with such paradigmatic sharpness in German thinking must be ascribed to the almost antithetical structure of German political life, where the interpenetration of parties and social strata as it occurred in England was impossible to anything like the same extent, and where – in addition and more importantly – conservatism could adhere strictly to its own inner dynamics. Not even in the later period, so far as we can see, when the oppositions sharpened even there as a result of the French Revolution, did England display any such approximation to the abstract schematics of polar opposition.

Further, in Germany, conservative ideology had about half a century of undisturbed intellectual development available. It had therefore had time to refine itself and to achieve philosophical sophistication without having to cope with the demands of a parliamentary life which, as a result of its inevitable practical conflicts, would certainly have compromised its purity and ideological consistency. As soon as parliamentary life begins,[16] the clear contours of world-views and ideologies increasingly lose their sharpness.[17] That these, though faded, nevertheless persist into the present, is due to the fact that the 'incubation period' of ideology formation was a very long one, so that there was time

46

during this formative period for the ideology to develop thorough-ly and consistently according to its own logical principles. Just the necessary minimum of ideological pressure was present: the distant threat of the revolution in France provided precisely the right inducement to stir people into occupying themselves with these policical and world-view matters, while the hard facts of reality were not yet mature enough to demand action. Action, as we know, always leads to compromises and to logical inconsist-ency.

This then is the situation: under the ideological impact of the French Revolution there developed in Germany a purely ideo-logical spiritual counter-movement which had at its disposal a long span of time to bring to fruition the conservative impulses and *to think them through* to their logical conclusion. The war cry against the revolution did not originate in Germany. Although it lacks a genuine German origin, it was there that it was pursued to its logical conclusion.

The main stimulus comes from England – ground which was far more politicised than Germany at that time. It comes from Burke. What happens in Germany is the process of 'thinking through to the end' – a philosophical deepening of the points which Burke initially posed, which are then combined with genuinely German elements. Even the way in which Burke is taken up is revealing. Burke was anything but what his first German translator, Gentz, and his friend, Adam Müller, deemed him to be. Müller makes him a reactionary, whereas Burke, even as he becomes increas-ingly conservative as he got older, retained so many liberal elements that even contemporary English liberals can claim him.[18]

In a word, Germany achieved for the ideology of conservatism what France did for progressive Enlightenment – she worked it out most fully to its logical conclusions. The Enlightenment had its start in England, arose in its true guise in the most progressive place for capitalist development, and then moved over to France, to achieve only there its most radically abstract and atheistically materialist form. The counter-revolutionary critique of the French Revolution similarly originated in England, and achieved its most consistent exposition on German soil. The most important intellectual seeds of 'historicism', for instance, are to be found in Burke. But 'historicism' as a method is a product of the German conservative spirit, so far as we can see; and when it does appear in England, much later, it is as a result of German influence. Maine, in his *Ancient Law* (1861), is the disciple of Savigny.[19]

That in Germany conservatism could be carried to its logical conclusion and that the polarities in the predominant world-views and ways of thinking of the time are so clearly visible, can be

47

attributed (as we shall see) partly to the lack of a substantial and uncompromised middle stratum (*Mittelschicht*), which could, in accordance with its own social centre of gravity, bring about a synthesis, a point of balance. Insofar as such a middle stratum existed at all, its mentality either expressed itself within the framework of conservatism, where it played a moderating role of which we shall have to speak again later; or it succumbed to an extreme liberal, professorial, and doctrinaire position, which in turn exacerbated the polarisation of the extremes. To these factors making for separation must be added another, geographical, one. While the Rhineland and Southern Germany came within the direct French sphere of influence, and were thus the seat of German liberalism, Prussia and Austria were the main citadels of conservatism. This geographical difference, to say nothing of the economic differences, also intensified the polarisation which concerns us.

Thus it is clear, taking all these factors together, why the antithesis between liberal and conservative thought is to be found in its most logically consistent form in Germany in the first half of the nineteenth century, and why it is precisely in Germany that sociological forces made their distinctive contribution to bringing it about that that which presents itself in far more involuted form in France and in England was able to achieve a certain logical structural consistency. This is why it is in Germany that we can observe in almost paradigmatic clarity the impact of social forces upon the logical structures of thinking itself, and why we have chosen this topic as the starting-point for our analysis of the significance of political elements for the development of thought.

3 Modern structural relations

After this somewhat extended explanation of our reasons for choosing to study the various dominant styles of thought within the German cultural complex, and the ways in which these are connected to existence, we are now ready to return to a few more *general* problems for a sociology of knowledge analysis, problems which provide the larger context for our particular inquiry.

Our principal interest lies in the study of the structural configuration within which a particular spiritual universe and the universe of thinking internal to it arise and take form. This requires us to get at the foremost problems for the history of ideas as well as for the sociology of knowledge: how and in what form did all the ways of thinking, currents of thought, meanings of concepts, and categories of thought come about that constitute the present state of our knowledge and the totality of our world-views? This does not mean that we are primarily interested in thought within the scientific disciplines or that which is in general 'exact' in the manner of the natural sciences; we are rather interested in the thinking of everyday life and, insofar as it is closely linked to this, in thought within the historical cultural sciences. What interests us, in short, is *historical thinking*.

We distinguish such 'historical thinking' from natural-science thinking because it has a developmental structure very different from that of natural-science knowledge. In the case of the 'exact' sciences, thinking and knowing seem to develop more nearly divorced from the social corpus and in accordance with their own dynamics. In these sciences, we appear to have a development in which, once the fundamental designs, initial problems and axiomatics are given, the thought process unfolds according to logical laws of inconsistency. This thinking is not 'socially unattached' either, from a sociological point of view, since the basic impulses out of which the exact sciences arise are bound to a specific stage of social development and to certain general constellations;[20] and the need of the social whole continues to enter into the makeup of the lines of inquiry and objectives of research in this type of knowledge. But apart from these factors determining the framework of the research agenda, thinking proceeds by way of immanent unfolding. One problem follows from another in a sequence consistent in subject-matter and logic, and sociological determination strikes us as important and grasp-able only at starting-points and at important turning-points. This is by no means the case in the domain of 'historical thinking', which is always rooted in the ways in which the historical entity defines its historical and social problems, and which is a sphere having an immediate function for the growth of that entity. As noted, such historical thinking is already registered in everyday life. The historical cultural sciences represent a more refined, elaborate and consistent knowledge, but this knowledge arises and develops from attitudes which are related to the experiential knowledge of everyday, and which are thus an integral part of the complex of social growth. Historical thinking is thinking connected to exist-ence *par excellence* – a circumstance which does not, in our opinion, reduce the validity of the knowledge it achieves, but which simply differentiates the structure and nature of this part of the intellectual universe from the thinking which links technical and natural-scientific concerns.[21]

If this hemisphere of the intellectual universe represents the phenomenon of connectedness to existence in its most finished expression, then it must become our task to investigate the inner

49

growth of this knowledge in search of its structure. We could attempt to do this by way of general observations. But since it is our view that structural relationships always take historically distinct forms, it seems more fruitful to pose the more general questions within the framework of a concrete analysis restricted to a narrowly bounded segment of time.

Some justification is required for the fact that in the course of this investigation we will be treating such categories as 'conservative', 'liberal' and 'socialist' thinking as *political* categories. This characterisation is not meant to suggest that in our view the political element is somehow always predominant in the development of the spiritual universe, but merely that the constitutive spiritual tendencies in the era under consideration are best characterised and comprehended on the basis of political ones.

The spiritual universe of a given period, with its existing store and forms of knowledge, is an incredibly complex structure. We can only succeed in envisioning it and following it in its growth if we are able, at first with the aid of the history of ideas, to sort the conceptual elements and forms of thinking derived from other periods of intellectual history into a classification according to historical origin. But we cannot be satisfied with such a schematic classification. We must further establish in which connection and through which real-world impulses the different concepts and elements of thought arose. So much seems certain: observations, contents and forms of thinking do not arise as isolated, sporadic chance ideas. They come into being on the strength of collective projects, always as parts or 'elements' within the larger design of an integral tendency of observation. It is not isolated pieces of thinking that are to be observed in their rise and career, but clusters of ideas (their contents and forms, etc.) which grow up and develop grouped coherently around a given problem-complex in life.

Even the most solitary thinker does not think in discrete intuitions, but on the basis of a more comprehensive design of thinking which somehow commands his life. And this design of his own is always part of a collective design which goes far beyond him. This fact does not deny the reality of the creative aspect, nor does it diminish the extent of irrational elements in our life. It merely means that even the 'genius' does not think in a vacuum, but can only choose the starting-point for his thinking from among the concepts and problems with which history presents him. These concepts and problems express a spiritual and experiential situation which, just as much as the other constituents of our life, has its rise in the historical stream. However radical the novelty of what he brings to life, the thinker will always do it on the basis of the then-prevailing state of the question concerning life, the store of his concepts will be only a modification of this collective possession, and the innovation will inevitably be taken up in turn within the on-going historical current.

Even where the experiencing subject believes that 'insights' and 'designs' come to him from himself alone, 'inspirationally' and 'in a flash', they nevertheless originate in collective fundamental designs, which are alive in him as well, although he is not self-reflectively conscious of it. It is, however, one of the most important tasks of the sociology of thinking to press on to the level of collective designs – which sustains itself, as it were, behind the individual's back, not entering into self-reflective consciousness – and to bring out the deeper contextures of discrete individual observations which come about within an age or current. This is a reconstruction.

The biographer may be interested in the specific heroic uniqueness of a creative genius (the reality of which we are not in the least denying), but the sociologist is much more interested in his 'integral blocks of thoughts' and 'impulses to form worlds', – all of which belong to the age as a whole.

If such collective designs are presupposed for the history of thought, as they have long been considered proven for all other levels of the spirit, we are immediately faced with the question: what holds these masses of ideas together, and the forms of thinking that develop with them, even though they are commonly also in movement towards or against one another? What is the seat of the volitional centre of these designs, from which the different cognitive tendencies and styles of thinking form themselves, and which alone allow us cognitively to enter into the social and spiritual universe?

Every epoch which has been even slightly complex has been marked by more than one tendency and style of thinking, more than one standpoint, and even such seemingly uniform periods as the Middle Ages are filled with a number of tendencies and standpoints in thinking. But the distinctive feature of modern development is that, beginning in the seventeenth century and culminating in the nineteenth, *the political element increasingly becomes the point around which all of the currents in the ideological universe crystallise*.

The religious definition of all problems forms the kernel of crystallisation in the Middle Ages. One has the impression that the various currents move like lines upon a global surface, crossing one another, but without any clear signs of direction. Looking at the early modern period, in contrast, one is persuaded that the

51

currents of ideas are more unambiguously comprehensible here, if only because they stand in a univocally comprehensible relationship to the total social and political process.

It is at least tendentially the case that every ideological element, and especially every more comprehensive current, more or less directly defines itself as a function of one of the social and political tendencies, and that it consequently develops in close connection with it.

This means, at the same time, that the global unity of the universe of world-views, within which the most varied elements had been present in amalgamation, underwent a split, that the elements which have entered into the new associations are now free of their former connections and group themselves around the socially determined fundamental designs, now become central. This leads to a splitting and regrouping in the ideological universe, whose tendencies increasingly become a mirror image of the social whole and its main currents.

Viewing the result of this process in retrospect, one might also express the facts of the case as follows: we are no longer concerned with a unified, though internally variegated world-view; from now on, in accordance with the plurality of strata in the social whole, a number of worlds confront one another.

This gradual departure of political and social designs from the religious framework can best be observed by looking at the course of the English Revolution of the seventeenth century. Once freed – and becoming ever more autonomous from this point on – the political turns into the unifying element within the various tendencies, which had come into being through the division in the religious world-view and which will from now on permeate the world. This does not mean that from then on each individual thinker is consciously concerned with politics, but that the total spiritual universe in all its currents, is borne by political designs, when seen from the viewpoint of the collective.

This is not to suggest that the medieval ideological universe is anything like a free-floating one, but merely that the 'social problem' does not play nearly such a predominant role, and that the relationship of the ideological to the 'base' is one entailing much more 'mediation', i.e. it is not comprehensible in terms of direct causal relations.

We are arguing, in short, that there is a realignment in the world of spirit and knowledge, a realignment and reordering of the structure of growth in the world of ideas, corresponding to the transformation of the hierarchically organised society of estate into a class-stratified society; and that the realignment in the spiritual universe takes place in a relationship to the class-stratification which is complex but which can nevertheless be directly traced and imputed.

The most important of the changes constituting the structure of modern spiritual and social life will first be briefly summarised: (a) The structure of the modern world is no longer that of an enclosed cosmos, but a process. History is not the cyclical, if also polyphonic, fulfilment of a basic design, but a continuous progression from one state to a later and 'higher' one.

*Emphasis on this element of progression was fully in character for the Enlightenment, the exponent of the bourgeois world, because it thereby hypostatised its own partial function as bearer of the growth of the new, elevating this function to the structure of the world as a whole. Condorcet is the chief representative of this idea of progress. In its conception of a progressive, processive universe, bourgeois thinking was hypostatising not only its partial function as the 'element for growth' but also its orientation to science and to the 'civilisation sphere', two historical factors which in fact had such a progressive structure. But it exaggeratedly took a part for the whole, since cultural formations (art, religion etc.) do not become processive even within a development which is processive overall.

Progressive thinking considers the elements of the past which survive in the present to be 'moribund remnants'. This is a point of view typical of the one-sided determinations of a partial and particular standpoint. The present which is now is always a cross-section of the preserved past – present and future at once. What has passed never dies out, but changes to accord with the newness that is coming into being.

In our analysis of conservative thinking in Germany we will see that there exists a modern conservative thinking, adapted to the new situation. The problem of conservatism really only begins at this point. The difference between 'conservative' and 'progressive' forces in the present consists primarily in the fact that, in a progressive world, the conservative element is not the bearer of events, authentically creative, but rather 'reactive' in the sense that it first becomes aware of itself as antitheses, as antithetical to the new, and that it can become creative only in this form.*

(b) The process-like character of historical development is not linear but marked by antinomies: it is dialectical.[22] Mutually counter-working tendencies yield the new. The prevalence of process itself, as well as an ever greater number of the elements in

53

process, are functionalised into factors furthering or impeding the process of growth. Every element must be considered as a part, and it is understandable only on the basis of its function with regard to the emerging whole. One element points to the future; another carries the past forward into the present; the third strives to stabilise the current situation.

(c) That such a thing can happen, that it becomes possible for all the elements of the spiritual universe to be ever more function-alised, is due to the fact, as mentioned, that the social process itself is reconstituted into class-related strata of development. An important factor in this transformation is the gradual growing together of smaller territories to form a coordinated, more inclusive historical unit. The emergence of the absolutist unitary state, precursor of the nation state, already implies, through the system of the international balance of power, the problem of even more comprehensive associations of peoples, but its immediate effect is to relativise the meaningfulness of separate territorial developments and to subsume entities which almost resemble mosaics *within the dynamics of an all-inclusive stream of develop-ment*. It is hardly necessary to emphasise that this unification falls first of all to the account of economic development. Through this process, in any case, the membraneous, segmented organisation is increasingly superceded by a stratified one. From now on, a historical unit reacts to external stimuli in accordance with its social makeup, far more than its territorial one. At the cultural level this means the achievement or at least a tendency toward a unified culture, and this in two senses: in the sense of a melioration (not abolition) of provincial differences, and in the sense of a gradual inclusion of ever more strata in the cultural process, above all through the entry of their fundamental designs and world-projects into the resulting overarching dynamics. With this interplay of active forces, the ensuing movement then takes the form that some strata are forced, in keeping with the primary weight of their interests, to desire a preservation of an earlier state of the social whole (so that, for example, the stratum of landowners readily becomes the centre of reaction); other strata become the upholders of the new world (as is the case with commercial, industrial, and financial capitalists); and still others – who are disadvantaged in the new world but can no longer return to the old state of things, because the framework within which they had existed there, the system of estates, has been demolished – bear what is first coming into being (viz., the proletariat).[23]

(d) This dynamic restructuring process of the social whole into classes need not, in and of itself, have caused a split in world views. It is easily conceivable that there might be only a *single*

54

world-view (ideological universe), even while the different strata oppose one another, in pursuit of their individual interests, simply by drawing different conclusions from the same ideological reasonings and upon an agreed state of the principal questions. But the fact is that, for example, political conservatism in defense of interests comes with a conservative world-view, that an historically later stage in the conception of the world accompanies political progressiveness, and so on. It is simply the case that interests do not merely oppose interests: worlds struggle against worlds.

The conservative does not want satisfaction of his interests alone, but also his own world, a world in which his interests are at home. The bourgeois does not want only his demands fulfilled, but also a world shaped by his own mentality. The proletarian is not content to secure his future; he wants a future in keeping with his spirit.

For the moment, it may suffice to establish this point by indicating that the political theories of the various political parties are historically rooted in different world-views, and that this historically rooted core, while revealing an incredible capacity for adaptation to the emerging new world, continues to live as foundation and starting-point of further development. Liberal theory is based on the mentality of the eighteenth-century Enlightenment,[24] while conservative theory rests primarily on romanticism,[25] although it must be noted that it has also worked fundamental designs from earlier stages into its own. In this way *the different strata are not merely bearers of different world designs, but also representatives of different historical stages of the past*. A struggle among the various historical stages of the cultural entity in question, accordingly, accompanies the contest of forces and the designs of the contesting strata, with the unceasing formation of the 'new' as the objective.

(e) For the specific problem of the sociology of knowledge, all this means that *a specific design of thinking comes with every particular fundamental world-view design*. Rationalism's style of thinking is completely different from that of romanticism; and with the retention of the different elements of world-views, the distinctive character of thinking and axioms of different historical stages are to a large extent also preserved. The conservative style of thinking and manner of reasoning continues to differ from that of a liberal or socialist one, even at a later stage. This continuity is naturally more pronounced in the *forms of thinking* than in the contents of thinking, so that a certain persistence is much more evident and traceable in matters of form than amid the fluctuations of the contents. But absolute continuity cannot be presumed in this

55

respect either: conservative and liberal styles of thought change over time even in their logical structure. Moreover, they often interpenetrate one another, and this factor in particular introduces complications into our inquiry. For us it is important not only that we attentively isolate and distinguish the diverse styles of thought, but also that we observe with equal care every synthesis that may come about.

What conservative thinking 'learns' or takes over from liberalism (and vice versa) is not to be underestimated, but it must already be indicated that *a complete amalgamation never takes place*. The differences in historical starting-points and basic intentions are too vast to allow a *complete synthesis*. Everything else concerning these questions is left for later treatment. We will return to these themes as soon as the next chapter, where we will be concerned with the more detailed specification of the nature of conservatism. To give some additional support, for the time being, to the last substantive assertion, we will next call attention to a difference in the styles of thought which manifests itself in the ways they define central problems.

(f) Nothing characterises the differences among styles of thought more fully than differences at the level upon which problems are defined. Where the same questions are at issue, such as the justification of rule or the interpretation of history, it is often more material to notice how the reasoner addresses the question (how he defines the problem) than how he answers it. The differences among the styles of thought that occupy us here can be characterised by the following three ideal-typical schemes for defining problems, each of which has an affinity with a different style of thought.[26]

In addressing the question concerning the legitimation of rule, conservative thinking tends to favour theological-mystical, or, in any case, transcendental definitions of the issue. The argument from 'divine right' belongs to the basic store of conservative thinking, even when the latter has become pantheistic, which is to say, actually unbelieving. History then takes the place of divine transcendence. The line of inquiry followed by conservative justifications accordingly operates predominantly upon a plane of *mythical transcendence*. In contrast, liberal-bourgeois thought sets the problem predominantly upon a *juristic* plane, specifically in conjunction with natural law. The *legitimacy of a form of rule* is justified by means of purely ideological, hypothetical constructions, which generate the meanings required, always at *the juristic level of validity* (social contract). Socialist thinking, on the other hand, defines problems primarily upon the plane of economics. With this it renders the approach by way of juristic constitution irrelevant by definition, stigmatising it as 'ideology'. Hypostatising of the mythical-metaphysical plane in the case of conservative thinking, stating the issues in terms of juristic validity in the case of bourgeois thinking, and hypostatising of the economic sphere in the case of proletarian thinking – these are typical, understandable constellations, which indicate that the dispute about the legitimacy of a given rule or forms of government does not proceed in a homogeneous way where the problems are defined differently.

The reason for this lies in the differences among the axiomatic structures of the different styles of thinking. In the case in point, bourgeois thinking hypostatises the juristic, natural-law element only in order to relativise the mythical-transcendental approach as a whole.[27] The proletarian opposition hypostatises the economic element for the same reasons, in order to relativise the natural-law-juristic approach as merely ideological. But the bourgeoisie's preference for remaining upon the legalistic plane can also be understood in a positive way. The balance of its own interests does not allow the bourgeoisie to go beyond juristic-natural-law reasonings on behalf of economic and political liberty and equality. For upon this plane, private property can still be legitimated as a natural right; as soon as the problem of liberty and equality is posed at the economic level, however, the most fundamental purpose of the bourgeois world is defined. But this was precisely why proletarian reasoning had to press this line of questioning and to hypostatise the economic definition of issues.

What could be shown directly in the ideological conflict over the legitimation or delegitimation of rule has its parallels in the variety of ways questions are defined when the task is the *interpretation of history*. All tendencies of thinking must eventually face up to the task of interpreting the process of history. At the same time, however, the interpretation of history becomes a weapon, to be employed upon the most exalted field of conflict between the parties, because it is not interests which confront one another here, but rather, it seems almost as a matter of choice, the diverse authentic world-views and socially and politically rooted designs upon the world.

The fundamental conservative design of seeing things under the aspect of transcendence also comes into play here, and it is the *metaphysical philosophy of history* which most adequately corresponds to it. Bourgeois thinking, on the other hand, with its focus of concentration on the juristic plane, makes the state into the bearer of the historical. All history becomes state history, and all events are construed in relation to the state. Even when bourgeois history is cultural, it strives to comprehend its subject-matter on the 'level of validity', as if it were construing laws. 'Proletarian thinking' appears here too as third contestant, and here too it hypostatises – as the others had hypostatised transcendence or the state – the economic plane, and it brings the so-called 'materialist' interpretation of history into action against the other two, construing them as merely ideological interpretations.[28]

We can already see from this example how different styles of thought are either created or at least maintained in ideological conflict, and that not only are different substantive elements seized upon according to the basic designs of the strata in conflict, but also formal logical elements (viz., the definition of problems and the hypostatisation of different ontological levels: the hypostatising of mythical-transcendental, juristic or economic elements) are brought forward by these different designs.

If to this is added the consideration that the philosophical and logical element, which reaches up into the various political reasonings, inherently presupposes correspondingly varied systems of philosophy and world-view, it becomes clear that the contexts of philosophy and world-view, linked to the social process, themselves also have their development within this political medium. This situation is not, however, to be envisaged as though, for instance, a specific philosopher were always deliberately fabricating ideologies for a political and social tendency when working on his system – although, of course, this frequently happens. The point is, rather, that the intellectual achievement of the philosophising individual, no matter how unpolitical and 'lonely' it may appear, is part, by virtue of its starting-point alone, of a more widely shared purposive design in thinking, which is, in turn, historically carried by a purposive design in society.

It is the nature of philosophical work to be structurally the 'underbuilding' for things which are immediately given; the philosopher does nothing more than to analyse and explicate that which everyday life accepts as unquestioned fact, with a view to the premises implicit in it.[29] Yet these givens are by no means eternal factors, but rather ones which are sociologically determined in history. Any particular philosophy has consequently no other meaning *from a sociological point of view*, than that of being the gradual systematic unfolding of a specific style of thinking, the style which the philosopher in question is said to represent.[30] When Kant builds up his system, he is not contriving an ideology for bourgeois thinking, but, in his intellectual achievement, he does presuppose axiomatic premises, as it were, and adopts tendencies in thinking which have reached him through history, borne by nothing other than bourgeois world designs and bourgeois rationalism. And what he accomplishes is merely a retroactive explication on a grand scale of all the systematic premises, as it were, which are integral to this design in thinking; that is, he provided a systematic 'underbuilding' for 'facts', which are unproblematically self-evident only for a specific tendency of thinking. The radical transcendence of a system of thought therefore never develops on the ground on which the system itself was created, but upon grounds of a different existential situation, which most often rests upon altogether contrary historical forces, able to call into question the factors which the system, like its animating tendency, accepts as self-evident facts.[31]

A philosopher – unless he is at the same time also a declared political writer – may therefore be imputed to a political tendency in thinking only in the sense that a tendency of thinking which is borne at the level of collective events by a specific political and social world design (*Weltwollungen*) is most intensively alive in him. The political element is thus – and this is a matter which we can already state with some precision at this stage of our inquiry – not necessarily creatively primary. Nor is it necessarily the originating cause in the emergence and growth of a tendency in thinking. The political element is simply, from the researcher's point of view, the element which can be most easily and clearly grasped for specifying the world designs and tendencies of thinking which are prevalent in an historical period. World design is more comprehensive than political design. Strictly speaking, the specific political design is contained within the encompassing world design, and nothing is further from us than to derive everything from politics. We let the political element be the starting-point for our analysis only because the vital conjunction (joint existence) between the speculative element and what happens in society is most clearly apparent in the political sphere and ultimately also because, during the historical period under study, the political did in fact largely become, as noted, the point around which the intellectual positions of the world-views accumulated.

4 The problem of modern rationalisation

The last preliminary inquiry to which we will submit the materials under study, the ideological universe of the historical period of interest to us, concerns the assumption, supported by many individual observations, that the differentiation of the social current into several counter-working, mutually opposed strata has corresponding to it a splitting, not only in the parts devoted to thinking, but also in the remaining dimensions of consciousness.

59

Corresponding to the social differentiations, in short, there is not only a reorganisation of structures of thinking but also, closely associated, a transformation in the structures of experience. What follows will explain this general assertion.

Attention has already been called to the fact that the distinctive characteristic of modern development is to be sought in the thoroughgoing rationalisation of the world. The rise of the exact science is accordingly nothing but a consistent elaboration of this basic intellectual design. There is no doubt that beginnings of such an effort already existed earlier, but it could not be carried through with this ruthless consistency until the modern age. No one could assert that there was a total absence of the element of rationality during earlier times (e.g., in the European Middle Ages) or in the world outside the Occident; but the point is that rationalisation in those times and places was only a *partial* one, which flowed all too soon once again into irrationalities.[32] Bourgeois-capitalist consciousness is marked by the fact that it knows of no principled limitation to such rationalisation.

This thoroughgoing rationalisation of the world has its unmistakable existence in a particular *design of thinking*, while, at the same time, it has a particular *form of experience* corresponding to it. The reshaping which brought about the present condition of the world was only achieved through the combination of both.

As far as the *design of thinking* is concerned, it can be grasped most directly and in its most radical articulation in the modern exact sciences. The clearest way of grasping the distinctive character of the new design in thinking which resides in the exact sciences, as well as its novelty in comparison to the design that immediately preceded it, is to inquire into the powers it has overcome in order to prevail. Such inquiry shows that the two adversaries of the newly rising natural sciences are, first, *mediaeval Aristotelian scholasticism*, and, second, the *Renaissance philosophy of nature*. We discover the plainest marks of the modern style of thinking if we find out just what it was that the pioneers of the new natural sciences opposed in Aristotle and the Renaissance philosophy of nature.

The *Aristotelian conception of the world* was opposed because it is *qualitatively* oriented, and because it involves the attempt to grasp each thing as having its own distinctive nature, and thus to grasp it on the basis of a teleological cause intrinsic to it, on the basis of an immanent determination of form. In opposition to this, the *new* intellectual project was directed towards a new conception of the world that attempted to explain the individual thing on the basis of *universal causes and laws* and sought to present the world as a composite of masses and forces. The recourse to mathematics, making it the foundation of the knowledge of nature, occurred precisely in order to overcome this *qualitatively oriented thinking*.

It was the *magical and analogising traits*, however, which were the targets in the attack on the Renaissance philosophy of nature, which had at first had a strong hold on the pioneers themselves. This struggle against magic and analogical thinking reveals, by its choice of targets, another side of modern rationalisation. And this fight on two fronts in fact serves to give rationalisation a dual character.

Rationalisation as contradiction to the experience and comprehension of the concretely *qualitative* and rationalisation as antithesis to magic are two fundamentally different phenomena, which are here joined together.

But there is a fundamental tendency which stands behind both and holds them together. This is a tendency to seek knowledge about things (and, to a large extent, also to manifest experiential interest in them) only to the extent that the findings about them are universally valid and universally demonstrable. The attempt is made to exclude from the results of cognition anything which is tied to a particular personality or which can only be demonstrated to a particular experiential community, and to retain only the determinations which are universally communicable. It is a matter of a striving for *socialisable knowledge*, in contrast to insights which can only be made accessible to particular, more restricted *experiential communities*. Only such certainties are to be sought as are universally demonstrable and not such as are evident only to a community of believers.[33] And because the calculable is the 'stratum' in consciousness which is universally demonstrable, the utopian ideal of knowledge lies in the mathematician's way of arriving at the sense of certainty.

This presents us with a peculiar identification of *truth* with *universal validity*. The approach to things rests on the completely unproved preconception that man only knows when his knowledge is demonstrable to everyone. In both types of rationalisation, then, that which imposes quantity as well as that which opposes magic, the sociologist finds *depersonalisation* and *decommunalisation* of knowledge, and these developments correspond to an *abstractness* which extends in several directions.

This knowledge involves indifference towards all concrete and particular elements in the object and towards all the sensitivities to knowledge which render the world comprehensible to the subject but which do not at the same time make that comprehension universally communicable. It further eleminates all *particular existential references* to man, nature, and things in which every piece of knowledge comes embedded. In man, only the subject constituted by epistemological theory, as it was later formulated, is capable of knowledge. The theory, in other words, heeds only universal experience, and this is *general* in two senses. It relates to many objects and is valid for many subjects. In objects, only the stratum which is general is of interest, and in the subject, only that has standing which renders it 'general', i.e., which 'socialises' it. This last is what is called 'reason'.

The material cause of the fact that this type of possible knowing could arise at all,[34] and more particularly, that it could be carried with such strictness to its final conclusions, lies in an existential transformation of the total subject. This 'rationalising' and 'quantifying' thinking is embedded in a psychic attitude and form of experience with regard to things and the world which may itself be described as 'abstract', although in a sense which is different from, if not unrelated to, that which pertains to the thinking. In itself, the quantification of nature goes parallel with the loss, or with the repression at least, of the pantheistic sense of the world; and this is symptomatic.

It has often been pointed out that the rationalism which manifests itself in the modern exact sciences has its parallel in the new economic system. With the substitution of a system of commodity production for an economy producing for need, there takes place a similar structural change in the attitude toward things as in the reduction of the qualitative to the quantitative, in thinking about nature. Here too, an orientation which is qualitative, the orientation to *use value*, is replaced by a quantifying orientation, in this case an orientation to *exchange value*, which considers goods merely in terms of their monetary equivalent. The orientation to abstraction which we have been discussing, accordingly, is manifest and dominant in both cases. In this as in every form of experience there is moreover a tendency toward expansion. This 'abstract' mode of orientation can first be observed with reference to nature and the world of goods, but it gradually broadens into a universal form of experience: it also becomes the basic form for comprehending the alien subject, the 'other'. In a world that is organised in a patriarchal or feudal way,[35] the 'other' is somehow a totality or at least a member of a hierarchically structured community, but in a commodity-producing society, he is a commodity too, with his labour power a quantifiable magnitude with which one reckons as with all other quantities.

It follows that the wider the compass within which man serves as a function of the expanding capitalist organisation based on calculation, the more commonly will he be experienced as an abstract calculable magnitude, and the more often will he himself experience the world around him as taken up with these abstract relationships. The psychological possibility of approaching men and things as something other than monetary equivalents remains of course, but from now on the possibility also exists of interpreting the whole world logically and consistently with only quantity in view. If it be asked to which sociological factor one may ascribe the rise and elaboration of a thoroughly consistent rationalism, one can well adhere to the frequently expressed view, that it was borne by the bearer of the whole modern capitalist world, the ascending bourgeoisie.

When making such sociological imputations, however, it is important to avoid a false naturalism. This is not meant to suggest that every individual bourgeois always and everywhere lives exclusively with this attitude towards the world around him. The point is rather, carefully expressed, that the predominant feature of the world project (*Weltwollen*) of the new social stratum, upon which rests the emergence of capitalism, brings into the realm of the possible a fundamentally novel form of experience, oriented systematically and consistently towards quantification and towards experiencing the world as abstract. Other social strata can share and increasingly manifest this type of attitude to the world and to their environment; but it becomes steadily more dominant, repressing all other tendencies, for the social stratum which stands in relations of this kind in the life-work which absorbs its everyday activities, the stratum for which the world created by these relations has become its immediate and pervasive environment.

5 The anti-capitalist opposition and the irrational

Most attempts to outline the general trend of the modern world tend to limit themselves to the rationalist line of development. The result is a picture of the contemporary world that strikes us as strange because it does not fit the reality we apprehend all around us, the facts and the world as we know it. This mechanised world and these abstract modes of experiencing and thinking are by no means all that is present in our time. When attempting to grasp the present in its fullness one will soon suspect that such a sketch has *only one tendency* in view, and that this tendency, while it doubtless exists, is accompanied by complementary phenomena of similar force.

And this is the point at which our inquiry truly begins and where our study of conservative thinking becomes genuinely relevant. We want to know: *what became of all the vital relationships and attitudes, as well as the forms of thinking corresponding to them, which were displaced by this increasingly thoroughgoing rationalis-*

ation? Did they simply sink into the past, or were they preserved in some place? And if they were preserved, in what form have they been handed down to us?

As one might expect, they did in fact persist, but as is usually the case in history, their existence became latent and manifested itself at most in complementary currents counter to the mainstream. They were taken up and reproduced, at first, by the social and intellectual strata which were not drawn into the capitalist process of rationalisation, or at least were not its main protagonists. The personal, concrete human relations which previously held sway were kept alive in varying, phenomenologically specifiable forms and degrees of intensity primarily in the peasant strata, in the petit-bourgeois groups which remained in touch with the experience of artisanship, and in the traditions of the nobility.

In particular, we find that the largely immanent and unbroken tradition of such religious sects as the Pietists[36] maintained, particularly in their inner life, manners of living, attitudes to life, and methods of learning from experience, which were bound to disappear from the style of life of the bourgeoisie, as it became increasingly drawn into the capitalist process, and from that of the industrial workers as well.

Even these strata, however, though primarily engaged within the rationalising process of capitalism, did not entirely lose their original bearing towards life. It merely disappeared from what we may call the foreground of their *public* and *official* life. Their *intimate* relationships, insofar as they remained untouched by the capitalist process, proceeded in a non-calculating, non-rationalised manner. The relationship to life did not become abstract in these spheres. In fact, the phenomenon of the gradual *recession into intimacy* of certain spheres previously of public concern (the spheres of life in which personal and religious feelings prevail), complements, as Max Weber has already suggested, the increasing rationalisation of public life in general, in the workshop, in the market place, in politics, and so on.

So the 'irrational', together with the original relation of man to man and of man to things, is now located at the *periphery* of a life become capitalist – and this in the two-fold sense of the word. In the first place, the irrational is at the periphery of the life of individuals, insofar as only the more *intimate* of human relations remain vital and alive in the old sense, while the experiences having public standing become ever more rationalised in structure. And secondly, it is at the periphery from the point of view of social stratification in the narrower sense, inasmuch as it is the bourgeoisie and the proletariat, the strata which sustain the new world, which immersed themselves with an ever wider expanse of their consciousness in the new style of thinking and living, and it is only at the periphery of the new world – in the lives of peasants, the nobility and the petit-bourgeois – that creation out of the old germs and traditions still occurs.

Here, at the periphery in both of these senses, slumber the germs of a style of thought and life which once constituted the world. For a long time these germs remained latent, and they did not emerge as a 'trend', as something conspicuous until later, when these suppressed elements were taken up in the social struggle. They were then revived by the forces of counter-revolution, who inscribed them on their banner.

The sociological significance of romanticism lies in its achievement, as experiential reaction against Enlightenment thinking (the philosophical proponent of bourgeois capitalism), in seizing on earlier, declining forms and contents of life, elaborating them at a conscious level, and setting them up against the rationalist style of thought. Romanticism took up just those attitudes and spheres of life that were surviving as mere residual undercurrents which bourgeois rationalism threatened to override. It made it its task to salvage these elements, to lend them new dignity and to save them from extinction. 'Community'-bound experience is pitted, in various forms, against manifestations of the turn to 'society' (to use Tönnes' terminology for the situation): family against contract, intuitive certainty against rationality, inner experience as a source of knowledge against the mechanistic. All the substances and contents which had, partly insensibly, formed the substratum of life are suddenly laid open to reflection. And they are fought for.

It is well known that romanticism developed from the Enlightenment as antithesis to thesis.[37] Since every antithesis is conditioned by the thesis it opposes, romanticism, as a counter-movement, suffered the paradoxical fate that its structure was fundamentally conditioned by the attitudes and methods of the very Enlightenment which had provoked it.

Romanticism wanted to rescue these displaced irrational life-forces by taking them up, but it failed to notice that paying attention to them *consciously* in and of itself served to rationalise them. Romanticism achieved a rationalisation which the bourgeois, rational Enlightenment could never have carried through, not only because its methods would have proved inadequate to the task, but also because it was not sufficiently alive to the contents in question to be able to conserve them. It is the fate of irrationalism, as of everything else, to be comprehensible only upon the plane on which the age rests. It is precisely because rationalism is the force which sustains and commands the age, that even the irrational can only become evident at the level of rationality, at the level of reflection.

Romanticism is thus a reception, a collecting of all the elements and ways of life, derived ultimately from the religious consciousness, which were pushed aside by the onmarch of capitalist rationalism. But it is a gathering-up of these elements and an encounter with them at the level of reflection. What the romantics achieved was by no means a reconstruction or resurrection of the Middle Ages, religion, or the irrational which made them once again into the foundation and substratum of life; it was rather a self-reflective comprehension of these contents, bringing them into sight and bringing them to knowledge. This was an achievement quite different from that which romanticism intended. It worked out methods, modes of knowledge, conceptual possibilities and a language capable of rendering into theory all the powers of life which would always escape the Enlightenment. With this, all the elements, ways of life and attitudes to people, things, and the world, which had been largely invisible for a whole epoch, were once more brought to the surface. But they were not conjured up in their quality as *humus*, as the substratum which shapes existence, but rather as a task, as a goal to be pursued.

We now have to show in detail how these contents, once restored and made visible at the level of reflection, simultaneously became associated, when considered from a sociological point of view, with the social currents hostile to capitalism.

All the social strata without interest in the capitalist process or even threatened by it with extinction, and which were, moreover, bound by tradition to the lost world forms (*Weltgestalten*) of the various stages of the pre-capitalist past – which were, in other words, more alive by tradition to its contents – made use of these romantic discoveries against the bourgeoisie and industrialism. The enlightened monarchy and the entrepreneur had an interest in rationalism by virtue of their historical connection with it, if nothing else. But the feudal powers, small peasant landowners and petit-bourgeois strata grounded in the tradition of the artisan guilds were all in some measure drawn to romanticism.[38] These strata already made some contribution to the rise of these contents to self-reflective knowledge. But it is especially during the socially-determined struggle over culture, when the conscious evaluation of such contents as these is at issue, that the representatives of these strata incorporate into their ideologies their takings from romanticism.

The most important tasks of our investigations then are to examine not only how the political and social 'right-wing opposition' took up arms against the political and economic system of rising capitalism, but also how it represented the first opposition to its spiritual universe, and takes to itself all the psychic and spiritual contents which would be displaced if the bourgeois-rational world were to rule alone, and, finally, how this adoption of the counter-forces goes so far as the elaboration of a 'counter-logic'.

We are commonly inclined to ascribe the critique of capitalism to the proletarian socialist movement, which only emerged later. There are many indications, however, that this criticism was initiated by the 'right-wing opposition' and that it was only subsequently transferred from here to the designs of the 'left-wing opposition'. And this naturally makes it important to investigate the shifts in the directions of criticism which make this 'transfer' possible. But here too we will pay attention primarily to the forms of thinking and their careers, because a position is characterised more thoroughly by its way of thinking than by the contents of its thought. Even if we limit ourselves at first to Germany, we come upon very interesting indications (without going into details) of the relationship between styles of thinking and the fundamental social designs which run through the social whole.

Although the type of thinking which arose in conjunction with the proletariat's world project and out of its basic designs has many features in common with the 'right-wing opposition' to the bourgeois world, the structural difference between them must not be overlooked. The proletariat grew out of capitalism; it is uniquely a creation of capitalism and has no other tradition. The 'fourth estate' is no estate but a class. Its members fused into a class formation when they were torn out of the organic estate associations, in which their ancestors had lived. Although all estate structures came apart with the rise of the new world and were steadily transformed into social units having the character of class, and although the conduct of collective action was ever more founded upon the determinacies of class and not upon the traditions of estates, this transition was only a gradual one for some strata, especially those which remained strongly rooted in the soil. Similarly, the experience of being an artisan generally preserved the mentality associated with guilds; but the proletariat, which is merely a mass when it is first thrown together in factories and only later become a class creating its own tradition, is a radically novel creation and a pure class. Since the birth of this novel social entity takes place within the rationalist epoch itself, the thinking of the proletariat manifests rationalism to a degree which is perhaps even greater than that of the bourgeoisie. Yet it would be a mistake to consider the rationalism of the proletariat as nothing more than a variant of bourgeois rationalism.

Proletarian rationality is disposed, by virtue of its own dynamic and by its own momentum, to invert itself into an irrationality of a distinctive type. It is true that the proletarian mode of conduct is so rationalistic that it designs even its uprising by plan and calculation, in keeping with the new world – and this to an extent greater than the bourgeois revolution had already done. The proletariat even bureaucratises its revolt, turning it into a 'social movement'. And yet this rationalisation and bureaucratisation cannot have the same sort of calculability as is sought by an *arriviste* bourgeois world. So long as proletarian rationalisation is in opposition, it cannot do without the irrational element which is necessary for any 'action'. The utopian ideal of all bourgeois action would be to make all enterprises so calculable that every element of risk is eliminated. If this ideal has not yet been realised, and if risk and uncertainty still adhere to all typical capitalist enterprises, this is merely because the capitalist world is still only partially rationalised, and not yet wholly based upon planning.

The proletariat, by contrast, would not restrict its actions to instances where calculation showed the prospects to be optimal, even if it were possible, say, to calculate the chances of a strike's success by means of strike-statistics and other analyses, because, as it is put, the indeterminate factor of revolutionary *élan* makes it impossible to calculate the probabilities of victory or defeat.

This is the point at which the openness of 'proletarian experience' to the irrational by virtue of its social location becomes most evident. It connects with the irrational in its revolutionary guise, the primeval 'chiliastic' element. This is also the connection in which its inner affinity to what is counter-revolutionary can be more accurately characterised.

Proletarian thinking has a significant affinity with conservative and reactionary thinking in many respects, an affinity which manifests common opposition to bourgeois-capitalist world designs and its abstractness, although the opposition derives in the two cases from designs which are themselves polar opposites.[39] As indicated earlier, an exploration in any depth of the relationship between the proletariat and the irrational would have to trace the fate of the irrational, originally 'chiliastic' elements, which ultimately derive from what may be called the 'ecstatic consciousness'. But this exploration cannot be undertaken here. One would have to show how this became the germ of all revolution since the peasant revolts, and how it entered into the 'proletarian view of the world' in time, however rationalised that view may be. There is here a fusion between the most extreme rationalism and irrational elements equally extreme, and this indicates that the 'irrational' is more diversified when examined more closely than we are at first inclined to suspect.

A more detailed analysis[40] would have to show that the irrational elements constituting the 'ecstatic consciousness', are fundamentally different from the elements which we have characterised in brief as traces of religious consciousness, and which later became the point of reference for the romantic consciousness.

But the proletarian revolutionary consciousness has its ties with the conservative line in Germany at yet another point, the one where Marx, impelled by the logic of his own position, was able to establish a connection with the conservative Hegel. And that is the dialectic.

The idea of the dialectic – the logical triad of thesis, antithesis, and synthesis – seems, on the surface, an extremely rationalistic idea, since it represents nothing less than an attempt to force the whole process of development into a single logical formula, and to present the whole of historical reality as subject to rational deduction. Yet this type of rationalism differs fundamentally from the type expressed in the bourgeois line of spiritual development by the natural sciences and by the search for universal regularities, as witness the fact that all natural-scientific and democratic thinking is hostile to dialectics, and that the most recent socialist generation, oriented to natural science and democracy, attempted, quite consistently from their point of view, to remove the dialectical element from Marx.

On closer scrutiny, then, it is evident that we must distinguish among the different varieties of rationalisation, just as we were led to draw a distinction within the realm of the irrational between 'chiliastic' and contemplative mystical elements (which appealed to romantic consciousness).

Already in Hegel, as we shall see more clearly later on, the dialectic is there in order to solve problems which are in fact romantic problems, problems which also live on in the historical school.

The chief function of the dialectic is first of all to provide a rational grasp on the 'historical individual'. While the uniqueness of the individual gets lost in all approaches which pursue generalisations and universal laws, the individual appears in dialectical thinking as integral to the unique growth which is history. What the dialectic is supposed to do is to bring out of itself a form of rationalisation in which rationalism, so to speak, transcends itself.

The second function of all dialectics, relating to its inner meaning more than to its external scheme, is the endeavour to trace the *inner line* of growth of a cultural domain. In this respect, too, we have a kind of rationalisation of an irrational dimension, the comprehension of which is altogether alien to naturalistic thinking.

69

In the third place, every dialectical approach is an approach which seeks to discern meaning in a process. It is a philosophical rationalisation of history and as such a form of rationality which is very difficult to reconcile with the 'value-free' and un-metaphysical spirit of a positivism oriented to natural science.

When all these elements are taken into account, it will be admitted that already in Hegel rationalism enters into a peculiar alliance with conservative thinking, and that this is anything but a straightforward expression of the naturalistic type of rationalisation, which calculates everything or at least aspires to do so. The fact that Marxism could go such a long way with historicism in its Hegelian guise and that, like the historical school – if also from another side –, it embodies an opposition to bourgeois consciousness, with its orientation to natural law, indicates commonalities which cannot be overlooked.[41]

But after all these affinities between 'proletarian' and 'conservative' thinking with regard to the irrational dimension suppressed by bourgeois consciousness are granted, the ultimate posture of the 'proletarian' nevertheless remains strictly rationalistic and intimately related in its basic tone to the positivist tendency of bourgeois philosophy. This positivist core can first of all be shown in the circumstances that in the proletarian philosophy of history the point of reference for historical interpretation was shifted to the social and economic sphere, as noted, and the movement of ideas was to be accounted for by the movement of society, seen as centered on the economy. In accepting this focal point of reference, at least, proletarian thinking adopts the hierarchy of spheres which had gradually become equivalent to reality for bourgeois consciousness. Proletarian thinking is therefore rationalistic to the extent that it must pass through capitalism; it is in a certain sense even more rationalistic, because it must not merely accept capitalist development, but actually accelerate its tempo. It is irrational, however, to the extent that it counts on an 'overturn' of this capitalism, when such a reversal appears as something inherently irrational, even hyper-irrational, when viewed in terms of the chains of individual causalities found in bourgeois rationality.

But it is not our task here to follow all of this up in detail. We found it necessary to look ahead to the project underlying proletarian thinking only in order to gain a better understanding of the past which interests us by viewing it in the light of events subsequent to it.

Our horizons now narrow themselves down. We shall be dealing with a strictly delimited phase in the development of thinking, and from an exclusively sociological point of view. Our problem is now exclusively to trace the development of 'early conservative' thinking (*das 'altkonservative' Denken*), which is the conservative thinking of the first half of the nineteenth century in Germany, through all its ramifications and various fates, in order to interpret these ramifications and fates on the basis of the social background of the age.

Part II Conservatism: its concept and its nature

1 Traditionalism and conservatism

Is there a historical and sociological entity which corresponds to the meaning conveyed by the word 'conservatism'? Is there a way of feeling, thinking and behaving which can be phenomenologically established and justly called 'conservative?'

We must start our inquiry in this way, to avoid the danger of playing with words, finding that their substance always escapes us and eventually even that they have no point in experience or knowledge. Although it is not possible simply to define concepts in the cultural sciences, we may properly be asked to evoke and to exhibit the contents intended by the concept. If there is a conservative way of experiencing and thinking, it must be experience and thinking in a very special sense, a way of thinking and experiencing with a very distinctive character. If conservatism is something that indeed exists, it must be asked if the word 'conservatism' refers to a timeless phenomenon, universal to all mankind, or if it is to be seen as a distinctly new modern occurrence that is historically and sociologically determined.

[We can speak of a 'conservative' style of thought as a unified tendency in the modern history of thought only after there is 'conservatism' as a coherent political and spiritual tendency; but this is of very recent origin.

To avoid confusion, the *historical-sociological* concept should be distinguished from the *generalising sociological* one, and it is therefore advisable to introduce two distinct terms. We distinguish between *traditionalism*, denoting a universal human attribute, and *conservatism*, denoting a specifically historical and modern phenomenon.

There exists a universal psychic inclination which expresses itself in the fact that we cling firmly to old ways and accept innovations only unwillingly. This quality has also been called '*natural conservatism*'.[42] But we prefer to avoid the risky term 'natural', and to designate it instead by the expression 'traditionalism' favoured by Max Weber].[43]

It may justly be said of such traditionalism, which simply refers to a clinging to old ways, that it is an earlier mode of conduct than reformism of any sort, than any deliberate striving for innovation. It can further be asserted that this mode is 'universally human', that its original form is linked with magical consciousness, as is evidenced by the fact that among 'primitive' peoples the clinging to inherited forms of life is closely bound up with the fear of magical evils which might attend change.[44] Traditionalism of this kind still exists in modern times, and even today is often connected with residues of magical thinking in our consciousness. Traditionalist conduct is therefore not tied, even today, to political or any other types of conservatism. Politically 'progressive' individuals, for instance, notwithstanding their political convictions, may bear themselves largely in a traditionalist way in some spheres of life.

It is clear from what has been said that, in contrast to traditionalism, 'conservatism' is not to be understood as a general psychological state of affairs. If we call to mind the example just offered, which presents the possibility of someone who is politically progressive acting very traditionalistically in his private or business affairs, or consider the converse possibility of a person who thinks and feels as a conservative politically but who is always progressive in his habits in everyday life, there must be an essential difference between the concepts 'traditionalist' and 'conservative'.

Quite evidently, *traditionalist* refers to a *formal psychic attribute* which is more or less present in every individual, while *acting conservatively* refers to action *in accordance with a structural contexture* which is objectively at hand. To act in a politically conservative way in any given historical period involves a way of acting whose structure cannot be determined beforehand. But how traditionalist conduct will manifest itself in any given case can be pretty well predicted on the basis of the formal determinants of this 'general mode of behaviour'. There is no doubt what the traditionalist reaction will be when something new – say, the railway – is introduced. But how a conservative, or someone who is acting in keeping with the political conservatism of an epoch, will conduct himself can be estimated only *on the basis of our knowledge of the distinctive character and structure of the 'conservative movement'* in the country and period under discussion. We are not yet concerned with enumerating the factors which must be considered as determinants of the structure and distinctive character of a particular type of conservatism, in a particular country and at a particular point in time, nor with assessing how far a specific tradition, a specific historical situation or specific social strata influence a concrete formation. What is already evident is that 'conservative action' (in the political sense, for now) does not simply involve *action which is merely a form of reaction* but a conscious or unconscious self-orientation to a manner of thinking and acting which can always be characterised historically in depth, as to contents and form, though it may well have undergone many vicissitudes before it reached a specific individual. The fate and form of this manner of thinking and acting may in some measure be altered by the individual's intervention and participation in it, but it will continue to have its own history and development when the particular individual of special interest to us is no longer there.

Political conservatism is, accordingly, an objective spiritual contexture (*Strukturzusammenhang*) as opposed to the 'subjectivity' of the isolated individual. It is not objective in the sense of eternal and universal validity, or in the sense that timeless *a priori* deductions can be made from the principles of conservatism. Nor does it exist apart from the individuals who actualise it and embody it in their actions. It is not an immanent principle with an inherent, self-evident law of development which the isolated individuals merely explicate, whether they are aware of it or not. In sum, while conservatism is not objective *in any rightly or wrongly understood Platonist sense of the pre-existence of ideas*, it does nevertheless somehow possess a definite objectivity in relation to the *hic et nunc* experience of the particular individual.

To grasp the distinctive mode of existence of such a spiritual entity, it is first necessary to make a clear distinction between timelessness and objectivity. Something may be objectively set apart, abstracted from the immediate experience of the here-and-now, and have its being as the contents towards which experience aspires and which it intends, without simultaneously being timeless. A spiritual structural complex (*geistiger Strukturzusammenhang*) is objective, in that it extends beyond the particular individual who takes it up for a time in his stream of experience, but it is nevertheless temporal, changing in history and reflecting the destinies of the community which is its bearer. *Psychic and spiritual contents are fitted to one another in such a structural complex in a distinctive way*. Although it can never be thought of as independent of its psychological bearer, if only because it is produced, reproduced and formed through his experiences and spontaneity, it is nevertheless objective, because the separate individual could never bring it into being by himself, growing up as he does into some stage of its historical existence, and also because it outlasts any of its separate bearers.

Both nominalism and realism miss the mode of existence of a spiritual structural complex: nominalism, because it always tries to dissolve it into the discrete acts of individual experience (cf. Max Weber's 'intended meaning'), and realism, because it always takes 'objectivity' and 'validity' to mean something metaphysically hypostatised, something *completed*, independent of the experiences and existence of the discrete individuals who bear it, a normative and eternal constant (something pre-existent).

There is a third alternative, beyond the stark alternatives of nominalism and realism, and we designate it as an *'historical-dynamic structural complex': an objectification which has its beginnings at some point in time, undergoes its destiny in time, and in time finds its end*, closely bound up with the actual existence and destinies of human groups and appearing as their product. This structural complex is objective because it is there 'prior to' any particular individual. *It displays its own distinctive structural integrity in relation to any particular course of experience.* Although a 'structural complex' in this sense exhibits an always present objective order, sequence, and belonging-together of possible experiences and contents, the structured interdependency must not be regarded as itself 'static'. A determinate form and a determinate structure of such interdependent contents and experiences can only be shown to exist during determinate cross-sections of time, and then only *approximately*, since the structural entity is *dynamic*, changing constantly.

And it is historical as well as dynamic, because every later stage of structural change is closely connected with the one before. It represents a change in *this specific* antecedent structured interdependency; it is not abruptly posited as something new. It is in this sense that we can talk about the progress of an unfolding. But this can be grasped and presented only as something decipherable *in retrospect*, something graspable in its inner core only after the event.

Within every historical-dynamic structural complex there dwells a *fundamental design* or stylistic principle, which one comes to possess together with the complex itself, when one orients oneself to it and incorporates it within one's own way of experiencing. But even this 'germ', this fundamental design, this stylistic principle, is not beyond time and history. It is rather something which has come into being in history and which is becoming what it is in close association with the concrete destinies of living human beings.

'Conservatism' is such an objective, historically embedded, dynamically changing structural complex, and, as such, is always part of the total psychic-spiritual structured contexture belonging to the social and historical reality of a specific epoch. The individual experiences and acts in a 'conservative' way (as distinct from a merely 'traditionalist' way) insofar, and only insofar, as he *orients* himself to one of the phases of this 'conservative' structural complex (usually the contemporary one) and bases his action upon this structural complex, either in that he simply reproduces it in whole or part or in that, adapting it to a specific living situation, he develops it further.

We are not in a position to distinguish 'conservative' from 'traditionalist' modes of action until we have grasped this peculiar objectivity of dynamic structural complexes.

Traditionalist action is *almost purely reactive behaviour.*[45] *Conservative action is action oriented to meanings*, and it is oriented to a complex of meanings which contains different objective contents in different epochs, in different historical phases, and which is always changing. This contrast lets us grasp why there is no contradiction involved when someone who is politically progressive reacts in a traditionalist way in his everyday life.[46] In the political sphere he orients himself to an objective structural complex, while in everyday life he merely reacts. But there are two considerations to note at this point. First, we cannot, in the discussions to follow, understand conservatism as a purely structural complex of political contents and modes of conduct, although the political aspect will receive a measure of preference. The structural complex of 'conservatism' also has reference to interdependencies among elements of world-view and feelings of a more general kind, and these go so far as to constitute a distinctive way of thinking. Secondly, we are not saying that 'conservatism' as a historical structural complex is unable to assimilate traditionalist elements – quite the contrary. We shall see in fact that conservatism is attempting to cultivate a certain historical form of traditionalism to the point of methodological coherence.

Notwithstanding this shifting of one of the phenomena into the other, or perhaps precisely with its help, we are now in the best position to show that behaviour which is merely traditionalist is something completely different from a conservative course of conduct. By virtue of its formally specifiable quasi-reactive nature, traditionalist action has no history, or at least none that can be clearly traced. 'Conservatism', in contrast, refers to a *continuity, historically and sociologically comprehensible, which has arisen in a specific sociological and historical situation and which develops in direct conjunction with living history*. That traditionalism and conservatism are different phenomena, and that conservatism first arises in a specific socio-historical situation, is already indicated by language, the most reliable guide to history. It cannot but be striking that the word 'conservatism' first came into usage during the most recent stage of development.

It was Chateaubriand who first lent the word its distinctive meaning when he called his periodical, designed to propogate the ideas of clerical and political restoration, *Le Conservateur*.[47] The word was not adopted in Germany until the 1830s,[48] while it did not obtain official recognition in England until 1835.[49]

Although we can take the emergence of this new usage to indicate that we are dealing with a novel historical formation, this obviously does not in itself enable us to grasp the distinctive sociological character of the phenomenon. Before we begin our sociological and phenomenological analysis of the phenomenon, we think that it will be instructive to review a few attempts at specifying the nature of conservatism. It is always fascinating and useful to follow the career of a social phenomenon in the mirror of the reflections of contemporaries. From among the ranks of theorists concerned with the nature of parties, we shall select three typical figures, representative for the German cultural continuum – Julius Stahl, Constantin Frantz and Gustav Radbruch – and we shall attempt to learn from them and to gain for our inquiry anything that they may have seen correctly.[50]

2 Historical note on the concept of political conservatism

We begin this critical excursus with Julius Stahl's *Die gegenwärtigen Parteien in Staat und Kirche* (Contemporary Parties in State and Church),[51] which is of special interest to us because German party life was just constituting itself in the course of parliamentary work precisely around the time when Stahl wrote his book, and also because in that development Stahl himself founded the conservative party.

Stahl approaches the problem of characterising the different parties by viewing them from their ideological side,[52] and he attempts to classify the parties of the time by comparing their programmatic objectives. He divides the different parties into two large groups: parties of revolution and parties of legitimacy.

But he defines revolution in the following special way: 'I take revolution in its world-historical sense, according to which it is not equivalent to revolt as such, not merely deed and event, but rather a system of politics.'[53] For us, the essential element in this definition is the insight that we are only faced with revolution when revolt is directed at the totality of the social system (Stahl calls it 'political' system), and thus, when there is rebellion against an order whose nature has been exposed and when the rebellion puts up a different, more or less explicit system of politics against that order.

Stahl then works out, in conformity with this principle of organisation, a distinctive *systematisation* of revolutionary ideas, beginning at the level of liberal ideas and then tracing revolutionary thought in the direction of steadily increasing radicalisation, through the 'constitutional' system and then the 'democratic' one to 'socialism and communism'. Correspondingly, he attempts to work out in the same way the systematic world of ideas for the conservative parties, the 'parties of legitimacy', moving from right to left, from 'absolute' to 'estate' and then to 'constitutional' monarchy.

For Stahl, then, revolution and conservatism oppose one another as different *systems* – a conception which has all the virtues and faults of the great systematic thinkers and of their spiritual mood, which still lingered in the Germany of the time.[54] The positive contribution of this insight is, to express it sociologically, that the modern era only begins when revolt is fought out by rationalistic means as well, and when not only the ideas in the name of which the uprising occurs but also those in whose name it is opposed both direct themselves towards a totality.

It is extremely dangerous ever to call these totalities 'systems', because a 'system' implies something static, an organisation of ideas, in which each constituent part retains its identity through time. But if these parts remained the same, their 'systematic' organisation would also remain the same. Contrary to this contention, it is to be shown that while the world of ideas belonging to each of the parties in conflict is certainly a totality of some kind, it is a changing, growing, dynamic totality.

Adapted to the constellation of real factors, every party is continually revising its programme, and every intellectual constituent may change within a certain period of time. It is nevertheless a totality that is at issue here, insofar as the intellectual world of a party displays coherent organisation in the cross-section of historical continuity which comprises a living historical moment. This coherence can be traced back to the fact (amongst others) that changes in professed doctrine, for example, develop in continuity with earlier doctrine, and that the new and the old are joined by one and the same fundamental design (although it too may gradually and incrementally undergo change). We have called such an intellectual totality, changing in all its parts over time but constantly remaining coherent, a dynamic totality or, in other cases, a dynamic structural complex. In equating 'dynamic totality' with 'system', Stahl commits two errors. First of all, he hypostatises the French Revolution of 1789, even though he had himself witnessed those of 1830 and 1848. Like the distinct historical phases and variations in the intellectual world of parties, these revolutions flow together into one in his mind.

Stahl thus hypostatises a single historical moment, lifting it out of time, as it were, and he refers the differences in system among parties, fixed and beyond time, to this unique central action. In consequence, ideas which are 'later' not only in temporal sequence but also in historical 'stage' are projected backward in time. This does observe two things correctly, even if it does not put them to proper use. First, he sees that the French Revolution of 1789 has to be given *preferential standing* in the development of political ideas, because it does in fact represent something like a symbolic turning-point in history. Something which had been spreading gradually but which is now visibly constituting itself here, as if by postulation – the splitting of the whole intellectual world over the questions of revolution – is already signalled by Stahl at this point. The emphasis on the Revolution of 1789 has another justification in the fact that the growth of the political to autonomy and, at the same time, to centrality in the structuring of the total process both are most clearly to be grasped in this case.[55]

There is moreover an element of truth in the suggestion that the *beginning* of clear divergences between party positions enjoins a certain predominance over the remaining phase of historical change. There is something to Stahl's assertion that the individual parties were not really constructively productive on matters of principle after the period of their inception. It is not literally true, of course, since change is always, as already indicated, under way; but the beginnings do weigh more heavily, since it was here that a current which had until then been growing latently first became conscious of itself with systematic clarity, and that it fixed *all the important points of departure*, at least, *out of which* all the later things grew.

Stahl's unhistorical, purely systematic way of treating the problem causes some surprise, because he was not only aware of the efforts of the 'historical school', but also praised them in almost glowing terms in his *Philosophie des Rechts* (Philosophy of Law). Yet in his own work, since his systematisation neglects national as well as temporal differentiations in the intellectual world (not to speak of sociological ones), the historical is at most occasionally anticipated.

What is even more surprising is the intellectualism of his study. Stahl, pioneer of irrationalism, is an extreme rationalist in his presentation of the parties, so that the reader gains the impression that political conflict does not concern anything but conflict between systems of ideas.

A contemporary reading of the book inevitably raises the question whether it would not have been possible to grasp *the fundamental designs* out of which these 'systems of ideas' grew, and to grasp these collective projects (*Willensintentionen*) in the form in which they differentiate themselves around the issues raised by the emergence of the modern historical-political organism. At the level at which he considers the matter, this problem of political will-formation and the role of *pre*-intellectual elements is still altogether absent.

But this is precisely the direction in which the *Kritik aller Parteien* (Critique of all Parties) by Constantin Frantz[56] initiates a new line of inquiry. In a distinctive way and to the neglect of the substantively rational differences among the parties, he puts into the foreground the fundamental designs which differentiate themselves in the face of the social process.

Frantz was a follower of Schelling, and readily hypostatised to a metaphysical level differences which are simply empirical and can only be shown for a particular period of time. Nor did he escape the danger of deducing the essence of a party from its concepts.

He accordingly defines conservatism, for example, as follows:

> If words and names are to retain some meaning and not to turn into arbitrary play, it is clear that conservatism cannot have any principle other than the preservation of conditions as they are. . . . Such a drive to preserve, however one-sided it may be, is nevertheless, as was remarked earlier, altogether indispensable in the economy of human society. Conservatism represents the *vis inertiae* of society, that is, a passive force, which has in itself no impulse to action.[57]

We are quite deliberately taking these sentences out of the context of the book, and simply want to show the distinctive character of such a line of inquiry. It is immediately apparent that, in contrast to Stahl's way of making distinctions, this approach does not address itself to the doctrines upheld by the parties, but rather scrutinises the 'drive' behind the ideas, from which everything else follows, as it were, and it seeks to characterise this 'drive' by its function in the social process. For us, what is valuable is the attempt in Frantz's work to reach back behind the intellectualistic element,[58] as well as the suggestion that this is a matter of collective designs, which are functionally related to the social process.

We shall call this definition a *formal definition* of conservatism. But in our opinion it is well-founded only so long as it can be shown that concrete social events are in the nature of a process – that there are always inhibiting and furthering elements present – and so long as such functional differentiations can be shown to be present in the designs of the groups concerned. The definition is moreover formal inasmuch as it only lays down that there are in every process elements which represent the *vis inertiae* and others which carry the process forward. But questions about the conditions under which this happens or who the respective parties may be, it leaves altogether open.

Such a way of specifying the nature of conservatism always remains a relative and formal one; and Frantz remarks quite accurately: 'This explains why experience also teaches that among progressives themselves there is a constant development of conservative fractions, which always want to remain at the point just reached.'[59] As a pure relational concept, such a formal definition has its justification. It gives notice that within every historical cross-section there are elements that carry and others that inhibit the development. *Which* ones these may be, however, depends on the circumstances of the times. Something which is progressive today may take on the function of conservation tomorrow.

We take note of this relational concept of 'conservative' and 'progressive' as 'useful', but point out that this is not the concept under discussion. We are not concerned with the character common to *every* kind of conservatism, but with the nature of a *particular* conservatism at a particular time. We are working with the historical concept of conservatism within a specific epoch.

Frantz's observations nevertheless call our attention to two matters which we must take into consideration in our own inquiry: (a) that a pre-rational element is behind any given set of contents in political theory – a fundamental design, which must nevertheless always be characterised by its present contents, and (b) that this pre-rational element can be studied in its function (i.e. whether it is conservative or progressive) within the social process.

As the last of the three attempts to characterise conservatism, we want to introduce a contemporary analysis, selected because it is suited to prepare us for our inquiry. We shall conclude, then, by discussing Radbruch's *Rechtsphilosophie* (Legal Philosophy),[60] which characterises the parties on the basis of a very interesting line of inquiry.

In the middle section ('The Purpose of the Law') of his book, Radbruch attempts to characterise modern party tendencies, in close conjunction with a previously stated philosophical systemisation of values. 'It is only through the coincidence between the system of possible starting-points for legal philosophy derived *a priori* and the classification of empirical, actual parties that the former system gains its ultimate validation.'[61] He deliberately chooses a narrow point of view, at the legal-philosophical level of inquiry. 'Only the party ideologies, *in their systematic connections with the world-views which are behind them* are relevant to legal philosophy, not the party-realities in their genetic connections to economic interests.'[62] What fascinates us in his investigation is the inquiry into the world-views behind political ideologies. We are given a full measure of systematic connections between political objectives and the aspirations embedded in world-views, as they were not yet present in Stahl, at least not to this extent. This is the part of the way where we can go along with Radbruch. But he is also instructive for us because he makes the attempt, if only incidentally, to show the way into the modes and structures of thinking which belong to the different political parties.

Our own investigation along the lines of sociology of thinking differs from his in that we do not want to presuppose an aprioristic philosophical system of values. This starting-point forces him, like Stahl, to touch up, for the sake of systematisation, the fundamental designs which live and struggle within partisan tendencies, and to hypostatise one stage of development. With regard to conservative thinking he usually picks the 'Tivoli-programme'[63] of the German Conservative Party as evidence for his points – and thus, the programmatically fixed state of conservatism as of the year 1892.

We also set out from the assumption of a 'systematic' connection between world-view and 'political' theory, but we presuppose that every current is distinguished by a world-view that is a dynamic, historically changing totality and by a gradually changing mode of thinking closely bound up with it. We are not concerned with *a general typology of political world-views and ways of thinking, but with a historically developing* gradual shift and *stratification* among thoughts and *total contextures*. And, in the final analysis, we are interested not only in how this gradual shift comes about but also in how these shifts are *connected with the sociological background* and how a common developmental pattern (*Werdeproblematik*) manifests itself in all this.

Where Radbruch by far surpasses Stahl is in not only realizing that modern parties give expression to systems of ideas but in sensing as well that, in closest association with these political theories, whole worlds are in conflict.

3 The sociological background of conservatism

If we view these attempts to grasp the nature of modern conservatism as self-reflections about the process by participants in the process itself, we gratefully learn from their insights, because we are then looking at these insights as incremental advances of social knowledge into the emerging historical formations themselves. Each of these attempts discerns something about the nature of the newly emerging entity, but each in its own way is misled into an excessively one-sided view by the prejudice peculiar to particular systematic assumptions. Without deluding ourselves into thinking that we are in a position to address the problem without ourselves having a point of view, we now want to make use in our own analysis of everything that seems right to us in the literature we have been analysing.

'Modern conservatism' differs from 'traditionalism in general', as we saw, first of all in that it is a function of *one particular* historical and sociological situation. While 'traditionalism in general' refers to a general psychological attitude which manifests itself in the individual as a clinging to old ways and expresses itself in a fear of innovation, this fundamental inclination (*Grundintention*)† gains, in the course of modern development, a special function in shaping the process as a whole. What formerly played some sort of part in every human being now becomes the unifying factor for *particular tendencies* within the total process. This psychological attitude accordingly now takes sides in the totality of events.

This transformation of the traditionalist attitude to life into a function of a historical situation so as to make it into the nucleus of a particular tendency, does not take place spontaneously, but is rather a response to the prior functionalisation of the 'progressivist' basic inclination. The fact that traditionalism turned into conservatism – in other words, that traditionalism changed from being a formal attitude more or less actively present in all individuals, into the source of emanation or energising nucleus of a 'movement' displaying a determinate if also historically changing structural contexture in its spiritual and psychological contents – is due to the immediately antecedent similar transformation of the 'will to progress' into a 'tendency' having its own distinctive substantive structure. Traditionalism had been a tendency dor-

---

†Elsewhere in the text, '*Grundintention*' has almost always been translated as 'fundamental design', in order to communicate Mannheim's deliberate avoidance of an unambiguously psychological (or social-psychological) concept, but here the more psychological term is clearly appropriate. *Trs.*

mant in each individual, not at all conscious of itself, and it existed in this vegetative character in its original form. Conservatism, in contrast, is a counter-movement, and this fact alone already makes it reflective: it is after all a response, so to speak, to the 'self-organisation' and agglomeration of 'progressive' elements in experience and thinking.

[The emergence of conservatism as a consciously cultivated and designed tendency within the complex of events (*Gesamtgeschehen*) is thus already a symptom of the fact that the way in which the social and spiritual world comes into being takes on a distinctive structure in the course of modern development. The mere existence of conservatism is already expressive of the fact that the course of history is increasingly borne by such sweeping tendencies and the corresponding counter-tendencies, some of which constitute themselves in the name of progress and others in the name of restraint.

The emergence of such sweeping tendencies, however, in turn presupposes the structural fact that social and cultural developments increasingly merge into a novel and dynamic unity, at the expense of the previously dominant, relatively self-contained provincial and estate-related (*ständisch gebundenen*) units, whose importance, while not altogether superseded, is nevertheless increasingly diminished. Locally bound and provincial units coalesce into national units. Although at first nations remain to a large extent socially and culturally autonomous, the fundamental economic and social complex of problems is structurally so similar in all modern states that it is not surprising that the social and intellectual party-formations oriented to these ultimate questions of social destiny parallel one another.

These structural problems common to all modern states have been very well summarised as follows:[64] (1) full development of the unitary nation state, (2) participation of the people in directing the state, (3) integration of the state in the world economic order, (4) solution of the social question.

And it is precisely these structural problems which appear to become so important for the social as well as the intellectual life of the newly emerging cultural and social entities that, correspondingly, party alignments everywhere ever more *display a tendency* to refer themselves to these *fundamental tensions*, derived from the structural problems here noted. Just as religious conflicts gradually turned into political ones, and just as we can already clearly see social and political alignments under the guise of religious alignments in the English revolutions, it seems ever more possible, as we approach the period extending from the eighteenth into the nineteenth century, to characterise the remaining spiritual phenomena in terms of party alignments more or less directly referable to this social and political problem-complex.

Once a deliberately functionalised conservative political will becomes possible, accordingly, this inclination toward conservatism entails not only an orientation to certain political contents but also a particular way of experiencing and thinking. With the appearance of an integrated conservative politics, or perhaps even somewhat earlier, a corresponding world-view and way of thinking emerge, which may be similarly classified as conservative. In our terminology and in relation to the first half of the nineteenth century, then, 'conservative' and 'liberal' refer to quite specific affinities to distinctive philosophies and to an associated distinctiveness in the manner of thinking, and not only to distinctive political aspirations. A distinctive overall structure of the world may thus be said to be implicit in the term 'conservative'. The sociological definition of the term, inevitably more comprehensive than the historical-political one, must necessarily also refer to that historical structural situation in which this term could arise to designate a new fact].[65]

In our view, the socio-historical precondition for the emergence of conservatism is, in brief, a conjunction of the following factors:
(1) The historical social whole (*Sozialkomplex*) must have become explicitly dynamic (processive). Individual happenings within the totality of events must to an increasing extent be in every sphere oriented to the same set of basic questions about the growth of the social whole. This orientation to the central issues of the overall movement happens unintentionally at first; but later it will become conscious and intentional, whereupon the significance of each element for the development of the whole will become increasingly clear. There will be accordingly a steady decline in the number of the discrete, self-contained social units which had previously predominated. Even the most commonplace action will now contribute something, however little, to furthering or inhibiting this development, now integrated into a single unified dynamic.[66] That is also why it becomes increasingly possible to describe every event and every psychic attitude (*Seelenhaltung*) in terms of its function in relation to the whole.
(2) A further condition for the emergence of modern conservatism is that this dynamic process must increasingly proceed by means of social differentiation, i.e., horizontal social strata must arise, reacting to events in a more or less homogeneous way. Some of these will support the forward-driving tendencies, while others will promote stability or (ever more consciously) even retrogression.
(3) The world of ideas as well as the basic designs upon which it rests must be differentiated, and the resulting thought-tendencies,

whatever combinations and syntheses may be produced, must correspond – in ways that must be analysed for each individual case – to this social differentiation.

(4) This differentiation into elements promoting change on the one side and stability on the other must take on an increasingly political (and later purely economic) character,[67] so that the political factor becomes the primary nucleus around which the new strata crystallise.

To put it briefly, the development and the shared characteristics of modern conservatism – as distinct from mere traditionalism – in the different nations, are due in the last resort to the dynamic character of the modern world; to the basis of this dynamic in social differentiation; to the fact that this social differentiation affects the entire intellectual cosmos; and to the fact that the fundamental designs of the decisive social strata do not merely crystallise ideas into actual movements of thought, but also create different antagonistic world-views and, embedded in these, different antagonistic styles of thought. In a word, the transformation of traditionalism into conservatism can only come about in a class-differentiated society.[68] The phenomenon we call 'conservatism' could only arise once the conditions outlined above were given, at that stage of development where intellectual and social growth took on the structure we have described.

After this analysis of the *sociological constellation* within which modern conservatism arose, we shall now turn to its contents.

4 Morphology of conservative thought

Once we have established the sociological constellation out of which conservatism constituted itself as a distinctive dynamic structural complex and as a style of thought, we can characterise the nature of conservatism in two ways. We can either regard it as a relatively self-contained and fully emerged totality, or we can emphasise its historical *growth* and trace this dynamic totality in its development.

We shall have to pursue both ways. In this second part of the investigation, where the objective is a general characterisation of the German conservative style of thinking, we shall attempt to bring out its internal consistency by taking its historical development for granted, by considering it in its final form. The third part will then trace the actual career of this style of thinking. In its attempt to place every distinctive type and variation of conservatism in its own distinctive historical and sociological location within the process of growth (*Werdeprozess*), the next part will also attempt to reproduce the stratigraphy and makeup of the *process of growth* itself.

But we cannot proceed to this purely historical part unless we first, in keeping with normal procedure in humanistic historical investigations, provisionally work out some essential points of reference for our study of individual cases within the overall development. We thus turn to our first task, which is to offer a general account, relatively undifferentiated as yet, of early nineteenth-century German conservative thought.

This part of the inquiry – taking the early conservative style of thought as it has come to be, and neglecting its individual ramifications for the present – is itself divided into two phases. First we shall attempt to bring into view the pre-theoretical, experiential element, the *fundamental designs* out of which the style of thought grows. Then we shall turn to the mature theoretical constructions belonging to this style of thought, in order to extract the *central problem-complex* which, as the inner theoretical core, integrates the style of thought as a unified whole – the core which is the source of its growth and which is also the point of reference best enabling us to comprehend it in its distinctive theoretical character.

(a) *The fundamental design of conservative thought*

[If we want to grasp the *stylistic unity*, the *inner formative principle*, we must of course neglect, for the time being, the features differentiating the diverse currents, although we are obliged to give them their due weight in the procedures for a full historical reconstruction, like those applied in the next chapter.

We are trying to grasp the unifying principle, the purposive direction of the soul (*intentio animi*), which links conservatives of the old estates, in the unconscious designs of their thinking, with conservative romantics, conservative Hegelians with followers of Haller, and so on.

To keep from arriving at nothing more than a vacuous general concept, we are not stretching this stylistic unity too wide but are setting out to grasp it exclusively within German developments, and even here only within a period which is historically relatively self-contained and unified: *the first half of the nineteenth century*].[69]

In analysing the unity within spiritual formations, nothing can take the place of an attempt to penetrate to the inner core by means of interpretive understanding. And there is only one safeguard against arbitrary constructions, which is that we adhere so far as possible to the objective manifestations and self-reflections of the currents of thought in question and that we stay as close as possible to this evidence in our attempts to establish what is to be demonstrated.

This inner core of modern conservatism, its distinctive design in thinking, doubtless has a certain kinship with what we have called traditionalism, since, as we have already noted, conservatism in a certain sense grew out of traditionalism. Indeed, it is at the outset quite clearly nothing more than traditionalism become self-reflective. And yet the two are not identical, since traditionalism takes on specifically 'conservative' features only when it becomes the expression of a very definite, consistently maintained attitude towards life and thought (as against revolutionary experiencing and thinking), and when it functions as such, as a relatively autonomous movement in the social process as a whole.

One of the most essential characteristics of this conservative way of experiencing and thinking seems to be its clinging to what is immediate and *concrete* in a practical way. The result of this is a novel, almost empathetic experience of the concrete, reflected in the consistently anti-revolutionary connotations of the modern term 'concrete'.[70] To experience and to think *concretely* now comes to signify a specific mode of conduct, a desire to be effective only within the particular immediate environment in which one is placed, and a total aversion to all things that are merely 'possible' or 'speculative'.

Non-romantic conservatism always starts out from the particular case at hand and never broadens its horizon beyond its own particular environment. Its aim is immediate action, change in concrete details, and it is therefore not really concerned with the *structure* of the world in which it lives. All progressive action, in contrast, is increasingly animated by a *consciousness of the possible*; it transcends the given immediacy by recourse to a *systematic possibility*, and it fights against the concrete *not* by seeking to put a *different concreteness* in its place, *but* by wanting *a different systematic starting-point*.

Conservative reformism consists in the exchange (substitution) of certain individual facts for others ('improvements').[71] To deal with a single undesirable fact, progressive reformism is inclined to transform the whole world built up around that fact, the world in which such a fact is possible. This distinction enables us to understand *the inclination of the progressive to system and the inclination of the conservative to the individual case*.

The conservative only thinks systematically when he is moved to reaction, perhaps because he is forced to set up a system counter to that of the progressive, or because the process has progressed to a point where he has lost touch with the present state of things, so that he is compelled to intervene actively in order to reverse the process of history.[72]

From this contrast between the concrete and the abstract, which is in fact a contrast between experiences of the world more than it is an intellectual difference, and from a showing that a fundamental political experience is hidden within the modern form of this logical contrast, it becomes evident, at a crucial point, how far two types of experience are functionally related to the social. The production of change in its modern form seems to require that whole strata work at the loosening of the existing framework. Their thinking is necessarily abstract: it lives on possibilities. The thought and experience of those who work at preservation and retardation, in contrast, is *concrete* and does not advance beyond the existing framework of life.

This contrast and the distinctive character of the conservative concrete experience of things can hardly be shown more plainly than in the conservative experience of *property*, in contrast to the bourgeois-modern experience of it. In this connection we possess a most instructive document, an essay by Justus Möser, which offers what is in effect a phenomenological specification of the disappearance of a specific relation to property, and contrasts it with the modern concept of property, which had already superseded the old one in his own time. In his essay 'Von dem echten Eigentum' (Of Genuine Property)[73] he shows that the old 'genuine property' was bound up with its owner in an entirely different way than is the case with modern ownership. There was a definite, vital, and reciprocal relationship between the owner and his property. Property in its old and genuine sense carried with it certain privileges for its owner; it rendered him eligible, for instance, to have a 'voice' in the state, it bestowed hunting rights, and it qualified for membership on the jury. Hence it was closely bound up with the proprietor's personal honour and in this sense inalienable. Even when the proprietor sold his estate, the right to hunt – for example – could not be transferred with it, and the continuation of the old proprietor's hunting rights upon an alienated estate was a living testimony to the fact that the new owner was not the 'real' proprietor of the estate. The obverse also applied. Just as an old property could not endow a social upstart (*homo novus*) with the honour pertaining to genuine proprietorship, so was it also impossible for a man of established honour, if he bought an estate back from such a mere proprietor (*proprietarius*), to endow the acquired estate with the character of genuine property, as if by virtue of his personal honour. There existed, accordingly, a *non*-fungible reciprocity between a particular property and a particular owner, and all property was experienced as possessing such personal reference.

Möser adds to his presentation of this mode of experience, here merely recounted, a sentence of regret to mark the fact that, while the feeling for this mode still survived in his time, the linguistic expression of the distinction had gone: 'How impoverished must language and philosophy have become when these fundamental distinctions can no longer be expressed in a specific way!'[74]

Here we see clearly what a wealth of pre-theoretical and existence-related relationships of the most concrete kind subsist between person and property in a society based upon estates, which were then replaced by the abstract bourgeois concept of property suppressing the concreteness of experience. Möser registered the nature of estate-conservative experience of proprietorship at the last possible moment; and subsequent conservatism, especially of the romantic type, likes to come back to it, if also in altered form.

Adam Müller[75] regards things as extensions of the limbs of the human body; and he describes feudalism as a fusion of person and thing. He attributes the corruption of this condition to the adoption of Roman law, and speaks of a 'Roman-French Revolution'[76] which is to be blamed.

These are all mere echoes of the past in an openly partisan vein. Their significance lies in the fact that such living relationships extending to things did once exist. This emphasis on the 'intimacy' between owner and possession continues right down to Hegel.

For Hegel possession means that I have put my will into a thing,[77] and 'the rationale of property is to be found not in the satisfaction of needs but in the supersession of the pure subjectivity of personality'.[78] It is also interesting to note here something which we shall have occasion to observe again later – how the Left opposition to the bourgeois capitalist mode of experiencing things learns from the conservative opposition. The repeated insistence by Marx and others, on the abstractness of human relationships in the capitalist world, was originally the discovery of early estate-based (*altständischen*) conservative thought.

We are not suggesting that the distinction between 'concrete' and 'abstract' was previously unknown; we are merely calling attention to the peculiar phenomenon whereby two ways of experiencing history gradually took form as polar opposites and were each taken up into the experiental designs of socially distinct strata, differentiated according to their locations within the stream of social happening.

To trace the differentiation between ways of thinking and

experiencing within the same social space in the case of another central concept, we turn next to the distinction between the liberal and conservative *concept of freedom*.

Revolutionary liberalism understood by freedom in the economic sphere the release of the individual from all his bonds to either state or guild. In the political sphere, liberalism understood freedom to mean the right of the individual to do as he wishes and thinks fit, but particularly the possibility of exercising the 'Rights of Man'. This freedom was thought to be limited only by the freedom and equality of fellow-citizens.[79]

This concept of freedom, then, can only be understood in conjunction with its complement, the idea of equality; it can be properly grasped only by starting out from the assumption of the political equality of all men. A correct understanding of revolutionary thought, moreover, shows that it proposed the equality of men as a postulate and not as a statement of empirical fact, and that it demanded that men be rendered equal only in the contests within the economic and political spheres and not that they be equalised in all spheres of life. When conservative thinking takes this postulate to represent an allegation of fact, as if revolutionary liberals had claimed that all men are equal in fact and in all respects, the reinterpretation typifies the kind of shift in frame of reference which we presented earlier, in the course of our analysis of the different levels of problem-formulation associated with the different political tendencies of thought.

But this sociologically determined misunderstanding gives rise, as is so often the case in the political thinking on both sides, to a new insight into the state of things. As with the concept of property, conservative experience and thinking here self-reflectively grasp an earlier way of experiencing things, and they keep it alive and thus available to subsequent thought. Since conservatism could not fail, under the pressure of political necessity, to set up an explicitly *conservative concept of freedom*[80] in opposition to the revolutionary concept, a new concept of freedom was worked out, which we shall call the *qualitative concept of freedom*, in view of the distinctive way in which it opposes itself to the revolutionary-egalitarian concept. The counter-revolutionary opposition, on sound instinct, does not attack 'freedom' itself, but rather the principle of equality upon which it rests. The contention is that human beings are *unequal* in their nature, in their innermost being, and that freedom consists in the condition in which each and every one, in accordance with his innermost principle, actualises the laws of development uniquely peculiar to himself. Müller accordingly says:

Nothing can be more antithetical to freedom, as I have described it . . . than the concept of an external *equality*. If freedom is nothing more than the universal striving of the most varied natures for growth and life, it is impossible to think of a greater contradiction than that of suspending, at the very moment of establishing freedom, all unique peculiarities, i.e., all the variety in these natures.†[81]

This is also the romantic conservative idea of freedom. Although traces of Aristotle, Goethe, and others are active within it, it takes on a distinctly political connotation in this formulation. The liberal thinker, thinking abstractly and reasoning on the basis of the possible, in keeping with his revolutionary function, holds firmly to the equality of all men in principle – or at least, on the grounds of an 'abstract optimism', to the thesis of equal opportunities for all –, and limits the freedom of the individual only by the freedom of his fellow-citizens. The romantic thinker, however, finds such a limitation of freedom already in the '*individual law*'[82] of development, in which everyone recognises his potentialities and limitations.

But this kind of freedom, vested in the nature of individuality, is typically romantic and dangerously close to an anarchist subjectivism. Although there is achievement in a conservative sense in the transfer of the problem into the inner sphere, since the restriction of demands to the inner life deprives them of their world-transforming implications, in effect transforming external political anarchy into an anarchy of inwardness, there remains the enormous danger that this internalised anarchy can nevertheless endanger the state. (Liberal thinking, in contrast, does not concern itself with inwardness, comprehending this as the 'private sphere', and it consequently poses the problem of 'freedom' only at the level of public life.) This difficulty explains the growing tendency, already present within romantic thinking as it became conservative, to detach this 'qualitative freedom' from the individual and to find for it a true bearer, a 'true subject' of freedom, in comprehensive collective formations, 'organic communities', and, ultimately, *the estates*. It was now the estates which harboured the inner principle of growth whose unfolding was said to comprise freedom. This uncovers what is at least one of the roots of the qualitative concept of freedom, its origin in the regime of estates. The connotation of 'liberties' (*Freiheiten*) of estates,

†These arguments work better in German than in English, at least in rhetorical effect, since there is no clear linguistic distinction between 'inequality' and 'dissimilarity', the word '*Ungleichheit*' serving unforcedly for both. The translation cannot avoid sacrificing some of the plausibility. *Trs*.

where the word also refers to 'privileges' and presents itself as qualitative and inegalitarian in make-up, clearly returns in this sense of 'freedom' or 'liberty'.[83] In the course of development, however, conservative thinking in all its major currents notices the danger of the maintenance of the state and prevailing relations of domination which lies in even this form of the romantic concept of freedom. The attempt is then made so to select these individual or corporative qualitatively diversified freedoms that they are simultaneously embedded in a supervening totality. The historical school, Stahl, and Hegel differ among themselves only in the conception of this totality; the fundamental structure of their solutions to the problem is the same.

The solution consists in rendering the principle of freedom inward while subjecting external relationships to the principle of order. But this raises the problem of what is to guarantee that the two spheres – the spheres of 'inwardness' and 'order' – will not collide. A solution for this is found in the presupposition of a kind of 'pre-established harmony', which is guaranteed either directly by God or by national energies within society. On this point, conservatism has taken instruction from liberal thinking, from which it has adopted two methods of thinking, the 'separation of spheres' and the 'idea of harmony'.

In the historical school, the 'people' (*Volk*) or 'spirit of the people' (*Volksgeist*) above all provide the totality which keeps the freedom of the individual or of the various parts from degenerating into mere arbitrariness. Rothacker has recently shown how later, in Ranke's writings, the concept of the state replaced that of the nation.[84] In any case, the solution of the problem offered by Savigny and Ranke is even more clearly characterised by an upward shift of this qualitative freedom from the individual and the estates to the nation and the state respectively. It is only this 'higher' entity which is completely free within the limits set by its own law of development. This binds the individual, whose life can only be worthwhile within these encompassing wholes and in accordance with the meanings they constitute.[85]

The tension between order and freedom is at its greatest in Hegel, who, as always, tries to preserve both sides. He transforms the revolutionary, negative, abstract concept of freedom (as he calls it) into an intermediate stage on the way to the true one.

This negative freedom,[86] or freedom as the Understanding conceives it, is one-sided; but a one-sided view always contains one essential factor and therefore is not to be discarded. But the Understanding is defective in exalting a single one-sided factor to be the sole and the supreme one.[87]

93

As we follow his argument, it soon becomes evident what is to be understood by this negative, abstract freedom:

> For instance, during the Terror in the French Revolution all differences of talents and authority were supposed to have been superceded. This period was an upheaval, an agitation, an irreconcilable hatred of everything particular. Since fanaticism wills an abstraction only, nothing articulated, it follows that, when distinctions appear, it finds them antagonistic to its own indeterminacy and annuls them.[88]

This opens the way for Hegel to concrete freedom,[89] which represents a synthesis, a third moment, between this abstract freedom and its opposite, straightforward external determination:

> Now the third moment is that, in its restriction, in this other, the will is by itself. In determining itself, it still remains by itself and does not cease to keep hold of the universal. This moment, then, is the concrete concept of freedom, while the two preceding moments have been found to be through and through abstract and one-sided.[90]

Applied to our problem, this means that man is free by virtue of taking upon himself the will of the state as a whole.

Stahl too had to struggle with the romantic concept of freedom.[91] Like Hegel, he tried to encompass the entire conservative tradition, but he sought to achieve this on the basis of the idea of authority (*Obrigkeitsgedanke*). His solution takes the following form:

> Freedom is not the liberty of acting as one pleases, on the basis of unfounded, accidental decision; freedom is the ability to live and act in accordance with one's innermost self. Yet the innermost self of a human being is his individuality,[92] which cannot tolerate external rule or regulation, while an essential component of political freedom is the right of individuality comprising both an independent private sphere[93] as well as a part concerned with the regulations laid down by public authority. The innermost self of the individual, however, is not only his individuality but also his nature as a moral being.[94]

Stahl then proceeds to state his solution of the problem:

> Precisely this content-rich freedom [!] is the aim in the political realm. It must not isolate the individual from the physical power of the state or from its ethical substance and historical tradition in order to ground the state upon mere individual will.[95]

Enough examples. All these different solutions of the problem which arises for conservative thought display the same fundamental tendency.[96] Everywhere the point of departure is a 'content-rich freedom' (Stahl), a 'concrete freedom' (Hegel) a 'positive freedom' (Müller), all inclining towards the 'concrete' and 'qualitative', just as in the case of the conservative concept of property. 'Concrete', 'qualitative' and the like are nevertheless expressions which by no means suffice to comprehend the fundamental design common to all these ways of thinking. The accumulation of examples is merely meant to serve as a circumscription of the fundamental design which lives and develops within them and which can be comprehended as a growing self-awareness of a fundamental attitude to things, which originates, just like the experiencing of property, in an earlier mode of relating to the world.

Closely related to the contrast between 'concrete' and 'abstract' is the contrast which arises from the fact that progressive thinking not only sees the actual in terms of its potentialities, but also in terms of the *norm*. The conservative, on the other hand, tries to comprehend the actual in its contingency or attempts to understand the normative in terms of the existent.[97]

In the case of freedom as in the case of property, we are ultimately confronted by two archetypical ways of *experiencing* things and the world around them, from which subsequently two tendencies of thought arise. Our attitude towards things, persons, and institutions is different, already at the level of experience, when we view them from some standpoint of how they 'ought' to be from what it is when we accept them as 'something which has grown' or as an 'existent' which has become necessary. The effect of the former of these attitudes is that we will never do more than to glance off the world around us: we do not bring it a forgiving love, and we lack the interest in its existence which would arise from solidarity with it. But the latter attitude, on the other hand, will always tempt us to overtenderness towards all that exists. The former way of experiencing and judging always addresses itself to institutions in their entirety, while the latter loses itself in details. To learn the significance of these two ways of relating, we must first see clearly that it is in the nature of formations belonging to the spirit that we can never grasp them by taking them 'in themselves', in isolation, but only when we expand upon them to form more comprehensive totalities. We can only find out what something is, what it means – and the 'being' of every object of the *spirit* consists of its meaningfulness – when we experience it as a phase or an element within some purposive tendency.

By virtue of its fundamental feeling for the principle of passivity, *quieta non movere*, the conservative attitude would prefer to avoid meanings altogether;[98] it would like simply to accept all that exists as mere being, whence its streak of fatalism.[99] As in other aspects of conservative thinking, the impulse towards attributing meanings, towards viewing things in terms of their meaning, arises in opposition to revolutionary attribution and projection of meanings. Conservative 'attribution of meanings' can also only proceed in the form of expanding upon the particular to make a more comprehensive whole. *But the process, the 'method', of this expansion upon the given is an altogether different one from that employed in liberal revolutionary experience and thought*, which is another indication that in this sphere the forms of experience develop in conjunction (*seinsgebunden*) with existence. This conservative method of expanding upon the particular is characterised by the fact that it approaches the particular in some way from *behind*, from the past. For 'progressive thinking', every individual thing gains what is usually its ultimate meaning from something either above or beyond itself, from a utopia of the future or from a norm transcending existence. But conservative thinking derives the meaning of the particular from something that lies behind it, from the past or from what has been prefigured in germ. The meaning which the future has for the interpretation of particulars in the one case, the past has in the other; what the one approach achieves with 'the norm', the other accomplishes with the idea of 'prefiguration in germ'.

It appears, then, that this 'what lies behind us' can be experienced and expressed in two ways: as something that is antecedent in time and lies in the past, or in the sense of the 'germ', the 'germinal essence', of which the particularity to be understood appears as an unfolding. For the former of these approaches, everything which exists has meaning simply because it has come about as a result of a development in the past, and for the latter, because everything with a common history and every objectification of a culture exhibits a single basic direction, one purposive tendency of growth in soul and spirit.

In this latter case, the particular can only be understood 'characterologically', i.e., as a manifestation of a fundamental design, as a mode of unfolding the germinal origins. Both kinds of conservative expansion upon the particular, accordingly, tend towards an intuition of totality (*Totalitätsschau*) and the wider whole which is reached in this way is usually a *concrete totality* (*anschauliche Totalität*).[100]

The expansions upon the particular which the progressive undertakes are mostly derived from the utopia of rationalism and lead to a *structural* view of the existing and developing totality.[101]

A simile may help to make matters clear. When the conservative way of experiencing is compelled to form a comprehensive image of the whole, its view of things resembles the inclusive sort of picture of a house which one might get by looking at it from all sides, corners, and angles – from every conceivable perspective relevant to concrete focal points of life. The comprehensive view characteristic of the progressive, in contrast, looks for the *blueprint*, it searches for a pattern of connectedness which is not intuitively concrete but rather rationally analysable.[102]

This 'difference in direction' between the two experiences of expanding upon the particular itself contains a further radical difference between conservative and progressive modes of experience: their different *experience of time*. To express this difference[103] schematically, we could say that the progressive always experiences the present as the beginning of the future, while the conservative regards it simply as the latest stage reached by the past. The difference is the greater and more radical by virtue of the fact that such linearity of the historical process is by no means native to the conservative mode of experiencing.

[The conservative is in fact either drawn to the ancient theory of the eternal cycle[104] or he is subject to a form of experience in which past and present merge into one. Perhaps the most attractive formulation of this experience of historical time is to be found in the following statement by Droysen:

Every point in our present has come to be. What it was and how it came to be is the past; but this past remains within it, in an ideal sense. . . . It is not the things of the past that become apparent, since they are no more, but rather what there is of them that has not passed away in the here and now.[105]

In this kind of experience, where one in effect possesses the past within the present, the picture of historical time takes on something of the quality of an imaginary space. The succession characteristic of the speculative experience of time is undone, and the 'intermingled state' (*Ineinandersein*) of the contents which is native to the reality of experience breaks through.]

The inclination towards such a spatial experience of history, towards such a resolution of every temporal succession into a spatial contiguity or inclosure, is also ever more strongly furthered by the fact that the land and the soil serve as the substratum of history for landowning stocks (nobility and peasantry), and that each individual among them appears to himself, to express it spinozistically, as nothing more than a mode of this eternal substance. For Möser, for example, the state is not so much a 'personal association' as it is a 'real association',[106] since land and

97

soil are the substrata upon which the life of the state – and thus of history as well – truly rest. In this experience of history, then, land and soil take over the place of the shortlived individual as substratum. This provides the background required to understand Möser's important remarks in the introduction of his *Osnabrück-ische Geschichte* [1768]:

> In my opinion, the history of Germany could look forward to an entirely new turn if we were to trace the fate of the landed estates, as the true constituents of the nation, if we were to make them into the body of the nation and to consider the high and the lowly incumbents of this nation as mere evil or good accidents of this body.[107]

Next to this compacted, spatial substratum, every discrete event and each individual is actually nothing more than an accident. And this spatial experience of history clearly influences Adam Müller when, with the romantic's facility, he coins the conservative expression *Raumgenossen* (fellows in a shared space) to oppose the democratically tinged concept of *Zeitgenossen* (contemporaries) as hallmark of politically relevant association:

> In reply to the question, 'What is the people?' they answered,[108] 'the collection of ephemeral creatures with heads, two hands, and two feet which happens to be standing, sitting, or lying side by side, displaying all the external signs of life, at the present miserable moment upon that stretch of earth called France', *instead of answering*, 'a people is the sublime community of a long succession of bygone and living generations, together with generations yet to come, all of whom are bound together in a great, intimate association for life and unto death, in which each generation – and within each generation, every single human individual – stands surety for the association as a whole and in turn is given surety by the association for its own existence in its wholeness. And this beautiful and immortal community presents itself to the eyes and to the senses by means of a common language, common customs and laws, thousands of beneficent institutions, many long-flourishing families singled out to tie and even chain the ages together, and, finally, the one immortal family placed at the centre of the state, the reigning family and – to come even closer to the very heart of things – the present head of this family and bearer of its estate.'[109]

Here the participation of past generations is emphasised, and the present sampling taken from the larger whole is experienced as a quite insignificant episode.[110] Such raising of spatial, corporate

98

units, unconfined by time, to the level of historical substratum is a trait which conservative thinking has in common with subsequent proletarian and socialist thinking. There too, not that which is individual is considered to be the real substratum of history, but rather such entities as 'relations of production' and 'classes'. Möser's approach also has much about it that is sociological, if we take sociology to mean an understanding of individual events in terms of more comprehensive, underlying factors.

The difference between these two types of 'non-individualistic' interpretation of history consists in the fact that the conservative tends to construe historical life from the point of view of organic collective associations (of which the family is the prototype),[111] while proletarian thinking builds on the newer forms of collective association, which are mainly (though not wholly) agglomerative rather than organic in character – i.e., classes. The place occupied by family and corporation in conservative thought is taken by classes in socialist thought; industrial and productive relations similarly take the place of land and soil.

Only 'bourgeois thought' – which may be said to stand midway between the other two and which has its starting-point in an historical stage where the old associations are in dissolution while the new stratification is still in its early development – builds an interpretation of society upon the isolated individual and achieves a picture of the whole which is merely the sum of its parts. The bourgeois-democratic principle which corresponds to this view of society dismembers time in the same way: although it does experience movement, it is only able to master this dynamicism by segmenting the movement into *discrete instants (Momentanquer-schnitte)*. Each ballot taken indicates the given momentary state of the 'general will' without reference to past or future; and *continuity*, which here appears just as atomised as the *totality* of the national community, can similarly be reconstructed only in approximation and *by addition*, on the basis of periodic samplings taken by ballot from the constantly changing general will.[112] But even this momentary totality of the national community can only be grasped as a sum.[113]

In short, while conservative thought is oriented towards the past surviving in the present, and bourgeois thought, because it bears the present,[114] nourishes itself on new developments, as they transpire from moment to moment, proletarian thought attempts to consider and to further the future within the present, by putting into the foreground those present factors which herald the future structural forms of social life.

Having penetrated to this point, we have reached the root of the difference, as it were, between the modes of experience fundamental to conservatives and progressives. Each case analysed shows ever more clearly that the historical and social events of every chronological present can be experienced and comprehended on the basis of divergent substantive starting-points. It is possible for people themselves to stand at different points within the historical stream, as it were, when they apprehend and experience events, when they take in history. Every chronological present holds contents which are originally native to constellations of the past and which extend into the present from that source. Other contents arise in the struggle for mastery of the present situation, while yet other factors are those which, though generated in the womb of the present, will prove their power to give shape to the world only in the future. Everything depends upon which of these contents determines one's view of what has happened and is happening now.

So far, then, we have attempted to lay out some of the features characteristic of the conservative way of experiencing things and thinking about them, including its experience of the qualitative, its concrete rather than abstract ways of experiencing, its experiencing on the grounds of what is and not of what ought to be, its experience of imaginary spatial relationships in contrast with the linear experience of historical development, its substitution of landed property for the individual as the substratum of history, its preference for 'organic' associations over 'classes', and others. All these individual features, however, are not meant to add up to a reconstruction of conservative experience as such.[115] Our claim can only be to establish, by way of these manifestations, the basic design, the fundamental impulse which animates this style of thought, to trace it in its course of development, and – from now on – to understand as well this basic design in its functional importance for the process as a whole. The 'inclination toward the concrete' (*Wollen des Konkreten*), the aversion to an interpretation grounded upon what ought to be in society, the rejection of the linear construction of time, the empathetic experience of land and soil and organic associations can all be comprehended from the central fact that conservative experience takes in historical happenings from the standpoint of contents surviving from the past, and at the same time acquires its *tensio* – the direction towards which it is physically tensed – from this source. Conservative experience in its authentic mode therefore means to draw sustenance from the foci of experience whose origins are rooted in past constellations of history,[116] and which maintained themselves relatively unchanged until modern conservatism constituted itself, because they were located in portions and sections of the social stream which were not yet borne along by the current of modern happenings. Conservative thinking derives its fullness and its dignity as something more than mere speculation from these authentic germs of life and forms of experience.

Conservative thinking has distinctive character only because it is embedded in this way of experiencing the outer and inner world. Hence, this authentic conservative mode of experience is best studied where the traditional continuity of the vital germs and spheres of life which nurture its spirit and soul is not yet broken. Authentic conservatism first becomes self-reflective and conscious of its own nature when other ways of life and thought come upon the scene within the same life-space where it is situated, against which it must distinguish itself in ideological struggle.[117] Conservative thinking and experiencing is already self-reflective at this first stage of ideology-formation, which is at the same time a stage of methodological reflection, and its subsequent fortunes are increasingly marked by a heightening of this self-reflection. Möser, who stands at this first stage of development in Germany, is characterised precisely by the fact that even though he still lives entirely on tradition, he is already striving to grasp the nature of this authentic conservative thought at the level of reflection.

In the measure, however, that specifically modern social structures not merely co-exist with old ones, but increasingly draw them into their orbit and transform them, authentic conservative experience tends to disappear. In place of the simple habit of living more or less unconsciously, as though the old ways of life were still appropriate, we now find a deliberate effort to maintain the old ways by raising them to the level of reflection, to the 'level of recollection'.[118] *The conservative mode of experience thus preserves itself, as it were, by raising to the level of reflection and methodical control those attitudes to the world which would otherwise have been lost to authentic experience.*

Only here, at the stage where direct experience based on tradition began to disappear, was the nature of history discovered by means of reflection, while the most intense efforts were devoted toward the development of a method of thinking which could somehow rescue the old fundamental attitude towards world and surroundings. By grasping this fundamental experiential attitude methodically, however, conservatives gave shape to an entirely new way of thinking, capable of interpreting the course of things in a new way. We do not share the view consequent on an interpretation construing the overall course of things on the basis of progressive aspirations, which holds that old forms of life and ways of thinking simply die out, cast aside as ballast which has become superfluous. On the contrary, insofar as these elements of the past are grounded and active in material social life, they will always transform themselves, in accordance with the new stages of consciousness and social development, and thus keep alive a 'line' in historical continuity which would otherwise become extinct.

For modern conservatism to develop into a current of thought and to constitute itself as a comprehensive counter-current to liberal Enlightenment thinking, and thus to provide, in its character as self-transforming entity and dynamic structural configuration, guidelines for one of the main currents in the modern history of the spirit, it was necessary for its *fundamental design* – a precondition for everything else – to have been vitally and immediately experienced by identifiable strata and circles within an historical life space. Our central task, accordingly, is to explore this fundamental design of conservatism even in its original form, prior to its abstraction from its place of origin. This is the significance of Möser, among others, who represents a conservatism still in its original state, not yet become recollection, indeed a 'traditionalism' linked to estates. Only when this attitude to life removes itself from its original and 'natural' breeding place and takes on a self-reflective character do we encounter the problem of its transformation into a current of thought freed of local attachments and possessing fixed maxims and methodological insights of its own.

At this point, it is clearly no longer enough to identify the '*pre-theoretical fundamental design*' out of which this style of thought grows. Now it is necessary to explicate as well the *theoretical framework* which henceforth becomes the *theoretical* focal point for the development of this style of thought.

(b) *The theoretical core of conservative thought*

This brings us to our second question. Is there not, quite apart from the fundamental design of a pretheoretical and experiential kind which we have already described, a theoretical core as well, out of which conservative thinking, having become a distinguishable current of thought, steadily grows? In other words, is it possible to identify a central problem within the complex of issues which constantly preoccupies conservative thinking in its capacity as methodological inquiry, a central problem on the basis of which the leading methodological ideas of this thought can best be organically grasped?

This is indeed the case. Conservative thought emerged as a distinguishable entity and dynamic structural configuration when it placed itself into conscious opposition to the bourgeois-revolutionary style of thought, *to the natural-law mode of thinking.*

By finding itself faced with a systematic opponent, the thought impulse which had been more or less latent gained a theoretically comprehensible point of crystallisation. It eventually became necessary to raise up an emerging 'countersystem' against this system. It is important, of course, not to fall into Stahl's error of imagining that two finished systems of thought neatly distinguishable by their contents now confronted one another. On the contrary, it is a question of two ways of thinking in continuous process of development. Conservatism did not merely want to think 'something different' from its liberal opponents; *it wanted to think it differently.* And it was this impulse which provided that additional element which not only involved new contents but turned it into a new mode of thinking (which was still fed, however, by older elements in consciousness).

In order to grasp the central methodological problem of conservative thought, it is first necessary to find out something about the opponent, viz., thinking oriented to natural law. Modern natural-law thinking is by no means merely a pale theory of natural law; it is the natural-law theory inherited from antiquity, now incorporated into the bourgeois forms of thinking and bourgeois assumptions of the eighteenth century. This is the form in which it appears to the counter-revolutionary thinker and in which it affronts him. Just as the overthrow of the old regime and the execution of the royal pair serve counter-revolutionary consciousness as expressive symbols of the revolutionary happenings themselves, so do the Declaration of the Rights of Man and the revolutionary constitutions serve as the facts which symbolise the new way of thinking. This new mode of thought had to be extirpated, down to its systematic roots.[119]

As is well known, the *lex naturae*[120] refers to a complex of ideas going back to the Stoa in its original formation, a complex which enters into Christian doctrine from there, eventually coalescing with it, only to emerge once more from this religious guide in modern times and to become, newly constituted in the form of a secular natural law, one of the most important ideological forces in modern thought. Here, if anywhere, it is evident how doctrinal contents which appear identical can mean different things in the course of history and how, as a function of different sociological situations, they constantly assume a new mien. Originally the ideology of a dominant social stratum, this theory already manifested during the Roman Empire a way of thinking and experiencing which was wholly antithetical to that of the national religion.[121] This original tendency towards *cosmopolitan thinking*, constructed upon the dual focal points of *extreme individualism* and *extreme universalism* resurfaces in the modern version of the doctrine and defines the respect in which it is antithetical to the thinking of primary spheres of life. This doctrine had its authentic origins during the time when the world-view of the *polis* was in dissolution.[122] It arose as a counter to a localised world-view which respected the positive law and customs of a traditional community, and it grew out of the consciousness of a spirituality which was liberating itself from these ties. Set over against the prevailing laws and morality, characterised as being arbitrarily posited, was an ethics *which was to be derived from the universally valid lawfulness of reason*. The tension between 'absolute' and 'relative' law of nature (*Naturgesetz, lex naturae*), so fundamental to all natural-law thinking, already makes its appearance here. In the latest development of this way of thinking, then, it returns as a contrast between the 'natural' and the 'positive' systems of legal right (*Naturrecht, positives Recht*).

Also already present in Stoic thinking is the characteristic philosophy-of-history construction to which the events which have transpired in the world present themselves as being located along a line of decline, from a blissful state of nature (the 'golden age'), where absolute natural law – pure reasonableness – is thought to have still ruled, to a state of the present, in which, through the supremacy of human passions, the reasonable has been over-whelmed by power and greed. For Stoicism, which, with this theory, predicated the utmost tension between absolute norm and positive existence, this tension did not offer grounds for revolutionary conclusions, simply because the theory was put forward by a ruling social stratum. This stratum was quite content to understand all existing things, in particular property and family hierarchy, as a compromise between absolute norm and relative circumstances.

That Christianity was capable of incorporating such a doctrine is due to the fact that it arose out of the same world situation as Stoicism itself, except that Christendom was also a spiritual and psychic expression of an oppressed stratum. By the encapsulation of Stoic natural law in Christian dogma, the theological grounding of the doctrine becomes dominant. 'Absolute natural law' was now turned into the 'law of God', binding only upon the true 'children in Christ'. Relative natural law, here derived from the fall of man, provided the basis for understanding the actual condition of the world. As in Stoicism, the contrast between the norms laid down as absolute and those which are relative survives in the form of a contrast between two normative orders, one of which is valid for 'civil' and economic existence while the other comprehends the norms of personal morality and religiosity. This is not the place to retrace all the differences in function which Troeltsch has pointed out with regard to the ecclesiastical, sectarian and mystical line of development, nor to review the different ways in which Lutheranism and Calvinism accommodate these tensions – how in one case the conservative, and, in the other, the revolutionary resolution of the tension comes to the fore. We need only note that the starting-point of the newer mode of thinking is marked precisely by the fact that the idea of *lex naturae* gains its modern form by leaving theistic groundings behind. This first came about when modern state absolutism sought to justify its position of power in a secular way, independent of theological groundings. But this secular natural law quickly passed into the hands of those who, thinking on behalf of the bourgeois world, saw in this doctrine a weapon for revolutionary struggle against the dominant positive legal order. The more this thinking frees itself from theistic grounding according to revelation, the more it seeks ultimate legitimation for its demands in 'Nature' and 'Reason'. In this connection, Max Weber tellingly points out that this presupposes a parallelism between the two terms. The knowledge gained by human reason is regarded as identical with 'the nature of things' (as in the English expression 'reasonable', which retains the twofold connotations of 'rational' and 'practical').[123] In this way of thinking, now deprived of theological premises and no longer able to invoke the ecclesiastical-theological criterion as a source of validation, the isolated individual comes to the fore once again, as ultimate court of appeal and as end in itself. Precisely the elements within natural law which have their origins in Stoicism are thereby revived.

But Stoic natural law was accessible in two forms at the time, in the theological form of churchly doctrine and in the widespread tradition of Roman law which had also absorbed Stoic elements. The elements of *lex naturae* thus emphasised attached themselves to the Enlightenment's already pervasive faith in reason, with the methodological ideal of natural science, with the 'atomistic way of thinking', and with the 'speculative construct of the [social] contract';[124] and they broaden themselves out into a particular style of thought which already represents something more comprehensive than merely a new conception of *lex naturae*. This is then its form when counter-revolutionary thinking attacks this style of thinking.

The attack on natural-law-grounded thinking does not happen all at once, but appears scattered in the writings of various authors, animated by a fundamental design different from that of the revolutionary theorists. In Möser, who represents a starting-point for conservative thinking in Germany in so many respects – and especially by his historical mentality – we find the doctrine of the state of nature superceded,[125] for example, while the author continues to cling to the conception of the original contract.[126] The same is true for his student Rehberg, who remains on the premisses of Enlightenment philosophy when fighting the conception of natural law, who upholds Möser's doctrine of the original (social) contract among the possessors of land, and who relies on basic points derived from Kantian doctrine, interpreting them in a conservative sense.[127]

An interesting parallel example of a different kind of partial overcoming of 'natural-law' thinking is offered by Haller, who must also be referred to at this stage, at which natural law is only partially overcome. Although Haller comes chronologically later, he proceeds in just the opposite way: rejecting the doctrine of the original (social) contract, while believing in a natural state. He even asserts that we are still living in that state, since the rule of the stronger, which we find everywhere, accords with the will of nature and of God.[128] In an interesting turn, Haller replaces thinking and argumentation on the grounds of eternal laws of reason with a similar, statically structured argument on grounds of eternal natural laws of the drive for power. Clearly such 'overcoming' of natural-law thinking, which reshapes a building-block here or there – perhaps rejecting the doctrine of the state of nature which had already been rejected as historical fact by both Rousseau and, most emphatically, Kant, or which replaces the theory of the contract with something else, – does not represent a clean sweep of 'natural-law thinking' in general. This thinking was fed from many sources, and in all the many attempts it could only be attacked and dissolved in one or another of its aspects. The main thing is to note how one and the same fundamental politically conservative design is behind all these attacks, and, accordingly, how here too newly emerging methodological insights are existentially integrated by a fundamental political design.[129]

Since we cannot show the total refutation of the natural-law way of thinking in any one individual author, it is all the more important to work out the principal theoretical support and central point of reference which enables the intellectual counter-movement to think and to grow.

To replace the mere idea of *lex naturae*, we must therefore first classify all of the features of form as well as contents which distinguish natural-law thinking in the eighteenth century, constituting a style of thought and not simply an idea. Parallel contrasts then will open our way to the characteristics of the conservative style of thought.

Analysing 'natural-law' thinking, the style of thought as it appeared to conservative critics of the time, into its component parts, we can distinguish the following levels:[130]

A *The contents of natural-law thinking*:
1 The doctrine of the 'state of nature'.
2 The doctrine of the social contract.
3 The doctrine of popular sovereignty.
4 The doctrine of the inalienable Rights of Man (liberty, property, security, the right to resist oppression, etc).

B *Characteristics of natural-law thinking*:
1 *Rationalism*: establishing the results of any inquiry on the basis of *reason*.
2 *Deducing* the particular from a general principle.
3 A presupposition of *universal validity*, binding on all individuals.
4 A claim of *universal applicability* of all laws to all historical entities.
5 *Atomism and mechanism*: collective formations (the state, the law, etc.) are construed from the standpoint of the individual, the discrete.
6 *Static thinking*: right reason conceived as a self-contained autonomous sphere of the 'ought' suspended above history.

While the first group of characteristics reveals the contents of the doctrine, the second group points to the elements of form which characterise this style of thought. If the counter-attack is to be somehow systematised, with the scattered elements of the critique given a centering internal focal point, the inner coherence of the conservative counter-arguments can be grasped by classifying them as if they were responses to the positions analytically distinguished above.

The counter-revolutionary thinker conducts his offensive either by

A *attacking the contents of natural-law thinking*,
1 by questioning the doctrine of the original state of nature,
2 by questioning the doctrine of the social contract,
3 by attacking the doctrine of popular sovereignty,
4 by questioning the doctrine of the inalienable Rights of Man; or by turning against

B the *characteristic method of natural-law thinking* in that he
1 rejects the method of establishing the results of any inquiry on the grounds of reason and counters with *history, life, nation*. This confrontation gives rise to philosophical problems which dominate the whole epoch, problems which appear, when abstractly formulated, in the ageless form of the contrast between *thinking and being* but which, when seen concretely, give this problem a special meaning, graspable

when one bears in mind the overwhelming primal experience signified by the French Revolution. From a sociological point of view, most of the philosophical positions which accord primacy to '*thinking*' have their roots in either a bourgeois revolutionary or in a bureaucratic mentality, while most philosophies which give primacy to '*being*' are rooted in the ideological counter-movement of romanticism or, rather, in the form they assumed then, in counter-revolutionary experience. This last was the soil out of which such basic correlations as Müller's 'idea and concept' grew (i.e., in the distinctive form they then took, of course, and not with regard to the elements which originate in the philosophical tradition).

2 To the deductive bent of natural-law thinking, the conservative opposes the many-sided *irrationality of reality*. The *problem* of the irrational is the second great problem of the age. In the form it assumed at the time, it too has its sociological roots in the French Revolution. The problem of the relationship between genesis and system also acquires its modern significance in these ideological struggles.

3 The problem of *individuality*, radically formulated, is counterposed to universal validity.

4 The idea of the social *organism* is put forward by the conservatives to counter the idea of the universal applicability of political innovations to any historical and national entity. This 'category' has a special significance,[131] since it arose from the conservative impulse to stem the spreading tide of the French Revolution by pointing out that political institutions can only develop organically and cannot be arbitrarily transferred from one national organism (*Nationalkörper*) to another. The emphasis on the *qualitative* which is so characteristic of conservative thinking also grows out of the same impulse.

5 Against the interpretive construction of collective formations on the basis of individuals, the conservative opposes a *mode of thinking* which starts *from the standpoint of totality*. The whole (the state, the nation) is not to be understood as the sum of its individual parts, but the discrete individual is to be regarded as part of the totality (as in the concept of *Volksgeist*, for example). This is also the place to note that concepts of the 'subject' vary with the currents of thought, and that, in the cultural sciences as well as in the logical philosophical disciplines, primacy is accorded to either an 'I-structure' or a 'we-structure', depending on the style of thought which is at work. Other methods of making analytical

distinctions – such as those whereby liberal Enlightenment thought isolates the various cultural fields such as law, state, economy – are also opposed, in this case by a *synoptical view*; and the significance of synthesis rather than analysis is insisted upon in all fields. One of the most important problems occupying the nineteenth century, not only on the level of theory but also in political reality, is how elements can be forged together into a totality. Problems of national unity pressed for resolution, as did problems of the total structure in the common life of states. Such vital experimentation goes hand in hand with the rise and fall of different synthetic conceptions.

6 Finally, one of the most important logical weapons against natural-law thought is the *dynamic conception of reason*. At first, the conservative merely opposed the rigidity of the static theory of reason with the movement of 'life' and history. Later, however, a much more radical method of avoiding the eternal norms of the Enlightenment was discovered. Instead of regarding the world as revolving around a static reason, reason itself and rational norms were conceived as changing and moving. At this later stage, the impulse against natural law achieved the most radical innovations and gained insights of great novelty. We shall come back to the steps by which these – as well as the other forms of thinking here classified – were worked out.

If we began by attempting to figure out the internally integrative element in conservative thinking within the sphere of fundamental designs of an experiential kind, we are now, before turning to historical detail, trying to grasp, in the materials just presented, the intellectual framework which can best provide a reference point for an orientation able to comprehend the methodological ideas of conservative thought in their innermost interconnections.

In none of the conservative thinkers do we find, as already noted, an all-out attack upon the natural-law way of thinking methodically effectuated; each attacks and corrects certain aspects of it only. But this is precisely why such a theoretical framework is necessary if we are to see things with reasonable clarity; it indicates the logical locus, so to speak, of the individual overturnings which historically commence at quite diverse points. It is by no means our intention thereby to juxtapose two static, completely developed systems of thought. All that can be done is to juxtapose two methodological lines of inquiry at work on the problems they have in common, in order to gain a perspective on the logical sequence of events in time.

In our view, the only thing that can be offered in lieu of a definition of conservative thinking is to offer a vivid demonstration of the theoretical and pre-theoretical element that holds it together. This structural orientation concerning the nature of early conservative thought, more like a systematic presentation than anything else, is now to be followed by a purely historical and sociological presentation, which will attempt to show in detail how the rational and pre-rational impulses, only sketched until now, concretely expressed themselves within a specific historical and sociological entity, which specific types and standpoints in thinking confronted one another within that entity, and which living forces were behind them in each case, as motive powers.

Part III Early conservatism in Germany

All concrete thinking occurs within a specific historical life-space (*Lebensraum*) and can be adequately grasped in its concreteness only by reference to it. The initial task of sociological investigation is to work out the distinctive character of this historical life-space.

In essence, the identity of a life-space can be characterised and is upheld, first of all, by the *social bearers* (social strata) of the newly emerging spiritual and psychic cosmos; then also by the *traditions* surviving from earlier times (since they always represent a point of departure for new developments); and finally, by the *specific course of events* to which the particular life-space under investigation is subjected during the time in question.

If we want to analyse conservative thinking in the first half of the nineteenth century in the German cultural world, we must first investigate the factors just indicated. But we do *not* want to approach this task in the systematic and even schematic sequence just indicated. Instead, we shall address the proposed questions from case to case, in direct connection with the primary problem which concerns us here: the formation of the most important styles of thought and intellectual positions which comprise conservative thought in this epoch.

By 'styles of thought' we mean the main currents in the world of thinking which, when they are present, move against or towards one another in historical variation, and occasionally merge in whole or in part. The syntheses brought about in this manner must not be imagined to be impervious to further change, since their constituent elements invariably split up again and may enter into new combinations, their variability reflecting the changing vicissitudes of the living whole in which they arise.

By 'intellectual positions' we mean a conjuncture where an especially important and representative synthesis of intellectual currents comes about. Like the view from a mountaintop, such a standpoint provides the best possible grasp of the ways which lead up to it. We want to collect our treatments of the above-mentioned sociological problems around characterisations of the socially determined development of such conjunctures in early conservative thought. Accordingly, we prefer a living presentation to a schematic architectonic design. In order to make certain of some points of reference in advance, however, we shall begin by marking out the most important 'junctures' or 'intellectual positions' attained by early conservative thought in Germany: the synthesis between the estates-related and romantic thought; the beginnings of the historical school; Hegel; the party of the *Politische Wochenblatt* (Political Weekly); Metternich's standpoint; Stahl; the later historical school; and late romanticism.[132]

1 The first conservative position: romanticism and the estates

The identity of an historical and spiritual life-space can be understood most readily (leaving closer analysis aside for now) by investigating what it absorbs from outside and how, but especially the manner in which it *redirects external influences* during a given cross-section of time.

If we examine, from this point of view, the German spiritual cosmos during the period of interest to us, the time immediately following the French Revolution, we find that in Prussia, the outstanding centre of conservative thought, the revolution precipitated a clash between the aspirations of the *feudal forces and old estates*, on the one side, and *bureaucratic-absolutist rationalism*, on the other. There was, no doubt, some revolutionary influence on the Prussian bourgeoisie, but the decisive effect of the French Revolution was its temporary weakening, to some extent, of the spiritual and political alliance between the absolute monarchy and the nobility, which had already been firmly established under Frederick the Great.[133] Not that the bourgeoisie was closed to the liberal ideas of the revolution: we know only too well the enthusiasm with which broad strata of the German intelligentsia greeted the outbreak of the revolution in France.[134] The biographies of most conservatives and reactionaries reveal a revolutionary period in their youth. It is also well-known that surprisingly many higher officials were imbued with liberal ideas, and that the 'reforms from above' after the battle at Jena were due to these inclinations. Yet this response was nevertheless an essentially ideological one; it was largely reversed by the subsequent development of the real historical factors.

What is unique about the constitution of a historically and socially conditioned life-space is precisely the fact that it reacts to external ideological influences in a definite manner which reflects its own distinctive makeup, and that it turns the influences received from outside in the direction of its own development. The ideas of 1789 – which sought, in contrast to absolutism, to build up the state from 'below', instead of from 'above' – set into motion and animated those elements of the German and, more specifically, the Prussian bodies politic which were in fact active there as historically and socially relevant forces: viz., the estates, and among them the nobility as the only politically potent force.[135] Every other influence was bound to remain merely 'ideological'.

In the first decades of the nineteenth century in Prussia we have a sociological experiment, as it were, which shows what happens when ideas which have their genuine nativity in a more advanced state of social development enter a socially undeveloped but culturally sophisticated life-space. Germany and especially Prussia, whose fate was decisive for conservative thought, were many decades behind in the economic development toward capitalism. Even if one is not prepared to be as drastic in assessing the backwardness of the Germany of those years as Frederick the Great was with regard to his own epoch,[136] Marx's estimate is probably correct, when he placed the social conditions of Germany in 1843 roughly on a par with the social situation of France in 1789.[137]

Let us consider what would then have been the equivalent to the fourth or third 'estate' in Germany, and especially in Prussia. The transformation of a stratification by estates into a *class* society was still in its early stages. The proletariat consisted of handicraftsmen who still lived to all intents and purposes in a system of guilds and did not react to external pressure as a class. Corresponding to the *tiers état* was the German *Mittelstand*, but it had, as Sombart has correctly noted, as yet nothing in common with *bourgeoisie* in the real sense.[138] This absence of development explains the fact that this stratum still lacked a clearly defined common goal and a conscious purpose, but was at the mercy of a variety of ideological currents and fluctuations. As yet, this intermediate stratum lacked 'real' ties of an interested kind. As a result, most of its members were politically indifferent. They were quick to welcome everything that was new, but also ready to abruptly change their mood when things went wrong or failed to live up to their abstract expectations. All these characteristics are clear symptoms of an interestedness which is still unattached. That the French Revolution, in its specific character as a revolutionising force, had no very great radicalising effect was, sociologically considered, due to

113

the fact that its reverberations could as yet only be ideological: the element least capable of action in the Germany of that time was precisely the stratum equivalent to the bourgeoisie.

An active response to the revolution came only from those strata in Prussia which, due to the special character of the country and the distinctive shape of its history, possessed the capacity for carrying real political weight – the nobility and the bureaucracy. If we may overstate the point: for our purposes, *the most important effect of the French Revolution in Prussia is that the French conflict between people and ruler is here reproduced on a 'higher' level.* It takes the form of a struggle between the estates, which build up the state from '*below*' (nobility), and the monarchy, which rules from '*above*' and is represented by its bureaucracy. The result is a curious intermixing of influences. The revolutionary element of the events in France gives life to the designs of the nobility, who want to build up the state from 'below' by invigorating the estates and by seeking an organic development.[139] The mechanistic, centralist, and rationalist impulse of the French Revolution, on the other hand, is taken up by officialdom and brought into play against the designs of the nobility. The situation is also given its character as an amalgam by the fact that the revolution is indeed initiated in Prussia from 'above'. (The expression, 'revolution from above', was coined by Hardenberg.) The bureaucratic absolutist state, borne by its officialdom, carries out reforms which are necessary in the interest of a state moving in the direction of capitalism. It implements them only partly in the interest of the common people, but in some measure *against* the nobility and its defensive positions.

In France the revolution brought about a defensive alliance between the nobility, the monarchy, and the Church. In Prussia, where actual pressure from 'below' was still negligible, the result was a partial weakening of the alliance between the nobility and the bureaucracy. The situation found its ideological expression in that Prussia of the first decade of the new century presents us with *a reaction based upon the estates, a reaction which operates at the level and cultural stage of the nineteenth century, which employs the most advanced intellectual resources to work out designs grounded in its social centre of gravity* – a reaction, in short, which finds a way of giving modern expression to fundamental designs resting far in the past. The ideological reaction to the Enlightenment allies itself with the social reaction of the nobility: *romanticism and the thinking of estates take on one another's qualities*. This combination generates the distinctive character which in effect marks 'German' thinking to the present day: a romantic trait on the one hand and, on the other, historicism, which similarly gained the power to give itself definition and form within the constellation and at the juncture where the thinking characteristic of the old estates entered into an alliance with romanticism.

*In general, we reject the views of those who posit national ways of thinking as ultimate and unanalysable units and who speak in this sense of a 'German' or a 'French' mode of thinking, which is to be deduced directly from 'national characters'. It is possible that at the end of a particular inquiry one may come up against national character as an irreducible residue, although even that residue would have to be regarded as potentially changeable. But one must first take into account all those factors which can be deduced from history and from social structures. Once one adopts this approach, one will increasingly realize that those who speak of a national way of thinking are in fact thinking of the thought of a particular period of national life, and within that period only the thought of a particular social stratum which happens to have a decisive influence on the national culture in that period. They elevate this thinking, which can be sociologically and historically much more closely defined, to the realm of national thought in general. In this form the view is mistaken. What is true is that certain periods and, within them, certain strata may have a lasting effect, especially if the period is a decisive one for the development of national history and culture. This is the spirit in which Alexis de Tocqueville[140] already quite correctly deduced French abstractness from the sociological importance of the pre-revolutionary era – and the mentality of that era, in turn, from the cultural predominance of the contemporary literary intelligentsia, which was excluded from administration and government. To the same extent, but in the opposite direction in matters of substance, the years of the Wars of Liberation and of the subsequent period of restoration have been decisive for the character of German thought. German thinking has been so thoroughly romantic and historicist since the nineteenth century that even the opposition to it, which grew up on the same soil, remains deeply involved in these forms of thinking. Heine was a romantic, although an opponent of the romantic movement, and Marx a historicist, although an opponent of the historical school.

When 'conservative thinking' is hypostatised to 'German thinking', the sociological differences are obscured. It is not correct to say that German thinking is conservative. What can be argued, however, is that the conservative element in European culture was most consistently developed in all its implications in Germany. It is equally wrong to claim that

115

oppositional thinking is essentially 'French'. It is correct, however, that the oppositional elements of consciousness were most highly developed in France[141] owing to the specific situation there.[142*]

[We return from this excursus on the general problem of 'national character' to our detailed consideration of the alliance between romanticism and the estates in the early nineteenth century.] In order to understand this peculiar combination, it is necessary to look more closely at the distinctive sociological character of the strata which took part in this intellectual struggle. Let us begin with the bearers of the romantic and estates-oriented opposition, which consists, first, of the nobility and, second, of the 'ideologues', i.e., middle-class writers and literary aristocrats who become the spokesmen of this movement.

Romanticism must be seen as reaction against the Enlightenment mode of thinking, and, at least at the outset, more as an immanent, ideological movement rather than as a movement which is socially and politically determined in a direct way. Enlightenment thinking was indeed borne in part by the upwardly-striving bourgeoisie, but by the enlightened monarchy and its officials as well.[143] A compact and cohesive ideological counter-movement, irrational in inclination, could arise as a current only because the tendency towards rationalisation had advanced to its outermost limits in the Enlightenment. It had succeeded in constructing a comprehensive picture of the world which was radically and logically grounded in reason. It thereby eliminated the 'irrational' from every corner of the world-conception (*Welt-bild*); and at the same time, in its triumphal march, it excluded life-elements which were enabled, just by virtue of this exclusion, to flow together and to become a unified counterpole.[144] This assembling of elements opposed to the Enlightenment at first proceeded wholly without a political fundamental design.[145] Quite the contrary, the pre-romantic stage which we find in most countries is borne within the same milieu and often by the same individuals who stand in the midst of Enlightenment rationalism.

The romantic movement is not simply an antithetical counter-movement, fueled by diverse forces; it is rather far more comparable to the movement of a pendulum, which, having swung to an extreme point, abruptly reverses itself. This turnabout of the rational into the irrational (in emotional life as well as in the way of thinking) accordingly sometimes occurs even among major representatives of the Enlightenment itself. In Rousseau and Montesquieu,[146] we find extremely rational ways of thinking peacefully alongside of their contraries. In Germany the precursors of romanticism, the *'Sturm und Drang'*, Hamann and Herder already appear at the time of the high tide of Enlightenment. It is only on the basis of this pendular movement, which let the counter-stroke emerge out of the same driving force as the one from which rationalism drew its energies, that we can account for the many traits of romanticism which are – despite the radical differences which are also present – reminiscent of rationalism: viz., [its excessive subjectivism and its tendency towards rationalising all the irrational forces of consciousness which the rationalism of the Enlightenment could never have grasped with its purely speculative means, a tendency which is present *de facto*, notwithstanding all of the programmatic irrationalism of the romantic movement].

This romantic current, by the time it takes the form of a 'movement', is mainly borne by *socially unattached intellectuals*[147] and thus, in a sociological sense, by the stratum that was also committed to the Enlightenment. But while the stratum as represented in the Enlightenment remained inwardly connected, as it were, with at least its historical social origins, and while the bourgeois writers of the Enlightenment could still, as it were, fall back on the bourgeoisie for support with regard to their world-view, the conversion to romanticism meant for the intellectuals an increasing sociological as well as metaphysical alienation and isolation. Nowhere is it more apparent to what extent the 'intelligentsia' (*Intelligenz*) constitute a very distinct sociological phenomenon. The extremely unstable outer circumstances of the intelligentsia and the fact that they lack a place where they belong in the economic division of labour, greatly complicates questions of sociological imputation regarding this sociological phenomenon. The German 'intelligentsia', insofar as it was socially unattached, was indeed very badly off during that time; its members literally suffered hunger pangs. There were no newspapers in our sense, and the last years of Kleist's life show what it meant to keep alive a journal such as the *Berliner Abendblätter*.[148] One could try to survive as a professional writer, but this was only a very recent possibility. Klopstock, Lessing, and Wieland[149] were in fact the first German writers to attempt to make a living by their literary production. In view of the many difficulties which life as an independent intellectual involved, it is not surprising that the lives of most literary men of the time show, after a period of stormy youthful opposition to the world and to their environment, a tendency toward a career in officialdom.

Precisely by virtue of this uncertainty of outer circumstance, together with a spiritual horizon stretching far beyond their own narrow sphere of life, these romantic *literati* possessed an

117

extraordinary sensitivity combined with moral unsteadiness, a constant readiness for adventure and obscurantism. As we have seen, they could not maintain themselves on their own, socially unattached. They hired out their pens to the government of the day, oscillated between Prussia and Austria, and a number ended up with Metternich at the time, who knew how to use their services. Never properly employed as officials, their assignments essentially in secret service and the influencing of public opinion, their thinking takes on a characteristic half-concreteness, intermediate between the unworldliness of the idealist and the official's single-minded concentration on immediate tasks. They are neither abstract enthusiasts nor narrow-minded practical men. The 'signs of the times' form the insignia of their inquiries; they are the born philosophers of history.

This is certainly the positive side of their activity, for there must and should always be people who are not so bound by their immediate ties that they care only for the 'next step'.[150] It also seems that the intellectual elucidation of the social process becomes ever more necessary as that process becomes increasingly complex. At the beginning of this line of development – or at least at an important point in its path – which represents, as it were, the creation by history of an organ of self-observation, we find the speculations in the philosophy of history advanced by the philosophy of the Enlightenment. Romantic thought fulfils just the same function, though it starts out by transporting the valuations with a change of signs. From the dreams of a Novalis, the way leads to Hegel, only to pass smoothly on to Marx. And these are also the sources from which German sociology takes its dominant tone heavily weighted towards philosophy of history. In contrast to Western sociology (which has gradually taken off the philosophy-of-history framework from its inquiries into totality), German sociology retains this characteristic inclination toward the philosophy of history as an essential trait, at least in those of its currents which are authentically native. If this is the positive element in romantic political thought, its negative feature is its readiness to justify anything and everything.

These unattached intellectuals are the archetypical apologists, 'ideologists' who are masters at providing a basis and backing for the political designs whose service they enter, whatever these may be. Their own situation does not produce any attachments, but they have an extraordinarily refined sensitivity for all the collective designs present in their life-space and the ability to ferret them out and to enter into their spirit. On their own, they know nothing; but as soon as they catch hold of something from outside and identify with it, they know it *better* – better indeed than those who have a design imposed upon them by their situation, by the dead weight of their existence.

It is sensitivity, then, which is the distinguishing characteristic for this style of thought. Not thoroughness, but a 'good eye' for events in the realm of spirit and soul, is its virtue. The constructions it places on things are therefore always false or even falsified; but some thing or other is always 'astutely observed'. This is the respect in which romanticism had a fecundating effect on the human sciences.[151] It threw up problems for discussion, it discovered entire fields; but the task of distinguishing actuality from mere construction was left to subsequent research. The enlightened intellectuality of the French *philosophes* had to substitute wit and *esprit* for the scientific foundation which it lacked. At the stage of romanticism, this acuity turns into a special sensitivity – a faculty for detecting *qualitative* subtleties, a virtuosity in empathy. Out of the intellectual current of literary *esprit* and romanticism, then, there arises one component of what we shall call '*qualitative thinking*' or the '*thought of the qualitative*', whose other component springs at the same time, although in a wholly different way, from the feeling for the world (*Weltgefühl*) associated with the old estates.[152]

As we have seen, it was because of their lack of social roots that intellectuals failed to have ultimate goals and substantive materials as their own immediate possessions, that their thinking always sought to *approach* something rather than departing from settled grounds, and that the things they sought to justify were taken from elsewhere, from more vital sources. It is the typical fate of the intelligentsia in the modern world – clearly traceable since the eighteenth century – that the destiny of the spiritual universe is in the keeping of a stratum with few roots or none and impossible to refer unambiguously to some one class or status; a stratum which does not ground its designs in itself, but engages itself, when it is engaged at all, on behalf of designs borne by strata which are socially more intensively attached. This fact is significant for thought because for every spiritual tendency the ultimate grounds in orientation and intention are existentially fixed in place by social positions. If these fundamental levels of designs were also to be left to the disposition of this socially unattached intelligentisa, they would be used up and exhausted all too soon. If, on the other hand, there were no such unattached and socially emancipated literary stratum, it might easily happen that, in a society becoming ever more capitalistic, much of our spiritual substance would disappear, leaving nothing but naked self-interest. For it is, as

Alfred Weber has observed, the intellectuals who are the bearers of ideals as well as of ideologies – and it is hard to decide which of these predominates.

If, in delineating the distinctive intellectual characteristics of this romantic literary stratum, we want to go beyond the two features already noted (the point of view based on philosophy of history and sensitivity to the qualitative differences) there is hardly a definition of romanticism that is better fitted to the peculiar nature of this way of thinking than the one given by Novalis himself. He declares:

> The world must be romanticised. That is how original meaning is recovered. *Romanticising means nothing but raising to a higher qualitative power*. In this operation, the lower self is made equal to a higher one, as we consist ourselves of such a series of qualitatively different 'powers'. This operation is still completely unknown. *In giving an exalted meaning to the vulgar, a mysterious aspect to the commonplace, the dignity of the unknown to the familiar, the semblance of infinity to the finite, I romanticise it.*[153]

We should like to characterise this 'technique' of thinking by saying that it elevates a given state of things to a level of explication higher than the one that is usually associated with it, and we think that this formulation merely expresses in different words what Novalis himself (although with apologetic intent) said in the passage cited above. It also indicates that the state of things or the complex of events in question is not creatively produced or discovered by the romantic thinker himself, but is rather simply caught hold of or taken over by him from some other source. A typical instance of romanticising of this sort is the romanticising of Catholicism or of the nobility. The existence of the nobility is an empirical fact. Accepting all the historical faults and virtues of the nobility as given and known, romantic thinking makes its contribution by discovering an inner principle there and by presenting the historical development of the nobility as a struggle between conflicting principles. The facts which in themselves simply appear as parts of a complex of causal linkages, especially for a thinking which is positivistically-inclined, are thereby converted into contextures of meanings. Such 'romanticising' no doubt sheds new light on the facts ('something is always astutely observed') but it obscures the material interconnections.

*We have emphasised the obscurantist quality of romantic thought. It could also be shown, however, that the romantic method of thinking is fruitful in the spheres where interpretation is appropriate. This is by virtue of the fact that it is in the nature of the spirit and of the soul that they may be penetrated to different *levels of depth*. The positive meaning of Novalis' remark and of the whole romanticising way of thinking lies in their awareness, in contrast to the Enlightenment, of these different levels of depth. For reasons of space we must refrain here from a phenomenological analysis which would show this in detail. But such an analysis would also have to show that the romantic directedness towards the deepest level is not an 'authentic' one. The preponderance of subjectivity permits an element of arbitrariness to enter surreptitiously into the interpretation and prevents the subject from giving itself fully to the object. This also explains the possibility of abuse, mentioned above, to which 'romanticising' lends itself: the tendency to interpret relationships of cause and effect which ought not to be subjected to interpretation at all, that is, to interpret them in defiance of their objective nature – and thereby to glorify even that which is mean. Significantly enough, the possibility of two readings are already implicit in Novalis' remark: one which attempts to penetrate to ever greater 'depths', and a second which leads to putting an ideological gloss over existing conditions. Romanticism realised both possibilities.*

It would not be necessary to spend much time on this method of 'romanticising' if it were confined to political contents. The most peculiar thing is, however, that it led to the rediscovery and explication of an *older style of thought* which would otherwise have remained latent. Romantic thought did not only romanticise certain *contents* of politics and of world-views, but it also employed the same process in romanticising an older *way of thinking* as well. Just as romantic thinking had not created its political objectives out of its own resources, so it took over, at a certain stage of its development, many of the major supports of 'non-Enlightenment thinking' from the *thought of the old estates*. It romanticised what had already been tentatively elaborated there into a full-fledged methodology, and adapted it to political purposes.

At the important juncture in intellectual and social history where the union between literary romanticism (as ideological counter-tendency to the Enlightenment) and the thought associated with the old estates comes into being, stands Adam Müller with his *Die Elemente der Staatskunst* (The Principles of State-craft).[154] Müller is not an author who merits attention on account of the substantive importance of his achievement on account of his creative originality. But he is one of those historical figures who have done a great deal to shape the thought of their age, or at least of one of its dominant tendencies. He is the born ideologist and romanticist in the sense just indicated above – essentially dependent on outside sources, but also a connoisseur, endowed with an exquisite flair for gathering up what belongs together from the teeming welter of contemporary ideas.

Since we are here concerned only with the main constituents of the stylistic development, we cannot discuss in detail the beginnings of political romanticism, and little need be said about the early political writings of Novalis and Friedrich Schlegel. Everything they contain that became relevant for the subsequent ideological development is in some way incorporated by Müller. Novalis' beautiful essay 'Die Christenheit oder Europa' (Christianity or Europe)[155] is a real gem, but it is more daydream than political ideology. Its ideological point was discovered by Müller: its criticism of Protestantism and its praise for the hierarchy of the Catholic Church. The eruption of the curious Protestant longing for the forsaken church, which precipitated a movement of conversion and which had its sociological basis in the interests of Austria, in the Holy Alliance, and in ultramontanism, dates back to Novalis.

A feature prominent in the beginnings of the romantic movement, which Müller took up and which became immensely important for the style of thinking then in formation, is the *pantheistic element*[156] in thinking, which had entered into a remarkable state of tension with the hierarchical organisation of the Catholic conception of the world and of the Catholic structure of thought. In the experience of modern times, the pantheistic element was first predominant in the Renaissance, whose philosophy of nature was the intellectual counterpart of such an attitude to life. As mainstream, this style of thinking was displaced by the exact natural sciences, but there were apparently thousands of tributaries in which this manner of experiencing the world survived. The *Sturm* and *Drang* period marks its first powerful reappearance; and how deeply Goethe too was immersed in it can merely be mentioned here. This attitude to life entered into early romantic thought, and there seems to be some truth in the assertion that when Protestantism becomes atheistic it tends to turn pantheistic, while Catholicism, when it becomes atheistic, turns into materialism.[157]

The pantheistic attitude to life, then, is dominant in early romantic thought and gives it a special cast. To limit ourselves at the outset to the pith of the matter, it should be noted that the essence of the pantheistic ways of experiencing as well as thinking is that God is not experienced and presupposed as being 'in the beginning' and only *as* the beginning, but rather as present in everything in the world.[158] The dogmatic thinking of Catholicism and the general, law-seeking, and positivist thinking of the natural sciences stand together, in a sense, against this style of thinking, however they may differ in other respects. They are akin in that both conceive at least the internal relations of the world as rationally determined and as rationally intelligible (which is why the Church and Positivism are well able to join forces, as has often been observed). For Catholic thought, the miracle (the irrational) is in the beginning, as the person of the Creator, while for the generalising natural sciences, the irrational is either completely eradicated or relegated to a kind of transcendental sphere of 'things-in-themselves'. In any case, both ways of thinking hold that there is a rarified sphere which is thoroughly amenable to rational analysis. In contrast to all this, the living and the divine pulsate everywhere for pantheistic feeling; and static thinking, with its abstract, general categories, cannot get close to this vitality. Thinking, where it plays a part at all, undergoes a change of function here. Its task is no longer to recognise and register the general norms or laws which govern the world, but to move along with that which is coming into being and with the fluctuations of all that is contained in the world.†

One tendency that grows out of pantheistic thought is analogical thinking.[159] It was already present in alchemy and astrology, as well as later in romantic speculations on nature, and it was eventually introduced into political thought. This way of thinking, although it conceives the world as thoroughly brought to life, nevertheless presupposes hidden constitutive sets (*Bildungsreihen*) of an analogical kind. Analogical thinking is not yet altogether a polar opposite to ordinary, law-seeking thinking, since in it the search goes on, even if in a most peculiar way, for general laws of constitutive sets (*Reihenbildungsgesetze*). This thinking first becomes truly pantheistic when it drops formal lawfulness even in its analogical guise, experiences every emergence (*Werden*) as animated by its own inner vitality, and assigns to thinking the pure function of swinging with the movement. *Thought must not copy, but move along.* Everything we call '*dynamic thinking*' grows out of this tendency. This pantheism of the nineteenth century is distinctive because it became a historical

---

†Mannheim intentionally uses allusive, imprecise language both here and in what follows below. His point is that pantheism is to be portrayed as not talking about 'development' or 'contents' as these concepts occur in 'rationalistic' thinking. Later, according to Mannheim, such concepts are presumably reinstated, thanks to the syntheses between rationalism and irrationalism he claims to be tracking. *Trs.*

pantheism by shifting the high point of all that is living to the sphere of experiencing the historical.

This early romantic pantheism has had its own vicissitudes, which we shall later on observe in detail. For the present, however, it is enough to establish that this pantheistic-dynamic thinking was Müller's principal inheritance from early romanticism. At the same time, it is interesting to observe the struggle which takes place in his thought between the hierarchic and static principle of Catholicism and these dynamics, pagan in spirit. It is almost possible to put one's finger on the exact passage in the *Elemente der Staatskunst* where this pantheist conception of things gradually fades away and makes room for hierarchical thinking. (Baxa has indicated them in his notes to the new edition of the work).[160] As has been already noted, there are more lines which intersect and amalgamate in Müller's position (represented by the *Elemente* at the stage which interests us). The romantic tendency (i.e., the ideological reaction to the abstract rationalism of the Enlightenment) is joined by two other currents, which can be personified by the names of Edmund Burke and Justus Möser.

Before turning to the analysis of this particular representation of different ways of thinking, it is necessary to investigate the *concrete sociological situation* out of which Müller's book grows, since only this can legitimate the position as a historically representative one. As the title-page announces, *Die Elemente* consists of public lectures delivered in the winter of 1808/9 in Dresden, 'before His Highness, Prince Bernard of Saxe-Weimar and a gathering of statesmen and diplomats', and printed in the same year in lecture form. The book anticipates a general mood which did not find expression in practical politics until somewhat later, in the estates' opposition to Hardenberg in 1810/11.[161] A closer analysis of the contents shows it to be concerned essentially with a vindication of the nobility and of the estates' way of thinking. This is the nucleus around which is built up a whole theory of statescraft, with many brilliant arguments and unrivalled intellectual virtuosity. The immediate occasion for the choice of the subject was a pamphlet by the liberal writer Buchholz, *Über den Geburtsadel* (On Hereditary Nobility), which, according to Gentz, caused immense consternation among the older nobility.[162] We will not dwell on the often emphasised fact that Gentz encouraged Müller in the letter just cited to write a refutation of Buchholz's book and that he promised him an 'exceedingly pleasant existence' as a reward.[163] But neither can we agree with Baxa, an undiscriminating admirer of Müller, who sees his hero as morally vindicated because he neither destroyed the outer form of the *Elemente* on account of this offer nor 'wastefully scattered' his efforts in an 'attack on all fronts against Buchholz'. The sociological fact remains that the basic intention of the work can be traced to these external circumstances. This finding is important to us inasmuch as it brings the materially causal determinacy (*real-kausale Bestimmtheit*) of the union between romantic designs and those of the estates into direct view. Two ways of thinking which are connected by an inner affinity flow together here, pushed on by an external circumstance of life, and coalesce into a single whole. After these comments on the sociological situation we are ready to return to the *characterisation of the non-romantic components* of this position.

To understand the estates-oriented element in Müller's thought by reference to its sources, it is necessary to turn to two additional tendencies of thought, one represented by Burke and the other by Justus Möser. The influence of the former is much more obvious, not only because Müller often refers to him and praises him to the skies, but also because there is material evidence of his influence, i.e. one can show without difficulty that certain ideas are derived from Burke. The influx into Müller's work of elements grounded in the estates, on the other hand, is influential at a much deeper level, and probably just for this reason much harder to establish by 'positivistic' methods. Adam Müller does not cite Möser once.[164] Yet, reading Müller after Möser, one cannot help noticing how the former reproduces Möser's attitude of thinking on a romantic plane; and that Möser's writings contain, in a naive (unromantic) form, modes of thinking and ideas belonging to the estates which reappear in Müller, although transformed. The influence is so fundamental in this case, that the actual identity of the person does not matter. In other words, what matters is not whether Müller derived this fundamental attitude from Möser himself, but whether Möser does not represent a taken-for-granted, everyday type of thinking which may well have acted on Müller through quite different intermediaries.

We shall begin with the more straightforward of the patterns of influence, with Burke.[165] Here again the first thing to do is to determine his sociological location. The importance of Burke lies in the fact that he represents the earliest effective response to the French Revolution, that his is the first in a succession of anti-revolutionary conservatisms, and that he accordingly conditions the character of all later ones. Every modern conservatism which responds to the French Revolution is somehow influenced by Burke. His attitude to the great event of his time in some measure has affected all other attitudes hostile to the revolution. In this sense, he supplied both the tone-setting word as well as the battle-cry for his time. To all appearances, his *Reflections on the*

Revolution in France was a pamphlet directed against the pro-revolutionary clubs which were growing up in England. His arguments therefore grew quite directly out of that particular immediate situation. That Burke, in spite of the speed with which he composed the *Reflections*, could nevertheless catch sight of so much that was fundamental, so much that was to recur again and again, can only be explained by the fact that he was already able to look at the revolution from a vantage-point which virtually forced fruitful insights on the spectator. Observing the revolution from England with a political eye and good sense provided such a favourable opportunity, so favourable a vantage-point, that every particular observation turned of itself into a statement of principle, became 'philosophical' – even for a mind which was, by any serious standards, so essentially unphilosophical as Burke's. The special character of this philosophy lies in the fact that practice here turns into philosophy, while in the case of Müller command over practice is gained by starting out from philosophical first principles (and this is the only real point of resemblance, incidentally, between Möser and Burke as opposed to Müller).

It is quite amusing to observe that the first effective picture of revolutionary France, destined to orient entire generations, comes from England, and that England thus revenges itself, as it were, for the stereotyped representation of its own country once supplied by a Frenchman, Montesquieu, which similarly shaped foreigners' judgements of England for many years.[166]

To the question, which aspects of Müller's thought are already present in Burke, the answer must be that it is precisely the distinctively conservative attitude which Müller took over from him. First of all, it is the idea of 'history' – if it may be so called – which already existed in Burke, though on closer inspection one finds that 'history' in Burke's thought is not yet that complex, deeply romanticised construction, shot through with metaphysical elements, which we encounter in Müller as well as in Savigny. It is only one element of this complex whole, albeit an essential one: the element of 'continuity'.[167]

Although it was Burke who most profoundly stimulated conservative thought to reflect on historicity, we do not yet find in him the view of the historical which is refined to methodological subtleties, according to which every single thing that has come into being, every configuration in the course of organic growth, has its own unique value. The complexity of the problem of standards is not yet grasped: that fruitful relativism flowing out of historicism,[168] which renders even the observer relative to the process of becoming which moves over and through him. The idea of the organism and the intuition of totality (*Totalitätsschau*) are not yet present in their full profundity. All he sees is that permitting the slow ripening of events brings about far more useful arrangements (constitutions) than any sudden construction by individuals. He is aware of continuity – or, more precisely, of the place of gradual-ness within the historical – and he stresses the gradual accumulation of the historical resources of the past (compare that typically English simile with *Capital*).[169] He shows that reverence towards the past which one feels in a gallery of ancestral portraits.

> By this means our liberty becomes a noble freedom. It carries an imposing and majestic aspect. It has a pedigree and illustrating ancestors. It has its bearings and its ensigns armorial. It has its gallery of portraits; its monumental inscriptions; its records, evidences, and titles. We procur reverence to our civil institutions on the principle upon which nature teaches us to revere individual men; on account of their age; and on account of those from whom they are descended.[170]

But these are all still reflective remarks, set down as theses, rather than entering into the mode of thought itself, i.e., into its logical structure. At most, one can consider them as the first appearance of the phenomenon which may be called the '*positive-historical*' attitude to history, as opposed to the '*negative-historical*' conception which marks the Enlightenment, as Rexius[171] has so well shown. The Enlightenment could only find something negative in the fact that everything in history constitutes itself in gradual continuity. It was not history itself that conservatism had discovered, but a *specific sense* of becoming, of the past – the sense of tradition and continuity in it.

What makes the fact of its social bondedness (*sozialen Gebundenheit*) so immensely important for the understanding of history is that the knowing subject's commitments within the process he is trying to understand, the rootedness of his position in that process, create vital relations which provide the medium within which thinking first arises.[172] Without wanting something from the historical process, one cannot gain any understanding of it. If certain strata had not felt that their social existence was threatened and that their world might perish, the vital relation within which the growth of historical arrangements is sympathetically comprehended would never have come about.[173]

Historicism is, as already noted, an exceedingly complex and many-sided configuration, as well as a socially very differentiated one, but in its essential point it is of *conservative* origin. It arose everywhere as a political argument against the revolutionary breach with the past – and 'historical study' only turns into historicism when historical facts are not just passionately invoked

127

against the facts of the present, but when the process whereby things have come about (*das Werden*) is itself experienced with feeling. This is the meaning common to 'continuity' in Burke's sense, French traditionalism,[174] and German historicism. While this comprises a common element, various complicating factors, in addition to this fundamental experience, enter into the formation of the diverse offshoots.

[Briefly to overview the example of special importance to us,] the probable sociological and historical causes of the increasingly 'dynamic' character of German historicism are: 1. German conservatism, in its chief trends and in the periods under discussion (which decisively shaped modern consciousness), had no need to become reactionary, since there had, after all, been no revolution in the country. For a counter-revolution is compelled to confront reality with an ideal just as rigidly utopian as that of the revolution. The evolutionary attitude, however, favours the realisation of dynamic historicism. 2. Since the German middle class, with its static style of thought grounded in natural law, had not yet made its entry into politics, it played no part in the German conservatism of this period. 3. German conservatism was largely able to develop independently of Catholicism and could therefore avoid the latter's tendency toward 'static' thinking (as Rohden has also pointed out[175]). [We return to our more fundamental analysis of the original structure of historicism, as it is prefigured in Burke's work.]

While the process of growth, of continuity as such constitutes the most fundamental experience of the historicist, there is always another factor present as well, which is a preference for a particular historical epoch and for a particular historical collective actor. In this respect too, Burke set the example for Müller, in his preference for the Middle Ages and his assessment of the nobility as the pre-eminent bearers of historical events.

The meaning of the historical phenomenon 'nobility' became an important problem for post-revolutionary conservative thought. But only in exceptional circumstances are the contours of a form of social existence evident to those who are born into it. Sociology, even a sociology which merely 'interprets' and which bolsters existing institutions, requires a certain distance, a productive position, a fruitful angle of vision which is existentially created. We have already referred to the importance of the socially unattached intelligentsia for the elucidation of the structure of society. The example of Burke merely confirms this thesis. Burke was not a member of the nobility himself; he was a 'self-made man' seeking admission to the nobility, advancing himself socially. For that very reason he was able to offer an exemplary, if apologetic, account of the social significance and distinctive character of the nobility. In Germany, too, a member of the middle class, Adam Müller, became the interpreter of the nobility and the estates. France alone provides an example of a nobility which itself became aware of its own form of existence.[176] This without doubt can be explained by the fact of their emigration. When imposed by fate, detachment from one's own accustomed mode of existence also provides greater sociological and historical clearsightedness and penetration. The social and historical structure of society becomes most transparent to the individual during his ascent or his descent. In the ascent one understands what one aspires to, in the descent what one is losing.

What is true of the evaluation of different social strata is equally true of the evaluation of different epochs of the past. The defence of the nobility has as its pendant a defence of the Middle Ages. This is not so much, of course, an apologia either for the principles of the guilds and estates, or for the Middle Ages of the mystics, but rather involves an emphasis upon the value of chivalry.[177]

Burke's achievement in this respect consists of little more than his emphasis on the positive value of the Middle Ages at a time when these were simply the 'Dark Ages'. His writings show neither that empathy which is the mark of historical thinking, as opposed to the mere 'positive evaluation' of historical facts, nor the historicist attempt to revitalise those germs of the past that survive into the present, which alone make possible the existential rediscovery of the historical. In Burke, the defence of continuity, of the nobility, of the Middle Ages are deeply immersed in rhetoric. All these things indeed still remain on the level of 'reflections'; they do not yet constitute a distinctive mode of thinking.

Turning to Möser,[178] in his capacity as representative of the estates' manner of thinking, we are immediately struck by the difference between his attitude to life and that of the romantics. It is tempting to call his conservatism 'proto-conservatism' (*Urkonservatismus*), if this term can be used to denote the first transformation of mere traditionalism into a conservatism which is entering into a functional relationship to social and political life. There is here none of the dramatic despair (*Gebrochenheit*) and introspection of romanticised conservatism. The frontal attack of the French Revolution against the inherited, traditional attitude to life, had not yet struck. The leitmotif which sounds out of Möser's reflections is, first of all, his steady praise of the 'good old days'.[179] In a curious way, his person is completely enveloped in the atmosphere of the Enlightenment. His grandfatherly wisdom is sober, practical, and rational. And yet – and this shows us that rationalism too has its varieties – his rationalism is *not* the computing, calculating, speculative rationality of the bourgeoisie.

The capitalist mentality always possesses a dual soul, at least as long as the world has not grown into a planned economy:[180] a calculating, meticulous book-keeping mentality alongside a *speculative daring* to take the risks which appear at the boundaries of calculability. Möser's sobriety tends more towards the rationality of the peasant farmer – it is not a speculative calculation of abstract factors, but a *weighing*. It has its origins in caution and a spiritual narrowness of horizon, which does not want to consider dynamic factors in constant change. This sobriety, this kind of rationalism, rejects any leap beyond immediate fact, and it resists incursions by elements belonging to alien worlds. It fears the loosening of the conventional moral ties which make the surrounding world what it is. It is a conservatism which will not experiment beyond its own limits. The fact that this proto-conservatism becomes reflective at all in Möser is due not to any eruptive upheaval, but to the gradual infiltration from France of new and 'fashionable' ideas and attitudes to life. So even this conservatism became reflective. But Möser never 'romanticises' things. It may happen – and it happens constantly[181] – that he involuntarily imposes his own designs upon history, but never that he makes a conscious or half-conscious attempt to justify something by way of importing arguments from elsewhere, or to preserve it by shifting it to a 'higher' level of reasoning.

The romantics were full of enthusiasm for the Church, for the Middle Ages, and for the nobility, because something in their own wish-dream had brought them closer to these things. Some deprivation of their own was to be compensated by means of these objects. The relationship between the romantic subject and his object is not one of close observation, because the object is always only skirted from within an inner wish-dream.

> It was a lovely and glorious time when Europe was a Christian land, when *one* Christianity dwelled in this continent formed for man; *one* great common interest joined the remotest provinces of this farflung spiritual realm. [Novalis' emphases]

So begins Novalis' essay, 'Die Christenheit oder Europa'.[182] These lines suggest the fundamental mood, and in the remainder of the essay it is *this mood that is developed, and not the object* under consideration.

The case is altogether different with Möser. He does not go to his subject-matter; he *lives* in it. He does not return to the past; he

lives in those remnants of the past which survive in the chronological present. He lives within them and speaks from within them.
The past is not something that lies on a line behind him; it is a co-
presence – and not in the way of memory and return, but as an
intensification of something possessed, now under threat of being
obliterated.

This type of conservatism, which still lives directly on contents
of the past and does not possess them as yet at the level of
reflection and memory, has already been touched on in our
general discussion of the conservative attitude to life. We
indicated there that Möser exemplifies it in its purest form. Now
we must support this assertion.

We shall therefore begin with a passage from Möser, which
typifies this kind of attitude:

> When I come across an old tradition or old custom which simply
> will not rhyme with the conclusions of modern reasoning, I keep
> coursing around it with the idea in mind that, 'after all, our
> forefathers were not fools either', until I find some sensible
> reason for it . . .[183]

Now compare this attitude with that of Novalis. Möser's starting-
point is that which is concretely and immediately present – an old
custom, an old habit – and he then tries to discover its meaning.
For the romantic, it is the subject that is the given starting-point, as
it were, and the search is then for a possible world to complement
this subject. Such 'coursing around' an object is typical of Möser's
way of thinking, as is his characteristic rationalism which must
somehow find the *sensible reason*[184] for the deportment of the
forefathers. What is not rational is only the trust in all things old
and handed-down, the unwillingness to find fault with traditions.
But what is sought is a 'sensible reason', and not some 'higher'
justification initiated at some higher metaphysical level. Under
some circumstances, such coursing around the object could still be
romantic or at least aim at paradoxical conclusions. The French
traditionalists have been fittingly called 'rationalists with irrational
contents'.[185] Someone like Kierkegaard, for example, also shows
signs of this paradoxical sophistication, which brings irrationalities
into view by means of rational acuity. Möser, however, pursues
the paradoxical only in order to surprise by its means,[186] not in
order to invent irrational explanations. His intention is merely to
recover the obliterated 'sensible reason' underlying inherited
traditions. What is irrational is the presupposition of the conclusion that the forefathers probably acted wisely; only this faith is
irrational, not the explanations he is trying to find.

The contents of bourgeois calculation are always abstract.

Things and human beings only appear as factors in a speculative combination. Möser's 'weighing' is always *palpable* and *concrete*. He takes things into account, not simply by counting them or by treating them as functions in a process which can be calculated in advance, but by viewing them as binding in their concreteness, as constituents of a particular configuration of life.

His concept of *practice* also originates here – that recurrent praise of practice as opposed to theory (an element which is also present, though on quite a different level, in the romantics). He wrote an unfinished polemical essay against Kant with the title 'Über Theorie und Praxis'[187] ('Regarding theory and practice'). Its pivotal passage reads: 'Deduction from actual events often yields conclusions which are more correct than deduction from all too lofty premises.' A struggle is being waged here against speculative reasoning from 'all too lofty premises' on behalf of a palpable thinking which holds close to the circumstances given:

> Practice which adapts itself closely to every individual circumstance[!] and knows how to make use of it is bound to be more competent than theory which in its high flights is bound to overlook many circumstances.[188]

The purpose of the essay is a justification of serfdom. It is interesting because it shows so clearly how, in response to an immediate impulsion to preserve an old institution spiritually, two ways of thinking whose differences will continue to occupy conservative thinking for a long time to come are counterposed to one another and thereby phenomenologically explicated. At issue is the opposition between thinking which starts out from normative speculative premises and an intellect whose thinking proceeds from the circumstances of the case. The tension is increased by the fact that, in his justification of serfdom, Möser himself thinks along the lines of natural law, insofar as he too presupposes an original contract. But here, what is alive under the cover of the legitimation from natural law, is the fundamental intention not to deduce the matter to be explained from normative premises, but to comprehend it from the living and practical interplay of socio-historical phenomena.

Another example may be mentioned which illustrates how much Möser is constantly preoccupied with this tension between a palpably living, practical thinking and a thinking which is abstract. He wrote a short treatise entitled 'Von dem moralischen Gesichtspunkt'[189] ('Of the moral point of view'). In it he somehow tries to show, on an entirely different level – the moral sphere – that the value of a thing cannot be grasped on the basis of general principles, because measured by such excessively high standards everything must appear imperfect, but that everything contains *within itself* the point of view from which it can adequately be apprehended:

> Can you name me a single beautiful piece of the physical world which retains its former beauty under the microscope? Does not the most beautiful skin get ridges and furrows? the loveliest cheek a ghastly mildew? and the rose quite a wrong colour? There is, accordingly, a *unique point of view for every thing*, from which alone it is beautiful.

And at the end of the essay he says:

> Let us proceed in a straightforward way, then, and recognise virtue as nothing but the *suitability* or inner worth of every specific thing. A horse thus has its virtue, as has iron, and the hero too, who possesses the requisite steel, hardness, coldness, and heat.

Apart from the idea that everything prescribes its own standards and the distance required for seeing it correctly, Möser's thought contains still further elements that were to become part of the intellectual inheritance of conservatism and were to be absorbed by romantic consciousness as elements of estates-derived thinking. One is generally inclined to consider the tendency toward *extreme individualisation*, the demand that every person and every thing should be experienced and thought as from a starting-point within itself, as a trait typical of romanticism and the historical school. An analysis of Möser's writings, however, shows the extent to which this tendency of thinking already flows out of the designs of estates-thinking, and it shows that there are already method-ological insights in that thought – such as those which assign priority to 'qualitative thinking' – which address the problem of making the individual element accessible to thought. Such methodological reflections, moreover, already appear closely linked to political objectives. For all these reasons we are now concerned to show, first, that a consciousness which is still deeply immersed in the estates-constitution, carries on its life, precisely on the grounds of this structure of life, in forms of thinking which were just then being attacked by the bourgeois world; and, second, that this thinking became self-reflectively conscious of its own distinctive character precisely as a result of these attacks. Although the example above has already let us observe Möser's will to experience every thing as individual and to comprehend everything in its particular 'suitability' we have to consider a few more examples which show the *political* point of this direction of experience and thought. In his essay (1772) with the title 'Der

133

jetzige Hang zu allgemeinen Gesetzen und Verordnungen ist der gemeinen Freiheit gefährlich'[190] (The modern taste for general laws and decrees is a danger to our common liberty), the rootedness in the estates of the emphasis on individuality, as against the generalising tendency of the bureaucracy, is clearly apparent. Right at the beginning he declares:

> The gentlemen of the central administration, it seems, would like to see everything reduced to simple principles. If they had their way, the state would let itself be ruled according to an academic theory, and every councillor would be able to give local officials their instructions according to a general plan. . . . But in fact we thereby abandon the plan of nature, which displays its abundance in diversity, and we prepare the way for despotism, which aspires to force everything in accordance with a few rules, and thus loses the abundance of diversity.

This passage illustrates with great clarity how the struggle against the centralist and rationalist bureaucracy gives rise to insights into problems of method, and how clearly Möser recognised the spiritual affinities between this bureaucratic centralism and the enlightened monarchy and saw the essence of despotism precisely in its aspiration to force everything into conformity by means of a few rules.[191] Möser has a most delicate sense for stylistic unities. In his essay he attempts to show that the same stylistic principle which underlies this thinking, which wants to reduce everything to a few principles, also governs French tragedy.[192] He calls the tendency toward such generalising, which is designed to render things uniform, a 'new-fashioned mode of thinking'[193] and considers it suitable at most for use as a technical aid but never as a standard in judging a concrete case. Every native inhabitant should be judged according to the laws and customs of his local jurisdiction, and Möser practically sees the *meaning of freedom* in the observance of these *particularities*.

Voltaire had made fun of the fact that someone could lose his case by the law of one village and win it by the customs of the next. Möser addresses the same paradox and remarks:

> For purpose of ridicule, Voltaire need not have looked for the differences in lawfulness between two villages; he could have found the same diversity between two families living under the same roof.[194]

If the general decrees of the state are not obeyed, the cause lies in the fact 'that we are trying to cover too many things by a single rule and would rather deprive nature of her abundance than to change our system.'[195]

Having observed the sense for diversity and variety, individuality and distinctiveness arising from the consciousness of the world-design characteristic of the estates and of particularism (and simply becoming reflective in Möser), we are not surprised to hear that, in his judgement, every little town should be given a constitution of its own.[196]

Nor is it surprising that this impulse, so deeply rooted in the experience and the thinking of the estates, allowed the Prussian nobility to grow towards the idea of the nation state only very slowly; and that, for many years and even during the high tide of national and patriotic fervour in the first decades of the nineteenth century, their path to it was beset with inner tensions. It is only when confronted with the extreme particularism of this estate-rooted way of thought in its pure form, that one recognises the extent to which nationalism, in comparison with the particularism of the province, is already a stage of transition to internationalism. Consider, for example, a passage from Ludwig v.d. Marwitz which illustrates the *Prussian variant* of this particularistic individualism:

> Prussia is not a nation which has always been what it is now, nor is it a nation closed in upon itself in language, custom and law. It is rather assembled together out of many provinces, very diverse in laws and customs. It can also never become one nation . . . because every province adjoins other provinces which are foreign to its state, but to which it feels itself to be at bottom more closely akin than to the remote and alien other provinces of the Prussian state – Brandenburg, for example, to Saxony, Silesia to Bohemia and Moravia, East Prussia to Courland and Lithuania. To propose to weld them into one is to deprive them of their distinctiveness and to turn a living organism into a dead mass.[197]

In addition to the generational difference, there are many sociological differences between v.d. Marwitz and Möser.[198] First there is the fact that v.d. Marwitz, landlord of Friedersdorf, is spokesman for the Brandenburg nobility, while Möser, on the other hand, is the *son of a patrician* of Osnabrück, the son of a councillor in the chancellery, who had advanced so far as an advocate of non-noble birth that he *de facto* ruled the land for a while, alongside of aristocratic privy councillors. As son of a patrician, Möser showed only so much sympathy for the nobility as his position required.[199] He is a supporter of the corporative estate-order (*Ständestaat*), notwithstanding the fact that he locates the Golden Age in the time of the ancient liberty and community property.[200] But precisely because he did not so much defend the nobility as this entire world as a whole, comparatively undisrupted, hierarchically stratified, and organised by estates as it was,[201] and because he thereby most closely followed the way of thinking of the old, rooted peasant strata, the conjunction of his way of thinking with that of Müller can be taken as representative. It guarantees that if we find the *same emphasis on what is individual and qualitatively unique in Müller, at least one of the roots of Müller's mode of thinking rests in the older 'estate-oriented' level of thinking and experiencing.* Similarly, *the emphasis on life and diversity*, as the elements which cannot be comprehended by bureaucratic rationalisation and generalisation, anticipates a line of thought which consolidates itself into a single position of thinking, at first in opposition to centralism and subsequently in opposition to revolutionary natural law – and which points to the later 'philosophy of life' (*Lebensphilosophie*), to give it its modern name. It is precisely this *developmentally prior stratum of experience and thinking* that had already been damaged in several respects by bourgeois-absolutist and bureaucratic rationalisation and that was in danger of gradual extinction, *which was revitalised by its encounter and alliance with the romantic will to the world (Weltwollen)*, and was elevated to a modern level of justification.

This earliest stage of the conservative way of thinking moves beyond 'traditionalism as such' at least to the extent that the latter already appears 'functionalised' here, having discovered its political relevance in its opposition to enlightened bureaucratic rationalism. It now gains a new political relevance at the level of its 'romanticisation' in the struggle against revolutionary natural-law thinking.

At this point, in the eyes of his conservative opponent the two varieties of modern rationalism come together and, in the light of the experience of the French Revolution, the stylistic unity of bourgeois thinking also becomes more transparent to its conservative opponent. And struggle against it also appears to be demanded by the times. While the traditionalists in France, in their explorations of the ideological roots and causes of the revolution, tended to analyse and to make the starting-point for their reaction the *metaphysical* and *religious* premisses of the eighteenth century,[202] the romantics in Germany aimed their critique against the *logical and methodological* devices of liberal thinking. This had its cause in the fact, among other things, that in France the counter-revolution found its metaphysical dogma ready-made in Roman Catholicism; while in Germany – as has often been observed before – the schism between Protestant and Catholic dogma made the metaphysical foundations heterogeneous and therefore insecure. The result was a retreat into methodological inquiry. Moreover, since there was no revolution within their own walls, the German romantics could allow themselves the luxury of re-enacting the differences in world-view upon this very abstract plane. But as soon as the sociological situation became more uncomfortable (after 1830), and when conservatism, accordingly, even in Protestant Prussia, was compelled to withdraw to the grounds of theism, dogmatic and metaphysical contents returned to prominence. There was an awareness that the pantheistic methodological ground of romanticism had to be relinquished, and it is Stahl's achievement to have satisfied that requirement by establishing the monarchical principle once again on theistic foundations.

For the time being, however – during the first decades of the nineteenth century – this pantheistic and methodological consolidation of counter-revolutionary thought was still able to unfold freely, and thereby to put its mark upon the German conservative manner of thinking for a long time to come. Müller's ideological achievement consists, as has already been pointed out, in lending inner coherence to this methodological struggle, by drawing simultaneously upon romantic sources and the thought associated with the estates. It is in his *Die Elemente der Staatskunst* that the decisive importance of the struggle against natural-law thinking hits us for the first time in its full breadth and impact. And it is here that the phenomenon for the first time emerges which, later incarnated as the 'philosophy of life', storms against all kinds of rationalism to the present day.[203]

Having characterised one by one the most important currents which flow towards the juncture of interest to us, we can now inquire which new and comprehensive political impulses brought about the positional concentration of such diverse tendencies into a unified world-view.

At this stage, conservative thought derives its determination *to emphasise life rather than concepts*, no longer, as is the case in Möser, from reaction against bureaucratic rationalism alone, but also from the reaction against the other contemporary variant of rationalism, the rationalism of the bourgeoisie.[204] If we were to make our imputations by speculation alone, without historical investigation, it would seem highly likely that 'life' would be emphasised by the progressive will to the world and that the conservative one should cling to rigidity and to concepts. In fact, however, it happened the other way around. The reason is that the revolutionary thinking of the bourgeoisie arose in a definite alliance with rationalism (as is so often the case with revolutionary thinking) so that the counter-current was bound to adopt the ideological counterpole, if only for the sake of opposition. But the interpretable (*verstehbare*) connections lie even deeper. Revolutionising thinking derives its subversive force from the desire to realise a rationally well-defined model of rightness (*Richtigkeits-bild*) for the social and political order. Conservative thought, because it opposes the achievement of that utopia, is forced to consider why the actually existing state of society fails to correspond to such a rational model of rightness.[205] This inclination, initially simply a function of self-interest, also renders conservatism clear-sighted about all the factors which revolutionary thinking – again on grounds of its own vital interests – overlooks, viz., the non-rational factors within the flow of social reality. But while revolutionary thought considers such factors – insofar as it sees them at all – as defects of reality, in relation to the standard of reason (*Ratio*), conservative thinking, as we have seen, invokes its typical method of paradox to characterise these factors as supra-rational.[206] That all this is not simply a question of inversion of values-signs, but rather of different categories and contents of experience and of the knowledge to be derived from experience, is shown, for instance, by the fact that this 'nonrationality' which is experienced as 'supra-rationality' leads to that whole philosophy which might be called, to put it very generally and briefly, 'philosophy of life', and in which sometimes 'history', sometimes 'spirit', and sometimes 'life' are counterposed to the mere principle of reason. The great polarities of nineteenth-century philosophical thought (obviously only in the form they take on as product of the situations of the time) – 'being' and 'thinking', 'concept' and 'idea', 'speculation' and 'practice' – although they often first arose immanently within philosophical systems, are nourished and bound together to constitute positions by the corresponding political polarities of the liberal and conservative wills to the world (*Weltwollen*).

The most primitive form of struggle against the rationalist-deductive mode of thinking by means of an appeal to 'life' consists of confronting the 'written constitution' with an actuality which is always richer and more alive than the written word.[207] [Frederick William IV's later famous slogan of 'the mere scrap of paper', which was coined to ridicule the constitution, goes back to this most primitive kind of struggle against 'rationalisation'. Looked at more closely, however, this slogan already expresses an antithesis which may be characterised in philosophical language as the antithesis between 'posited norm' (*Satzung*) and 'being' (*Sein*). What conservative thought objects to here is the fact that the point of departure in such treatments as the 'Declarations of the Rights of Man' is in the 'rights of man as such'.[208, 209] This starting-point, the unfolding of thought by deduction and the goal of developing in order of rightness for the state in *this* way, are all found offensive, and a search for an alternative manner of reasoning is initiated. In the course of this search, in the course of the opposition to oppositional thinking, thought is given to the question of how state, society, order and laws had come about and assumed validity until then. It is noted that nowadays deliberation and voting decide matters, that nowadays 'reason' intends to set realities into the world, whereas formerly, in contrast, everything grew gradually and was preserved by usage. *Here then systematic beginnings and historical beginnings become distinguished.* The constructions of natural law still proceeded so that *the genesis of meanings (Sinngenese)* and *actual genesis (Realgenese)* coincided; the theory of the social contract was at once a meaning-genetic interpretation and a fiction concerning actual genesis. Not until Kant were the two quite clearly distinguished. This turns the relation between being (becoming) and norm into a living problem, occupying the collective thought of the entire epoch.

Because the opposition grounded in the estates was confronted with bureaucratic rationalism, it mainly had reason to criticise modern rationalism with regard to its questionable tendency toward generalisation and mechanisation. The range of aspects under attack in this 'campaign' was widened, however, when in the shape of bourgeois revolutionary rationalism a more radical form of rationalism became the enemy. The rationality of the bureaucracy essentially consists in little more than 'homogenisation' ('*Gleichmacherei*'), in the abolition of territorial differences, and later also those among estates; and apart from this it does not expand beyond its own sphere. Bourgeois rationalism, by contrast, is revolutionary and radical precisely in that it wants, right from its systematic beginnings, the whole social world rationalised. It confronts the world as it has come to be with a *single, rigid, and static system of order, in the form of constitutional plans. The answer from the conservative side is to give the struggle against thinking in its guise as static system* a prominence equal to the struggle against generalisation.[210]

In such a contrast between *thought* as something rigid and immobile and *life* as that which is always changing and growing, there were two possibilities. One could either reject all thinking, deny its significance, and appeal to the irrational; or one could distinguish between a rigid and a mobile kind of thinking, with the latter able to keep up with the mobility of life because it is itself dynamic. The *historical school* chose the first path, coupling the experience of dynamics with a completely radical irrationalism. Adam Müller, in contrast, allied the dynamic elements, present as a parallel sociological manifestation in contemporary philosophy, with the political experience of dynamics, and thus conceived of the idea of a *dynamic thinking*. In this living, mobile thinking he saw the solution to political problems. This brings us to a fundamental methodological conception, the distinction between '*idea*' and '*concept*'.

The *antithesis between 'idea' and 'concept'* which is worked out by Müller in his *Elemente der Staatskunst*, is a late fruit of his earlier logical reflections, the beginnings of which go back to his work 'Die Lehre vom Gegensatz' (The Theory of Antithesis). The development of his thought brings out most clearly the successive steps, so to speak, in the 'working out' of the 'dynamic conception'. The most important stages might be demarcated as comprising a development which moves from thinking in terms of antitheses to dynamic thinking, to arrive finally at dialectical thinking.

The *first stage* in the development which seeks to resolve the problem of the rigidity of thought not by means of a somersault into 'total irrationalism', but by making thought mobile, is the experiment which opposes a thinking in polarities to linear deduction from a single principle.[211] Rigidity, which rests in 'linearity', is here overcome by dissolving all positions into antitheses. Enlightenment thinking was *linear*;[212] where the attempt was made constructively to postulate a line of continuity within philosophical history, the development was always the unfolding of a *single* principle. The idea of progress has its roots in a linear speculative construction – just as, in another aspect, the rights of man were to be deduced from a *single* idea, the 'idea of man'. Such a construction, however, is remote from reality, because the world cannot be understood on the basis of a single principle. It is undoubtedly a first step towards greater correctness to try to enhance the capacities of thinking by endeavouring to think from more than one position and to grasp the world on the basis of more than one principle. Such thinking, comprising antitheses and polarities, is of romantic heritage. It is a method of thinking in which the attempt is made to bring about a measure of mobility, even while remaining within the static framework.[213]

Adam Müller demonstrates the contrast between the two ways of thinking by the possibility of two alternative types of definition. He calls the first (the rigid one) the 'atomistic', the second, the 'dynamic' definition. While the first type of definition consists in describing 'the isolated nature of the thing to be defined, its qualities, the parts of which it is composed, the signs by which it is recognised', the dynamic definition consists in 'naming some other known thing which stands in direct opposition to the thing to be defined',[214] e.g. heat through cold, love through hatred, masculinity through femininity. In this conception, nature herself is nothing but 'a whole (organism) made up of an infinite number of oppositions'.[215] In any case, this type of dynamic conception still remains firmly embedded in speculations which are derived from pantheism and the philosophy of nature and which centre on the difference between the sexes. Although a purely dynamic thought-intention is already competing here with the tendency toward analogising, the dynamic germ of the method only comes truly to life when this thinking turns from the philosophy of nature towards historical reality.

The second stage, the dynamic conception of thinking, is actualised in the work of Müller in the correlation between *concept* and *idea*. In one of the most important passages in the *Elemente* he says:

> The state and all great human affairs share the characteristic quality that their essence will absolutely not let itself be enveloped within or compressed into words or definitions. . . . Rigid formulas, designed once and for all, such as those which the vulgar sciences drag and hawk around concerning the state, life, and man, we call *concepts*. But there *is no such thing* as a concept of the state.[216]

We ask ourselves, what there *is*, then, with reference to the state, and receive prompt answer:

> If the thought which we have entertained of such a sublime object expands, if it moves and grows, just as the object moves and grows, we then call the thought, not the concept of the thing, but the *idea* of the thing, of the state, of life.[217]

The complex situation concerning our relationship to thinking, once it has become clear that there is a discrepancy between flowing existence and rigid thought, is not resolved by simply rejecting thought altogether, but by designating only one type of thinking (the concept) as rigid and thus denigrating it, and by opposing to it the ideal of a mobile kind of thinking (the 'idea'). The 'idea' is naturally also a product of rationalisation, but of a *rationalisation in dynamic form*. There is nothing to say that thinking must necessarily grasp its living object by means of rigid, instantaneously fixed concepts – and this insight is contained in the sentences from Müller quoted above. While the individual concept may always be statically rigid, thinking is a process, and this process can *take part* in the change of the object. What is demanded is that thought should move and grow – and this already goes far beyond the first step towards dynamic thinking, beyond mere thinking in terms of polarities.[218] Implicit is no longer merely a proposal to grasp the object through its no less rigid opposite, but the breakthrough of the intention to make thinking just as mobile as life itself.

This solution differs from Savigny's solution of the same problem in the historical school, to be analysed in the next chapter, in that the romantic solution does *not* destroy the Enlightenment *faith* in *reason*, but merely modifies it. The faith in the power of reason, in the capacity of thought, is not abandoned. Only *one* type of thinking is rejected, the immobile thought of the Enlightenment with its deductions from single principles and mere combinations of rigid conceptual components, and the horizon of potential thinking is expanded only in contrast to this one type. In this respect too, romantic thought (though unintentionally) carries forward the line of development, though more radically and with new methods, which the Enlightenment will to the world had already hoped to bring to completion – the thorough rationalisation of the world.

What is rational and what is irrational is, after all, really a relative question, or rather – and this is a point which we have to get clear – the two terms are correlative. While the generalising and rigidly systematicising thinking of the Enlightenment prevailed, the limits of the rational had coincided with the limits of *that* thought, and everything beyond it had been conceived as irrational, as life, as a residue which, from the point of view of the Enlightenment, was irreducible. But the thought of 'mobile thinking' pushed the limits of the rational a good deal further, and thereby *romantic thinking completed a task of the Enlightenment* which the Enlightenment could actually never have completed by its own means. Müller gained access to experience of the dynamic and to a focused awareness of all that is alive (*Lebendigen*), to some extent from the pantheistic sources of romanticism, but largely from an empathetic re-experiencing of the attitude to the world characteristic of the old estates. By equipping this sense of life with means of thinking which corresponded to the most modern stage of consciousness – means of thinking which not only incorporated the intellectual project (*Denkwollen*) of the Enlightenment but also went considerably beyond it, to another stage –, he rescued this older way of thinking from eclipse. He helped to raise to a modern stage of consciousness a mode of experience and thought which historically even preceded the Enlightenment.

It would nevertheless be one-sided to assume that the passage cited above fully characterises Müller's conception of 'idea' and 'concept'. In it, the 'impulse to think dynamically' is in fact the only component that comes through with clarity and unconfused by romantic oddities. When additional passages are adduced in order to observe the method of thinking with 'ideas' at work,[219] it becomes apparent that he relapses again and again into the analogical thinking of romanticism, and that every concrete event is grasped by him only by taking it as an 'inter-living' (*Wechselleben*) of various powers which are usually opposed to each other in the manner of the masculine and feminine principle.

In one place he himself gives a pertinent brief characterisation of the method which he actually employs:

> The essense of the *state* had to be shown next. Once again
> without definitions of any kind, which are the poison of science,
> I described the inter-living of the four eternal estates, clerical
> and mercantile, noble and civic, and I mediated [!] among these
> inescapable differences in age and sex; and then the nature of
> the state unfolded itself more clearly and precisely than it could
> have after even the most ingenious analysis, and, what is more,
> it was alive.[220]

What we have then is a portrayal of living in interaction (*Wechselleben*) and a 'mediation' between differences. Everything that lives is comprehended as alive, in short, by being always displayed as a tension between several antagonistic principles. And every instant, every condition within the living flow is nothing for this interpretation but a momentary *mediation*, a *compromising* amid ever-present tensions. The following characteristic sentence by Müller proceeds wholly along these lines, and reveals as well the political bearing and source of this way of thinking:

> The fundamental contract is accordingly not a contract
> concluded in some definite time or place, but rather the idea of a
> contract which is being concluded always and everywhere, a
> contract which is everywhere revised at every moment by the
> new freedom stirring alongside the old, and which is being
> upheld in just this way.[221]

Here again it is quite apparent that this yearning to think dynamically has its sociological roots in the aversion to bourgeois natural-law thinking and hopes to thoroughly displace the latter most completely where it is superior not only in contents but also in method. Nowhere else can the fundamental differences between the two modes of thinking be observed more clearly. For bourgeois natural-law thinking, the state is constituted by a compromise (contract) between the contracting parties, recognised once and for all as just. For romantic estate-based thinking, in contrast, the state is a constantly fluctuating, dynamic arrangement among mutually conflicting collectivities. What seems familiar in this way of thinking is the now so widespread interpretation of the historical process on the basis of such antithetical and competing factors, and the comprehension of any given state of things in the present as a current synthesis (mediation) within the current coexistence of factors undergoing dynamic change. This form of thinking, which has in effect become *an historical a priori* for us, constituted itself here as a reaction against the linear model of Enlightenment rationalism. And at this point, the estates-based romantic 'philosophy of life',[222] with its method of thinking through ideas (to use Müller's terminology), did indeed succeed in creating a means for the orderly arrangement of the historical movement in flux and for grasping it as a totality.

The *third stage* in the development of conservative dynamic thinking is represented by the stage of the *dialectic*. It must be analysed in connection with Hegel, whose position for synthesis leads to a very special solution in this respect as well.

For the present, we must turn to a third important basic category which can only be understood in close conjunction with the contrast between 'concept' and 'idea'.

In the discussion of Müller's 'idea'-grounded dynamic conception of thinking, we have several times come across a favourite concept of his, that of *mediation*. 'Mediation' is a concept and category belonging to the romantic estates-grounded synthesis. All thinking is analytical, including that which resists it, and faces the task of reuniting the parts of reality which it has broken apart. But the distinctive character of a style of thought is never more clearly comprehensible than at the point where thinking is confronted by the task of synthesis. The rationalist thought of the Enlightenment analysed by dismembering and atomising; corresponding to this with regard to synthesis is *addition*. Estates-romantic thought, as has just been described, analysed by dividing a moving totality (e.g., the state, life, etc.) into mutually antithetical partial movements. This raises the question of how it is possible to arrive at a living dynamic synthesis. The answer to the problem lies in the concept of 'mediation'.

The word recalls the Christian idea of the 'mediator' and often also the distinctly Catholic idea of the mediating role of the Church.[223] But it is really a specifically romantic reformulation, which gains its distinctively modern meaning from the already described fundamental tendency of romanticism, from its striving for mobile thinking and for intellectual comprehension of the polyphony of life. But at the same time the concept also resonates to the other components, with their sources in the thought-impulse of the estates, a resistance to the subsumption of the particular under the general. This conservative thinking of the estates looks for some kind of determination of the relation between part and whole, between particular and universal, which is different from either addition or subsumption. *This* is the place where this impulse is incorporated into Müller's solution.

If we now ask ourselves what the concept of mediation signifies in the 'system' of Müller – its meaning alongside of the fundamental concepts of 'concept' and 'idea' – we have to return once more to the basic attitude which holds that every living totality is constantly developing and unfolding, that it is a dynamic product of contending forces and principles. Sometimes, as has been seen, it is the different estates that are in conflict, sometimes it is the contrast between the family and individual,[224] or between eternity and the moment[225] which are antithetically in contention. It is the task of the acting person, the judge as well as the thinker, *not* to comprehend a given concrete situation *as the particular instance of a general rule or concept*, but to experience the constantly changing situations as a *compromising* among dynamically changing factors, and to understand them and deal with them as such. Generalising thought works with the correlation: general law/particular case. Its cognition proceeds by way of subsumption. Dynamic thinking grasps the idea, i.e. the inner aim and purpose of the concrete whole, and conceives of the particular as a part of this dynamically changing total formation. Its way of knowing is 'mediation' *between the law and the case under dispute*. Müller writes:

> The lowest judge in your land should represent the will and striving of the whole, rather than the whole as such. In small things and within his *narrow* horizons, he should stand with plenary powers, like the sovereign in matters *great and broad*, both of them engaged in live mediation between the wishes of the ancestors and the needs of contemporaries, between the law and the case in dispute, rather than in lifeless comparisons and mensurations.[226]

The *sociological roots* of this aspiration of thought, already noted earlier, are clearly apparent here. In opposition to the justice of the bureaucratic administration, which merely subsumes cases, the threatened patrimonial jurisdiction of the land owner is brought forward, as a higher form, as a 'mediation'.[227]

It is no accident that the judicial decision is taken as the model. If the unspoken presupposition of rationalism is the purely intellectual, theoretical, spectatorial, passive subject who makes no decisions, but merely affirms or denies (which is not equivalent to deciding), then the model for the dynamic thinker, in contrast, is the man who *decides, judges, mediates*. The purely spectatorial, theoretical subject engages in subsumptions, while the subject who stands in the midst of the antinomic-vital polarities of life offers mediations and makes decisions. The very concept of 'dynamic synthesis', 'mediation', already contains *a breaking-through of the contemplative course of conduct*.[228] Dynamic thinking grasps the particular case by decision and mediation. What gradually becomes clear is that the diversity in forms of thinking, while largely effaced in our time by the homogenising effects of the written word, are still discernible here. *Thinking always has a different character, according to the living function which it performs*. The man who systematises and makes subsumptions thinks, as does the judge; but 'thinking' as a function of 'judicial decision' is something entirely different from contemplative subsumption.

To grasp the difference between the generalising rationalism of the Enlightenment and the dynamics of estates-based romanticism, it is not enough to bring out the element of movement. It is also necessary to reach down for the ultimate presuppositions; and these are the *existential premisses*, where the relationship between theory and practice in fact takes on a different character in the two cases. This is a problem, incidentally, towards which the two styles of thought also take a different stance at the level of theoretical reflection.

Before turning to this problem of the relation between theory and practice, however, we should cast a glance at the subsequent fate of the 'category of mediation'. Already in the *Elemente der Staatskunst* (where, as has been suggested, the pantheistic-dynamic aspect begins to give way to the Catholic-hierarchical one after a certain point) there are passages where mediation is not presented as a spontaneous, mutual engagement among the eternally moving polarities, but is rather given the meaning of *reconciliation*, and the Catholic clergy are introduced as a conciliatory court, standing *above* these moving elements. The clergy is said to be a 'mediative apostolic estate' whose task it is to interlink the various national states, and, within the separate states, to 'join' poverty and excessive wealth to society, and to preserve the spirit of 'ethical balance'.[229] Such mediation is here assigned its own distinctive organ, and that this should be the Catholic Church follows from the romantic inclination towards Catholicism which began, as we have noted, with Novalis.

Once again we can observe here clearly that even the most fundamental categories, the distinctive types of synthesis, will change as thinking makes a transition from one structural contexture to another one, whose socio-historical origin is different. One and the same thinker shapes his syntheses differently, depending on whether he is taking his stand on estate-based romantic or on Catholic grounds. The fundamental categories of the synthesis change with the substantive solutions. As long as thinking remains in any way pantheistic, the polarities will mutually engage themselves immanently. Catholicism can also point to philosophers in its history who thought in terms of polarity – as has been shown by the Jesuit scholar Przywara[230] with the delicacy of the genuine Catholic in regard to the nature of his own tradition. We find a philosophy of polarities in Pascal, as well as in Newman's doctrine of 'oppositive virtues'. Authentic Catholic thought, however, tends to join the polar elements by means of something higher, which is placed *above* them. Fundamentally it is God, but his place may also be taken by the Church as the third party standing *above* the polarities. Such hierarchical joining of the polarities already appears in romanticism with Novalis: 'It is impossible for mundane forces to bring themselves into equilibrium; this task can only be achieved by a third element, which is at once mundane and supermundane.'[231]

The more this thinking, with its combination of estate-grounded, romantic, and pantheistic elements moves across into the Austria of Metternich with its partially Catholic traditions, the more the first stratum of the 'dynamic' body of ideas is overlaid by a second, Catholic intellectual component which may provisionally and over-generally be characterised as hierarchical. 'Idea' and 'mediation' take on a new meaning.[232] Since we are here only concerned with the estates-grounded romantic position, we cannot deal with the subsequent fate of 'mediation' – that form of thinking and experiencing which creates synthesis – and we must now return to our analysis of the problem already introduced, *the relation between theory and practice* in estates-based romantic thought.

How bourgeois rationalism and estates-type conservatism relate to each other with regard to this problem we have already discussed in connection with Möser's polemic against Kant (cf. p. 132 of this book). The former stands up for practice and he reasons from there, while the latter separates the spheres only to establish a relationship between them eventually. We have also seen that 'practice' – the living element which Möser opposes to theory – is not only free from all mystical elements but that it is also something exceedingly sober, just as custom and usage, religion and tradition have for him nothing of the irrationality about them into which they will be transformed by romanticism and even more by the historical school. Möser merely denies to theory its sovereign supremacy. Romantic conservatism derived this view of thinking as a factor embedded in what is alive, from estates-types conservatism. The uniquely irrational, fluid element, in contrast, is an original contribution of the type of romanticism which linked bourgeois and estates components. Accordingly, we find a 'concept of life' in the romanticism of Müller in place of Möser's sober 'practice', and in this concept the 'practical element' is mingled in a peculiar way with emotional elements and with contents which are residual remains of the *contemplative mystical* consciousness.

The mere men of practice can satisfy Müller as little as the mere theorists, because the former 'are confined to such narrow spheres of action, cramped by such petty conditions, and compressed into such narrow-minded localities that they find it as hard to escape bigotry as it is for our theorists to escape enthusiasm'.[233] While a narrow sphere of action still had meant living contact for Möser, Müller sees the danger of pedantic narrow-mindedness in the man of mere practice. *From this point, Müller sets about 'mystifying', 'irrationalising', 'romanticising' the practical* in two directions. On the one hand, he stresses what we would now term 'sureness of instinct' in practical thinking. He sets out to prove that here 'principles are of no use, only the feeling for what is advisable and good which has been accumulated through long experience'.[234] Möser, too, was aware of this phenomenon – but we shall see in the next chapter in how different a manner the problem appears to him. The observation that a feeling accumulated by experience enters into every decision of concrete thinking provides Müller with an opportunity to emphasise the aesthetic element in living cognition, which brings – in typically romantic fashion – political knowledge close to art. The second direction in which he introduces irrationalisation is that he emphasises the quality of pure becoming, the 'protean' or 'fugitive' character of 'life', 'practice', or whatever else he may call that which counters rigid systematic theory:

> In just this way, the *statecraft* which I envision should treat the state *in flight, alive, in motion* and not simply throw a confusion of laws into the mix and then casually stand by to see what happens. The statesman should be the omnipresent soul of civil society, and his actions should be at once martial and pacific.[235]

The experience of the 'dynamic' is here laid over the soberly 'practical', as conceived by Möser. It is the quality of sheer flow and movement which is to be comprehended by means of this concept of life.[236] To characterise *practice*, it is not enough to cite the elements of concrete circumstances and locality (a concept, incidentally which appears in Möser as well as in Müller). *For the romantic, 'practice' is in fact not the activity of everyday but that pure 'becoming' which can only be experienced by beginning 'from within'.* The counter-revolutionary experience of the concrete, *now in an internalised form*, here allies itself with attitudes towards experience which had earlier, when they were still grounded in religion, corresponded to mystical modes of conduct, and whose remnants now reappear in a dynamicised form, grounded in pantheism.

This concept of this (a combination of 'practice', 'concreteness' and 'pure movement') is nevertheless similar to Möser's conception, insofar as he too absolutises something extra-theoretical, in relation to which theory is to be interpreted and assessed. *Thought is here a function of life and practice*, and not the opposite – as if practice were merely an application of theory to matters immediately given. It is not the case that the theoretical subject decides and the practical subject carries out the decision. Instead, comprehension of the concrete is decision, mediation by the practical subject who shares in the life of what is to be comprehended. *Cognition is action* and at the same time knowledge that arises out of action. While, therefore, the consciousness of the Enlightenment, which is oriented to pure theory, was inclined toward comprehending even action as a kind of subsumption (and accordingly covered even action under categories belonging to 'theory'), it is now possible that here a concept of life will serve even for the understanding of the concrete. Synthesis is not a compilation or addition, but a *mediation* carried out from within, as by a participant.

The most important determinations of estates-grounded romantic thinking thus form themselves into a closed circle: a distinctive conception of thinking in terms of ideas, of the relationship between theory and practice, as well as the concept of mediation mutually elucidate one another as constituents of this dynamic thinking and experiencing. At the same time, if we abstract this dynamic element in the thought of Müller (as it frequently abstracts itself, as we have seen, from the element of 'practice' in Möser's sense) and consider it by itself, we can grasp *the conservative origins of the modern concept of 'life'*, whose roots lie in the experiencing and absolutising of 'pure becoming'.

Although we can constantly observe in Müller an effort to grasp the concrete in its concreteness, he never arrives at a proper realism. At the point where it would be up to him to become truly concrete he always goes off into declamations about the 'living', 'becoming', the 'idea'; and his discussions are no less abstract (though in a different direction) than the 'normative abstractness' of the Enlightenment, whose antithesis they are supposed to be.

And yet, from this fiercely determined, if still only programmatic, impulse towards the dynamic emerged an important component of the *modern concept of 'life'*.

The realism of the second half of the nineteenth century had a romantic conservative component which originated in just this intense directedness towards what is alive. This *'dynamicism' was at first experienced by itself and in abstraction*; later it followed a dual direction, especially in its German development. In the 'romantic line' it became more and more 'internalised' and what is still allied in Müller, at least programmatically, with a directedness towards the concrete, the practical, the sober, is ever more abstracted from this and experienced purely in itself. *There arises a 'realism' which does not look for 'real being' in the empirical realm, in 'everyday life', or however else one might suggestively designate externalised reality, but in 'pure experience'.* (This expression is not to be taken in a psychological sense.) This tendency – after having been in eclipse for a while, particularly during the 'founding years' of materialism – has recently gained a new, fructifying impetus from the Bergsonian philosophy of life (whose notion of *'durée réelle'* is really a revival of the pure dynamics belonging to romanticism). Many currents of German intellectual history flow towards Bergson, and German spiritual life received back from him a piece of experience, in a more advanced stage, which it once already possessed.[237] In Germany, the Bergsonian impulse combined, on the one hand, with currents joined together in the *phenomenological school*, and, on the other, it allied itself with the *historicism* revived by Dilthey.

The various kinds of contemporary *Lebensphilosophie* can be characterised by variations in the tendencies amalgamated in them. However much the tendencies within 'philosophy of life' may differ from one another, they nevertheless all betray their origin in romanticism and counter-revolution by *their common opposition to Kantianism as well as to positivism*, the two variants of bourgeois rationalising thinking which both endeavour to uphold universal concepts and the natural-scientific, generalising mode of thought, although upon different epistemological foundations. All these varied philosophies of life are at root romantic, because the common opposition against generalising concepts survives in them and because they seek for the truly real in *pure experience*, phenomenologically freed from conceptualised models and not screened by reason. At the present stage, we can no longer speak of them as counter-revolutionary, since they have mostly become politically indifferent. But they live on the strength of designs of thought and experience which once sprang from the fundamental design of conservatism. Just because this originally romantic current lost the political ground under its feet (which is to say, the direct capacity for action, the concrete directedness towards the actuality around them), it could abstract the 'living' and 'the dynamic in itself', as they had been grasped at the stage of romanticism, from Möser's 'practice', and it could increasingly *internalise* this wholly abstracted 'purely dynamic' element.

The great significance of this philosophy of life lies in its constant emphasis on the abstractness of bourgeois rationalism, whose expansion gradually threatens to cover over (to 'reify') all elements of life. It steadily points out that the world of relations which we experience as realities in a rationalised world are actually rational relations which have been absolutised into a 'fetish';[238] in other words, that this allegedly real world is nothing but the world of capitalist rationalisation which covers over a world of underlying 'pure experience'. The conservative origin of this current still betrays itself today, however, in the fact that it is an inactive opposition to the rationalised world which surrounds us. Because it is depoliticised in the widest sense of the term, it cannot find the direct way to change. It has inwardly given up on the world which is in the state of becoming (if only along rationalised lines). But even in this character, it is naturally still a function of the contemporary becoming of the world, and a very important one at that. It serves to keep alive a germ of experience; and it remains for later syntheses to determine the combinations into which this germ may yet enter.[239] As a position for the cognitive penetration of the world, the philosophy of life is a fruitful counterpoise to the currents of thought which stand under the spell of absolutised rationalism. For it teaches us again and again to dismantle the rationalisations which conceal the real nature of things and to avoid orienting consciousness to the ideal of the theoretical attitude alone. It is always showing that the 'reasonable' and the 'objectified' are relative and partial.

The romantic experience of pure dynamics followed an entirely different path when it was taken up by Hegel, who sought for objectivity rather than for internalisation,[240] and thereby also associated the dynamic element with the concrete problem-complex of the political and historical world. This meant that he renounced the pure experience of dynamics. By means of an altogether novel kind of rationalisation, it was transformed into '*dialectics*'. But at the same time, he preserved the conservative discovery of mobility, now safe from loss, for use in a method for comprehending historical becoming. All this he accomplished by dismissing the alternatives as they had crystallised at the beginning of the new century: either rigid thinking or irrational dynamics. Instead, he answered, *there is a higher order of rationality than that*

151

of 'abstract', rigid thinking; there is dynamic thinking. That answer brought victory to the tendency already observed in Müller, i.e. the tendency to extend the sphere of potential rationalisation and to utilise the new method of rationalisation for the understanding of the historical. That Hegel succeeded in this, that he did not, like romantic thought, lose touch with the world as it was coming to be and consequently did not need to take refuge in mere 'internalised' experience, was due to the fact that he attached himself with indomitable perseverance,[241] to the historically existent (*Seienden*), which was then the decisive reality for conservatism.

Müller's type of romanticism developed at first in alliance with the estates-opposition. Since the latter could not get its way in the long run, since the future did not belong to it, the romantics were soon left without any real social backing and many had to flee to the Austrian camp, in order to keep alive. There, they sought to win Church and State to their side. That, however, meant the destruction of all the germs that had been native to romanticism, that gave it meaning and for which it had a special sense. As a visible entity, romanticism did not even last as long as Metternich. As a living influence in intellectual history, it had been done with in the 1840s, after having been found out in the criticism of Heine. But by the time of the *Hallische Jahrbücher*, it was little more than a shadow, even when viewed from outside.[242]

By turning the mere experience of dynamics into a rational method of thought of a higher order, Hegel posed the problem of dynamic thinking and the whole complex of questions concerning the problems of truth and standards, which occupy us to the present day. This entire range of problems, however, and the social background from which Hegel's thinking derives can only be dealt with later. At this point it is only important to show that it is precisely the *objective dynamics* of the Hegelian line which enters into the synthesis implied by *Marxism*, and that Marxist proletarian thinking therefore *also* possesses *a dynamic and dialectical conception of reality*. What Hegel and Marxism thus have in common with the philosophy of life is that for all of them it is possible to relativise 'everyday', 'static', and 'abstract' thinking by reference to a dynamic ground. But while this dynamic ground is something pre-theoretical (such as the pure '*durée*', 'pure experience', and so on) in the 'internalised' philosophy of life, in Hegel this ground – by reference to which 'vulgar' and 'abstract' thinking are relativised – is something spiritual (rationality of a higher order), and in proletarian thought it is the class struggle and the economically centred social process itself. *This is the direction in which Hegel's flight into objectivity has shifted.*

It is not necessary to go into all the details which might be mentioned here. Our purpose was merely to call attention to *the extent to which even the conceptions of reality of the two-fold opposition against bourgeois natural-law thinking were formed in opposition to it; the way in which a concept of life emerged here, which was characterised by mobility, by dynamicism; and the nature of the dual form in which the concepts of reality of both the philosophy of life and Marxism continued their development, in clear continuity with these origins.*

In addition to these two directions taken by the estates-grounded romantic element (viz., the discovery of the vital, the idea as the mobile, the discovery of history as antithesis to norm and system), there is also a third way, which was pursued by the *historical school*. It offers a distinctive solution to the conservative problem of the relationship between norm and history, between thinking and existence. The determination of its sociological position presents quite a distinct problem. It signifies a place between Hegel and romanticism, and without it Hegel cannot be understood. For these reasons, we must give special consideration to the problem complex it represents.[243]

2 The position of the 'historical school'

As noted earlier, the historical school represents the third type of problem-definition to arise out of conservative experience within the social and spiritual constellation just described. It does not flee from history into the purely internalised experience of pure dynamics, as romantic experience ultimately does, but seeks to connect these dynamics with what is historically coming into being. Like Hegel, it aims to become objective and concrete; unlike Hegel, however, it does not set abstract rationality over against dynamic development, as a higher form of rationality. Although the historical school deprecates 'abstract' rationality just as much as Hegel does, it sees as the antagonist of this rationality not the dynamic concept of 'higher order', but historical life as such, i.e., the irrational, which is purely dynamic.

In this connection, Hegel had taken over the romantic opposition to abstract rationality and confronted this rationality with a 'being' (*Sein*). But he immediately conceived of this being so that it itself becomes a rationality of a higher order. The same configuration appears in the historical school, except that this school renders the higher being of a dynamic sort which is to be upheld against bourgeois and bureaucratic rationality wholly irrational. In this *irrationalisation*, the historical school goes beyond the romanticism of Adam Müller. While favouring

153

irrationality, he devises a rationality able to track the course of the dynamic by following along with it. From this point of view, then, the historical school carries romanticism's irrationalist tendencies (with which it shares common sociological origins) to more radical conclusions.

The historical school shifts the centre of gravity of the 'actually existent' (*des wirklich Seienden*) into the irrational sphere, which takes on the character of the unconscious (a concept adopted from Schelling), while at the same time immersing itself in concrete history. It thus casts off the last remnants of rationality surviving in romanticism and looks for the essence of the world's historical events (*Weltgeschehen*) in the irrational sphere. Yet it does not depoliticise and internalise the irrational, but rather endeavours to read its signs in history. Here, the romantic subject does not turn to its inner self by retreating from the world's historical happenings, but *it renders these happenings inward* and therefore stays in contact with them, albeit in a peculiar fashion. But if the essence of these happenings is something wholly irrational, unconscious, *prior* to all rationalisation, then the problem becomes what thinking and knowing can mean, from this standpoint, and what they can achieve. From here, the way would seem to be clear to a thoroughgoing agnosticism. But the historical school does not follow this way, just because of its groundedness in the political. It neither denies that there is thinking nor that thinking has productive value. Instead, *it allocates a very special function to thinking*.

For bourgeois thought, rationality means calculation (deduction) of something which is valid once and for all, and which must then be put into effect by action. The knowing subject is enthroned, as it were, beyond history: he grasps what is theoretically true by contemplation. And it is left to the acting ego subsequently to actualise this truth. In *Müller's type of romanticism*, the knowing subject is immersed, struggling, in a flow which is inherently *incalculable*, but it comes to know this stream by thinking and acting in terms of 'ideas', *mediating* between the clashing, active cross-currents, while in their midst. Action and mediation are simultaneously also cognition.

While the knowing subject also stands within the process of reality for Hegel, the subject's everyday thinking – even when it is abstract and calculating – is *de facto* a realisation of the next step in historical development, according to Hegel's theory of the cunning of reason. Although itself rational, the plan of this development embodies a rationality of a higher order which never becomes apparent to the immediately acting and abstractly thinking subject, while it does become comprehensible to the philosopher who arrives, like the owl of Minerva, after the event. This rationalism, which deprecates calculating rationality but overcomes it by a rationality said to be higher, is a dynamic rationalism. It solves the problem of choosing between 'dynamic being or rigid thinking' by juxtaposing being to rational dynamics, true knowing to dynamicised rationality. Rigid, abstract, computing calculation is only an intermediate stage, a function of dynamic being. *We are thus constantly placed within the element of dynamic rationality*: philosophical cognition uncovers and comprehends its plan.

With Savigny, by contrast, we stand in the element of the irrational, and thinking has the function of groping forward, of *elucidation*. This thinking is not calculation or mediation or reconstruction of the world's plan. It is a clarification carried on within the element of something existing prior to thought. This thinking is differently placed in the world than the functions of thinking, themselves varied, with which we have hitherto dealt. It has a different function, both for the world and for the knowing subject. Until these distinctive specifications of function have been grasped, a comparison among these types cannot be definitive. Recorded statements are compared but not the different modes of thinking which are the element within which each of the statements has its existence.

Now we must fill out our sketchy characterisation of the historical school, and we shall proceed by drawing on Savigny, who sets the standard for its early stage. The program of the historical school was first reflected in Savigny's publication against Thibault, *Vom Beruf unserer Zeit für Gesetzgebung und Rechtswissenschaft* (Of the Vocation of our Age for Legislation and Jurisprudence)[244] and subsequently in the essay, 'Über den Zweck der Zeitschrift für geschichtliche Rechtswissenschaft' (On the Objectives of the Journal of Historical Jurisprudence),[245] programmatically anticipating the journal which Savigny founded together with Eichhorn and Göschen. Also relevant for this period is Savigny's publication against Gönner (1815).[246] His *System des heutigen römischen Rechts* (System of Modern Roman Law),[247] like the other writings of the historical school, has to be treated with caution at this point, however, since it stems from a later phase of the school's development.

The substantive core of the essay 'Of the Vocation of our Age' consists of a polemic against Thibault's proposal for the creation of a general legal code, which, like the Code Napoléon, would systematise all the provisions of law to which the judge would be bound in his judgment:

Men longed for new legal codes, which, by their completeness, should insure a mechanically precise administration of justice, insomuch that the judge, freed from the exercise of private opinion, should be confined to the mere literal application: at the same time, these codes were to be divested of all historical associations, and, in pure abstraction, be equally adapted to all peoples at all times.[248]

Savigny objects to this in the name of the newly awakened historical spirit,[249] for which it has become questionable whether there even is any such thing as a law of reason from which laws can simply be derived. Instead, he advises the examination of history, to see whether law has arisen anywhere in this declaratory and deductive way:

> Where we first find documented history, the civil law already has a specific character peculiar to the people, like its language, usages, constitution. Indeed, these phenomena have no independent existence; they are simply the various powers and activities of the people, in their nature inseparably interlinked and appearing as separable qualities only to our observation. What binds them into a whole is the common belief of the people, the shared feeling of *inner necessity*, which precludes any idea of accidental and arbitrary origins.[250]

We cited this passage earlier,[251] as evidence for the contemplative, characterological intuition of totality (*Totalitätsschau*) in conservative thinking. But now we are interested in the expression, '*the shared feeling of inner necessity*' as a characterisation of the source of legal validity. We continue with Savigny:

> This youthful period of peoples is poor in *concepts*, but it enjoys a *clear consciousness* of circumstances and condition. It *feels* and *lives in them* in full and in their entirety, while we, in our *artificially* complicated existence, are overpowered by our own wealth, instead of *enjoying and mastering* it.[252]

Here *conceptual knowledge* is expressly divorced from a *clear consciousness of circumstances and conditions* which leads to their being enjoyed and mastered. From this point of view, one can apparently know about conditions in the world in two different ways: first, by having conceptual command over them; second, by living inside them and being conscious of them, and having command over them in this way. At a time, then, according to Savigny, when there is still a scarcity of concepts, the place of abstract thought is taken by symbolic, palpable actions, whose function it is – comparable to a grammar of the law – to guarantee the 'preservation and precise application' of the law. It is not by way of knowing, then, but rather by preserving the sense of justice present in consciousness, that even modern times still retain juristic formulae. But Savigny finds them lacking in palpability.

This '*organic* connection between the law and the nature and character of the people' confirms its effectiveness in the fact that it does not lie quiet even for a moment and that it evolves by inner necessity. 'The law therefore grows with the people, forms itself as they do, and then eventually withers, just like the people loses its distinctive character.'[253]

This interpretation of the development of law runs into difficulties, as Savigny is quick to admit, at a differentiated stage of development. Having claimed that the 'real seat of law is the common consciousness of the people', he immediately acknowledges that this may be claimed for the most basic principles of marriage and property in Roman law but not for the many details contained in the Pandects. He solves the difficulty by stating that differentiation occurs with the growth of culture. The 'activities' which were carried out communally by the people in an earlier epoch are subsequently allocated to individual 'estates' (*Stände*), one of which is the estate of jurists.

> The law now takes shape in language, it takes a scientific direction. Having originally lived in the *consciousness of the whole people*, it is given up *to the consciousness of jurists*, who now represent the people in this function. From this point onward, the existence of the law is more *artificial and complicated*, in that it leads a *double life*: on the one hand, as part of the whole people's life, which it does not cease to be; on the other, as a special science in the hands of jurists.[254]

But it does not follow, according to Savigny, that this brings to an abrupt halt the organic character of the law's growth. It simply takes on greater complexity, in that the 'political' element (which is how Savigny now designates the organic connection between the law and the life of the people) is joined by the 'technical element' of juristic subtleties.

> The conclusion to be drawn from this view of the matter is that all law arises in the way that the predominant but not wholly adequate language calls *customary law*; i.e., that it is first generated by usage and tradition and only afterwards by jurisprudence. It is thus everywhere the work of inner, silently-acting forces, and not of the arbitrary decision of a legislator.[255]

In response to questions about the function assigned to the thinking of the 'legislator', Savigny identifies as permissible only one type of legislative activity: as individual legal propositions become uncertain, a type of legislation may properly arise which comes to the aid of custom, removes these doubts and uncertainties, and so brings to light and preserves the real law, the actual, contemporary will of the people.[256] This indicates once again, and perhaps most plainly, the function which genuine thinking has for Savigny – that of 'elucidation'.[257] That which is right is somehow present in our consciousness even if we do not know this. Thinking may explicate but cannot produce it.

To grasp the distinctive character of such elucidation, it is only necessary to ask about its opposite. Savigny addresses that question. He maintains that the great danger posed by legal codes is that they may be produced in times which do not possess this inner sense for what is organically right. In such a case, the legal code will

> unavoidably draw all attention to itself by its novelty, its inner link to the concepts prevalent at the time, and its outward weightiness; and it will *distract* attention from the genuine source of the law.[258]

The opposite of *elucidation*, then, is *distraction* or, more pointedly, *obfuscation*. Here too there are apparently two types of thinking: first, the elucidative thinking which is a primary component in the consciousness of the people; second, the thinking which distracts and obscures. It is necessary to learn more about the second type of thinking, which clearly corresponds to the abstract thinking discussed earlier. Speaking about the distinctive character of the classical period of jurisprudence, Savigny remarks the following:

> The concepts and tenets of their science did not seem to these jurists to have been brought about by their own arbitrary act; the law consists of *real entities, whose existence and genealogy have become known to them by long and intimate association.*[259]
> The depth to which this community of scientific property is rooted among the Roman jurists can also be seen from the slight value which they attached to the *outward expressions* of this community; *their definitions*, for example, are largely very inadequate, without the slightest loss in the precision and reliability of the concepts.[260]

The opposition, then, is formed as follows. On the one side, there are concepts which are substantive entities, have actual presence, possess a genealogy – concepts to which one relates in familiar associations. On the opposite side are concepts specified by definition alone. But something else must be made clear. How do the concepts wholly dependent on definition come about?

The law has no existence by itself: its essence is rather the life of people themselves, when seen from a certain aspect. When the science of law detaches itself from this, its object, scientific activity, is enabled to proceed along its one-sided course without being accompanied by a corresponding apprehension of the legal relationships themselves.[261]

Science will attain to a 'formal elaboration' and do without that reality which characterised Roman jurisprudence. But the Roman jurists, whenever they must decide on a legal case, begin with

the most vivid apprehension of it, and we see the whole complex emerge before our eyes and gradually change. It is as if this legal case were the starting point for the whole science, which is to be invented from this point. Theory and practice are not really distinguished for them. Their theory is refined to the point of the most immediate application and their practice is constantly enhanced by scientific treatment.[262]
And they have their unique value in this method of finding and interpreting the law, quite like the old Germanic jurors in that their art consists simultaneously of scientific finding and of pronouncing judgement.[263]

In sum, then, two types of thinking are being contrasted. There is, first, a thinking which operates with rigorous definitions, which can achieve nothing more than elaboration of form, which obscures organic thinking, and which has detached itself from the living law. We call this thinking 'an abstract thinking, detached from the organic'. Contrasted to this is a thinking which is, unlike the other, connected to the existence of the law. Initially we shall call it 'existentially-connected thinking (*seinsverbundenes Denken*)'. Its distinguishing characteristic is that the knowing subject must be existentially rooted in the community in which the living, always changing law is to be found. The function of this thinking is to elucidate this law – already present in existence – by means of concepts. Everything that is legally right is already present, although it changes dynamically and, strictly speaking, lacks conceptual being. Thinking can only *elucidate*: it can explicate immanent implications and insert missing terms. There are no such things as general formal implications. The law in being does not elucidate itself by abstract speculation, but only in the course of the *concrete individual cases* in which the law lives and evolves.

Savigny's invocation of the Germanic juror (*Schöffe*) as well as his conception of 'theory and practice' suggest Möser as the source from which he derived his conception of knowing.

It is known that Savigny owes much to Möser; Savigny himself recalls Möser in his *Beruf*[264] with gratitude. But that this conception of thinking has its origins in Möser has not been shown before, so far as we can see. Since the problem of the sociology of thinking is central to us, however, we must lay particular stress on precisely this issue of the origins of this way of thinking.

Möser's influence on Adam Müller cannot be supported by any express acknowledgements by Müller, and we therefore had to take recourse to the license of the sociologist, which allows him to establish connections by the indirect route of simply comparing two positions, two states of thinking. But Savigny expressly cites two articles for Möser to which we also want to refer.[265] 'Über die Art und Weise, wie unsere Vorfahren die Prozesse abgekürzt haben' (On the ways and means by which our ancestors shortened trials),[266] and 'Schreiben eines alten Rechtsgelerten über das sogenannte Allegieren' (Writings of an old jurisprudent concerning 'allegation').[267] We shall soon see how much the Möser in question here differs from the one that influenced Müller.

In the first of these essays, Möser begins, as is his custom, with an individual case in history and builds up his reasoning by constant reference to it. He starts out with a quote from an Osnabrück peace treaty in the year 1305, which concludes:

> And if in the future new conflicts should arise amongst them, they will each have some of their servants or liegemen assemble in some third place, where these will mediate or adjudicate the controversy within fourteen days; and if they cannot conclude within fourteen days, these eight arbitrators shall move on to Bielefeld, and if they still cannot come to an agreement there within fourteen days, they shall go to Hereford, and then move from one town to another after every fourteen days until they have agreed upon a verdict.

Möser builds his analysis upon this example – an example which he puts at the head of his account, with the familiar conservative partiality for paradoxes.

He does not find remarkable in this state of affairs either the choice of the arbitrators or the fact that each party has an equal number of votes; what fascinates him is that the arbitrators are given the power to come to a 'resolution by virtue of their office'. They did not have to adjudicate 'like our judges today' on the grounds of established laws, but rather had to travel back and forth between Bielefeld and Hereford until they had 'found' a verdict.[268] The verdict found in this way was, however, legally binding by virtue of their office.

The second thing that Möser finds remarkable in the settlement procedures is that they make it evident that there are generally two major ways of settling disputes. The first is 'that a man who is of equal birth and who is in fellowship declares how things must be, according to his judgement'; and the second, 'that a learned man who is neither equal in birth nor in fellowship with the parties declares what the laws have decreed for the case under dispute.' 'The former was the manner of our forefathers; the latter is our own . . .'[269] For Möser, and for ourselves as well, the most important thing is what the expression 'in fellowship' (*genoss*) is supposed to indicate. Möser offers the following explanation:

> This is an old German word, for which I cannot find a better one. A French and a German nobleman may be equal in birth, but they are not in fellowship with one another. Similarly, citizens of different towns are not in fellowship with each other.

In fellowship, then, are only those equal in status who come from the same life-community. In the same essay, Möser points out that this whole way of thinking is also linked with English traditions and that the English concepts of 'liberty' and 'property' contain this principle of 'fellowship' (*Prinzip des Genossenschaftlichen*).[270]

Here we clearly see the estate-orientation contained in this way of thinking, which we had ample opportunity to analyse in Savigny. We can now apply the term 'thinking-in-fellowship' (*genossenschaftliches Denken*) or 'communally-determined thinking' (*gemeinschaftsgebundenes Denken*) to this type of thinking, which is essentially elucidation and which we earlier provisionally called 'existentially-connected thinking' (*seinsverbundenes Denken*). Its distinguishing characteristic remains the distinctive function of elucidation, and it continues to rest upon the precondition that the 'elucidating subject' stands *with his whole personality* within the context of the community in which and for which he performs the elucidation.

With this, we have once again come upon one of our most important theses, namely that conservative thinking raises older ways of thinking and behaving to the level of reflection and thereby rescues them from being buried, but simultaneously creates a fruitful new method of thinking. It is also possible at this point to closely follow this process of a growing reflectiveness. We only have to observe in detail how the first stage (the early 'conservatism' of Möser) differs from the partially romanticised conservatism of Savigny, with regard to this conception of 'thinking-in-fellowship'. Such a comparison brings to light, in addition to the similarities noted, the following differences.

First, the circle of 'fellows' is narrower for Möser than for Savigny. For Möser, each estate is a distinct sphere of life, a distinct, existentially connected community. For Savigny, only the 'people' (*Volk*)† represent a cohesive spirit. This shows how the community of the people (*Volksgemeinschaft*) replaces the estate and the local community[271] in the course of the transition from the old estate-related conservatism to the modern. Savigny is already living in a world for which, mostly at the level of hopes and designs, national unity has become the problem.[272]

Secondly, although the 'people' is in part the discovery of a living unit with actual effectiveness, it is at the same time ideological protection against revolutionary demands.[273] The point is to confront the civic nation [in the French sense] with a totality of equal worth, a totality of a different kind, and this is 'the people' [in the German sense]. In the world of estates, the rule of the governing strata has not yet been called into question and one can quite peacably argue in a particularistic, estate-oriented way. With the rise of the idea of civic equality, any kind of particularism, Right or Left, must legitimate itself in the name of the whole.[274] Since the basic paradigm of this legitimation is the idea of natural representation, we want to differentiate this type of representation from popular representation based on choice. Clearly, just as the juristic estate appears, for Savigny, as natural representative of the 'spirit of the people' (*Volksgeist*) as soon as the people differentiates itself,[275] with the rise of 'culture', the remaining ruling strata (e.g., the nobility) also represent the spirit of the whole. Although Savigny marshalls the idea of organic association against totality by agglomeration, he does not see the people in realistic terms.[276]

The 'idea' of the people is more clearly seen in Savigny's work than anyplace else, but one does not feel in him a direct concern for this people, like the concern which is often naturalistically present in Möser's narrow-minded devotion – even when he is justifying serfdom.[277] In Savigny, something is existentially slipping away from conservatism. But the *idea* of this something which is slipping away becomes evident at the same time, as an abstraction; and this too brings something to light. Even at the early stage, Savigny's 'people' is in fact what we have come to understand by 'nation'; the destiny of the whole is conceived exclusively at the level of culture (language, custom, art, the law). In this instance, too, it can be clearly shown that even the romantic conservative counter-current, despite its programmatic aspiration

†The German word *Volk* often refers to a collective and substantive entity. It tends to exclude the individualist connotations which English usage often intends with the word 'people'. Nevertheless, the term 'folk' would be misleadingly archaic here, especially since Savigny is, after all, often writing about the *populus* of the Roman law. *Trs*.

to concreteness, can comprehend the contents of its experience solely on the level where the forces bearing the present development (i.e., bourgeois capitalist thought) possess their own contents – at the level of abstractness. The difference is that the contents which become apparent to romantic conservative thinking are different. It is no accident that this romanticised conception of 'the people' brought forth in practice a historiography which eventually came to possess a most sensitive empathy for precisely these cultural expressions, but that the conception proved incapable of creating a *new community*.

The second feature distinguishing Savigny's 'spirit of the people'[278] from Möser's 'fellowship' is the complete *irrationalisation* of the pre-theoretical element in which one must live if one is to elucidate it and if one is to find the law (as well as the other communally-determined verities). Here too, Möser is *sober*, and he is only concerned, so far as he is aware, with the purely practical question of preventing the gradual transfer of powers which formerly belonged to fellows to judges outside the fellowship.[279] It is a matter of safeguarding the rights of estates against incursions by territorial rulers.

There is not a single passage in the entire essay which characterises this pre-theoretical knowledge of what is right in even a remotely emotional way – quite the contrary. Once again, Möser puts forward utterly sober, peasant-shrewd arguments, this time against the introduction of judges from outside the fellowship:

If they [the fellows] think it right that he [the member of the market-fellowship to be judged] should not have more than two geese and one gander; if they prohibit him from mowing fodder on the village green; if they accordingly oblige him to slaughter his pig, he can at least be sure right away that those who lay down this law are in the same case as he is himself, and that they would have to abide by the law which they have declared if it should go against them. That is quite a different matter than when the commissioner of police orders him not to drink coffee, while proceeding noisily to slurp his own, and then can justify his order with nothing more than reason and prudence (those eternal procuresses of the human passions.[280]

Despite this interest-oriented account, the fact of an opposition between abstract deduction from the law and a concrete decision on the basis of the mutuality of fellowship is clearly brought out.

But where does Savigny get his irrationalisation of pre-reflective knowing, the irrationalisation of the being that stands behind reasoning? This question simultaneously poses the whole problem of the irrational in conservative experience and thinking.

Which 'locations' and 'conceptions' of the irrational can be uncovered in that period and life-space, and where does the irrationality in Savigny fit amongst them? The relation between 'rational' and 'irrational' is a problem common to all tendencies of thought and experience in the nineteenth century. Although this problem belongs, in some form or other, to the hard core of philosophical experience and thought as such, we have already pointed out that the nineteenth century puts a distinctive stamp on the correlation. The preoccupation arose not least because the eighteenth century had pushed rationalisation to such a logical extreme – and thereby had so stubbornly excluded all irrational elements – that these latter were bound, as it were, to be washed together on the banks of a stream. They could thus be compacted into an opponent displaying many varieties but common effects.

For the different variants of irrationalism of this epoch the decisive factor, when viewed from our problem perspective, *concerns the point and place in the contexture of thought and experience at which the irrational appears*. We shall see that, while progressive liberal thinking too has to grapple with the irrational and cannot completely avoid it, the irrational nonetheless takes on a different form here and appears in an entirely different context. We must attempt at least a classification of ideal types from this point of view.

The liberal rationalism of the Enlightenment tends to create *a pure and homogeneous sphere of the rational* in which no irrational factor has a place, and then must concede the existence of the irrational somehow outside these boundaries. This solution may present a number of variants:

(1) All rationalisation is a transformation in the categories applied to a given apprehendable matter. This tendency further divides into two types of solutions. In one, this matter (contents) is conceived to be irrational and is left in its irrationality. (This is most clearly expressed philosophically by the present Southwest-German School of Philosophy, whose positions can be traced back to Kantianism.) In the second, the irrationality of contents is seen to be something purely situational, and it is thought that with the progress of knowledge (here taken as an unending project) this irrationality will increasingly be transformed into rationality (the Marburg School is its philosophical expression).

(2) Only certain areas of the world can be consistently and thoroughly rationalised. The concordance of these discrete rationalisms, however, is already irrational. Here again there are two solutions: this adjustment is achieved either by a harmony among

these discrete spheres (optimistic liberalism), or it is determined by force (*Realpolitik* and imperialism characteristic of the epoch of the rationalised bourgeoisie). The irrationalisms here are consequently 'equilibrium' or 'harmony' in the one case, and 'power' (as a 'naturalistic' factor) in the other, which has gained dominance since the mid-1860s.[281]

What all these enlightened liberal irrationalisms share is their attempt to work out a pure sphere marked by calculability or by some different kind of rationalisability, a domain undisturbed by anything irrational. It is for this reason that they prefer the types of knowing which formulate their problems in so abstract a manner that such detachability from concretion becomes possible. Just as mathematics disregards the distinctive character of the objects it counts and considers them only insofar as they are quantifiable units, so do the other sciences which arise under this sign (making mathematics their ideal) strive to penetrate their objects merely from an abstract point of view. They therefore make themselves, as it were, a new 'scientific object' (a body is only *res extensa*, man is only *homo oeconomicus*, and so on). All the aspects of the concrete object which do not enter into these points of view appear to be accidental; and the accidental, too, is irrational. ('Accident' is a term correlative to 'necessary', as 'irrational' is to 'rational'. The meaning and inclusiveness of the former concepts vary with the scope assigned to the 'necessary' or, as the case may be, the 'rational'.) As usual, epistemology patterns itself on the concept of science; and it equates 'rational' with 'science' (that is, the sciences which are oriented to the ideal of the 'exact' natural sciences) and generally sees anything which reaches further as irrational and 'unknowable'. At this point, it is enough to indicate that epistemology thus overlooks the fact that we can know even when we are not 'knowing' scientifically, i.e., in the sense of the 'exact' natural sciences.

In contradistinction to all this,[282] it is a fundamental feature of the conservative tendencies of thought arising in this age that they do not turn the irrational into a *limiting concept*. The conservative sees and experiences the world as *permeated* by irrationalities. For him, rationalisation is only to be found in sectors, and even here the rational element is only a function of more comprehensive irrational forces.[283] At first, we simply want to enumerate several of the instances in which the irrational can appear and show that it is possible to distinguish a corresponding variety of irrationalities.

It is possible to seek the irrational, and to find it in:

(a) the *individual* (romanticism). While 'individual', for thinking in the manner of the Enlightenment, mostly means 'in-dividuum', that which cannot be further subdivided, for romantic thinking it

165

denotes the possession of a specific, incomparable, central essence.

(b) *Locality* (J. Möser, A. Müller). The mere *hic et nunc* of the enlightened man is here experienced in its incomparable uniqueness.

(c) *Application*. Universal law is rational, but that it can be at all *applied* to the world is an irrational fact.

(d) *Movement*. Movement cannot be broken down into its more or less specifiable phases.

(e) The *personality* in contrast to that which can be comprehended as mechanism, but also in contrast to that which history can comprehend. Stahl's thought, for instance, is rooted in this.

(f) The *qualitative*.

(g) The *totality*.

(h) The *divine*, the mystical, the revelation.[284]

(i) The *organic*, the vital core.

To begin with, then, we have simply enumerated the general possibilities for the displacement of the irrational, leaving it for later to analyse these types more closely in their appropriate historical and sociological place. But we had to enumerate such a sampling of types (of which there are still more) in order to help us to distinguish the irrational according to Savigny and the historical school. In such a typology, the irrational naturally appears only as polar opposite of the rational. And even a merely cursory listing of its variants makes strikingly apparent that *qualitatively* very diverse phenomena are subsumed under the term irrational, because there can be no doubt that there is very little essential connection between the irrationality of the individual or locality, on the one hand, and the irrationality of mystical ecstasy or of the organic vital core, on the other. That we are nonetheless content to classify the world of spirit and soul by reference to this contrast and that our philosophy formulates its problems in terms of it, merely shows that rationalisation has increasingly become our central problem, and that, in comparison, it is a rather secondary problem whether the irrationalities are wholly disparate in substance.

But for a consciousness which lives primarily in the 'irrational' element, these differences must be quite radical. And if one really wants to enter deeply into the distinctive character of the ways of thinking which move conservative thought in its early stage, nothing is more important than to strip off this concealing cloak, this concept of the 'irrational' which reduces everything to a common denominator, so as to be able to turn concretely to the individual types of irrationalities. (The fact that we constantly use the undifferentiated term 'irrational' is itself a sign that we have already begun to live this concept, that is, that we are only aware of irrationalities insofar as they somehow relate antithetically to the fact of rationalisability.)

Addressing the question, then, of specifying qualitatively which type of 'irrational' Savigny has in mind, we find that it is the one named last in our enumeration, the one we called '*organic vital core*'. It is a matter, in Savigny, of discovering that there are constructive forces alive in all of the objectifications of an individual, but also in those of an organic community, and that these forces act towards the same or at least towards closely related ends. The manner and the direction of this constructive force can subsequently be deciphered in the objectifications (which can be elucidated), but, strictly speaking, it acts latently in the unconscious. When we compare Savigny's own descriptions of these constructive forces, it must strike us – as was pointed out earlier[285] – that in his early writings of the time in question the term 'spirit of the people' (*Volksgeist*) itself does not yet appear; it occurs only in 1840, in his *System des heutigen römischen Rechts*, clearly only under the influence of Puchta.[286] In 1814/15 Savigny uses the following circumscriptions instead: 'the various powers and activities of the people, *in their nature* inseparably inter-linked',[287] 'the shared feeling of *inner necessity*',[288] 'this organic connection between the law and the nature and character of the people',[289] 'in an organic way without actual arbitrary act or intention',[290] 'inner, silently acting forces',[291] 'higher nature of the people',[292] 'higher common freedom',[293] 'inner constructive forces',[294] 'the law that exists independently of [the legislators]', 'the law that lives in the people without the help of any arbitrary act [by either the people or the ruler]',[295] the people are not inanimate material that one works upon, but an 'organism of a higher order'.[296]

We can see that the rendering of 'spirit of the people' into substance is here at first mostly avoided, due to the absence of the term, and that (with the exception of the last example, where he comes rather close) key importance is attached to pre-theoretical, unconscious, creative forces. What Savigny is here playing upon and at the same time discovering is the way in which every attempt to give shape to things, including creative thinking, moves *in the sphere of the unconscious, the supra-rational*. He then contrasts this thinking to a thinking alienated from its own unconscious origin. The irrational is here the unconscious, that which has not yet become conscious. From where does Savigny derive this conception of the unconscious, which first makes 'elucidation' possible? We cannot here rehearse the extensive yet instructive discussion concerning the historical origin of the concept 'spirit of the people'. In alluding to it, we simply want to remark that to us the origin in Schelling appears beyond doubt.[297] As in other cases, our claim merely means that it is not possible to trace such an element as the irrational in the form of an unconscious vital core further back than to Schelling. Our interest is directed towards discovering how and when these component parts assemble themselves together into a conservative position. Kantorowicz has identified and analysed the following passage in Schelling's 'System des transzendentalen Idealismus (1800)' which probably influenced Savigny.[298]

> A second nature and a *higher* one must be built, as it were, above the first. In it, a law of nature rules, but one which is wholly different from the one in visible nature. It is a natural law dedicated to *freedom*. Inexorably, and with the same iron necessity with which the effect follows cause in sensible nature, every intrusion upon the freedom of another must be followed, in this second nature, by an instantaneous counter against the selfish impulse. The established law is such a natural law as that which we have depicted, and the second nature in which this rules is the legal order.[299]

We quote Kantorowicz's commentary verbatim:

> Its 'realisation' is now deduced as 'the only object of *history*' and so the problem arises 'how can it represent the reconciliation of freedom and necessity', and 'how is it possible, since we are altogether free and act with consciousness, that something can unconsciously be brought about us, something which we never intended and which freedom, left to itself, could never have achieved?'; how then is it possible that 'something objective, a second nature, the legal order can emerge by means of my free action', even though 'everything objective as such arises unconsciously'? The problem is solved by Kant's theory of the '*organism*', which has a 'purpose' without having been brought about 'purposefully'. Nature must be such a product, and therefore also the 'second nature, the legal order'.[300]

Next Kantorowicz very pertinently brings out the following contrast: for Schelling and German idealism, there exists a rational entity, 'the state', while for Savigny there is instead a natural entity (*Naturwesen*), 'the people', the bearer of the organic development of the law. Savigny renders still more irrational the already irrationalist beginnings in Schelling, and for precisely this reason he eliminates everything reminiscent of the concept of 'reason'. Moreover, while Schelling recognises that the result of this initially unconscious process is affected by an immanent rationality

(*Vernünftigkeit*), Savigny merely takes over the element of the unconscious from Schelling's doctrine, and then only in order to sanction customary law. Further, while Schelling's idea of development knows a goal ('Herder's humanity, Hegel's freedom'), Savigny merely supposes perpetual change without change of substance.[301]

Kantorowicz thus works out with exemplary clarity the *spiritual angle of refraction*, as it were, of the modifications undergone by Schelling's theory when it was taken up by Savigny. It is therefore all the more surprising that he offers as explanation and interpretation of this redirection such grounds as Savigny's ostensible lack of philosophical talent and consequent inability to understand German idealism, or the assertion, meant as a 'sociological' explanation, that Savigny, as an aristocrat, had a 'need for dignity' and that he therefore could not bear the thought that his science, jurisprudence, should satisfy (according to the views ascribed to natural lawyers) nothing more than the subjective preferences of the ruler. This sort of assertion represents the worst and most primitive type of sociological explanation. This is not to deny, however, that it is sometimes possible that purely subjective, psychologically determined factors may lead an author to his theory or that Savigny's 'aristocratic background' is important. But the assumption that intellectual tendencies which follow a particular inner logic and persist over time, are nothing more than collections of the most varied, undirected, and subjective arbitrary expressions, is the kind of sociological observation that takes us back to the most primitive stage of Enlightenment thought. While the sociological relevance of Savigny's aristocratic origins must indeed be taken into account, it is nevertheless interesting only insofar as it brings about redirections which are typical and insofar as it can be linked up with typical impulses of the aristocratic mentality of the time. These, however, can be more easily derived from the nobility's positionally determined opposition to absolutism than from their formal need for distinction. And if there is embodied in the invocation of the 'people' – which served as an element of concealment for the nobility as well as reflecting the national patriotism which was generally awakening in Savigny's time – a disguised particularistic, estate-oriented argument, a self-justification hiding behind the totality of the nation, this can be explained by reference to the situation of the nobility at that time and by its collective, sociologically determined designs.

Kantorowicz himself seems to lose confidence in his own manner of argument. By asking himself why Savigny's ostensible petty scheming should have laid the foundation for a school, and why someone like Puchta, for instance, joined in, he invalidates one subjective, psychological explanation by another: 'A rationalist like Puchta would never have professed this doctrine if it had not already been the prevailing one.'[302] This is sociology along the lines of research into world-historical back-stage gossip.

All this cannot keep us from drawing Kantorowicz's valuable finding into our own analysis, namely, that here the elements of irrationality which came to life in Schelling and romanticism, and only they, were taken up in their full inner logic, to a clearly ascertainable end, and incorporated into the quite different context of legal theory. Our next question, then, concerns the point of this invocation, in Savigny, of unconscious creative forces, put forward with such special emphasis and with a marked evaluative stress. The answer is quite plain: to exalt the mere fact of 'positive law'. But why was it necessary to exalt this 'positive law' to the expression 'law of the people' (*Volksrecht*), to a formation which flows from the generative, unconscious ultimate ground? What was the state of the conception of 'positive law' in the period just before Savigny and what was the distinctive attitude to it within the conservative tradition prior to him?

This takes us to one of the most interesting figures in this development – Gustav Hugo. A sociological analysis of his doctrine will provide us with an answer to this question. Hugo was fifteen years older than Savigny.[303] Such generational difference was particularly significant in those years. Hugo was twenty-five in the year of the French Revolution, and had thus experienced the ascent of the whole line of development from Enlightenment to revolution during his intellectually most impressionable years; and though he emulated his father's arch-conservatism after only a few years of *Sturm und Drang*, he nevertheless came to know the revolutionary world-view during its most virulent epoch. Savigny was only ten years old at the time of the French Revolution, and so by no means as yet open to political impressions. In 1799, the year of the great style-change in German thinking, he visited the University of Jena, among others, in the course of the travels which were then customary between the years as student and as university teacher. Here he gained a personal impression of the younger generation, and especially of Schelling;[304] and at the age of twenty-nine, approximately the same age at which Hugo experienced the French Revolution, he experienced the fact of the Battle of Jena. The difference between the decisive experiences of their most impressionable years brings with it a difference in the makeup of the two types of conservatism which they severally represent. In this way, they are at the same time symbols of two stages of the same current; the change in destinies within the same life-space manifests itself in the difference between the attitudes to life of two generations.

The common element connecting their style of thought is first the sense of history already present in Hugo (although it is not yet possible to speak of historicism in this case), and, secondly, the affirmation of positive law as against the logical constructs of natural law, even though positive law (the law of the people) means something quite different for Savigny than for Hugo, and even though Hugo's attitude to natural law differs from that of Savigny in many details.

Characteristic for Hugo, in this regard, is a unique relativism which can be found, for instance, in his *Lehrbuch des Naturrechts als einer Philosophie des positiven Rechts, besonders des Privatrechts* (Textbook of Natural Law as a Philosophy of Positive Law, and Especially Private Law). Contemporaries had already called his manner of investigating the problem an '*indifferentist*' *natural law*. And although he preferred it to be known as a 'critical' natural law,[305] it seems that his opponents had sized him up better than he had done himself. What is the pivot of his way of thinking, and what is its technique? To summarise it briefly: *he relatives positive law (though in fact unintentionally) by reference to natural law, while at the same time relativising positive law by reference to natural law*. In this way, both are devalued for him and yet both remain. This is a technique which characterises most positions of synthesis and which finds its most sublime expression in Hegel's unified concept of negation and enhancement (*Aufheben*). But how does this happen in Hugo, and what does it achieve?

On the other hand, he does not deny that man is a rational being, and he is always somehow presupposing reason when he exposes one thing or another in history as irrational.[306]

The rational idea of a universal condition of right is everywhere to be found, albeit in the way in which rational ideas are to be found in passionate men, as legend from the past or as hope for the future.[307]

Or just before that:

The condition of right which is prescribed to us by reason ought by all means to be universal, and all rational beings who could do one another harm ought to be subject to a common highest authority.[308]

Or:

There is also something in every constitution which bears a great resemblance to the division into many constitutions, since it

too is an isolation, and one among members of one and the same
constitution, and since it is also commonly viewed as something
given *a priori*, although it too is nothing more than an
imperfection of the one constitution under a single authority.
This refers to the 'mine' and 'thine', according to which the
individual may possess many an external thing which happens to
belong to his sphere of operation.[309]

He is thus relativising private property here and holding it to be
contrary to reason; and in just this way his retention of the concept
of reason found in natural law, which he does not actually intend,
serves to relativise everything in history as contrary to reason.
Obversely, however, he causes the demands of reason to lose their
point by showing that they cannot be carried into effect. He
relativises the critical point, the actual sense of every demand in
the name of natural law, by showing that anything and everything
has been possible in history and has been equally subject to being
presented as rational. His aim is to show along this way that
natural law and reason cannot be touchstones for concrete
decisions. In a note, he refers to a work by Schmalz, in which we
can read: 'The law of nature can and ought to be invoked in courts
of law as little as the metaphysical doctrine of physical bodies ought
to be invoked in factories.'[310] This is precisely the view of Hugo;
he sees it as the sole use of his inquiry, 'to become secure against
false doubts, and not to be perplexed by allegations that something
is contrary to reason.'[311]

This state of spiritual suspension, which enables him to do away
with natural law by means of positivity, but, on the other hand,
also lets him relativise all stages of history, including the positivity
of his own times, by reference to the demands of reason, makes
available to him an immense freedom of movement, an independent judgement in all things, an interest in history. This relativism
also serves as a preliminary step towards the fruitful relativism of
historicism which, in its turn, relativises all ages in a similar way.
At least so far as we can tell from his *Lehrbuch des Naturrechts*, a
genuine historicism does not as yet grow out of Hugo's position,
but only comparative *historical investigation*. His book is in fact
one of the precursors of all those treatises which assemble their
materials from all corners of the world (disregarding the historical
locations of the individual objects) and work through this material
by means of a comparative method.

The free range of his vision lets him be more radical than the
radicals and more conservative than the conservatives of his time.
He is not compelled, like the bourgeois revolutionaries, to uphold
the rationality of private property. There are passages in his book

which surpass the most trenchant socialist critiques (he cites Rousseau, Diderot, Mably, among others, whom he obviously knew well).[312] As a sampling, we quote a few passages:

> Poverty is the most stringent prohibition of books. Many a virtue is so easy for the wealthy man and so hard for the poor that it is no less surprising when a rich man commits base acts in order to put aside another hundred Thalers per year, than when a poor one resists the temptation to help himself out of the most extreme necessity by some act of wickedness, or at least to appropriate illegally some portion of the surplus of the rich, in order to satisfy urgent needs.[313]

Or further on:

> Among the lower orders, young people of different sexes often share common sleeping places until quite late. This leads quite frequently to immoral intimacies. This is doubtless why such sleeping together has been prohibited, which is undeniably much easier than supplying the poor with more beds.[314]

But there are also in his writings such contrary passages as the following concerning slavery:

> The right to kill, mishandle, and maim *servi* is not substantial, and even if it occurs, it is not much worse than what the poor put up with, and, as far as the body is concerned, it is not as bad as war, from which *servi* must, as such, everywhere be exempt. Beauty is, if anything, more likely to be found in a Circassian slave-girl than in a beggar-girl. The danger of overwork arises at least as easily for the bitterest poverty.[315]

In and of itself, this would be a state of suspension without decision, in which one does away with one point of view by means of another, plays pro and con off against one another. And he does in fact do this inasmuch as he lets both points of view be valid for every institution, only to then nevertheless add his own solution, as a third. We must at least once follow word for word how this happens, and therefore cite the resolution of the problem of slavery which we have just discussed:

> *Decision*: Having balanced all these grounds off against one another, we are doubtless also entitled to the judgement which is already indicated in general terms and which will be encountered in quite a few doctrines: there is a condition in which even bondage is better as provisional right than its opposite, and that is when a positive law as it *happens in fact to be* contains bondage as a material part. Under such conditions,

reason commands us gradually to ameliorate the harshness of
bondage, but not to end it all at once.[316]

It is evident that the preponderant weight in this case (and in all
others) inclines, for Hugo, towards the established positivity of
that which exists (ameliorated by a moderate reformism).[317] We
ask ourselves what this technique of thinking, viewed sociologically, may mean, where it arises, and how its form of thinking is
connected with its social location.

Hugo represents, in his own distinctive way, a synthesis which
comes about – and can only do so – when two social worlds
confront one another within the same historical space, and where
the newly emerging world already has reality, so that its contents
and methods of thinking infiltrate its opposite.

Hugo was a conservative but had already absorbed French
cultivation in his youth.[318] Nevertheless he made his choice in
favour of the existent, in the guise of a very moderate reformism.

One could call this position and this stage of conservatism a
disillusioned conservatism, whose pathos resides in its intellectual
honesty, but whose commitment can be characterised by the 'how
it happens to be' which recurs in Hugo at every decisive point.[319]
From this we can glean something of decisive importance for our
further investigation. Within a social and spiritual development
which flows in more than one stream, syntheses will recurrently
become possible, making a contribution to the development of our
thinking which it is hard to overestimate, but these syntheses can
never float above the social positions (above the atmosphere, so to
speak), but are always effected from a specific position.[320]

For every synthesis, then, we must ask: *what is its starting point?*
from where is it effected? If we ask this question about Hugo, we
can say that he has his starting point in the life-impulses of the
ancien régime, but that he works into this the most essential parts
of the contemporary left-wing critique.[321] What applies to Hugo
with regard to contents, in this connection, is seen again in the
forms of his manner of thinking. The mutual 'relativisation' of two
ways of thinking is an expression of this situation. While
revolutionary natural law views the existent from the norm, the
conservative thinking of someone like Möser views the norm from
the existent, deprecating it as mere abstraction. Both happens in
Hugo, as we have seen: the norm is relativised by reference to
positivity, and positivity by reference to the norm. And by this
means we encounter one of the essential elements of a *conception
of reality* which must be recorded as a distinct type alongside of
those which we have already considered (e.g., reality=pure

experience; reality=the *transcendent* dynamics of the tendencies upon which history rests, etc.).

Reality is here the mutual negation and enhancement (*Aufheben*) of tendencies which are actually working against one another *in the empirical* world and which are in fact already negating and enhancing (*aufheben*) one another in that world. This kind of thinking rejects any mode of knowing which goes beyond the immediately given actuality, which seeks to comprehend the true nature of things in a transcendent factor (e.g., world-spirit, process of production, pure experience), which can only be done by breaking through immediate causalities, by letting the 'relevance' of the empirical actuality to the real development of things be determined in indirect ways (like the Hegelian category of 'mediation'). Even in Hegel, the empirical phases relativise one another only in order to be taken up (*aufgehoben*) within a dynamic totality (transcendent *vis-à-vis* the empirical).[322] In Hugo, it is *antithetical points of view* that mutually relativise one another, and these are then left in this state. All of reality consists, in this view, of an inert amassment of actualities, which are indeed repeatedly measured by a standard which transcends them, but this 'actuality' is only an indifferent manifold, much too inert really to move towards ends. It is quite possible to improve this or that, but one must leave everything in its subsisting framework. For this sense of life, then, *reality* does involve the existence of utopian goals, but these are not binding, because all being is ultimately indifferent to them, and their contests cannot be fixed. Norms serve to help understand what exists. Norms and demands can also, seen from the other side, be comprehended from the standpoint of the existing as integrally part of what is.[323] 'To be positive' and 'to see truly' accordingly comes down to balancing these two spheres of the existent off against one another.

This is where one of the important components of the conception of reality which we want to call a 'realism of disillusionment' (*Desillusionsrealismus*) has its origins. Such realisms mostly arise in periods where two or more social strata confront one another within the same historical space and in a form in which the world-views belonging to them are already present in equal weight. An incorporation of the opponent's insights within one's own system begins at this point, and one considers one's thinking to be 'realistic', 'sober', and 'free of illusions' when one balances two or more of the perspectives present in the life-space off against one another, thereby relativising them with respect to each other. Here value-freedom, the absence of utopia, become, as it were, the test of objectivity and proximity to reality. Hugo reaches this stage by virtue of the fact that he renders the revolutionary-bourgeois experience of reality (according to which the world develops in the direction of the norm) impotent and denigrates the norm itself as lacking in force and contents, while he simultaneously relativises the contents of his own world, for which he stands, by reference to these same norms.

According to the bourgeois sense of reality, actuality is itself inert, but there is nevertheless ceaseless progress towards the norm. That Hugo's sense of reality shows such a striking resemblance to the realism of disillusionment prevalent today arises from the fact that he was able to render the fundamental design of the original bourgeois-revolutionary sense of reality ineffective by depriving the normative element of its force. But in this, favoured by his specific social location, he implemented the same measure as did later 'arrived' bourgeois-rationalist thinking, when it itself also relativised this same utopian thrust. Naturally, in keeping with the changed constellation, this actually happened quite differently than with Hugo, since here bourgeois thinking took over from socialism the point of view of sociological critique. The view which socialism, starting from its utopia, had cast upon social factors saw the whole social process as a mechanism and intellectual contents as nothing more than functions of this process. Bourgeois sociology – i.e., the sociology which arose in direct continuity with Enlightenment thinking – adopted this angle of vision and, with one move, relativised its own contents as well as the socialist ones as equally utopian, while it simultaneously constituted this reciprocal self-relativisation of views as the criterion of truth.

*One of the outstanding representatives of this position is Max Weber, who is placed historically at a stage very similar to that of Hugo in his time. While Hugo is a representative of the *ancien régime* who works the bourgeois critique into this standpoint in such a way that the two world-views negate and enhance one another (*aufheben*), Max Weber is without doubt the most important representative of 'late bourgeois' thinking, and he, in turn, works the socialist critique into his own position. We can only show a few of the analogies to Hugo, which must naturally be treated with care. The illumination of facts as by twilight comes back in his work, when he soberly exposes the mechanisms of the world with the help of the socialist critique ('disenchantment of the world'), but at the same time, in this structurally like Hugo, relativises the socialist utopia as a mere utopia, by means of the bourgeois counter-critique, just as Hugo had once relativised natural law. Similar, too, is the fact that his concept of reality consists in the continuous mutual negations of volitions which are in constant conflict, a conception which Weber expressed in his portrayal of the world as unresolvable conflict between antagonistic gods. The similarities in method include his deliberate refusal to abandon positivism, his distaste for theoretical constructions of totality, and his coming to a position, just like Hugo in the work we have analysed, where he proceeds comparatively.[324]*

Such reciprocal relativisation illuminated reality as by twilight. That this process is not restricted to the play of thought but rather suffuses the most spontaneous sense of reality of the time is shown by nothing so well as by contemporary art, whose realism has this twilit illumination as its most essential component: 'the flight from pathos', 'that everyone is right in his fashion', are the leitmotifs of this way of looking at things, which believes itself to be nearing reality when it destroys all compositional lines (linear precision being possible only when the consciousness of norms is wholly intact), and which considers itself to have arrived at the reality it seeks when it illuminates every object from many sides.

In this connection, it may be noted that the sociology and philosophy whose thinking derive from Enlightenment rationalism have kept much in the axiomatics of its thinking intact. Decisive among these is nominalism, (1) whose constructions always take their start in the discrete individual, (2) which is logically committed to the level of immediate causalities, despised by opponents as 'abstract', and (3) which rejects all categories of 'totality', etc. At the same time, this thinking also incorporates varied elements originating in subsequent developments in the natural sciences and in positivism, while always preserving the framework of thinking just depicted. To subject these to analysis, however, will only be possible when we come to the historical setting in which these elements arose. We anticipate these later themes here only in order to gain a better understanding of Hugo's twilit view.

We return to Hugo after this digression. How far Hugo progresses in the incorporation of enlightened revolutionary thinking can best be illustrated by the way in which he works a typical Enlightenment argument into his construction of the world, namely his specification of the functions of '*usage*'. If Hugo is interrogated as to why he unconditionally upholds every actually established positivity in spite of his passionate contempt for all positivity, the ultimate justification is 'usage' (*Gewohnheit*).†

§91[325] bears the heading, 'Justification of this imperfect state of things', and it runs:

> The only thing that justifies this imperfection is that the present state of things, usage, decides in its favour. No single individual and no single people can think, with any prospect of success, of coercing others to adhere against their will to a uniform state of the law. If it is true, as Kant well says, that this differentiation and isolation is by no means 'peremptorily right', reason [!] nevertheless commands that we submit to it, respect it as 'provisionally right', as a remedy against an entirely lawless condition.

This heightened significance of 'usage' is already shown to be present in nature in the introductory parts of his juristic anthropology (which prefaces his overall inquiry in an interesting way, in the manner of a propaedeutic foundation).[326] Now such a manner of arguing is part of the basic store of enlightened revolutionary thinking, which is also familiar with a clinging to the long-established; but it assesses such clinging to the past as a negative element.[327] In Hugo's thinking, such clinging to the long-established receives a conservative positive twist, to the extent that it becomes grounds for justifying anything that is established. This may be said to be the first step in the development of conservative historicism.

We find the other source in Möser, where, right in the midst of the Enlightenment, a love for the past which is not yet bygone simply grows out of experience close to the soil and out of unmediated life. Here, history and its characteristic of gradual coming into being are no longer merely acknowledged in resignation, but they are already experienced with empathy. But there is as yet nothing of a romanticising, 'mystifying' trait; we are

---

†The German word '*Gewohnheit*' does not distinguish between 'habit' and 'custom'. 'Usage' is offered in the hope that it is a term which similarly leaves open the two possibilities, although it is not wholly satisfactory for either. The issue is worth noting because the contrast between the two concepts figured importantly in the literature to which Mannheim refers. 'Habit' was a key concept for David Hume, for example, greatly admired by the French *philosophes* of the Enlightenment, and Hugo's analysis of legal anthropology, quoted below, also clearly has 'habit' rather than 'custom' in view. The undifferentiated German term serves important rhetorical purposes in the ideological arguments under review but cannot be altogether effectively kept in view in English. Where the juristic expression '*Gewohnheitsrecht*' is employed, the ordinary translation of 'customary law' will be used. The fact that most of the sources discussed are juristic texts offers another argument against resolving the terminological difficulty in favour of 'habit'. *Trs*.

already aware that Möser always soberly inquires after 'reasonable grounds'.

If we now return to Savigny and remind ourselves that we left him in order to inquire into his purpose in abstracting the pure element of unconsciousness from Schelling's philosophy, we find that we now have the answer. It serves to hypostatise, but at the same time also to deepen the argument from usage. We asked ourselves further how conservatism stood towards 'positive law' prior to Savigny, and received the following answer by way of our analysis of Hugo: he tried to justify it by means of an argument from usage, while in a position of disillusioned resignation. For Savigny, the place which had been occupied by usage in Hugo – the same logical location, as it were – is filled by the 'silently working forces' of the people. Instead of resignation, we find empathetic, affirmative, content-rich experience.

What is the source of this *élan* in the conservative current? Whence this turn from Hugo to Savigny? This question gives point to the suggestions with which we introduced Hugo's doctrine and shows the significance of the problem of generations. Between Hugo's and Savigny's ways of reasoning we have the defeat at Jena, foreign rule, and the wars of liberation, which transformed theoretical discussion into real discussion and a national uprising (led by the nobility) into reality. Hugo lived to experience this uprising, and even lived long afterwards,[328] but the difference in generations prevented him from assimilating this complete transformation of the ways of thinking and experiencing. Hugo's book, which would have had resonance if conditions had remained calm, was not understood by the new generation.[329]

This also identifies the social and political constellation under which the 'element of the unconscious', 'the idea of the people' (*Volksgedanke*) entered into romanticism. The experience of unconscious creative forces existed in this setting not only as an experience which concealed (although it was that as well) but also as something which could be positively experienced. But no one can see and experience this, as is also true for the positive element in revolution, who is not situated, with regard to social location and generation, at the appropriate place in the course of history, at the point where these forces are coming into being. It is not just the 'weave' of history that reveals itself only to certain 'standpoints of experience'. The 'depths' of historical growth can also only be experienced from a place which is adequate to them. To this must be added, that these 'depth-contents', these 'ultimate substances' are not always the same.

*While analysing the differences between Hugo's and Savigny's

179

ways of thinking, it may be possible to shed some additional light on a problem of more general importance. In periods like ours, in which self-reflectiveness and a many-sided relativism are reducing themselves to absurdity, as it were, a fear grows up instinctively about where all this will lead. How can relativism be overcome in history? If we can learn from the example just analysed above, the answer would have to be: not by way of immanent theory, but by way of collective fate – not by a refusal to think relativistically, but by throwing new light on new, emerging contents. Here the fact of the generational growth of culture is of immense significance. Although considerable individual latitude is possible, it can be phenomenologically ascertained that the newly arising faith has quite a different character in the most recent generation than it has in those who, coming from an earlier generation, do not take part in this upsurge.[330*]

There are differences between the conservatism of Hugo and that of Savigny other than the difference between the conception of 'usage' and that of 'silently working forces'. And we must, so far as is feasible, try to understand even this difference on the basis of the overall historical and sociological constellation.

(1) Hugo still had a generally applicable system of valid right, thought out in the manner of natural law, which he doubtless struggles against but keeps applying. If not, where would he have got the judgement that all positivity is bad? While he relativises this system in its virulence and blunts its effectiveness, he retains it nevertheless.[331] This natural law disappears completely in Savigny and does not even persist as standard. Its last remnants survive in the recognition that there is a type of thinking, serving to conceal and operating with defined concepts, which lives out its life divorced from the living law. The disappearance of natural law, even in a resigned and relativised guise, is to be explained by the fact that the criterion of truth (which continues to reside in natural law for Hugo, despite all relativisation) has shifted to the sphere of the silently working forces for Savigny. The place of static, speculative natural law is taken by the spirit of the people.[332]

(2) Hugo carried out his deprecation of natural law in order to hypostatise the actually existing positive law. Savigny similarly destroyed speculative natural law for the sake of another one. But this is not positive law, since Savigny opposes that as well. He deprecates natural law, rather, for the sake of the people's law, the customary law. The question then is why Savigny replaces positive law with customary law, or at least views the whole of the law on

the basis of customary law. Why does he relativise, as it were, the law posited by the governing authorities? Even if we were not acquainted with the historical facts, the analysis of meaning that we have undertaken should point us to a correct imputation of the source.

Hugo's conservatism is decidedly submissive to the governing authorities.[333] He is striving to legitimate positive law in their interest.[334] In Savigny, the estate-minded basic design of pitting customary law against bureaucratic absolutism survives, but at the same time there is awake in him the newly roused patriotic opposition which rebels against an imposed foreign law (*Code Napoléon*). Now that the problem has been narrowed down and we must inquire whether this imputation on the basis of meanings can be causally explained on the basis of individual fates as well as the parentages and traditions of those who put forward these meanings, it is in order to ask, 'who in fact were Hugo and Savigny?'

Hugo comes from a prosperous family of officials; his father was a judicial and administrative official in Baden.[335] His conservatism is a bureaucratic conservatism, whose be-all and end-all is the positivity of law. Savigny's family belongs to the imperial nobility of knights. His ancestors and their castle can be traced back to the middle of the fourteenth century, in their location on a small tributary of the Moselle[336] – hence the germs of estate-minded thinking, which survive despite his own later induction as official (we are thinking of his professorship). Savigny does not absolutise positive law; he lives in quiet, moderate opposition to it. He absolutises the customary sources of law, the estate element, at every point. We have seen how estate-reasoning already appeared at that time, in part on genuine experiential grounds and in part on ideological ones, under the banner of the nation and no longer as particularist reasoning, but nevertheless continued to argue in accordance with the old way of thinking. For Savigny represents, like Adam Müller at the stage of his *Elemente*, a synthesis of 'estate' and 'romantic' elements, although of a different variety.

Whence, then, does the difference between them originate? Before answering this, we must bring out what they have in common. Adam Müller belonged, like Savigny, to the circle of the romantics. Savigny was not only very friendly with the romantics but also connected with two of the outstanding members by ties of family.[337] But if we want to search out the community of spirit among the nobility, romantic literati, and a part of officialdom in its sociological place, as it were, we must consider the '*Christlich-Deutsche Tischgesellschaft*' ('Christian-German Dining Society'), where one can find the chief representatives united in sociable intercourse. Achim von Arnim and Adam Müller had founded this society, to gather fortnightly for cheer and sociability, and to be restricted in membership to 'eminently respectable' and 'suitable' people.[338] The circular says about this: 'By this eminent respectability, the society understands that a man is a man of honour, good morals, and Christian birth, and by this suitability, that he is no dull philistine, since such are forever banned.'[339]

Looking at the signatures of those who entered themselves as members, it is evident that the membership was recruited from the circles of the hereditary nobility, the military, the bourgeois elite, educated artists, literary men, officialdom, and aristocratic writers (H. v. Kleist and A. v. Arnim),[340] and what interests us most of all is that Müller and Savigny are included in the circle. Savigny had taken his doctorate at Marburg, after the study-trip mentioned earlier, and had at first taught there. After a journey to Paris and a teaching post in Landshut, he was called to the University of Berlin in 1810; and this was precisely the time of the founding of the Christian-German Dining Society. A. von Arnim, Müller, Hauptmann v. Röder I, and Professor von Savigny were elected to its 'legislative committee'.

This society was the spiritual connection that bound them together. The ideas which are especially prominent in the ceremonial songs have to do with Christianity, loyalty to the king, the safeguarding of historically vested rights, liberation of the fatherland from foreign rule, and devotion to Queen Louise.[341] The society was anything but a scientific academy. To the accompaniment of beer and joking, there was conversation about the questions of the day; and the high point of each meeting was a short talk (consisting mostly of anecdotes) given by 'the speaker', followed by a sort of half-humorous and half-serious discussion.[342]

Here, then, we see the world of estates and romanticism in fellowship, we see Müller and Savigny in the same circle. And what is common in their forms of thinking and their contents, here accounted for by external factors, does indeed extend deep into the work of both. The express rejection of natural law, the sense for what pertains to the old estates, the emphasis on the historical, on nationalism, etc. can be found in both. The difference between their ways of thinking consists rather in the fact that in the *Elemente*[343] the praise of estates (or of the nobility) lies openly on the surface, while in Savigny, the origins in the old estates, the membership in the nobility, manifests itself rather in the structural forms of his thinking. (One need only recall the phenomena analysed earlier, such as elucidation, the aversion to abstract systems, the experience of silent growth, etc.) Savigny was no politician. But despite his often noted and mostly well-observed quietism, he lived instinctively secure within the way of thinking and the traditions of his origins; this is the source of his unconscious, spontaneously adequate response to events, and this is also the source of the applicability and timeliness of his conservatism. If he was not, like the British aristocracy, progressive, in the sense of anticipatory preemption of changes, neither was he reactionary, like the Prussian Junkers of the Mark, nor overbearing, like the ambitious Müller, who was forced to outbid even the Junkers. The difference, then, is that Savigny's programme is a subdued evolutionary one, while the *Elemente* have a reactionary ring.

This is reflected as much in the most abstrusely logical categories as it is evident in the theses expressly upheld. While Müller, more or less openly, seeks a return to or an extension of[344] the Middle Ages, nothing could be further from Savigny than turning back the wheel of history, despite his preference for the time of the origins. He writes:

> But there is a blind overestimation of the past, among those on the other side, which is almost more dangerous than this vain presumption [of progress], because it altogether paralyses the forces of the present; and the historical sense must guard against this as well, if it is put into action and not merely in words.[345]

He is thus a conservative evolutionist, for whom the evolutionary emphasis is laid on the preservation of the original substance. The acceptance of new elements is reconcilable with this as well as that the possessions of strangers are considered, once assimilated, as national possessions. Nothing expresses this difference more clearly than the fact that Savigny was a scholar of the Roman law while Müller thundered against its reception.[346]

The very same difference revealed in their substantive theses is repeated in their conceptions of the distinctive character of historical study and in their concepts of knowledge. For Müller, history is an unceasing and productive conflict among estates, while for Savigny, what comprises the productive element in history is that the inherited substance should elucidate itself in its encounter with concrete actuality.

> The reflective activity of every age must however be dedicated to getting to the heart of all this matter, transmitted out of an inner necessity, renewing it, and keeping it fresh.[347]

This also makes understandable the difference between their *concepts of knowledge*, which is further evidence for the fact that the forms of thinking develop in close connection with the

183

contents, and that it is in the final analysis not possible to view them 'in themselves'. While Müller's concept of knowledge culminates in the term 'mediation', for Savigny true knowledge consists in what we have called 'elucidation'. All political knowledge is purely activist for Müller, mediating between living polarities, mediating the conflict. Savigny's 'elucidation' is a peaceable immersion in the substances alive within us, a discarding of alien matter and alien postures of thought. And this way of knowing fails to be contemplative only to the extent that the thinking involved is not conceived of as speculative either, but as something that can only be accomplished in living community and with regard to concrete individual cases. A 'theoretical subject as such', detachable from the whole human being, would be unthinkable for either.

The same contrast between the activist and the more nearly genetic elements manifests itself in the fact that, as we saw, Müller never altogether dispensed with the rationalist element in his thinking (he tries to get at the liveliness of life by putting the logic of reasoning in motion), while Savigny already conceived of the vital principle in life in quite a different way. What is essential is not its characteristic *quality of fluidity* but its unconscious evolutionary nature. In the one place, conflict, in the other, an unfolding; in the one place, extending the capabilities for rationalisation, in the other, a far-reaching irrationalisation of thinking itself. One way out of Müller's position leads, as we saw, to the dialectic. What has come of Savigny's method of elucidation is the richly elaborated method for subjecting cultural formations to elucidative *interpretation*, which sustains all of the cultural sciences of the present day. To find an epitome of this method, it is only necessary to think of the distinctive features of method in interpretive art history.

But what is the source of the difference between Müller and Savigny, if both represent, from a sociological point of view, the same synthesis between romanticism and the estates? Two fairly important external differences should be considered first of all. Müller wrote his book at the time of greatest unrest, when the nobility was being attacked from above and from below and when the first signs of estate opposition to Hardenberg could be felt. Immediately after the appearance of the book, when open opposition broke out, Müller became a secret ally of the Marwitzes and of the Junkers of the Mark.[348]

When Savigny wrote his own book, the period of restoration was under way after the defeat of the enemy. The internal opposition was paralysed at first, and there had to be some readjustment. This was Savigny's moment. It is useful here to bring in Meinecke's argument that the national idea was bound to slip away from the state, as it were, and to hide itself behind 'the people', in a land which was powerless in external affairs, as Germany had come to be, and whose rights were to be guaranteed by the guardianship of the Holy Alliance.[349] The external political constellation will also have played its part in the emergence, but especially in the reception of this particular version of the concept of 'popular spirit'. When one combines all these factors, the overarching reason for the differences subsisting between Müller's and Savigny's ways of thinking gradually becomes clear, for all the individual events just reviewed took place and had their effects in the element of a single overall sociological constellation.

Granted these individual historical facts, it is nevertheless possible and indeed necessary to ask why Müller attached himself specifically to the Junker opposition, and why Savigny arrived at his conception specifically at the beginning of the restoration period. The ultimate meaning of individual facts can appear only when they are grasped as stages in the emergence of more comprehensive factors. We are brought close to the solution when we reduce the differences between Savigny and Müller to the single point that Savigny represented a *silent opposition* of the estate element while Müller stood for a more radical and straightforward rebellion of this spirit. Why Müller serves as representative of a 'more straightforward rebellion against rationalism and despotism' has already been explained on the basis of his sociological position. He belonged to that 'unattached intelligentsia' which became counter-revolutionary at that time and which initially sought shelter with the newly aroused nobility, and with its most radical wing at that. We have already indicated at the beginning of our historical account the things that contributed to this radical loosening, if only for a short time, of the alliance with the monarchy. The whole of the conservative movement treated so far stands in the sign of this partial loosening. It revives the repressed ambitions of the estates, along with the corresponding forms of thinking.

Savigny, however, represents an altogether different wing of the nobility from that of the Junkers of the Mark. Quite apart from his different descent – he was born in Frankfurt am Main, and his family, which came from Lothringia, emigrated to Germany in 1630[350] – we must in his case consider not only the traditions of the nobility but also those of officialdom.[351] This brings us to the sociological analysis of officialdom, whose significance for the sociology of intellectuality in Germany is of special weight.

Schmoller praises as the greatest achievement of the Hohenzoller dynasty that they were first able to create an anti-feudal officialdom within a feudal society, and then, through the army and the academy which qualified nobility for office, to convert the nobility from being a major enemy into being once again a prime support of the crown.[352]

Frederick the Great already selected higher officials exclusively from among the nobility (only cabinet councillors and lower officials were drawn from the bourgeoisie).[353] Such an officialdom, always newly amalgamating aristocratic-estate and bourgeois mentalities, was of enormous importance and capable of radiating influence in many directions. The synthesis between bourgeois and estate mentalities welded together in this way paralysed the antithetical tendencies of movement of the initially contrasting mentalities, and it moulded them into a new, autonomously moving tendency.

They come together in objective tasks, in a mental attitude required by the matter at hand. The mentality of officials is reactionary only in exceptional cases; its centre of gravity is situated so that it is moderately progressive; it inclines towards revising everything, through administrative channels. It never seeks to overthrow: the whole system is not to be overthrown, but, within the system, it is always prepared for corrective measures. If these are, so to speak, the natural tendencies in the mentality of officials, coming out of the range of tasks and social location within the state, then all the other modifications as well as deviations can only be derived from the various specific constellations.

Among these suggestions (which will concern us in connection with Hegel in more detail later) the only thing important for us right now is that it is quite evident that during the period in question the officials' mentality was not left unaffected, and that the elements of bourgeois rationalism and estate-irrationalism, which had been happily welded together until then, began to diverge, with each of the amalgamated elements moving off in the direction of its own intrinsic dynamics.[354] Surprisingly at first, we see on the one hand spirits strongly moved by liberalism. It has already been remarked that it was mostly the higher officialdom which was influenced by Kraus, a follower of Adam Smith,[355] and that these Smithians (Kühne, Hoffman, Kessler) held on, especially in the finance section, until late into the period of restoration.[356] On the other hand, the estate-grounded elements[357] in Savigny's thinking indicate just how much these too had received, although a professor can admittedly be placed only at the outer edge of the officials' mentality. Insofar as one wants to

186

impute Savigny's spiritual makeup to its sociological sources, one can consider it as an estate-romantic mentality coming alive within the framework of the spirit of officialdom. The one form of the synthesis between the spirits of romanticism and the estates, which is reflected in Müller and v.d. Marwitz as two extreme examples and which failed to become wholly radical in fact only because the rebellion was peacefully put down, does not necessarily stop short at the higher interests of state. The romantic and estate elements as they have revived in Savigny, in contrast, may be said to be encapsulated within that which pertains to both bureaucracy and state. This can be seen right away in the fact that there is only silent opposition to be observed in him. The mentality of the official, which is most susceptible to the hypostatisation of the state,[358] announces its presence in Savigny in that it sets limits which appear self-evident to him. Savigny views positive law (bureaucracy) from the standpoint of customary law (estates), but he does not reject the former; he only asks that it systematise the customary law. Despite his aversion to systematisation, he does not repudiate codification. He merely wants to postpone it to the Greek kalends.

We have already shown the extent to which this silent opposition to bureaucracy, together with the stopping short of the final consequences, manifests itself in the forms of his thinking. We have shown with this, at least for these two positions, how far the different currents, even within the unity of conservative thinking, are connected with the social and spiritual structures that stand behind them. All this is not to say that we are to consider Savigny's achievement as nothing more than the sum of its sociological parts. The creative genius which reacts to the specifics of a situation, assimilates them, and creates something upon this foundation is an ultimate additional factor, more remarkable in this way than if it had been created in the empty spheres of 'ideality'.

We can give them some indirect indication of the characteristics of this creativity. Even if we grasped all of the components of his situation, we would not be able to predict Savigny's mental world and his forms of thinking. It is only when the completed work lies before us that we can make evident the extent to which – ranging even into the manner of thinking – the most important factors in the spiritual and social situation have been taken in and worked through.

The fact that all concrete thinking exists in historical time, in a determinate life-space and in a determinate situation, and that it is not indifferent to these, does not in the slightest diminish the spiritual significance of this thinking or its qualities as knowledge. This circumstance bestows on it, rather, the highest dignity and importance.[359]

[*Editors' Note*: The manuscript breaks off at this point. The last sentence reads:

> We now turn to Hegel, whose way into the common social and spiritual problem-constellation of German conservative thinking which we have been analysing represents a third type of this thinking. And we are right to expect that new light will also be shed on the ways we have already described from this attempt at a synthesis which somehow works its way through all of the problems of the time.

This final sentence is followed by a page introduced between the text and the notes of the manuscript, where Mannheim writes: 'The present work is only part of a still incomplete book; many an unevenness in exposition and treatment may be excused by this fact.']

Notes

1 **Editorial Note**:
Mannheim's 'Das konservative Denken', first published in 1927 in the *Archiv für Sozialwissenschaft und Sozialpolitik* ['Conservative Thought', *Essays on Sociology and Social Psychology*, ed. Paul Kecskemeti, London: Routledge & Kegan Paul, 1953], which is excerpted from the present work, contains an introduction in which Mannheim writes:

[The emergence of a specific conservative style of thought (although channelled into several tendencies) is one of the most cogent factors in the spiritual life of the first half of the nineteenth century in Germany.

The sociology of knowledge faces a series of tasks, in an inquiry with such an orientation in mind: to determine the specific *morphology* of this style of thought; to reconstruct its *historical* and *social roots*; to explore the *change of forms* in this style of thought *in relation* to the social fates of the *bearing groups*; to show its pervasiveness and sphere of influence in the whole of German intellectual life until the present. Here we highlight only a few groups of problems from such a more widely ranging context of inquiry and portray them as contributions to an overall solution . . .

Such a more widely reaching sociology-of-knowledge exploration of historical and political thought is necessary, for it alone puts us in the position to discern the formation of modern consciousness in conjunction with life in all its vitality. Philosophers and historians of ideas continue to portray the formation of thought as if it were a contexture which unfolds by its own inner logic – or, put more simply, as if the history of thought simply proceeded from one book to another. In contrast, the sociologist is intrigued by the opposite viewpoint: he seeks to show that even those works which originate in the scholar's closet, seemingly totally remote from the arenas of life (and, therefore, pretend to timelessness and spacelessness), are themselves part of a *more comprehensive* contexture of *experience* which reaches beyond them.

Just as language is not merely the language of the individual who happens to be speaking, but is something that arose behind his back, as it were, so the problem definitions, concepts, and categories, by way of which the individual approaches historical reality, are nothing but samples taken out of the fabric of experience which have become historical. These contextures of experience on their part, however, are nothing more than the results of preceding attempts by collective forces committed to historical development, to orient themselves in a world of forever changing social and spiritual realities.

The 'everyday experience of life' and the human sciences, which are very attuned to it, represent a very different type of knowledge than the knowledge of the 'exact' natural sciences, and it is very questionable whether their desire to embrace the paradigm of the natural sciences even makes sense. Do not the social and human sciences owe their powerful attractiveness precisely to their closeness to life? Are they not more subtle and penetrating precisely because all the points of view, perspectives, concepts, classificatory principles and categories with which they work originate as self-changing and transformative creations of life seeking clarity about itself?

We therefore have to be aware of all the historically variegated ways of thinking which active life itself produces. The wider implications of acquaintance with the sociologically investigated history of political thinking arise from the fact that it presents us with historical knowledge at every point at which the volitional impulses, otherwise latent, break through, where thinking becomes active and the formative powers reveal their social rootedness.

Every bit of political knowledge is certainly perspectivistic, a one-sided overstatement, but it too can only be overcome if we contrast the different biases and allow their mutual elucidation. In this sense a thorough combing through the different ways of thinking associated with the different standpoints also helps to *revise all those fundamental concepts and categories* by means of which we think of and investigate historical life today. Only such a comparison can reveal to us the extent to which perspectivism cannot be avoided in every bit of historical knowledge and where propagandist exaggeration, as it were, is in play.

In this task we must begin with *conservative thought*, because the modern perception of history was largely the creation of just this tendency, and because the most significant achievement of this style of thought is in our opinion to be sought precisely in the fact that here a transformation of the modern religious consciousness and of the other ways of thinking which were supplanted by modern rationalism was turned into an organon for comprehending the irrational elements in history. This is an achievement with which neither liberalism nor socialism would ever have concerned themselves had they remained faithful to their original impulse.

On the other hand, it is precisely in the conservative concept of history and in the whole categorical apparatus associated with it (which to a large extent permeates our writing of history) that there also reside biases which are bound to existence. It is for this reason that criticism becomes an ever more urgent issue for the historical human sciences. (*Archiv für Sozialwissenschaft und Sozialpolitik* (1927), 57: 68–142, 470–95).]

2 We use 'sociology of knowledge' (*Wissenssoziologie*), 'sociology of thinking' (*Denksoziologie*), 'sociology of cognition' (*Erkenntnissoziologie*) interchangeably since these differences may be neglected in our opinion so long as the epistemological problem is not introduced.

3 Heinrich Rickert, *Die Grenzen der naturwissenschaftlichen Begriffsbildung* [1902], Tübingen: J. C. B. Mohr, 1921; cf. also Wilhelm Windelband, *Präludien*, vols. 1–2, Tübingen: J. C. B. Mohr, 1911 (particularly 'Normen und Naturgesetze', 1882; 'Kritische oder genetische Methode?', 1885; 'Geschichte und Naturwissenschaft', 1884). A methodological investigation of the same question was initiated in the wake of Dilthey from a different perspective.

4 That is to say, this sharp contrast can only arise as a problem for methodological self-reflective consciousness once both a duality of attitude and a duality of ways of thinking have been apprehended and asserted in direct as well as in self-reflective experience. Even Windelband (*Lehrbuch der Geschichte der Philosophie*, 5th edition, Tübingen: J. C. B. Mohr, 1910, pp. 543 ff., S 45 'Natur und Geschichte') locates the beginnings of this contrast in French traditionalism.

5 We refer to a *style of thought* as distinct from the mere variety of schools of thought, when the perceptible differences in thinking do not merely turn on theoretical differences, but rather when differences in the comprehensive world-view underlie the theoretical differences which can be readily made apparent; and – more importantly – if we can establish a different set of mind and a different existential relation to the object of knowledge. The assumption here is that not all thinking is thinking in the same sense, but that hidden behind this homogenising and concealing concept are the most varied existential relations, for which thinking serves in the most varied ways, and further, *that all living thinking derives its distinctive make-up from this existential function*.

These, too, are differences which can be ignored by pure theory, but which the sociology of knowledge as the science of the existential connectedness of thinking must emphasise.

For want of a better expression we talk about a 'style of thought', whereby 'style' is a term taken from the history of art. Nothing is further from our minds than 'analogising' thinking with artistic creation. We can only learn something from the history of styles in so far as there are, in spite of the differences, also commonalities that are shared by the disciplines relating to intellectual and cultural history.

6 The analysis of meanings as well as the theory of the change of meanings represent a special problem for linguistics. Husserl's phenomenology has recently refined the method of the analysis of

meanings to the point of perfection. Yet in both cases it has constituted an end in itself. For our purposes it must become a research tool of the sociology of knowledge by way of which we can demonstrate the coherent change of the conceptual elements within the historical whole as it takes form.

7 Our distinction between 'adequate on the level of meaning' and 'causally adequate' agrees with the distinction made by Max Weber, *Wirtschaft und Gesellschaft*, Tübingen: J. C. B. Mohr, 1922, S7, p. 5, but it is not totally identical with it. [*Economy and Society*, ed. Guenther Roth and Claus Wittich, Berkeley Los Angeles, London: University of California Press, 1978, §7, p. 11.]

8 Cf. Wilhelm Dilthey, 'Das 18. Jahrhundert und die geschichliche Welt', *Deutsche Rundschau*, (1901) 108: 481–93.

9 Johann Eichner, 'Das Problem des Gegebenen in der Kunstgeschichte', *Festschrift für Alois Riehl. Von Freunden und Schülern zu seinem siebzigsten Geburtstag dargebracht*, Halle: M. Niemeyer, 1914, p. 203.

10 Karl Marx, 'Zur Kritik der Hegelschen Rechtsphilosophie', in Franz Mehring, ed., *Aus dem literarischen Nachlass von Karl Marx und Friedrich Engels 1841 bis 1850*, vol. 1, 4th ed., Berlin-Stuttgart: J. H. W. Dietz, 1923, pp. 389 ff. ['A Contribution to the Critique of Hegel's "Philosophy of Right",' in *Critique of Hegel's 'Philosophy of Right'*, ed. Joseph O'Malley, transl. Annette Jolin and Joseph O'Malley, Cambridge: Cambridge University Press, 1970, pp. 135 ff.]; Franz Mehring, *Geschichte der deutschen Sozialdemokratie*, vol. 1, Berlin-Stuttgart: J. H. W. Dietz, 1922, p. 72.

11 Cf. de Maistre: 'Nous ne voulons pas la contre-révolution mais le contraire de la révolution' [We do not want the counter-revolution, but the opposite of the revolution].

12 These ideological differences are certainly not yet adequately worked out. As soon as we have completed the task of characterising the distinctive character of German conservative thought in detail, we shall compare the different types of conservatism. The preceding assertion is insufficiently grounded as yet, although several previous investigations make it seem probable. Cf. Ernst Troeltsch, 'Der Historismus und seine Probleme', *Gesammelte Schriften*, vol. 3, Tübingen: J. C. B. Mohr, 1922; Ernst Troeltsch, *Naturrecht und Humanität in der Weltpolitik*, Berlin: Verlag für Politik und Wirtschaft, 1923; and Peter R. Rohden, 'Deutscher und französischer Konservatismus', *Dioskuren* (1924) 3: 90–138.

13 Otto Hintze, 'Das monarchische Prinzip und die konstitutionelle Verfassung', *Preussische Jahrbücher* (1911) 144: 387.

14 'England was the only country in which the caste system had been totally abolished, not merely modified'. (Alexis de Tocqueville, *L'ancien régime et la révolution*, 8th ed., Paris: C. Lévy, 1877, p. 125. [*The Old Régime and the French Revolution*, transl. Stuart Gilbert, Garden City, N.Y.: Doubleday Anchor, 1955, p. 82]).

15 Cf. on this problem Fritz Meusel, *Edmund Burke und die französische Revolution. Zur Entstehung historisch-politischen Denkens*

zumal in England, Berlin: Weidmann, 1913, pp. 13, 14, 143; Gottfried Salomon, *Das Mittelalter als Ideal der Romantik*, Munich: Drei Masken Verlag, 1922, pp. 47, 59. Cf. also Luckwaldt, *Mitteilungen des Institute für österreichische Geschichtsforschung* (1903) 24: 325 ff. Both are quoted in Meusel.

Even the social composition of these parties is different than it is in Germany. The Whigs became the party of the great traders, industrialists and landowners towards the end of the seventeenth century (cf. Felix Salomon, *Englische Geschichte von den Anfängen bis zur Gegenwart*, Leipzig: K. F. Köhler, 1923, pp. 134 ff.); hence, from the German perspective, this constitutes a 'conservative' stratum, and precisely because both parties were actually both 'conservative' and 'progressive' at the same time, we cannot make a strict ideological distinction between them. From our point of view, their similarity extends so far that only their firm clinging to Kingdom and Church can be regarded as the unchanging trait of the Tories (cf. Lord Hugh Cecil, *Conservatism*, Home University Library of Modern Knowledge, vol. 11, London-New York: Williams & Norgate, 1912, p. 41).

16 The Prussian Diet (*Vereinigter Landtag*) in 1847 may be regarded as a first beginning of conservative parliamentary party work.

17 Cf. Alfred W. D. von Martin, 'Weltanschauliche Motive im altkonservativen Denken', in Paul Wentzcke, ed., *Deutscher Staat und deutsche Parteien* (Festschrift in Honour of Friedrich Meinecke), Munich-Berlin: R. Oldenbourg, 1922, pp. 382 ff.

18 Cf. Fritz Meusel, *Edmund Burke und die französische Revolution*, p. 141; further Frieda Braune, *Burke in Deutschland*, Heidelberg: C. Winter, 1917.

19 Cf. Sir Ernest Barker, *Political Thought in England from Spencer to the Present Day*, New York: Holt & Co., 1915, pp. 161 ff. France also had a 'historical school' which was, however, something of an import (Cf. Gunnar Rexius, 'Studien zur Staatslehre der historischen Schule', *Historische Zeitschrift* (1911) 107: 497, 537 ff.). The party of the *Doctrinaires* Royer-Collard and Guizot, under the German influence and that of Burke, had attempted to legitimate this constitution by way of history. But this 'historicism' was neither genuine nor could it attain a consistent form in France, due to the structure of political development. This too has been convincingly shown by Rexius.

Troeltsch as well, in his *Naturrecht und Humanität in der Weltpolitik*, lays stress on this distinctive character of German spirituality.

20 The significance of such connections for the emergence of occidental science was also of interest to Max Weber. Cf. Max Weber, *Gesammelte Aufsätze zur Religionssoziologie*, vol. 1, Tübingen: J. C. B. Mohr, 1920, pp. 1 ff. More recently also Max Scheler, ed., *Versuche zu einer Soziologie des Wissens*, Munich-Leipzig: Duncker & Humblot, 1924.

21 On this see Karl Mannheim, 'Historismus', *Archiv für Sozialwissen-*

schaft und Sozialpolitik (1924) 52: 1–60 ['Historicism', *Essays on the Sociology of Knowledge*, ed. and transl. Paul Kecskemeti, London: Routledge & Kegan Paul, 1952, pp. 84–133.]; 'Das Problem einer Soziologie des Wissens', *Archiv für Sozialwissenschaft und Sozialpolitik* (1925) 53: 577–652 ['The Problem of a Sociology of Knowledge', *Essays on the Sociology of Knowledge*, ed. and transl. Paul Kecskemeti, London: Routledge & Kegan Paul, 1952, pp. 134–190.]; Alfred Weber, 'Prinzipielles zur Kultursoziologie', *Archiv für Sozialwissenschaft und Sozialpolitik* (1921) 47: 1–49.

22 Romanticism characteristically adopted the conception that coming into being is not governed by laws, and thus went beyond the Enlightenment conception of linear development. We shall discuss the emergence of this structure of thinking and its subsequent fate in greater detail at a later point.

23 This is presented here entirely schematically. As a result of our concrete investigation it will become evident that this schema is greatly in need of very precise differentiation in accordance with the particular constellations of historical factors.

24 Cf. Ludwig Bergsträsser, *Geschichte der politischen Parteien in Deutschland*, 2nd ed., Mannheim: J. Bensheimer, 1921, p. 8.

25 *Ibid.*, p. 22.

26 The following three ways of stating the problem are 'ideal-typical' cases. We therefore do not assert that exceptions and transitions cannot be established. But the exceptions can only really be comprehended and explained as exceptions in terms of particular constellations once the major ideal-typical tendencies have been worked out.

For example, the fact that enlightened absolutism was founded upon secularised natural law in order to preserve its autonomy from the Church is such an exception. In crisis situations, the monarchical principle nonetheless seeks refuge in a theological grounding; and precisely in Stahl we can observe that not even the historicist variant of conservatism legitimates rule (*Herrschaft*) in a sufficiently radical manner. It should also not be forgotten here that enlightened absolutism must be regarded as a progressive force.

27 Cf. my essay 'Das Problem einer Soziologie des Wissens', pp. 580 ff. ['The Problem of a Sociology of Knowledge', pp. 137 ff.], for more on the means derived from logic for 'relativising' the various definitions of issues in political struggle.

28 Here – where we are only concerned with the establishment of general trends – these examples too are cited as ideal-typical cases. Each specific concrete case should, of course, be analysed independently.

29 Note, for instance, the characteristic turn in the formulation of the question, 'how is an "exact" science possible?'

30 This is the intellectual position which the sociologist of knowledge as empirical researcher must adopt. Such an understanding of thinking does not imply relativism. But we do not need to elaborate this now, since we are side-stepping all epistemological questions here.

31 On this my essay 'Historismus', pp. 7 ff. ['Historicism', pp. 88 ff.].
32 Cf. Georg Lukács, *Geschichte und Klassenbewusstesein. Studien über marxistische Dialektik*. Berlin: Malik Verlag, 1923, pp. 125 ff. [*History and Class Consciousness. Studies in Marxist Dialectics*, transl. Rodney Livingstone, London: Merlin, 1971, pp. 113 ff.].
33 Cf. on this my analysis of Möser in Part III, Chapter 1.
34 It was already present in antiquity and the modern period merely took up the possibilities developed there. On this see Erich Frank, *Plato und die sogenannten Pythagoräer*, Halle a.d.S.: M. Neimeyer, 1923, pp. 143 ff.
35 'Whatever we may think, then, of the different roles in which men confront each other in such a society [Marx means the Middle Ages], the social relations between individuals in the performance of their labour appear, at all events, as their own personal relations, and are not disguised as social relations between things, between the products of labour.' Karl Marx, *Das Kapital* [1867], vol. 1, 9th ed., Hamburg: Otto Meissner Verlag, 1921, p. 44. [*Capital*, vol. 1, transl. Ben Fowkes, New York: Random House, 1977, p. 170].
36 On the strata behind the romantic movement cf. Gottfried Salomon, *Das Mittelalter als Ideal der Romantik*, pp. 118 ff. Cf. also Franz Oppenheimer, *System der Soziologie*, Allgemeine Soziologie, vol. 1, Jena: G. Fischer, 1922, pp. 3 ff.
37 Oppenheimer suggests the replacement of 'romanticism' by the term 'spiritual counter-revolution' (*System der Soziologie*, pp. 4 ff.) and explains its genesis in terms of Tarde's principle of '*imitation par opposition*'. There would be nothing wrong with this if romanticism had not had positive contents of its own rather than being mere negation, namely those preserved from past ages (Oppenheimer, incidentally, is aware of this). We must therefore distinguish between two factors in romanticism: firstly, a factor which gives romanticism the appearance of a spiritual counter-movement to the Enlightenment (it is determined in regard to all these points by the adversary against whom it struggles), and secondly, its function as heir of a style of thought and life which capitalism had pushed aside.
38 Cf. also Gottfried Salomon, *Das Mittelalter als Ideal der Romantik*, pp. 111, 188 ff.
39 *Ibid*.
40 A detailed analysis of this will follow later (Part III, Chapter 2).
41 One of the most important questions of the inquiry which follows is why Marxism was able to take up precisely the Hegelian line of historicism.
42 [Cf. Lord Hugh Cecil, *Conservatism*, pp. 9 ff.; as well as P. R. Rohden, 'Deutscher und französischer Konservatismus', pp. 94 ff.].
43 *Editorial Note*: The passage bracketed in the text has been taken from the *Archiv*-essay. It replaces the following passage contained in the *Habilitationsschrift*:
 [Our answer is: *Both exist* – a conservatism which can be regarded as by and large generally human, and a 'modern conservatism' which arose in a specific historical situation and which is part of a specific

tradition, possessing a very specific structure and form. If the term 'natural' were not so overburdened, the former type might be called 'natural conservatism', the latter 'modern conservatism'. We therefore prefer the expression *traditionalism*, frequently used by Max Weber, to signify the former phenomenon, and when we speak of conservatism we mean to signify a modern formation which differs from mere traditionalism in significant ways.

In this usage of traditionalism – where in its abstractness it does not mean anything but a vegetative clinging to tradition – it refers to an attitude which may well be assumed to be generally present and widely held.]

44 Cf. Max Weber, *Wirtschaft und Gesellschaft*, p. 19 [*Economy and Society*, p. 37]. That this traditionalism has nothing to do with the 'French traditionalism' of a de Maistre or de Bonald hardly needs to be emphasised.

45 On 'reactive behaviour' cf. Max Weber, *Wirtschaft und Gesellschaft*, p. 2 [*Economy and Society*, p. 4].

46 Even the *clinging to* a politically progressive programme is based on a form of traditionalism.

47 Cf. the article by Rackpfahl, 'Konservativ', in Paul Herre, ed., *Politisches Handwörterbuch*, Leipzig: K. F. Köhler, 1923.

48 *Ibid*.

49 [Cf. Lord Hugh Cecil, *Conservatism*, p. 64. The other term which characterises conservative party formation, 'legitimism', emerged late, at the Vienna Congress. On this see H. O. Meissner, *Die Lehre vom monarchischen Prinzip im Zeitalter der Restauration und des deutschen Bundes*. Untersuchungen zur deutschen Staat- und Rechtsgeschichte, ed. Otto v. Gierke, issue 122, Breslau, 1913, p. 116, note 2. On the term 'liberal', cf. Adalbert Wahl, 'Beiträge zur deutschen Parteigeschichte im 19. Jahrhundert', *Historische Zeitschrift* (1910) 104: 537–94. On the term 'reactionary' – for instance, in the sense of 'they are reactionary, they seek to turn back the wheel of history' (*Communist Manifesto*) – cf. *Politisches Handwörterbuch*]. Cf. also Oskar Stillich, 'Die Konservativen', in *Die politischen Parteien in Deutschland*, vol. 1, Leipzig: W. Klinkhardt, 1908.

50 Rather than discussing here all the attempts made in the study of parties (Rohmer, Abt, Treitschke and so on), we will confine ourselves to those which are relevant to our problematic. The difficulties inherent in the conceptual definition of parties are well treated in Alfred Merkel's excellent *Fragmente zur Sozialwissenschaft*, Strasbourg: K. J. Trübner, 1898, which represents a fresh attempt of coming to terms with the problem.

51 *Die gegenwärtigen Parteien in Staat und Kirche*, Berlin: W. Hertz, 1863.

52 The 'sociological' point of view is *not completely* alien to him, since he never fails to refer to the 'natural bearers' – as he calls them – of political ideas. However, he never goes beyond mentioning them.

53 Stahl, *Die gegenwärtigen Parteien*, p. 2. We are in complete agreement with the passage cited. It does not, however, do full

justice to Stahl's position. We intentionally leave unconsidered such passages as the following: 'Revolt means shaking off an existing rule, revolution means a reversal of the *relations of power* themselves: authority and law are now fundamentally and permanently subjected to men rather than being their superiors.' (*ibid*). We ignore such passages since in them his conservative theory of authority is already evident.

54 Stahl was a disciple of Schelling, and although he attacked Hegel, he nevertheless learned much from him.

55 This is also true for England which had, of course, experienced her revolution as early as the seventeenth century but had witnessed a more radical rift between the ideologies in her internal engagement with the French Revolution. The English Revolution occurred in a historical situation in which politics was still very much wrapped up in the religious problems of the Reformation period. Lord Hugh Cecil, *Conservatism*, pp. 393 ff., fixes 1790 as the date of the emergence of conservatism since it is the position taken *vis-à-vis* the French Revolution which first gave rise to distinct groupings.

56 Constantin Frantz, *Kritik aller Parteien*, Berlin: F. Schneider, 1862.

57 *Ibid.*, p. 16.

58 We cannot, however, go along with this talk about 'drives'.

59 *Ibid.*, p. 5.

60 Gustav Radbruch, *Grundzüge der Rechtsphilosophie*. Leipzig: Quelle & Meyer, 1914.

61 *Ibid.*, p. 96.

62 *Ibid.*, p. 97 [Mannheim's emphasis].

63 Cf. Felix Salomon, *Die deutschen Parteiprogramme* (Quellensammlung zur deutschen Geschichte, vol. 2) [1907], 2nd ed., Leipzig: B. G. Teubner, 1912, pp. VI ff.

64 Ludwig Bergsträsser, *Geschichte der politischen Parteien in Deutschland*, 1922, p. 5.

65 *Editorial Note*: The passages in square brackets are taken from the *Archiv*-essay. They replace the less detailed text contained in the *Habilitationsschrift*, which reads:

[That the course of history is increasingly borne by such comprehensive tendencies and counter-tendencies which are distinguished from the unmediated locus of everyday life, and which expressly constitute themselves in the name of progress or restraint, is initially due to the fact that the then existing manifold territorial and otherwise scattered units and the disconnected centres of life begin to grow together to a certain degree and to unite at a national level, but subsequently towards an even more comprehensive unit in the form of a social community sharing a common destiny.

And precisely because this multitude of individual nations, which becomes increasingly united in the sphere of culture, must each resolve the same fundamental social structural problems – viz., (a) the establishment of national unity, (b) the participation of the people in directing the state, (c) the incorporation of the state in the world economic order, (d) the solution of the social question – it is hardly surprising that in regard to this decisive issue, the spiritual cosmos becomes ever more divided and differentiated.

If, then, we ask ourselves why the specific phenomenon of 'modern conservatism' has emerged so late in history, our attention is drawn to the elaboration of the convergence of particular historical and sociological factors which constitute the precondition of modern conservatism.]

66 In the Middle Ages, too, there existed progressive centres, bearers of the dynamic principle: the towns. They were, however, still 'enclaves' within a larger whole. That they later were to become cells of growth for more comprehensive tendencies, does not alter the fact of their insularity. So far as we can judge, the international religious culture, as represented by the Church, does not have the same process-like and dynamic character, in which every tendency assumes a direct function which affects the whole.

There existed, furthermore, powerful obstacles militating against the formation of political parties both in the state of the feudal era, as well as in the time of the estates. Lamprecht sums it up as follows: 'The feudal state was unable to generate parties since it bound to the ruler, by way of the personal tie of the oath of fealty, those forces which were becoming effective within the state, each for itself and individually. From the point of view of the ruler, and thus from the viewpoint of the state, every party formation amongst the vassals therefore immediately appeared as factious and as constituting a threat to the state, as a form of factionalism. This point of view still holds for the "estates" since in this order too most members were, as vassals, tied to the sovereign by the oath of fealty.' (Karl G. Lamprecht, *Deutsche Geschichte*, Freiburg i.B.: H. Heyfelder, 1904, Supplement II, Part 2, p. 53).

67 On the increasing dominance of the economic element in modern party life cf. Emil Lederer, 'Das ökonomische Element und die politische Idee im modernen Parteiwesen', *Zeitschrift für Politik* (1911) 5. That the philosophical life of the mind is a function of politics becomes evident and enters consciousness in Germany only after 1840. With this, a tendency, which had existed already since the French Revolution, finally comes into the open: the division between styles of thought and world-views which run in accord with political polarities. In this sense we can already talk of conservative and liberal styles of thought in the first half of the nineteenth century in Germany, even though the corresponding political party formations are not yet present. During this epoch 'ideological' developments are, in Germany, antecedent to social and political developments, a fact which can be partly explained by the fact that important ideological stimuli and psychic and spiritual tendencies were adopted from the socially progressive West at a time when, sociologically speaking, the maturity of her own social organism was not yet adapted to these contents. Only this provides an explanation for the fact that the spiritual cosmos already contains tensions and structural relations which are not yet evident in the social sphere, and which

must be regarded as early symptoms of a social structure which only emerged at a later stage.

68 [A separate investigation would be required to determine if and to what extent early forms of a corresponding stage were already present in antiquity.]

69 *Editorial Note*: The text in square brackets is taken from the *Archiv*-essay and replaces the following much shorter version in the *Habilitationsschrift*:

[The pre-theoretical centre *out of which* the specific *current of thought* grows and which we call conservative, can only be something pre-theoretical, the animating purpose of the soul, which has its being in objectifications (*intentio animi*), from which it subsequently must be extracted.]

70 On Burke's differentiation between 'abstract' and 'moral', which was taken over and completed by Hegel, cf. Fritz Meusel, *Edmund Burke und die französische Revolution*, pp. 12, 137, note 7.

On the political point of the concept 'abstractness' we can read in Hegel: 'In Paragraph 5, it is only one side of the will which is described, namely this unrestricted possibility of abstraction from every determinate state of mind which I may find in myself or which I may have set up in myself, my flight from every content as from a restriction. When the will's self-determination consists in this alone, or when representative thinking regards this side by itself as freedom and clings fast to it, then we have negative freedom, or freedom as the Understanding conceives it. This is the freedom of the void which rises to a passion and takes shape in the world; while still remaining theoretical, it takes shape in religion as the Hindu fanaticism of pure contemplation, but when it turns to actual practice, it takes shape in religion and politics alike as the fanaticism of destruction – the destruction of the whole subsisting social order – as the elimination of individuals who are objects of suspicion to any social order, and the annihilation of any organisation which tries to rise anew from the ruins. Only in destroying something does this negative will possess the feeling of itself as existent. Of course it imagines that it is willing some positive state of affairs, such as universal equality or universal religious life, but in fact it does not will that this shall be positively actualised, and for this reason: such actuality leads at once to some sort of order, to a particularisation of organisations and individuals alike; while it is precisely out of the annihilation of particularity and objective characterisation that the self-consciousness of this negative freedom proceeds. Consequently, what negative freedom intends to will can never be anything in itself but an abstract idea, and giving effect to this idea can only be the fury of destruction.' (*Grundlinien der Philosophie des Rechts* [1821], ed. G. Lasson, Leipzig: F. Meiner, 1911, §5, pp. 28–29. [*Hegel's Philosophy of Right*, transl. T. M. Knox, London, Oxford, New York: Oxford University Press, 1967, p. 22.]).

Stahl: 'It is not, then, idle contemplation that moves us to assume such creative freedom. . . . We are moved, rather by the practical need to preserve the value of that which is positive, concrete, individual, the value of the factual.' (Friedrich J. Stahl, *Die Philosophie des Rechts*, 5th ed., Heidelberg: J. C. B. Mohr, 1978, vol. 2, p. 38.)

The category of the 'concrete', as has often been the case with contents as well, has been taken from the conceptual and categorical apparatus of conservative thought and is subsequently adopted by socialist and communist thought. The 'left opposition' to bourgeois liberal thought has contact points with its 'right opposition'; bourgeois liberal thought is opposed to concrete thinking by both the 'right' and the 'left', except that the 'concreteness' of the right opposition is based on an entirely different ontology than that of the left opposition. To see something 'concretely' means for the dialectical Marxist to understand the historical phenomenon under investigation in terms of the totality of the class struggle. The 'concrete', that which is ultimately real, coincides here with the class struggle. Thus Lenin, for instance, states: 'A Marxist must be a materialist, i.e. an enemy of religion, but a dialectical materialist who struggles against religion concretely upon the foundation of class struggle, rather than abstractly, on the basis of an abstract, purely theoretical, forever unchanging sermon.' (Vladimir I. Lenin, *Sämtliche Werke*, Vienna: Verlag für Literatur und Politik, 1925, p. 281.) The 'concrete' in the sense of viewing things *not* in '*isolation*' but rather as a comprehensive way of seeing is the dominant usage already in Hegel, e.g. 'that legislation both in general and in its particular provisions is to be treated not as something isolated and abstract but rather as a subordinate moment in a whole . . .' (*Grundlinien der Philosophie des Recht*, p. 21 [*Hegel's Philosophy of Right*, p. 16]).

The entire social history of the nineteenth and twentieth centuries is to some extent reflected in the change of meaning which the term 'concrete' has undergone. An exhaustive sociological analysis of meanings relating to this would have to always ask itself in the investigation of each case, at which point of the spiritual and social process this term appears, which particular meaning it assumes, and which spheres of actual existence are accordingly experienced as 'concrete' and 'real'. This is important because the point at which a social and spiritual current locates the 'concrete' (that is, the 'actual') reality constitutes the centre of its ontology. A history of the social differentiation of ontologies is also, however, the focal point of a sociological history of the mind. We shall, incidentally, encounter this problem later in another context.

71 'And finally one more thing, perhaps the most important of all: we placed a good administration above the best constitution.' (Bekker, the Pandectist, in an obituary on Böhlau, *Zeitschrift der Savigny-Stiftung*, Germanistische Abteilung, vol. 8, pp. VI ff. Quoted in Georg v. Below, 'Die Anfänge der konservativen Partei in Preussen', *Internationale Wochenschrift für Wissenschaft, Kunst und Technik*, 1911.) Cf. also the passage from Hegel cited last.

72 Even when the conservative has a system, he prefers not to admit this; Metternich, for instance, who more than any other conservative had something like a system, nevertheless was inclined to deny this (cf. Heinrich v. Srbik, *Metternich der Staatsmann und der Mensch*, vol. 1, Munich: F. Bruckmann, 1925, p. 322. The references given there are in Metternich's *Nachgelassene Papiere*, vol. 7, 6391; 8, 200). The following statement by Metternich is typical: 'The so-called Metternich system was not a system, but a *world order*. Revolutions are based upon systems, but eternal laws stand without and above that which with justification may be called a system.' (Clemens L. W. Fürst v. Metternich, *Denkwürdigkeiten*, ed. Otto H. Brandt, Munich: G. Müller, 1921, vol. 2, p. 461.)

Further references: Adam Müller, 'Die Lehre vom Gegensatz' [1804], in *Ausgewählte Abhandlungen*, ed. J. Baxa, Jena: G. Fischer, 1921, pp. 4, 89 ff. Ranke's dislike of systems is well-known. Savigny's rejection of codification also belongs here. The two important exceptions are Hegel and Stahl (Haller merely reacts and is therefore rather systematic). Stahl has a system, but his system, rather than striving for deduction from reality, is, in his own view, 'the genuine spiritual knowing, an envisioning [!] of the totality in every individual human or in every existing thing in the world of existences' (*Die Philosophie des Rechts*, p. 62), and in a note he comments: 'Only this constitutes the true system'. In the case of Hegel, the deductive tendency originates in German idealism which itself originated in revolutionary rationalism. The systematising tendency in Hegel should not be attributed to his conservative side, but rather to these idealist origins.

We could then show (in a conclusive discussion of these cases the various types of the 'system' concept should be kept apart; on this see the interesting discussion in Stahl, *ibid.*, 'Anmerkung'), that the liberal rationalist conception of system (which alone we have in mind here) can be clearly delimited. Every particular thinker, further-more – in our case, e.g., Hegel – would have to be investigated in regard to the question whether his thought does not represent a 'synthetic position', and an inquiry into the causes of the individual components of his way of thinking would always be called for. It seems very clear in the case of Hegel – as indicated above – that the rationalist desire to systematise in particular is *not* of conservative origin: most conservatives object, after all, precisely to it.

We need not strive for such concrete and detailed analysis here, where our concern is not with detail, but rather with revealing a fundamental intention.

Only an analysis of individual cases by means of the history of style has the task of inquiring into the constitution and internal stratific-ation of the (more complex) individual cases. It is precisely the appeal of phenomena within the sphere of cultural history that they cannot be conclusively comprehended in terms of universal laws but can be fully concretised only by a complementary structural style-historical analysis of the levels which comprise it.

73 Justus Möser, *Sämtliche Werke*, ed. B. R. Abeken, Berlin: Nicolai, 1842/43, vol. 4, pp. 158 ff., no. 43.

74 *Ibid.*

75 Adam H. Müller, *Die Elemente der Staatskunst*. We quote the new edition by J. Baxa, Vienna-Leipzig: Wiener Literarische Anstalt, 1922. Two volumes were published as Volume 1 of the collection *Herdflamme*. Cf. vol. 1, 8th lecture, pp. 156, 162 ff.

76 *Ibid.*, p. 281.

77 *Rechtsphilosophie*, p. 302 [*Hegel's Philosophy of Right*, addition to §44, p. 236].

78 *Ibid.*, p. 297 [addition to §41, p. 235].

79 Cf. the French 'Declaration of the Rights of Man and of the Citizen': 'La liberté consists à faire tout ce qui ne nuit pas à autrui: ainsi l'exercice des droits naturels de chaque homme n'a de bornes que celles assuren aux autres membres de la société la jouissance de ces mêmes droits. Ces bornes ne peuvent être déterminés que par la loi'. ['Liberty consists in doing anything that does no harm to others; thus, the only limits to the natural rights of any man are those which guarantee the same rights to the other members of society. These limits can only be fixed by law'.] Reprinted in Georg Jellinek, *Die Erklärunge der Menschen- und Bürgerrechte*, 3rd ed., Berlin: Duncker & Humblot, 1919, pp. 21 ff.

80 Cf. on this also Baxa's note in his edition of Adam Müller's *Elemente*, vol. 2, p. 334. On Müller's concept of freedom see also: *Elemente* I, pp. 156, 313; more recently also Erich Rothacker, 'Savigny, Grimm, Ranke. Ein Beitrag zur Frage nach dem Zusammenhang der Historischen Schule', *Historische Zeitschrift* (1923) 128: 440, who rightly talks of an 'early conservative' concept of liberty.

81 *Elemente*, p. 151.

82 An expression by Simmel.

83 Cf. also Alfred v. Martin, 'Weltanschauliche Motive im altkonservativen Denken', p. 345, note.

84 Erich Rothacker, 'Savigny, Grimm, Ranke', p. 433. Cf. also the references there.

85 *Ibid.*

86 Already in Adam Müller, *Elemente*, vol. 1, p. 313, it is called 'negative freedom'. Cf. also Gunnar Rexius, 'Studien zur Staatslehre der historischen Schule'.

87 *Rechtsphilosophie*. Addition to §5, p. 287 [*Hegel's Philosophy of Right*, p. 228]. This is the addition to the same paragraph we quoted earlier in our note 70.

88 *Ibid.*, p. 288 [pp. 227 ff.].

89 *Ibid.*, addition to S7, p. 288 [p. 228].

90 *Ibid.*, pp. 288–289 [p. 228].

91 Cf. on Stahl's concept of liberty, his *Philosophie des Rechts*, vol. 2, pp. 26 ff.

92 Here an acknowledgement of the romantic principle, yet also fear of its consequences.

93 Here a reception and an intrusion of liberal principles into conservative thought.

94 Stahl, *Die gegenwärtigen Parteien in Staat und Kirche*, pp. 5 ff.

95 *Ibid.*, p. 10. Incidentally, exactly the same constraints on freedom, but more in the direction of religion, can be found in Ludwig v. Gerlach. E. Jedele, *Die kirchenpolitischen Anschauungen des Ernst Ludwig v. Gerlach*, Ph.D. Dissertation, Tübingen 1910, characterises Gerlach's concept of freedom as follows: 'Gerlach's freedom is the fusion of one's own with the supreme will of God, and reincarnation consists of the deliverance from isolation.' (p. 13).

96 It will be the task of the next part of our inquiry to link the changes among them to the development of the social whole.

97 [Cf. Hegel's comment in the Preface to the *Rechtsphilosophie*: 'To comprehend what is, this is the task of philosophy, because what is, is reason. Whatever happens, every individual is a child of his time; so philosophy too is its own time apprehended in thoughts. It is just as absurd to fancy that a philosophy can transcend its contemporary world as it is to fancy that an individual can overleap his own age, jump over Rhodes. If his theory really goes beyond the world as it is and builds an ideal one as it ought to be, that world exists indeed, but only in his opinions, an unsubstantial element where anything you please may, in fancy, be built.' (p. 15 [*Hegel's Philosophy of Right*, p. 11]).

Hegel in his revolutionary youth, however, had commented, for instance: 'With the spread of the ideals of how things *ought* to be, the apathetic tendency of the solid citizens to accept everything always just as it *is*, will disappear.' (Hegel to Schelling [in a letter written from Berne on April 16, 1795]. Quoted by Franz Rosenzweig, in his *Hegel und der Staat*, Munich-Berlin: R. Oldenbourg, 1920, vol. 1, p. 31.)

The religious conservative has yet another, entirely different, motivation to keep to that which concretely exists, since he believes thereby to comprehend the decree of God. Stahl is an example: 'The merely moral person acts only in accordance with universal moral principles and his individuality; the religious person in addition seeks to ascertain the will of God for each particular case while remaining within the bounds of the reality prescribed by the general moral code and his own individuality.' (*Rechtsphilosophie*, vol. 2, 4th ed.)

Adalbert Wahl ('Beiträge zur deutschen Parteigeschichte', *Historische Zeitschrift* (1910) 104: 629, note 1) already seeks to determine the distinction between liberals and conservatives in terms of their relation to the normative sphere.]

98 In Ranke's *Political Dialogue*, Friedrich, the spokesman of conservatism, declares: 'I hope I did not express myself as if I had wanted to describe the ideal state; I merely sought to characterise the one we have.' Cf. Leopold v. Ranke, *Das politische Gespräch und andere Schriften zur Wissenschaftslehre*, Halle: N. Niemeyer, 1925, p. 29.

99 This fatalism repeatedly makes its appearance at the different stages.

At first it occurs as *theological fatalism* (that things are as they are by the will of God); in the age of the naturalist ideology of power it occurs as *fatalism of scientific natural* laws, and *'historical fatalism'* may be seen as the most important form.

100 Some examples of the variety of the conservative *construction of the totality*:

Savigny: 'Where we first find documented history, the civil law already has a specific character peculiar to the people, like its language, usages, constitution. Indeed, these phenomena have no independent existence; they are simply the various powers and activities of the people, in their nature inseparably interlinked and appearing as separate qualities only to our observation.' (*Vom Beruf unserer Zeit für Gesetzgebung und Rechtwissenschaft* [1814], quoted from the reprint in the third edition (1840), Freiburg: Mohr, 1892, p. 5). 'That is to say, the law has no independent existence, its nature is rather the life of the human beings themselves viewed from a specific aspect.' (*ibid.*, p. 18).

Hegel: 'As for the historical element in positive law . . . Montesquieu proclaimed the true historical view, the genuinely philosophical position, namely that legislation both in general and in its particular provisions is to be treated not as something isolated and abstract but rather as a subordinate moment in a whole, interconnected with all the other features which make up the character [!] of a nation and an epoch. It is in being so connected that the various laws acquire their true meaning and therewith their justification.' (*Rechtsphilosophie*, p. 21 [*Hegel's Philosophy of Right*, p. 16]).

101 ['There cannot be a revolutionary movement without revolutionary theory.' (Lenin, *Sämtliche Werke*, p. 38). Revolutionary theory signifies for Lenin an economic and sociological structural account of the class-determined constitution of society, having a theory of the revolution as integral part.]

102 [This is not the place to expound in detail upon the difference between the bourgeois-liberal and the socialist view of structure. From the point of view of the *conservative* at any rate, the socialist view is 'mechanistic' since it endeavours to understand the growth of that particular sphere in history which can be controlled like a mechanism and which can be rationalised. Conservative thought, by contrast, adopts an *'interpretive'* approach; it seeks to understand and interpret everything wherever possible, and earlier interpretations of *religious consciousness* are increasingly transformed in the direction of this approach. This is the *most important* difference between the conservative view and the liberal and socialist views. But like the immensely important problem of the attitude toward the 'irrational', it can only be explained by close reference to actual development.]

103 We do not claim that every conservative experiences time in a different fashion from a progressive. Such an assertion would be completely unverifiable. What we do say is that it is an ascertainable fact that in conservative constructions of the historical, time usually

appears in a different form than in progressive constructions. Here, too, we are (as always) concerned with structural contextures which – to the extent to which each specific individual re-experiences them and actualises the forms of experiencing time embedded in them – are always lived anew.

104 ['The social whole does not move forward in a straight line, but in a circle, and when it reaches a point which may be seen as a goal, it turns out that this was the point of departure.' (Metternich, *Nachgelassene Papiere*, vol. 8, p. 164, quoted by Heinrich v. Srbik, *Metternich der Staatsmann und der Mensch*, vol. 1, p. 355). This cyclical theory is vividly described in Heinrich von Kleist's, 'Über das Marionettentheater', *Berliner Abendblätter*.]

105 [Johann G. Droysen, *Grundriss der Historik*, new edition by von Rothacker, Halle: M. Niemeyer, 1925, p. 8. The quoted passage represents, in my view, a late formulation of the historical experience of time. Droysen was a student of Hegel's. Ranke writes: '. . . every important moment [in history, K.M.] inevitably affects us: one could say that it is never entirely over, it never ceases to have consequences.' (Introduction to *Historisch-politische Zeitschrift*, ed. Leopold Ranke, Berlin: Duncker & Humblot, 1832, vol. 1, p. 7).]

106 Cf. Brandi's introduction to Justus Möser, *Gessellschaft und Staat. Eine Auswahl aus seinen Schriften*, p. XXIII. Rehberg adopts the same theory of the state from Möser. Kurt Lessing, *Rehberg und die französische Revolution. Ein Beitrag zur Geschichte des literarischen Kampfes gegen die revolutionären Ideen in Deutschland*, Freiburg: C. A. Wagner, 1910, pp. 24 ff.

107 *Sämtliche Werke*, vol. 6, pp. IX ff.

108 [He means the representatives of the revolutionary theories of reason.]

109 *Elemente*, vol. 1, pp. 145 ff. Cf. also vol. 1, p. 179.

110 The direct opposite of this is to be found in the theme of the 'pouvoir constituant' in revolutionary consciousness, which acknowledged the right to change the constitution; so that – as Condorcet put it – 'no race could subjugate future ones [!] to its laws.' Cf. on this Rosenzweig, *Hegel und der Staat*, vol. 1, p. 143.]

111 Cf. on this Hans Freyer, 'Die Bewertung der Wirtschaft im philosophischen Denken des 19. Jahrhunderts', *Arbeiten zur Entwicklungspsychologie*, ed. Felix Krüger, vol. 5, Leipzig: W. Engelmann, 1921, p. 166, note 19 to Chapter III. We cannot deal here with those conservatives whose thought is still influenced by natural law (Haller, Metternich and so on). The separate development of their thinking represents a special theme in the sociology of knowledge interpretation of the development of conservative thought in Germany.

112 [Already Müller characterises democratic thought in this way: '*Vox populi, vox dei*, i.e. the people as a whole always strives for the good. The will of this whole is still far removed from Rousseau's *volonté générale*, in which it always only refers to the same generality of people inhabiting the same space at the same time, and not the sum

total of the immortal generations.' Cf. his *Über König Friedrich II und die Natur, Würde und Bestimmung der preussischen Monarchie*, Berlin: J. D. Sander, 1810, p. 3. The expression 'summation of the will' is characteristic, *ibid.*, p. 4.]

113 In *Die geistesgeschichtliche Lage des heutigen Parlamentarismus*, Munich-Leipzig: Duncker & Humblot, 1923, e.g., p. 15, Carl Schmitt has shown some other characteristic traits of the democratic argumentation.

114 What is meant here is not an 'eternal' but a 'dynamic' structural relationship. This already emerges from the fact that bourgeois thinking and desiring is not always present-minded. This allocation of functions only applies to the extent that the present, as it were, belongs to the bourgeois scheme of things. It is probably unnecessary to emphasise that there are conservative democracies. This problem, however, does not arise for the period in German history which concerns us here.

115 A few remarks are appropriate here to counter possible misunderstandings: it is not our view that all the traits we have mentioned were absent in the historical past and are to be regarded as original creations of conservative consciousness. In history every formation is always preceded by earlier forms. 'Nullum est jam dictum, quod non sit dictum prius.' (Terentius, *Eunuchus*, Prologue 41.) It is, however, less important always to want to 'trace back' everything than it is to discover how and in what form the elements of the spirit and the soul are connected within a particular historical segment with social and political collective forces. The problem of differentiating the ways of thought and experience and their changing forms and function in the overall make-up of historical and social reality alone is capable of lending the necessary concreteness to a history-of-ideas approach. It should also be noted here that we do not claim that conservative and liberal thinking in all countries and at every historical stage possesses this concrete structure and form. In order to do justice in this sense too to the full adaptability of social and historical phenomena, we must achieve a concrete *historical analysis of strata*, of which the next chapter means to offer a selective example. What emerges clearly from what has been said so far is, finally, that we consider the 'political' not as the *prima causa* of events, but as that sphere which best opens to view the structure of the process as a whole.

116 We largely agree (with the one reservation mentioned below) with Max Scheler's phenomenological observation that 'in effectively "traditional" behaviour, the past experience is not present in its individuality; its value and meaning, however, appear as "present" and not as "past", as in the case of recollection.' (*Vom Umsturz der Werte*, Leipzig: Der Neue-Geist-Verlag, 1919, vol. 2, pp. 202 ff.) Something similar holds for progressive experience: 'Now there is a phenomenon analogous to tradition in the givenness of our future which is "expectation" as little as tradition is "recollection": precisely those vital "anticipatory effects" of that which is, "in progress",

analogous to the living after-effects of the past without "recollection".' (*ibid.*)

117 In this context it should be remembered that precisely in this period the concept of 'becoming *reflective*' emerges as a dominant and fundamental category of thought.

118 Scheler, as we have seen, distinguishes 'recollection' from 'tradition'. We would assert that conservative experience and thought moves from the pole of experience in terms of tradition to the pole of life as it is recalled.

119 'The hydra of revolution has been destroyed in its methods and, to a large extent, in its results: let us destroy its source as well . . .' (Karl L. v. Haller, *Restauration der Staatswissenschaft oder Theorie des natürlich-geselligen Zustandes, der Chimäre des künstlich-bürgerlichen entgegengesetzt*, vol. 1, 2nd ed., Winterthur: Steiner, 1820, p. III.) Haller, as we shall see, is still deeply influenced by natural-law thinking.

120 The following presentation of the most important stages in the history of the *lex naturae* is indebted to the sociological analyses of Ernst Troeltsch. Cf. his 'Die Soziallehren der christlichen Kirchen und Gruppen', vol. 1, *Gesammelte Schriften*, Tübingen: Mohr, 1912, pp. 53 ff., 60 ff., 672 [*The Social Teachings of the Christian Churches*, transl. Olive Wyon, New York: Macmillan, 1931]; his 'Das stoisch-christliche Naturrecht und das moderne profane Naturrecht', *Verhandlungen des ersten deutschen Soziologentages vom 19.–22. Oktober 1910*, Tübingen: J. C. B. Mohr, 1911, and the discussion of this paper there; and his *Naturrecht und Humanität in der Weltpolitik*. Cf. also his 'Besprechung von Seebergs Dogmengeschichte', in Ernst Troeltsch, *Gesammelte Schriften*, vol. 3, Tübingen: J. C. B. Mohr, 1922, pp. 744 ff.; Georg Jellinek, *Die Erklärung der Menschen- und Bürgerrechte*; Max Weber, *Wirtschaft und Gesellschaft*, pp. 495 ff. [*Economy and Society*, pp. 866 ff.].

121 Troeltsch, 'Die Soziallehren der Christlichen Kirchen und Gruppen', *Gesammelte Schriften*, p. 54.

122 Troeltsch, 'Das stoisch-christliche Naturrecht und das moderne profane Naturrecht', *Verhandlungen*, p. 176.

123 Cf. Max Weber, *Wirtschaft und Gesellschaft*, p. 496 [*Economy and Society*, pp. 869 ff.].

124 On the historical roots of the idea of contract cf. Otto v. Gierke, *Johannes Althusius und die Entwicklung der naturrechtlichen Staatstheorien*, 3rd ed., Breslau: M. & H. Marcus, 1913, pp. 77 ff. On the relation between the 'idea of the social contract and the bourgeois spirit' cf. Werner Sombart, *Der moderne Kapitalismus*, vol. 2, first half-volume, 2nd ed., Berlin: Duncker & Humblot, 1916, pp. 29 ff.

125 'Man is destined for society and it is of little use to consider him in his isolated condition.' (Justus Möser, *Sämtliche Werke*, vol. 3, p. 68).

126 *Ibid.*, p. 177.

127 Thus, for example, one finds in him the antithesis of general laws and living particularities (which will preoccupy all subsequent conserva-

tive thinking), still formulated along the lines of the Kantian conceptual framework as the antithesis of *reason* and *understanding*. *According to him, reason*, which comprehends general and abstract laws without reference to experience, inheres in every human being, while *understanding*, which requires experience and makes judgements on the special character of the individual case, is distributed in every individual human being in different measure, which is why a subordination of one under the other is appropriate in this domain. The later antithesis between reason and the irrational individual case is still worked out in the realm of rationalism, in the terminology of the belief in reason, and the conservative point is assigned to understanding. Cf. on this Kurt Lessing, *Rehberg und die französische Revolution*, p. 40.

128 'Instead of the abandoned state of nature, I propound its uninterrupted continuation and even pronounce it the order of God.' (Haller, *Restauration der Staatswissenschaft*, vol. 1).

129 The same tendency can, of course, be observed in the philosophical literature. Baxa regards Fichte's *Naturrecht* (1796/97) as a first indication of this change and of a turn away from the doctrine of natural law within German idealism. One should add, however, that this, too, represents only a partial overcoming of the doctrine of natural law.

  On the other hand, it must be emphasised that in conservatism too there are intellectualistic tendencies which do not succeed in leaving behind the rationalist style of thought based upon natural law (e.g., Gentz and Metternich). They are too deeply rooted in eighteenth-century thought to achieve this (and there are other reasons as well which we will subject to sociological analysis later on). On Metternich cf. Srbik's fine analysis in his *Metternich: Der Staatsmann und der Mensch*, vol. 3, Part 2, 'Das Wesen des Systems').

  In the historical-sociological sections of the present work we will have to identify those currents in German conservative thought which did not radically depart from their embeddedness in natural law and inquire why this did *not* happen. We also need to explain why natural-law thinking, as has been pointed out by Troeltsch in his *Naturrecht und Humanität*, was never left behind as completely in the Western democracies as in Germany.

130 A passage from Rehberg, one of the earliest critics of all natural-law thinking, may serve as evidence for how this way of thinking is reflected in the consciousness of contemporaries. He defines natural law as follows:

  'The conditions of men in civil society, just like the *natural* ones, must be judged solely on the basis of the laws of moral necessity. Everything that is set up to be law in civil society and ought to be so can be derived from the original laws of reason. *One* constitution and *one* legal code for all nations on earth is therefore not merely the best but also the only rightful one. It is characterised by unlimited, universal freedom under the rule of that moral necessity.' (August Wilhelm Rehberg, *Untersuchungen über die französische Revolution nebst kritischen Nachrichten von den merkwürdigsten Schriften welche darüber in Frankreich erschienen sind*, two vols., Hannover: C. Ritscher, 1793. Quoted by Lessing, *Rehberg und die französische Revolution*, p. 40.)

131 Cf. the lucid observations by Erich Kaufmann in *Über den Begriff des Organismus in der Staatslehre des 19. Jahrhunderts*, Heidelberg: C. Winter, 1908.

132 The figure on p. 210 provides a preliminary scheme of orientation. It shows (very roughly, limiting itself to the most important characteristics how the tendencies proceed. Circles signify the most important positions. As a basis we have selected the distinctive character of thought (the style of thought). Since in our analysis we do not, for the present, explore the later period, the following references may provide a first orientation:

For Hegel: Friedrich Meinecke, *Weltbürgertum und Nationalstaat*, 6th ed., Munich-Berlin: R. Oldenbourg, 1922, pp. 278 ff., whose other works are also very important; Herman Heller, *Hegel und der nationale Machtsstaatsgedanke in Deutschland*. Ein Beitrag zur politischen Geistgeschichte. Leipzig-Berlin: B. G. Teubner, 1921; Franz Rosenzweig, *Hegel und der Staat*.

For the *Berliner Politische Wochenblatt* and Ranke's *Historisch-politische Zeitschrift*: the essay by C. Varrentrapp, 'Ranke's *Historisch-politische Zeitschrift* und das Berliner *Politische Wochenblatt*', *Historische Zeitschrift* (1907) 99: 35–119.

For the fate of the later historical school: Otto v. Gierke, *Die historische Rechtsschule und die Germanisten*. Rede zur Gedächtnisfeier des Stifters der Universität, König Friedrich Wilhelm, Berlin: G. Schade, 1903; and Rothacker's essay, 'Savigny, Grimm, Ranke', in the *Historische Zeitschrift*; also Rothacker's *Einleitung in die Geisteswissenschaften*, Tübingen: J. C. B. Mohr, 1920; further Troeltsch, *Der Historismus*.

For Metternich: Srbik, *Metternich: Der Staatsmann und der Mensch*.

For Stahl: v. Martin, 'Weltanschauliche Motive in altkonservativen Denken'.

133 Frederick the Great wrote in his *Die politischen Testamente* of 1752: 'One object of the policy of the King of Prussia is the preservation of his nobility. For whatever changes may come about, he may perhaps find a richer but never a more courageous and loyal nobility. In order to assist the nobility in maintaining their property, commoners should be prevented from acquiring noble estates. They should be encouraged to invest their capital in trade so that only a nobleman may buy an estate when another one should be forced to sell.' (Friedrich II der Grosse, *Die politischen Testamente* [1752; 1768], transl. from the French by Fr. von Oppeln-Bronikowski, ed. G. B. Volz [1920], Berlin: R. Hobbing, 1922, p. 33). For the later development, cf. Friedrich A. L. v.d. Marwitz, *Ein märkischer Edelmann im Zeitalter der Befreiungskriege*, ed. Fr. Meusel, two vols. (in 4 half-vols.), Berlin: E. S. Mittler, 1890–1913, vol. 2, part 2, pp. 80 ff.

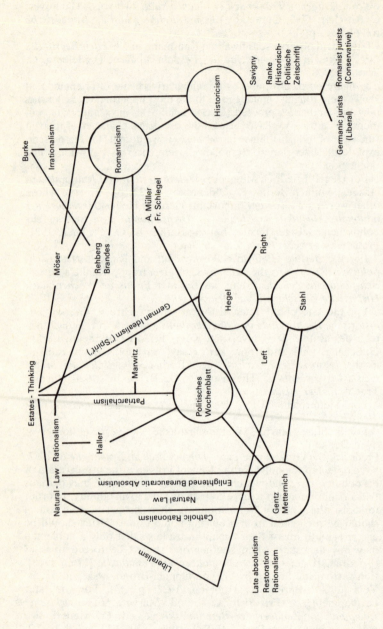

210

134 Cf., for example, Jakob Venedey, *Die deutschen Republikaner unter der französischen Republik*, Leipzig: F. A. Brockhaus, 1870.

135 Cf., for example, Erich Jordan, *Die Entstehung der konservativen Partei und die preussischen Agrarverhältnisse von 1848*, Munich-Leipzig: Duncker & Humblot, 1914, pp. 9–10. Further, Georg Kaufmann, *Geschichte Deutschlands im 19. Jahrhundert*, Berlin: G. Bondi, 1912, p. 48.

136 Cf. Ernst von Meier, *Französische Einflüsse auf die Staats- und Rechtsentwicklung Preussene im 19. Jahrhundert*, vol. 1, Leipzig: Duncker & Humblot, 1907, p. 6. Meier considers Frederick the Great's claim that the spiritual condition of Germany corresponded to the condition of France under Francis I correct if applied to the early years of Frederick's life.

137 Karl Marx, 'Zur Kritik der Hegelschen Rechtsphilosophie', in Mehring, *Aus dem literarischen Nachlass von Karl Marx und Friedrich Engels*, vol. 1, p. 385 ['A Contribution to the *Critique of Hegel's "Philosophy of Right"'*, in *Critique of Hegel's Philosophy of Right*, p. 132].

138 'In the view of those earlier ages, the *Mittelstand* united everyone who did not belong either to the nobility or to the lower orders. It did not have the explicit character of a class in our sense of the term. Sometimes it appeared as the group which comprised all the moderately well-to-do; sometimes more as the educated sections of the population.' (Werner Sombart, *Die deutsche Volkswirtschaft im 19. Jahrhundert und im Anfang des 20. Jahrhunderts*, Berlin: G. Bondi, 1921, p. 444.) Cf. also Friedrich Carl Moser's frequently quoted remark: 'We lack that mediatory power which Montesquieu considers the very support and defence of a good monarchy, protecting it from decay or from a change into depotism: *le tiers état.*' – Lack of space prevents a more thoroughgoing economic analysis of the social whole here.

139 The following sentences from v.d. Marwitz may serve as an illustration: 'However active and benevolent a government may be, it is dead to the state unless the governed understand and share in its life' (*Ein märkischer Edelmann im Zeitalter der Befreiungskriege*, vol. 2/2, p. 58); or (*ibid.*, in the footnote): 'The state does not consist of men who live *side by side*, of whom some command and others obey, but of men living *within each other*. It is the *unified* spiritual direction of their will.'

140 Alexis de Tocqueville, *L'ancien régime et la révolution*, p. 217 [*The Old Régime and the French Revolution*, p. 148].

141 *Editorial Note*: the preceding text in *petit* has been taken from two notes in the original manuscript. Since these notes overlap, a part of one of the notes has been cut out, even though it is contained in the German edition of this book. Cf. *Konservatismus*, Frankfurt: Suhrkamp, 1984, p. 142.

142 The view that the French *national character* can be gleaned from the French inclination towards abstractness was already attacked, as noted, by Tocqueville, who rightly pointed out that this abstractness

was determined by the sociological position of the pre-revolutionary stratum of the *literati* and was due to their exclusion from administration and government. He formulates this very concisely: 'I have heard it said that the penchant, not to say the passion, of our politicians during the last sixty years for general ideas, systems, and high-flown verbiage stems from a national trait, the so-called "French spirit" – the idea presumably being that this alleged propensity suddenly came to the fore at the end of the last century after lying dormant throughout the rest of our history.' (Alexis de Tocqueville, *L'ancien régime et la révolution*, p. 217) [*The Old Régime and the French Revolution*, p. 148].

In such cases a particular tendency of thought which becomes dominant for specific sociological and historical reasons in a particular epoch always leaves its mark on the other tendencies as well. Thus it can be shown that romantic conservatism in particular, which was the commanding tendency in Germany in the first decades of the nineteenth century, also strongly influenced the structure of the counter-currents. We can speak of a 'cohesive spirit of the age and nation' only in this sense.

143 *Editorial Note*: In the *Archiv*-essay, Mannheim substituted the passage printed below for the preceding two sentences in the original text:

[Romanticism, *in terms of its internal structure*, began as an ideological counter-movement to the Enlightenment.

Its *social* basis, especially in the pre-romantic period, seems to have been in strata (which might be called 'petit bourgeois') which stood apart from the general current toward modern capitalism. In this connection it seems increasingly probable, in accordance with the thorough investigations of Herbert Schöffler, that the Protestant parsonage played a particularly important part. It is especially the son of the parson in whom the wave of Enlightenment stirs doubt of traditionalist religiosity, but who does not therefore succumb to the opposite extreme of conservative rationalism. It is primarily his religious consciousness which is transformed. All those accustomed ways of thinking and experiencing, which were fostered by the religious life of the paternal home, survive the impact of the Enlightenment. Deprived of their positive contents, they are directed with redoubled strength against the rationalist atmosphere of the time. The new approval of irrationality for its own sake was made possible by the preceding tendency to thoroughly concentrate and emphasise the rational elements of consciousness.]

144 *Editorial Note*: Here Mannheim's published version of 1927 differs from the original text in an interesting respect. While the original emphasises the 'immanent' character of this ideological development, arguing the importance of a 'pendulum-effect' in the swing away from excessive rationalism, Mannheim's revision points towards a more sociological type of 'extrinsic' explanation for romanticism. The contrast is a matter of nuance, but it is nevertheless marked enough to render problematic a direct combination of the

two texts, such as is useful in other passages and as was also still done with this passage in our German edition of this work. The revised text at this point is as follows:

[But it was precisely these elements which were taken up by those who still retained, by virtue of their traditions, a way of access to these modes of experience and thought, just as, conversely, the rationalistic tendency was borne by the progressive portions of the bourgeoisie, monarchy and bureaucracy.

Pre-romanticism and even early romanticism itself are still only loosely connected with *political tendencies*, and, in keeping with the dominant mood of the pre-revolutionary epoch, are rather disposed to be revolutionary themselves. After the French Revolution, there is a parting of the ways, along the lines of the diverging structures of the various countries. The fact that in Germany romanticism issued in hostility to the Revolution, in conservatism, and in reaction, is a function of Germany's specific situation. At all events, this turn to conservatism implied a reinforcement of all the tendencies within romanticism which had always stood for opposition to the emerging new world, so that the distinctive character of German romanticism consists in the fact that in it the ideological opposition against the modern world coincides ever more with the political one.

This ideological and political opposition to the forces that sustain the modern world must not, however, conceal the fact that this movement is something more than a reaction based in the past. The modern and the rationalistic are already accommodated within the romantic consciousness, and transcended by it.]

145 On *Pre-romanticism* cf. Herbert Schöffler, *Protestantismus und Literatur. Neue Wege zur englischen Literatur des 18. Jahrhunderts*, Leipzig: B. Tauchnitz, 1922; Paul van Tieghem, *Le préromantisme. Études d'histoire littéraire européenne*, Paris: F. Rieder, 1924; further Alfred Weise, *Die Entwicklung des Fühlens und Denkens der Romantik auf Grund der romantischen Zeitschriften*, Ph.D. Dissertation, Leipzig: R. Voigtländer, 1912.

146 Adalbert Wahl, 'Montesquieu als Vorläufer von Aktion und Reaktion', *Historische Zeitschrift* (1912) 109: 129–48. Franz Oppenheimer, *System der Soziologie*, pp. 4 ff., suggests the replacement of the expression 'romanticism' with 'spiritual counter-revolution' and wants to explain it in terms of Tarde's law *imitation par opposition*. This brings out one aspect of romanticism very well.

147 An expression of Alfred Weber's.

148 Cf. the vivid account in Reinhold Steig, *Heinrich von Kleists Berliner Kämpfe*, Berlin-Stuttgart: W. Spemann, 1901.

149 Cf. Karl Lamprecht, *Deutsche Geschichte*, vol. 8(I), p. 209. The other writers who were Lessing's contemporaries – Weisse, Engel, Moritz, Dusch – soon took refuge in positions which set them up better for life. Conditions in Schlegel's and Novalis' time, furthermore, were more favourable than in Lessing's days. Cf. Wilhelm Dilthey, *Leben Schleiermachers* [1870], vol. 1, 2nd ed., Berlin-Leipzig: W. de Gruyter, 1922, pp. 193–255.

150 If one wanted to figure out in a speculative way – that is to say, without calling upon the facts of history – at which social locations a philosophy of history (in other words, an interest in the totality of the movements of history) is most likely to arise, one would think it probable that it is those who, by their social position, are responsible for the whole, who would reflect on these themes, i.e., high officials, diplomats, kings, etc. Experience, however, shows that this conjecture is only partly correct, if at all. High officials may possess the necessary practical experience and knowledge of the forces at work, but their view of the whole has the tendency to see society in terms of administration or of strategies of power. *Such* a rise of society to visibility, however, brings about neither philosophy of history nor sociology. The 'unattached intelligentsia' is doubtless in danger of hatching out empty speculations. Yet the best chance for the achievement of comprehensive views of history appears when socially unattached intellectuals, with their inherent sense of system and totality, bind themselves to the designs of social forces which are concretely manifest. It is irrelevant in this context whether these real forces which they join show society from above (Ranke, Treitschke) or from below (Marx). The first generation of romantics still lacked this sense of the concrete. Even in its late period (Fr. Schlegel, A. Müller, etc.), a speculative bend and sense for reality are found, unrelated, side by side. This fusion of the two forces is much more powerful in Ranke, Treitschke, Marx; it is almost possible to speak of progress. How very much the 'first servant of the state' is inhibited by the distinctive character of his social position from achieving the awareness of structure typical for philosophy of history or for sociology – even where he is personally endowed with a gift for 'philosophy' – can be illustrated by a few sentences from Frederick the Great. He writes in his *Die politischen Testamente* of 1752: 'Political schemes that are too ambitious and complicated are no more successful than excessively ingenious manoeuvers in a war.' He then gives some historical examples and continues: 'All these examples show that grand schemes which are tackled too soon never attain their objective. Politics is too much subject to accidents. It gives the human spirit no command over future events and over anything that belongs to the domain of chance. It consists more of using favourable opportunities to advantage than in bringing them about by careful planning. For this reason I advise you not to conclude treaties which refer to uncertain events in the future, but to preserve your freedom of action, so as to be able to take your decision in accordance with time, place, and the state of your affairs: in one word, as your interests will require at the time' (pp. 61 ff). Even the 'political phantasies' which follow do not interfere with the 'tactical point of view'. The actor himself stands much too close to be able to break through the effective disguises of men and conditions and to penetrate to the structural condition.

151 [On the importance of romanticism for historiography cf. Georg v. Below, 'Wesen und Ausbreitung der Romantik', in von Below, *Über*

historische Periodisierungen mit besonderem Blick auf die Grenze zwischen Mittelalter und Neuzeit, Berlin: Deutsche Verlagsgesellschaft für Politik und Geschichte, 1925, Cf. also Georg v. Below, 'Die deutsche Geschichtsschreibung von den Befreiungskriegen bis zu unseren Tagen', *Handbuch der mittelalterlichen und neueren Geschichte*, 2nd ed., Munich-Berlin: R. Oldenbourg, 1924.]

152 [When two currents of thought merge into each other, it is the task of the sociology of knowledge to discover those elements in both currents which showed an inner resemblance even *prior to* the synthesis and which thus made amalgamation possible. This is one of the guiding considerations in the style-analytical part of our presentation.]

153 Novalis (Friedrich v. Hardenberg), *Schriften*, ed. J. Minor, Jena: E. Diederichs, 1907, vol. 2, pp. 304 ff. ['Logologische Fragmente (II)' [1798], *Schriften*, ed. Paul Kluckhohn and Richard Samuel, Stuttgart: Kohlhammer, 1960, p. 454]. Mannheim's emphases.

154 [The literature on *romanticism* and on A. Müller is too extensive to be fully cited here. Some of it is collected in Jakob Baxa, *Einführung in die romantische Staatswissenschaft*, Jena: G. Fischer, 1923, pp. 176 ff., and in the second volume (pp. 586 ff) of Baxa's already cited edition of Adam Müller's *Elemente*. The relevant articles in Meinecke, *Weltbürgertum und Nationalstaat*, and Troeltsch, *Der Historismus und seine Probleme*, are also useful. The recent literature includes: the special issue on romanticism of the *Deutsche Vierteljahresschrift für Literaturwissenschaft und Geistesgeschichte* (1924) 2, 3; Carl Schmitt-Dorotić, *Politische Romantik*, Munich-Leipzig: Duncker & Humblot, 1919; Kurt Borries, *Die Romantik und die Geschichte*, Berlin: Deutsche Verlagsgesellschaft für Politik und Geschichte, 1925; and Gottfried Salomon, *Das Mittelalter als Ideal der Romantik*. Cf. also Albert Poetzsch, 'Studien zur frühromantischen Politik- und Geschichtsauffassung', in Karl Lamprecht, ed., *Beiträge zur Kultur- und Universalgeschichte*, vol. 3, Leipzig: Voigtländer, 1907].

155 ['Die Christenheit oder Europa' [1799], *Schriften*, ed. Paul Kluckhohn and Richard Samuel, vol. 2, pp. 507–524 [*Christianity or Europe*, transl. John Dalton, London: Chapman, 1844]. *Eds*.]

156 [On the history of the ideas of pantheism cf. Wilhelm Dilthey's essays in the second volume of his *Gesammelte Schriften*, Leipzig-Berlin: B. G. Teubner, 1914, as well as the relevant parts in his *Leben Schleiermachers*.]

157 This connection was already noted by Friedrich von Schlegel ('Signatur des Zeitalters', published in *Concordia*, a journal edited by him, 1820/23, pp. 45 ff.). Also Friedrich Stahl, *Die gegenwärtigen Parteien in Staat und Kirche*; Alfred v. Martin, 'Weltanschauliche Motive im altkonservativen Denken', pp. 374 ff.

158 [The following passage portrays the mood as well as the structure of pantheistic thinking: 'Feel how a spring day, a work of art, a loved one, how domestic bliss, civic duties, human deeds weave you, in all the dimensions of the globe, into the Universe, where one art follows

the other and the artist lives for ever . . .' (A. Müller, 'Die Lehre vom Gegensatze', p. 92).]

159 Schmitt-Dorotić, in his *Politische Romantik*, analyses this tendency to think in terms of analogies and the technique of 'transcending dualisms by invoking a third which is higher' very cleverly from the Catholic point of view. We believe that Schmitt fails to do justice to the essential feature, the 'dynamic element', which is contained in this type of thought.

160 Cf. Adam Müller, *Die Elemente der Staatkunst*, half-volume 1, p. 218, and Baxa's comment on this.

161 [Cf. on this Wilhelm Steffens, *Hardenberg und die ständische Opposition 1810/11*, Veröffentlichungen des Vereins für Geschichte der Mark Brandenburg, Leipzig: Duncker & Humblot, 1907; Friedrich Lenz, *Agrarlehre und Agrarpolitik der deutschen Romantik*, Berlin: P. Parey, 1912.]

162 Cf. *Briefwechsel zwischen Friedrich Gentz und Adam Heinrich Müller, 1800 bis 1829*, Stuttgart: J. G. Cotta, 1857, p. 140.

163 Cf. *ibid.*

164 Cf. Jakob Baxa, 'Justus Möser und Adam Müller. Eine vergleichende Studie', *Jahrbücher für Nationalökonomie und Statistik* (1925) 123: 14–30. Baxa confines himself chiefly to an elaboration of the common contents of ideas, while we must attempt to discover much more radical similarities, viz., in the general mode of thought.

165 [On Burke cf., for example, Fritz Meusel, *Edmund Burke und die französische Revolution*; Frieda Braune, *Edmund Burke in Deutschland*, Heidelberg: C. Winter, 1917; Richmond Lennox, *Edmund Burke und sein politisches Arbeitsfeld in den Jahren 1760–1790*, Munich-Berlin: R. Oldenbourg, 1923; John Morley, *Burke*, English Men of Letters Series, London: Macmillan & Co., 1923]

166 The [German] image of England, of course, has also had its adventures. The anglophilism of the young Müller emphasises the estate structure [of English society], but the same Müller characteristically abandons his favourable judgements as a result of the changes in English foreign policy. Cf. on this Friedrich Engel-Jánosi, 'Die Theorie vom Staat im deutschen Österreich 1815–48', *Zeitschrift für öffentliches Recht* (1921) 2, 1/2: 386, note 3).

167 Some characteristic passages from Edmund Burke's 'Reflections on the Revolution in France':
'You will observe, that from Magna Charta to the Declaration of Right, it has been the uniform policy of our constitution to claim and assert our liberties, as an *entailed inheritance* derived from our forefathers, and to be transmitted to our posterity.' (Burke, *Works*, vol. 5, pp. 77 ff., London: C. and J. Rivingston, 1801). 'The policy appears to me to be the result of profound reflection; or rather the happy effect of following nature, which is wisdom without reflection, and above it. . . . The people of England well know, that the idea of inheritance furnishes a sure principle of conservation, and a sure principle of transmission; without at all excluding a principle of improvement.' (*ibid.*, p. 78) 'You [the French] had all those

advantages in your ancient states; but you chose to act as if you had never been moulded into civil society, and had every thing to begin anew. You began ill, because you began by despising every thing that belonged to you. You set up your trade without a capital.' (*ibid.*, p. 82)

168 *Editorial Note*: In the published *Archiv*-essay, Mannheim changed 'relativism' to 'relationism'. This term was to take up an important place in his later work.

169 Burke, *Reflections on the French Revolution*, p. 82.

170 *Ibid.*, p. 116.

171 Gunnar Rexius, 'Studien zur Staatslehre der historischen Schule', pp. 500 ff.

172 *Editorial Note*: The slightly more detailed formulation in the *Archiv*-essay is as follows: [At this point we can clearly see the importance of historical thinking being somehow bound up with the historical mainstream in a living political sense. It is the direct rootedness of a standpoint in the historical process which alone is capable of creating those living relations in which thought and its categories can become possible. In order to extract knowledge from the historical process one has to desire something from it.]

173 Gentz, in a comment on his own translation of Burke's *Reflections*, speaks of an 'affectionate return to the past'. Cf. Burke, *Betrachtungen über die französische Revolution*, translated by Fr. Gentz, new edition, vol. 1, p. 408, Hohenzollern, 1794.

174 Richard Rohden, in his introduction to the German edition of Joseph de Maistre's 'Betrachtungen über Frankreich' in *Klassiker der Politik*, vol. 2, Berlin: R. Hobbing, 1924, p. 24, after having analysed the fundamental experience of the French traditionalists, the '*durée*', points out that the *durée* is conceived 'statically', not 'dynamically'. We agree with this and regard as the fundamental characteristic of German historicism that it *had become dynamic*, and that precisely for this reason it was able to carry the most fruitful potentialities of conservative thinking to their conclusions.

175 *Ibid.*

176 Rohden, in his introduction to [the German edition of] de Maistre, 'Betrachtungen über Frankreich', p. 14, points out that French traditionalism had its origins without exception in the landed nobility, and he attributes special importance to this fact.

177 Just one sample [from Burke's 'Reflections']: 'The age of chivalry is gone. That of sophisters, economists, and calculators has succeeded; and the glory of Europe is extinguished for ever. Never, never more shall we behold that generous loyalty to rank and sex, that proud submission, that dignified obedience, that subordination of the heart, which kept alive, even in servitude itself, the spirit of an exalted freedom.' (Burke, *Works*, vol. 5, p. 149) The guild system of the Middle Ages found its apologists in Tieck and Wackroder.

78 [On Möser cf. the introduction by K. Brandi to Justus Möser, *Gesellschaft und Staat. Eine Auswahl aus seinen Schriften*, which also contains a detailed bibliography of Möser, *ibid.*, pp. 265 ff. Cf. also

NOTES TO PAGES 129–34

the recently published essay by Hans Baron, 'Justus Mösers Individualitätsprinzip in seiner geistesgeschichtlichen Bedeutung', *Historische Zeitschrift* (1924) 130: 31–57.]

179 A typical example of this is 'Die Spinnstube, eine osnabrückische Geschichte', in *Sämtliche Werke*, 1, 5.

180 Werner Sombart, *Der Bourgeois. Zur Geistesgeschichte des modernen Wirtschaftsmenschen*, Berlin: Duncker & Humblot, 1920, distinguishes 'entrepreneurial spirit' from 'civic spirit' and analyses the two separately as component parts of the 'bourgeois spirit'.

181 The *Osnabrückische Geschichte*, although based on original sources, is nevertheless largely speculative history.

182 [In *Schriften*, ed. P. Kluckhohn and R. Samuel, vol. 3, p. 507. *Eds.*]

183 *Sämtliche Werke*, vol. 5, p. 144.

184 Cf. also Hans Baron, 'Justus Mösers Individualitätsprinzip in seiner geistesgeschichtlichen Bedeutung', p. 49.

185 Rohden says: 'If the traditionalist asks the question: "What is a nation?", the naive reader necessarily expects the answer, which to de Maistre represents the banal solution, "The totality of all citizens". The answer of the traditionalist, however, is: "The king and the bureaucracy". The art of the traditionalist thinker consists in taking a problem from the armoury of the adversary and connecting it by logical reasoning to an answer provided him by his strongly felt sense of life. The discrepancy between the expected "enlightened" result, which is constantly present in the subconscious, and the actual answer produces a state of anxious tension.' (Rohden, introduction to his [German] edition of de Maistre, 'Betrachtungen über Frankreich', in *Klassiker der Politik*, p. 23.)

186 [The sentence just quoted is taken from a fragment in Möser's literary remains entitled 'The Right of Man: Serfdom'. In an allusion to that title the fragment begins: 'Indeed a paradox! many a reader will think when he sees this title'. To that extent, Möser, too, employs the method mentioned by Rohden.]

187 *Sämtliche Werke*, vol. 9, pp. 158 ff.

188 *Ibid.*, vol. 9, p. 168.

189 *Sämtliche Werke*, vol. 1, 17, pp. 196 ff.

190 *Sämtliche Werke*, vol. 2, pp. 20 ff.

191 This goes back to Montesquieu.

192 '. . . and what is more, the most noble of all works of art, the constitution of the state, is supposed to be reducible to a few general laws; it is supposed to take on *the classical simplicities of beauty of a French play* . . .' (Möser, *Sämtliche Werke*, vol. 2, p. 21. My italics.) That the problem of the unity of style, which seems relatively modern to us, greatly preoccupies him, and that he is very conscious of the fact that there is such a thing as a unity of style, is evidenced by the following passage in his introduction to the *Osnabrückische Geschichte*: 'The style of all the arts, even of the dispatches and love letters of a Duke de Richelieu, displays closely related characteristics. Every war sets its own tone, and the affairs of state have their own local colour, costume and manner in common with religion and

the sciences.' (*ibid.*, p. 86; *Sämtliche Werke*, vol. 6, p. 22.) Cf. on this also H. Baron, 'Justus Mösers Individualitätsprinzip in seiner geistesgeschichtlichen Bedeutung', p. 45.

193 *Sämtliche Werke*, vol. 2, p. 21.

194 *Sämtliche Werke*, vol. 2, pp. 23 ff.

195 *Sämtliche Werke*, vol. 2, p. 26.

196 Cf. the treatise: 'Sollte man nicht jedem Städtchen seine besondre politische Verfassung geben?', *Sämtliche Werke*, vol. 3, p. 67.

197 Quoted by Wilhelm Steffens, *Hardenberg und die ständische Opposition 1810/1811*, p. 30. Cf. also *ibid.*, note 2, where it is pointed out that some national feeling, though infused with tensions grounded in antitheses, continued to survive.

198 Möser was born in 1720, Marwitz in 1777.

199 'Too many princes, too many noblemen, too many scholars, are the ruin of the state.' (*Sämtliche Werke*, vol. 5, p. 37.)

200 Cf. the introduction by Brandi to Möser's *Gesellschaft und Staat*, p. XXI; further, Otto Hatzig, *Justus Möser als Staatsmann und Publizist*, Quellen und Darstellungen zur Geschichte Niedersachsens, vol. 27, Hanover-Leipzig: O. Wigand, 1909. For v.d. Marwitz, see the essay by Meusel, in vol. 1 of his edition of v.d. Marwitz's *Ein märkischer Edelmann im Zeitalter der Befreiungskriege*; also Willy Andreas, 'Marwitz und der Staat Friedrichs des Grosen', *Historische Zeitschrift* (1920) 122: 44 ff.

201 Cf. 'Der Staat mit einer Pyramide verglichen. Eine erbauliche Betrachtung' (1773), *Sämtliche Werke*, vol. 2, p. 250.

202 A typical example of the distinctive character of the 'campaign' against revolutionary thought which was carried on by the French traditionalists is Louis de Bonald's interesting essay 'De la philosophie morale et politique du 18e siècle', *Oeuvres*, vol. 9, Paris: Adrien Le Clerc, 1817, pp. 104 ff. In it he attempts to draw parallels between theism, atheism, deism and the various forms of government. A few passages may be quoted which indicate his conclusions: 'Democracy properly so-called furiously ousts from political society all visible and fixed units of power, and does not perceive the sovereign in anyone but *the subjects*, or the people: just as atheism rejects the sole and first cause of the universe, and only sees it through its effects or in matter. In the latter system, matter has done everything; in the former, the people has the right to do everything, so much so that one could call democrats the atheists of politics; and atheists, the *enragés*, or the *Jacobins* of religion.' (pp. 128 ff.) 'Royalism' has its counterpart in 'theism or Christianity', and on the Gironde he says this: 'The *impartial*, moderate, constitutionalists of '89 placed themselves between the democrats and the royalists, like deists between the atheists and the Christians: and that caused the constitution they had invented to be given the name of *royal democracy*. They wanted a king, but a king without an effective will, without independent action; and as Mably, the doctor of that party, said to the Poles, *a king who would receive respectful homage, but who would have only a shadow of authority*. In these features one

may recognise the ideal and abstract god of deism, without will, without action, without presence, without reality.' (pp. 129 ff.) [de Bonald's italics].

203 Cf. on this Baxa's introductory comments in Müller's *Die Elemente der Staatskunst*, vol. 2, p. 293. Rothacker points out the roots of the concept in the historical school, in his *Einleitung in die Geistes-wissenschaften*, pp. 62 ff., especially note 2, p. 71.

204 [On the distinctive character and structure of modern rationalism cf. the works of Max Weber and Sombart, as well as Georg Simmel's *Philosophie des Geldes*, Leipzig: Duncker & Humblot, 1900, and Georg Lukács' *Geschichte und Klassenbewusstsein*, especially 'Die Verdinglichung und das Bewusstsein des Proletariats'].

205 That is the stage which German conservatism has reached, for example, in Gustav Hugo's *Lehrbuch des Naturrechts als einer Philosophie des positiven Rechts, besonders des Privatrechts* [1799], 4th ed., vol. 2, Berlin: August Mylius, 1819.

206 It is not our task as sociologists to pass judgment on the metaphysical question whether this is a matter of bestowing or discovering meaning. Our own opinion on the value of irrationality must be left aside.

207 This was formulated in an ideal-typical manner by de Maistre in his 'Considérations sur la France' [1796]: 'No constitution results from a deliberation. Popular rights are never written, or at least constitutive acts or written fundamental laws are always only declaratory statements of anterior rights, of which nothing can be said other than that they exist because they exist.' (J. de Maistre, *Oeuvres Complètes*, vol. 1, pp. 67 ff. Lyon: Librairie Générale Catholique et Classique, 1891. [English translation in Jack Lively, ed. and transl. *The Works of Joseph de Maistre*, London: Collier-Macmillan, 1965, p. 77]). Or: 'A written constitution of the kind that today governs France is nothing more than a mechanism with the external appearance of life.' (p. 81 [p. 82]). In his struggle for the idea that it is impossible to construct something upon bare ground consciously and in accordance with a rational plan, he works out for himself the phenomenological distinction between '*creating*' and '*changing*': 'Man can change everything in the sphere of his activity, but he creates nothing . . .' (p. 67 [p. 77]). Here again the emphasis on '*growing*'. He goes so far in his aversion to planned '*making*' that he rouses himself to the following sentences: 'Not only do I doubt the stability of American government, but the peculiar institutions of English America inspire no confidence in me. For example, the towns, inspired by a rather unworthy jealousy, were not able to agree on a place where the Congress should sit; none of them was willing to surrender this honour to another. Consequently, it has been decided to build a new town as the seat of government. The site was chosen on the banks of a great river; it was decided that the town should be called *Washington*; the situation of all the public buildings was marked out; the work has been set in hand and the plan of the capital city is already circulating throughout Europe. In essentials, there is

nothing in this beyond human powers; a town can very easily be built: nevertheless, there is too much deliberation, too much of mankind, in all this, *and it is a thousand to one that the town will not be built, or that it will not be called Washington, or that Congress will not sit in it.*' (pp. 87 ff. [pp. 84 ff.], my italics). This bet he surely would have lost. For this struggle against 'making' cf. also Burke: 'The very idea of the fabrication of a new government is enough to fill us with disgust and horror.' (Reflections on the Revolution in France', in *Works*, vol. 5, p. 125.) Cf. also A. Young, who in his diary makes fun of the French because they want to make a constitution, 'in accordance with a recipe, like a pudding'. The last two references are in Adalbert Wahl, 'Beiträge zur deutschen Parteigeschichte', p. 550. Cf. also Wahl's discussion on this topic (*ibid.*)

208 'The 1795 constitution, like its predecessors, was made for *man*. But there is no such thing as *man* in the world. During my life, I have seen Frenchmen, Italians, Russians, and so on; thanks to Montesquieu, I even know that one can be *Persian*; but I must say, as for *man*, I have never come across him anywhere; if he exists, he is completely unknown to me.' (De Maistre, *Considérations sur la France*, German ed., p. 72 [p. 80].)

209 [Here too we can see that this way of thinking is assimilated by the 'left opposition': 'But man is no abstract being, squatting outside the world.' (Karl Marx, 'Zur Kritik der Hegelschen Rechtsphilosophie' in Franz Mehring, *Aus dem literarischen Nachlass von Karl Marx und Friedrich Engels 1841 bis 1850*, vol. 1, p. 384) ['A Contribution to the Critique of Hegel's Philosophy of Right', in *Critique of Hegel's 'Philosophy of Right'*, p. 131].]

210 [There is a paradox in the fact that it is the progressive, the liberal – who was after all more receptive to the new elements produced by change than the conservative – who appeared to his contemporaries as 'rigid', while the conservative and the old traditionalist forms of continuity appeared as more mobile and 'alive'. This paradox is due to an optical illusion to which the immediate participants in the process (the contemporaries) were bound to succumb. Lukács, with reference to law, suggests a solution to a similar paradox: 'This is the source of the – apparently – paradoxical situation whereby the 'law' of primitive societies, which has scarcely altered in hundreds or sometimes even thousands of years, can be flexible and irrational in character, renewing itself with every new legal decision, while modern law, caught up in the continuous turmoil of change should appear rigid, static and fixed. But the paradox dissolves when we realise that it arises only because the same situation has been regarded from two different points of view: on the one hand, from that of the historian (who stands 'outside' the actual process and, on the other, from that of someone who experiences the effects of the social order in question upon his consciousness.' *Geschichte und Klassenbewusstsein*, p. 109 [*History and Class Consciousness*, p. 97]. To this essentially correct explan-

ation, however, it should be added that the forms of thinking of the closed, static system are in fact more rigid than those which the romantic adversary opposed to it as more 'alive'. If conservative thought proved nonetheless more impervious to the 'new', the reason must be sought not in the *forms* of conservative thinking, but in the fact that this current remains unreceptive to the new '*contents*'. This is precisely the other aspect of the paradox which has just been discussed: that the contemporaries paid attention to the way of *thinking* (to the forms of thinking) while as historians we focus on the *contents*.]

211 [Here is an example for the early stage: 'The *listener* is the true *anti-speaker*; which of the two we call the active, which the passive or counter-active partner, who is to be called object and who subject, is completely arbitrary. One thing alone is essential: if one of them is called object, the other must be called subject.' (A. Müller, 'Die Lehre vom Gegensatze', pp. 38 ff.)]

212 [The excessively unilinear form of rationalism itself gives rise, at a certain late stage, to a tendency towards antithetical thinking. Since unilinear thought splits up everything into sets of exclusives, it already contains within itself the notion of overcoming such a state of thinking. In this sense Lublinski points out correctly that at a late stage of the Enlightenment the possibility of going beyond Enlightenment was sought within the Enlightenment itself. He shows how both Kant and Schiller attempted, in different spheres, to overcome unilinear thought by means of the category of 'interaction'. The reference to Schiller is very apt as well. In Lublinski's view, Schiller's endeavour to portray the hero as bound up with his environment by interaction and mutual influence represents the same breakthrough of a new vision as Kant's endeavour to establish the category of interaction in thought. In both cases, the point is that isolated units are no longer merely placed side by side. Here it is once again apparent that new forms of thought are emanations of a more comprehensive factor, of new forms of experience. Cf. Samuel Lublinski, *Literatur und Gesellschaft im neunzehnten Jahrhundert*. Berlin: S. Cronbach, 1899/1900, vol. 1, p. 57.]

213 Wilhelm Metzger, *Gesellschaft, Recht und Staat in der Ethnik des deutschen Idealismus*, Heidelberg: C. Winter, 1917, pp. 260 ff., points to the romantic roots of this dynamic thinking. He mentions Friedrich Schlegel's *Ironie und antithetische Synthesis* (*ibid.*, note 1). Meinecke (*Weltbürgertum*, p. 131, note 2) refers to Fichte for its origins. H. Heller tries to establish Hegel's influence on Müller through Schelling, on the one side, and Gentz, on the other (*Hegel und der nationale Machtstaatsgedanke in Deutschland*, pp. 139 ff). The only influence that is definite is Schelling's philosophy of nature. This has been pointed out by Metzger (*ibid.*, note 2), who follows Arno Friedrich's *Klassische Philosophie und Wirtschaftswissenschaft*, Gotha: F. A. Perthes, 1913. Müller himself acknowledges this influence when he discusses the problem of the antithesis in his essay 'Vom Wesen der Definition' (published in *Phöbus*, edited by

Heinrich v. Kleist and Adam Müller, reprinted in *Neudrucke romantischer Seltenheiten*, 1924, p. 37): 'It was in 1803 when I accomplished the decisive step in constructing a dynamic logic, the need for which I had felt in the name of the philosophy of nature.' (Cf. also 'Die Lehre vom Gegensatz', pp. 9, 11.) For a sociologist the determination of priority does not have the same cardinal importance that it has for the pure historian of ideas. For isolated discoveries are for him always expressions of more comprehensive, mutually antagonistic positions. Whether the dynamic logic which was achieved at roughly the same time by Hegel, Schelling and Müller was arrived at independently or by way of mutual influence is of lesser importance to us than to locate those sources in social and spiritual existence from which arose the impulse to search for a dynamic logic.

214 'Vom Wesen der Definition', p. 37.
215 *Ibid.*
216 *Elemente*, vol. 1, p. 20.
217 *Ibid.*
218 [Already in Müller's first publication, 'Die Lehre vom Gegensatz', antithetical thinking has the tendency to turn into dialectical thinking, i.e. into a way of thinking which in this way attempts to comprehend the whole development of consciousness. He writes: 'It follows clearly from our assumptions that if we can easily let the whole world take its course through each of the two elements of our formula, and if we ourselves, as true antithesis, as unity in the manifold of the world stand against this our thesis, which is itself a contradiction between thesis and antithesis, in whatever form it may appear, that then the only possible explanation of the world, always and everywhere sufficient, the true history of self-consciousness, must be before us.' (pp. 51 ff.) Engel-Jánosi, 'Die Theorie vom Staat im deutschen Österreich 1815–48', p. 380, notes correctly that the 'rhythmic organisation' of the dialectic is still missing, so that the end-result is arrived at only by means of an arbitrary breaking-off the 'antithetical movement'.]
219 Cf., for example, *Elemente*, vol. 1, pp. 351, 354, 355, 356 (the 'idea' is here contrasted with the 'system').
220 *Elemente*, vol. 2, p. 178.
221 *Elemente*, vol. 1, p. 147.
222 We are here quite consciously speaking retrospectively from the standpoint of the 'philosophy of life'. Even though the terms 'alive' and 'life' can already be found to occur frequently in this period, there are nonetheless enormous differences between that earlier and the present-day philosophy of life. We will later on attempt to spell these differences out. It is, however, important to realise even now that the modern beginnings of this position must be sought here.
223 The passage in the *Elemente*, vol. 2, p. 175, recalls the religious context. On the religious origin of the term 'mediator', cf. more recently Paul Kluckhohn, *Persönlichkeit und Gemeinschaft*. Studien

zur Staatsauffassung der deutschen Romantik, Halle a.d.S.: M. Niemeyer, 1925, p. 17.

224 *Elemente*, vol. 1, p. 179.

225 *Ibid.*

226 *Elemente*, vol. 1, p. 143.

227 For further examples of the term 'mediation' in Müller, see his *Elemente*, vol. 1, pp. 148, 205. Note in the latter passage the expressions 'calculating wisdom', and 'not only weighed and determined by quantity but . . . mediated'; also vol. 1, pp. 206, 286, 305: 'constant peace-making'; and then applied, by analogy, to money (p. 361).

228 [Here too a far-reaching agreement between the 'right' and 'left' opposition to the bourgeois rationalist world. Cf. for instance the denigrating stress upon the calculating and ungenerative nature of the conduct of the capitalist as subject, for instance in the legal sphere, in Lukács, *Geschichte und Klassenbewusstsein*, p. 109 (*History and Class Consciousness*, p. 97)].

229 *Elemente*, vol. 1, p. 288.

230 Cf. his preface to Müller's *Schriften zur Staatphilosophie*, ed. Rudolf Kohler, Munich: Theatiner Verlag, 1923, pp. VI ff.

231 Novalis, 'Die Christenheit oder Europa', in *Schriften*, vol. 2, p. 42. Even Baxa refers to this passage (without analysing it as similar (note to Müller's *Elemente*, vol. 2, p. 350).

232 Hence, Baxa is wrong when he interprets the meaning of the notion of 'idea' in the *Elemente* by way of quotations from Müller's later works, such as the *Theologische Grundlagen*; for in the latter the 'idea' has already received a platonistically archetypal, theological meaning. Attempting to make sense of the Müller who wrote the *Elemente* by way of the later Müller was as serious a mistake as Gentz's attempt to explain the concept of ideas contained in the *Elemente* simply on the basis of Müller's work of 1804. (Friedrich v. Gentz, *Schriften*, ed. Schlesier, Mannheim: Heinrich Hoff, 1838–40, vol. 4, p. 359.) On all this cf. Baxa's comments on the *Elemente*, vol. 2, pp. 292–3. The point is to see even the thought of a single author *dynamically*. It must always be the task of the sociologist of knowledge to observe how the thought of a thinker is modified when it moves from one sociological position toward another within the same social movement. On the other hand, it will be necessary to observe in what forms certain fundamental concepts such as 'idea' and 'mediation' appear in other currents of conservative thought. Here, of course, the analysis of Hegel becomes important.

233 *Elemente*, vol. 1, p. 15.

234 *Ibid.*, Introduction, p. XII.

235 *Ibid.*, p. 11 [Mannheim's italics].

236 For further examples of this pure experience of dynamics, see *ibid.*, p. 4: 'In movement then . . .'; p. 144: 'In a state which claims to be free . . .'; p. 155: '. . . an active approach to the things upon whose behalf I have come to speak'; p. 193, on the contradictory element

within that which is alive; p. 348: 'whatever wealth may be . . .'

237 The prevalence of this experience of the '*durée*' (if only in an early version) in French traditionalism would have to be explored separately.

238 [Here again parallels, though of a very different structure, can be found in the 'left' opposition: Cf. Lukács, 'Das Problem der Verdinglichung', *Geschichte und Klassenbewusstsein*, pp. 94–228 ('Reification and the Consciousness of the Proletariat', *History and Class Consciousness*, pp. 83–222).]

239 As far as it is possible to judge at present, it has the tendency – when it regains political significance – to provide a foundation for the modern eruptive activist currents (whether in a reactionary or progressive sense). This is at any rate true of the Bergsonian trend which provided the *impetus* both for fascism and for the direct action of syndicalism (Sorel, for instance).

240 On his struggle against inner-directedness cf., in addition to the passages cited below, his *Grundlinien der Philosophie des Rechts*, additions to §§ 136 and 137, p. 319; also addition to § 138 (p. 320 [*Hegel's Philosophy of Right*, p. 255]): 'It is only in times when the world of actuality is hollow, spiritless, unstable, that an individual may be allowed to take refuge from actuality in his inner life'[!].

241 The following passage from the *Rechtsphilosophie* sounds like a confession in this direction: 'A will which resolves on nothing is no actual will; the characterless man never reaches a decision. . . . Only by resolving can a man step into actuality, however bitter to him his resolve may be. Inertia lacks the will to abandon the inward brooding which allows it to retain everything as a possibility. But possibility is still less than actuality. The will which is sure of itself does not *eo ipso* lose itself in its determinate volitions.' (*ibid.*, addition to § 13, p. 290 [*Hegel's Philosophy of Right*, pp. 229 ff.])

242 Cf. for instance Heinrich Heine, 'Die romantische Schule' [1833], *Gesammelte Werke*, vol. 5, Leipzig and Vienna: Bibliographisches Institut, 1898, pp. 207–364, and Theodor Echtermeyer and Arnold Ruge, 'Der Protestantismus und die Romantik. Zur Verständigung über die Zeit und ihre Gegensätze. Ein Manifest', *Hallische Jahrbücher für deutsche Wissenschaft und Kunst* (1839) [Reprinted as Th. Echtermeyer and A. Ruge, *Der Protestantismus und die Romantik*, ed., Norbert Oellers, Hildesheim: H. A. Gerstenberg, 1972].

That Hegel himself sees this process very clearly is evident from some remarks in which he describes the fate of romantic and Enlightenment thought on the occasion of his discussion of a specific problem which concerns the relation between law and morality. The abstract notion of the good – this should be pointed out from the beginning by way of interpretation – signifies the Enlightenment principle, while 'conscience' signifies the romantic principle. 'Each of the two principles hitherto discussed, namely good in the abstract and conscience, is defective in lacking its opposite. Good in the abstract evaporates into something completely powerless, into which

225

I may introduce any and every content, while the subjectivity of mind becomes just as worthless because it lacks any objective significance. Thus a longing may arise for an objective order in which man gladly degrades himself to servitude and total subjection, if only to escape the torment of vacuity and negation. Many Protestants have recently gone over to the Roman Catholic Church, and they have done so because they found their inner life worthless and grasped at something fixed, at a support, an authority, even if it was not exactly the stability of thought which they caught.

The unity of the subjective with the objective and absolute good is ethical life, and in it we find the reconciliation which accords with the concept.' (*Rechtsphilosophie*, addition to § 141, pp. 324/5 [*Hegel's Philosophy of Right*, pp. 258 ff.]). It is a well-known fact that in Hegel morality refers to the absolute power of the association of the state, and ultimately to the Prussian state. Cf. on this Heller, *Hegel und der Machtstaatgedanke*, p. 88, note 22.

243 The concept of actuality in bourgeois thought will have to be discussed later, after the meaning of modern relativism has been historically analysed.

244 Savigny, *Vom Beruf unserer Zeit für Gesetzgebung und Rechtswissenschaft*, Freiburg: Mohr, 1892 [*Of the Vocation of Our Age for Legislation and Jurisprudence*, transl. Abraham Hayward, London: Littlewood & Co., 1831].

245 Savigny, *Vermischte Schriften*, vol. 1, Berlin: Veit & Co., 1850, pp. 105–26.

246 *Ibid.*, vol. 5, pp. 115–72.

247 Friedrich C. von Savigny, *System des heutigen römischen Rechts*, vol. 1, Berlin: Veit & Co., 1840 [*System of Modern Roman Law*, vol. 1, transl. William Holloway, Madras: J. Higginbotham, 1867].

248 *Vom Beruf unserer Zeit*, p. 3 [Cf. *Of the Vocation of Our Time*, p. 21].

249 *Ibid.*, p. 4 [Cf. p. 22].

250 *Ibid.*, p. 5 [cf. p. 24] (Mannheim's emphasis).

251 p. 204, note 100.

252 *Ibid.*, p. 6 [cf. p. 25] (Mannheim's emphasis).

253 *Ibid.*, p. 7 [cf. p. 27] (Mannheim's emphasis).

254 *Ibid.*, pp. 7–8 [cf. pp. 28 ff.]

255 *Ibid.*, p. 8 [cf. p. 30]. It should be noted that the whole fundamental problematic of Tönnies' contrast between *Gemeinschaft* and *Gesellschaft* is already presupposed here.

256 *Ibid.*, p. 10 [cf. p. 32].

257 'This youthful period of peoples . . . enjoys a clear consciousness of circumstances . . .' (*ibid.*, p. 6 [p. 25]). '. . . the political element of the law has long since had its full effect and this effect needs only be acknowledged and articulated, which is the proper task of juristic technique . . .' (*ibid.*, p. 12 [cf. p. 36]). Juristic technique (thinking), then, only *articulates* that which has already previously grown (organically and unconsciously) out of the political element. 'Each part of our law [has] a sort of components which are the premisses

upon which the others rest: we may call them guiding principles. To sense these out and to recognise the *inner* connection as well as the fact and manner of the interrelationship among all juristic concepts and tenets, is one of the hardest tasks of our science . . .' (p. 13 [cf. pp. 38 ff.]).

258 *Ibid.*, p. 14 [cf. p. 39].
259 *Ibid.*, p. 16 [cf. p. 45]. (Mannheim's emphasis).
260 *Ibid.*, p. 18 [cf. p. 46]. (Mannheim's emphasis).
261 *Ibid.*, p. 18 [cf. p. 46].
262 *Ibid.*, p. 19 [cf. p. 47].
263 *Ibid.*, p. 20 [cf. p. 47]. Rothacker's interpretation of this passage comes closest to our own. He has attempted (for the first time in the extensive literature on the concept of the 'spirit of the people'), to pay attention to the distinctiveness of the thinking which underlies the assertions, rather than just dealing with disconnected individual fragments. He describes the thought which Savigny represents as 'finding' (*Finden*): 'Just as the artist *searches* for "his" style, or the poet creates a new language out of the *depth* of the common language, so the jurisprudence of Savigny *finds* the truly living law in the social corpus of the people.' (Erich Rothacker, 'Savigny, Grimm, Ranke', p. 425). In order to build up a phenomenological analysis on the basis of Rothacker's valid insights, we suggest the term 'elucidation' in place of 'finding'. 'Finding' is too general a term (one finds an object which has been lost, but in finding it, one does not change it); 'elucidating', by contrast, signifies a mode of conduct and an achievement which is only possible in regard to contents which pertain to the spirit and the soul. In a curious way it is necessary first to possess these things, to make them one's own, before they can be elucidated. And this is precisely what Savigny means. It is for this reason that such thinking is only possible in the cultural sphere, and inapplicable to the sphere of spiritless nature as well as to entities which are merely civilisational in character. It is the great achievement of Savigny to have discovered this method of thinking which is unique to the human sciences. We also consider every comparison with art dangerous, because the artist does not merely elucidate but he also creates; he brings into the world new spiritual realities. Savigny's way of elucidating law, however, does not create or fashion new works, but merely clarifies that which already exists; it is therefore not a 'work' but merely represents an access through knowledge. The element which refers to fellowship in this thinking, which we shall analyse later, may also contribute to this phenomenological analysis.
264 *Ibid.*, p. 9 [p. 31].
265 *Ibid.*, p. 69, note.
266 Justus Möser, *Sämtliche Werke*, vol. 1, pp. 274 ff.
267 *Ibid.*, pp. 217 ff. We shall not analyse this essay in greater detail, although it could help in characterising this way of thinking.
268 *Ibid.*, p. 376.
269 *Ibid.*, p. 377 [Mannheim's emphasis].

270 'They do not intend to say any more by this than that their freedom and property do not depend on the wisdom of a judge, but on their judgement of the others in the fellowship.' (*ibid.*, p. 334, note).

271 On the survival of particularistic sympathies in Savigny cf. the following interesting passage: 'Since God has ordained (however regrettable this may be) [!], that Hanover, Nassau or Isenburg have no language and literature of their own, but that there is only a German one.' (*Vermischte Schriften*, vol. 5, p. 164).

272 'Secondly, all know, even those who have closed their hearts, that there has arisen a new and living love for the common fatherland in all German lands.' (*ibid.*, p. 124).

273 Most 'ideas', whatever 'party' they may belong to, have two sides: they contain something that is accurately seen, which is discoverable only from their particular standpoint, but at the same time they also serve the function of concealment. Accordingly, every sociological interpretation must approach ideas by way of both 'intrinsic' and 'extrinsic' interpretation. For more on this cf. my forthcoming study 'Ideologische und soziologische Interpretation der geistigen Gebilde', *Jahrbuch für Soziologie* (1926) 2: 424–440 ['The Ideological and Sociological Interpretation of Intellectual Phenomena', transl. Kurt H. Wolff, *Studies on the Left* (Summer 1963) 3,3: 54–66. Reprinted in Kurt H. Wolff, ed., *From Karl Mannheim*, London: Oxford University Press, 1971].

274 Cf. on this Emil Lederer, 'Das ökonomische Element und die politische Idee im modernen Parteiwesen', p. 536.

275 *Vom Beruf unserer Zeit*, p. 7 [p. 27].

276 Even on the revolutionary side, of course, it was not only a question of a totality by agglomeration. Note the difference between *volonté de tous* and *volonté générale*.

277 *Sämtliche Werke*, vol. 5, p. 144.

278 While the term 'spirit of the people' (*Volksgeist*) does not yet occur in *Beruf*, it is clearly present in substance. Cf. on this E. von Moeller, 'Die Entstehung des Dogmas vom dem Ursprung des Rechts aus dem Volksgeist', *Mitteilungen des Instituts für österreichische Geschichtsforschung* (1909) 30: 45; Hermann U. Kantorowicz, 'Volksgeist und historische Rechtsschule', *Historische Zeitschrift* (1912) 108: 301.

279 *Sämtliche Werke*, vol. 1, p. 385.

280 *Ibid.*, p. 379.

281 Wilhelm Metzger, 'Gesellschaft, Recht und Staat in der Ethik des deutschen Idealismus', pp. 42 ff., has a good description of the irrational nature of the factor of power and the historical location of this type.

282 It must be emphasised again and again that such observations merely tend to establish tendencies. In the case of every thinker who might serve as a counter-example, it must first be historically determined whether he has not in fact achieved a synthesis of styles of thought, and whether it is not precisely this which explains his deviation. There exists a generally reliable method for establishing this, which employs historical and sociological reasoning. Cf. my discussion on

the problem of imputation on pp. 39 ff. of this volume.
283 In this respect as well Lukács has seen much that is correct.
284 The irrationalities which explicitly originate in religious experience will be discussed later.
285 For example, von Moeller and Kantorowicz, in the just cited passages. [cf. p. 228, n. 278].
286 *System des heutigen römischen Rechts*, pp. 19, 21 [*System of Modern Roman Law*, pp. 15, 17].
287 *Vom Beruf unserer Zeit*, p. 5 [cf. p. 24].
288 *Ibid.*
289 *Ibid.*, p. 7 [cf. p. 27].
290 *Ibid.*, p. 8 [cf. p. 30].
291 *Ibid.*, p. 9 [cf. p. 31].
292 *Vermischte Schriften*, vol. 1, p. 110.
293 *Ibid.*
294 *Ibid.*, p. 128.
295 *Ibid.*, pp. 128 ff.
296 *Ibid.*, p. 131.
297 Cf. also the already quoted writings [note 278, p. 228] of von Moeller and of Kantorowicz (who also summarise the results of this discussion); Siegfried Brie, 'Der Volksgeist bei Hegel und in der historischen Rechtsschule', *Archiv für Rechts- und Wirtschaftsphilosophie* (1908/9) 2: 1 ff., 179 ff.; E. Löning, 'Philosophische Ausgangspunkte der rechtshistorischen Schule', *Internationale Wochenschrift für Wissenschaft, Kunst und Technik* (1910): 65 ff., 115 ff.; Ernst Landsberg, ed., *Roderich von Stintzing 1825–1883. Geschichte der deutschen Rechtswissenschaft*, Munich-Leipzig: R. Oldenbourg, 1910, pp. 209 ff., notes pp. 102 ff.; 412; also Franz Rosenzweig, *Hegel und der Staat*, pp. 232 ff.; Friedrich Meinecke, *Weltbürgertum und Nationalstaat*, p. 221, note 2.
298 Kantorowicz, 'Volksgeist und die historische Rechtsschule', pp. 314 ff.
299 Friedrich Wilhelm Joseph Schelling, 'System des transzendentalen Idealismus (1800)', *Sämtliche Werke*, vol. 3, Hamburg: Felix Meiner, 1856–61, p. 583 [cf. *System of Transcendental Idealism (1800)*, transl. Peter Heath, Charlottesville: University of Virginia Press, 1978, p. 195. We have decided against using this English translation, however].
300 The passages quoted are from Schelling, *ibid.*, pp. 583, 596, 606 [pp. 203, 205, 231].
301 In our presentation of his analysis, below, we closely follow Kantorowicz.
302 *Ibid.*, p. 318.
303 Hugo was born in 1764, Savigny in 1779.
304 Cf. Savigny's letters in Adolf Stoll, ed., *Friedrich Karl von Savignys sächsische Studienreisen 1799 und 1800*, Leipzig: 1891, p. 14.
305 Gustav Hugo, *Lehrbuch des Naturrechts als einer Philosophie des positiven Rechts, besonders des Privatrechts*, p. 34.

306 Cf. *ibid.*, the whole second section 'Der Mensch als vernünftiges Wesen', pp. 70 ff.
307 *Ibid.*, § 86, p. 105.
308 *Ibid.*, § 85, p. 103.
309 *Ibid.*, § 93, p. 116.
310 *Ibid.*, § 29, p. 35, note 1.
311 *Ibid.*, § 34, pp. 40 ff.
312 *Ibid.*, p. 28.
313 *Ibid.*, p. 123.
314 *Ibid.*, § 195, p. 125, note 3.
315 *Ibid.*, pp. 251 ff.
316 *Ibid.*, pp. 259 ff. [Mannheim's emphasis]
317 Relativism tends to be self-limiting. The relativity of revolutionaries remains radically relativist only as long as they seek to dissolve the established orders of things; they give up their relativity as soon as it becomes a question of the credibility of the things they uphold. The condition of suspended judgement just described is equally untenable on the conservative side, but must be set aside as soon as it is a question of volitional implementation of the underlying conservative design.
318 Ernst Landsberg, *Roderich von Stintzing*, pp. 1 ff.; also H. Singer, 'Zur Erinnerung an Gustav Hugo', *Zeitschrift für das Privat- und öffentliche Recht der Gegenwart* (1889) 16: 274 ff.
319 'From this condition, however it happens to be . . .' (Gustav Hugo, *Lehrbuch des Naturrechts*, S 112, p. 143). 'If nothing more should come out of this investigation than that we must submit to the law as it happens to be . . .' (S 113, p. 143).
320 When we speak of positions of synthesis we refer to positions which seek to bring together two socially and politically radically opposed powers and their ways of thinking, as, for example, when conservative thought assimilates liberal elements, or enlightened bourgeois thought socialist perspectives. Although, in a broad sense, a connection of older 'estate' and 'romantic' tendencies constitutes a synthesis as well, we nevertheless exclude it from the concept of synthesis that interests us here.
321 Karl Marx, 'Das philosophische Manifest der historischen Rechtsschule', in Frank Mehring, ed., *Aus dem literarischen Nachlass von Karl Marx und Friedrich Engels 1841 bis 1850*, pp. 268 ff. ['The Philosophical Manifesto of the Historical School of Law', in Marx/Engels, *Collected Works* vol. 1, New York: International Publishers, 1975, pp. 203 ff.], illustrates Hugo's position most pointedly (precisely with the one-sidedness of the adversary), even if his bitter animosity prevents him from seeing the positive achievements.
322 If Hugo cannot without qualifications be directly compared with Hegel, this is not least because the standpoint of conservative synthesis is complicated in Hegel by the problem of 'dynamic thinking' which had in the meantime arisen. We shall come back to this comparison later.

323 The last sentence already characterises a later stage of this tendency of thought and experience. It points to the positivist concept of ideology.

324 Cf. Max Weber, *Wirtschaft und Gesellschaft*; we cannot explore to what extent the *Religionssoziologie* represents a breakthrough beyond this stage.

325 Gustav Hugo, *Lehrbuch des Naturrechts*, p. 114.

326 § 52 (*ibid.*, p. 67) reads as follows: 'Usage. In organic bodies much depends on the previous condition, hence not only on what the individual is used to do, but also on that of the larger setting that brings it about.'

327 Gunnar Rexius, 'Studien zur Staatslehre der historischen Schule', accordingly calls the approach to history which results from this a 'negative-historical' one.

328 Hugo died in 1844.

329 Cf. Ernst Landsberg, *Roderich von Stintzing*, § 3, half-volume 2, p. 24, note 51. Cf. Hugo's preface to the tenth edition.

330 French sociology in particular has recently been preoccupied with the problem of generations, since France around the time of the Dreyfus Affair underwent a psychic transformation whose design could be observed at close hand.

331 Here we should mention that he had in mind not only the revolutionary variant of modern natural law, but also the variant upholding authority, which served at that time to provide a systematic overview of that which has positive legal effect. In Hugo's words: 'Natural law thus was a more or less complete encyclopedic catalogue of our positive law, which worked against all free-thinking philosophy of proclaiming the essentiality of everything that now exists.' (*ibid.*, p. 9). Cf. on this the entire § 6.

332 It is for this reason that Max Weber claims in *Wirtschaft und Gesellschaft*, p. 496 [*Economy and Society*, vol. 2, p. 867], that the conception of the historical school is also a type of natural law.

333 Cf. Gustav Hugo, *Lehrbuch des Naturrechts*, §§ 78, 79, 80, pp. 97–100.

334 He had not opposed the *Code Napoléon* either.

335 H. Singer, 'Zur Erinnerung an Gustav Hugo.'

336 Ernst Landsberg, *Roderich von Stintzing*.

337 His wife Kunigunde was the sister of Clemens and Bettina Brentano; the latter, however, was the wife of Achim von Arnim. Thus Clemens Brentano and Achim von Arnim were his brothers-in-law. His friend Friedrich Breuzer had close connections with the Heidelberg circle of romantics (cf. on this Ernst Landsberg, *Roderich von Stintzing*, p. 212; Adolf Stoll, *Friedrich Karl von Savignys sächsische Studienreisen*, p. 1).

338 Cf. on this Reinhold Steig, *Heinrich von Kleists Berliner Kämpfe*, pp. 21 ff.; what follows is based on Steig's presentation.

339 Reprinted in Steig, *ibid.*, pp. 21–2.

340 *Ibid.*, p. 23.

341 *Ibid.*, p. 29.
342 A sociological analysis of the structure of *German sociability* would be worthwhile. The *Christlich-Deutsche Tischgesellschaft* (Christian-German Dinner Society) had connections to the *Zeltersche Liedertafel* (choral society). See Johann Wilhelm Bornemann, *Die Zeltersche Liedertafel in Berlin, ihre Entstehung, Stiftung und Fortgang nebst einer Auswahl von Liedertafel- Gesängen und Liedern*, Berlin: Verlag der Deckerschen Geheimen Oberhofbuchdruckerei, 1851 (quoted by Reinhold Steig, *Heinrich von Kleists Berliner Kämpfe*, p. 19). But the early German conservative movement had yet another very important place of associational crystallisation: *Die Maikäferei* (the May buggery), which however had an entirely different character. On this cf. Fr. Wiegand, 'Der Verein der Maikäfer in Berlin', *Deutsche Rundschau* (1914): 279 ff.
343 This is undoubtedly also true of Adam Müller's *Über König Friedrich II*. We must not, however, be misled by the fact that he too always refers to 'totality'; reasoning from a particularistic standpoint had already become impossible. We have not analysed this work, already written in Berlin, in detail, since its position is basically similar to that of the *Elemente*.
344 An expression used by Gottfried Salomon.
345 Friedrich Savigny, *Vermischte Schriften*, vol. 1, pp. 117 ff.
346 Adam Müller, *Die Elemente der Staatskunst*, vol. 1, 14th lecture.
347 Friedrich Savigny, *Vermischte Schriften*, vol. 1, p. 113.
348 Cf. the collected works of v.d. Marwitz, *Ein märkischer Edelmann im Zeitalter der Befreiungskriege*, vol. 2, 1, pp. 252 ff.
349 Friedrich Meinecke, *Weltbürgertum und Nationalstaat*, chapter IX, especially pp. 220 ff.
350 Ernst Landsberg, *Roderich von Stintzing*, p. 186.
351 Even though the sense in which professors are state officials is on the outer limits of the notion of the 'bureaucratic'.
352 Gustav Schmoller, 'Der deutsche Beamtenstaat vom 16.–18. Jahrhundert', *Jahrbuch für Gesetzgebung, Verwaltung und Volkswirtschaft* (1894) 18: 712.
353 Karl Lamprecht, *Deutsche Geschichte*, vol. 8, p. 221. For further detail cf. also the instructive explanations by the author.
354 Some useful information about the parties at court around 1814 can be found in Heinrich v. Treitschke, *Deutsche Geschichte im 19. Jahrhundert*, Leipzig: S. Hirzel, 1886, part 2, pp. 183 ff.
355 Reinhold Steig, *Heinrich von Kleists Berliner Kämpfe*, pp. 54 ff.
356 C. Varrentrapp, 'Rankes *Historisch-politische Zeitschrift* und das Berliner *Politische Wochenblatt*', pp. 87 ff.
357 Freiherr vom Stein's distinctive intellectual make-up and the structure of his thinking requires special structural analysis. The controversy between Lehmann and E. von Meier already suggests the difficulty of the problem. (Mannheim refers here to two books on Freiherr vom Stein by Lehmann and by von Meier offering conflicting interpretations of vom Stein: Max Ludwig Eduard

Lehmann, *Freiherr vom Stein*, Leipzig: S. Hirzel, 1902–1905, 5 vols.; and Ernst von Meier, *Französische Einflüsse auf die Staats- und Rechtsentwicklung Preussens im 19. Jahrhundert*.

358 The officialdom's loyalty to the dynasty is gradually transformed into allegiance to the state precisely in this period. Cf. Max Lenz, *Geschichte der Kgl. Friedrich-Wilhelms-Universität zu Berlin*, vol. 1, Halle: Buchhandlung des Waisenhauses, 1910, vol. 1, p. 9.

359 *Editorial Note*: The *Archiv*-essay contains the following concluding paragraph: [As we have just shown, the social differentiation of experience and of thought reaches deep into *ontology*; even the concept of reality is historically, politically and socially differentiated. We have seen how political and historical thought is formed alongside of and in closest connection with a sociologically defined real basis; how the delicate web of forms and ways of thinking contains and has 'preserved' within itself the entire destiny of the social whole as it exists in history. We have seen that at an important juncture of events, where an historically and sociologically determined alliance between the previously separate spheres of life comes about, this alliance expresses itself in a conjunction of the corresponding forms of experience and thought. It is a task of the sociology of knowledge to refine both the method of social analysis and the method of the phenomenological analysis of meaning in such a manner that the course of political and historical thought, but also of historical consciousness in general, becomes a problem which can be investigated with a considerable degree of accuracy.]

Bibliography

[This bibliography contains only those titles which are expressly referred to in *Conservatism*. Missing bibliographical information has been added or completed. Where Mannheim refers to 2nd or later editions of a book, the date of the first publication has been added in square brackets. Available English translations have been added as well, again in square brackets – Eds.]

ANDREAS, WILLY, 'Marwitz und der Staat Friedrichs des Grossen', *Historische Zeitschrift* (1920) 122: 44–82.

BARKER, SIR ERNEST, *Political Thought in England from Spencer to the Present Day*, New York: Holt & Co., 1915.

BARON, HANS, 'Justus Mösers Individualitätsprinzip in seiner geistesge-schichtlichen Bedeutung', *Historische Zeitschrift* (1924) 130: 31–57.

BAXA, JAKOB, *Einführung in die romantische Staatswissenschaft*, Jena: G. Fischer, 1923.

BAXA, JAKOB, 'Justus Möser und Adam Müller. Eine vergleichende Studie', *Jahrbücher für Nationalökonomie und Statistik* (1925) 123: 14–30.

BAXA, JAKOB, 'Introduction' to Adam Müller, *Die Elemente der Staats-kunst*, Vienna-Leipzig: Wiener Literarische Anstalt, 1922.

BAXA, JAKOB, ed., *Gesellschaft und Staat im Spiegel deutscher Romantik*, Jena: G. Fischer, 1924.

Below, GEORG VON, 'Die Anfänge der konservativen Partei in Preussen', *Internationale Wochenschrift für Wissenschaft, Kunst und Technik*, 1911.

Below, GEORG VON, 'Die deutsche Geschichtsschreibung von den Befrei-ungskriegen bis zu unseren Tagen', in Georg von Below, ed., *Handbuch der mittelalterlichen und neueren Geschichte*, Munich-Berlin: R. Oldenbourg, 1924.

Below, GEORG VON, 'Wesen und Ausbreitung der Romantik', in von Below, *Über historische Periodisierungen mit besonderem Blick auf die Grenze zwischen Mittelalter und Neuzeit*, Berlin: Deutsche Verlagsge-sellschaft für Politik und Geschichte, 1925.

BERGSTRÄSSER, LUDWIG, *Geschichte der politischen Parteien in Deutschland* [1921], 2nd rev. ed., Schriftenreihe der Verwaltungsakademie Berlin, Mannheim: J. Bensheimer, 1921.

BONALD, LOUIS G.A. DE, 'De la philosophie morale et politique du 18e siècle', *Oeuvres*, vol. 9, Paris: Adrien Le Clerc, 1817.

BORNEMANN, JOHANN WILHELM, *Die Zeltersche Liedertafel in Berlin, ihre Entstehung, Stiftung und Fortgang nebst einer Auswahl von Liedertafel-Gesängen und Liedern*, Berlin: Verlag der Deckerschen Geheimen Oberhofbuchdruckerei, 1851.

BORRIES, KURT, *Die Romantik und die Geschichte*, Berlin: Deutsche Verlagsgesellschaft für Politik und Geschichte, 1925.

BRAUNE, FRIEDA, *Edmund Burke in Deutschland*, Heidelberg: C. Winter, 1917.

Briefwechsel zwischen Friedrich Gentz und Adam Heinrich Müller, 1800–1829, Stuttgart: J. G. Cotta, 1857.

BRIE, SIEGFRIED, 'Der Volksgeist bei Hegel und in der historischen Rechtsschule', *Archiv für Rechts- und Wirtschaftsphilosophie* (1908–1909) 2: 179–202.

BRINKMAN, CARL, 'Carl Schmitts politische Romantik', *Archiv für Sozialwissenschaft und Sozialpolitik* (1926) 54.

BURKE, EDMUND, 'Reflections on the Revolution in France' [1790], in *Works*, Vol. 5, London: C. and J. Rivingston, 1801. [*Betrachtungen über die französische Revolution*. Nach dem Englischen des Herrn Burke neu bearbeitet mit einer Einleitung, Anmerkungen, politischen Abhandlungen und einem kritischen Verzeichnis der in England über diese Revolution erschienenen Schriften von Friedrich Gentz. Hohenzollern, 1794.]

Bund deutscher Gelehrter und Künstler, eds., *Deutsche Freiheit*. Five lectures by Harnack, Meinecke, Sering, Troeltsch, Hintze, Gotha: F. A. Perthes, 1917.

CECIL, LORD HUGH, *Conservatism*, Home University Library of Modern Knowledge, vol. 11, London: Williams and Norgate, 1912.

DILTHEY, WILHELM, 'Das 18. Jahrhundert und die geschichtliche Welt', *Deutsche Rundschau* (1901) 108: 481–93.

DILTHEY, WILHELM, *Leben Schleiermachers* [1870], vol. 1, 2nd enl. ed., Berlin-Leipzig: W. de Gruyter, 1922.

DILTHEY, WILHELM, 'Weltanschauung und Analyse des Menschen seit der Renaissance und Reformation', *Gesammelte Schriften*, vol. 2, Leipzig: B. G. Teubner, 1914.

DROYSEN, JOHANN GUSTAV, *Grundriss der Historik*, Halle: M. Neimeyer, 1925 [*Outline on the Principle of History*. transl. E. Benjamin Andrews, Boston: Ginn & Company, 1893].

ECHTERMEYER, THEODOR and ARNOLD RUGE, 'Der Protestantismus und die Romantik. Zur Verständigung über die Zeit und ihre Gegensätze. Ein Manifest', *Hallische Jahrbücher für deutsche Wissenschaft und Kunst* (1839). Reprinted as Theodor Echtermeyer and Arnold Ruge, *Der Protestantismus und die Romantik*, ed. Norbert Oellers, Hildesheim: H. A. Gerstenberg, 1972.

EICHNER, JOHANNES, 'Das Problem des Gegebenen in der Kunstgeschichte', *Festschrift für Alois Riehl: Von Freunden und Schülern zu seinem siebzigsten Geburtstag dargebracht*, Halle: M. Niemeyer, 1914.

ENGEL-JÁNOSI, FRIEDRICH, 'Die Theorie vom Staat im deutschen Österreich 1815–48', *Zeitschrift für öffentliches Recht* (1921) 2, 1/2: 360–94.

FRANK, ERICH, *Plato und die sogenannten Pythagoräer*, Halle: M. Niemeyer, 1923.

FRANTZ, GUSTAV ADOLPH CONSTANTIN, *Kritik aller Parteien*, Berlin: F. Schneider, 1862.

FREYER, HANS, 'Die Bewertung der Wirtschaft im philosophischen Denken des 19. Jahrhunderts'. *Arbeiten zur Entwicklungspsychologie*, vol. 5, ed. Felix Krüger, Leipzig: W. Engelmann, 1921.

FRIEDRICH II DER GROSSE, *Die politischen Testamente* [1752; 1768], transl. from the French by Fr. von Oppeln-Bronikowski, ed. G. B. Volz [1920], Berlin: R. Hobbing, 1922.

FRIEDRICHS, ARNO, *Klassische Philosophie und Wirtschaftswissenschaft*, Gotha: F. A. Perthes, 1913.

GENTZ, FRIEDRICH VON, *Schriften*, ed. Schlesier, Mannheim: Heinrich Hoff, 1838–1840.

GIERKE, OTTO VON, *Die historische Rechtsschule und die Germanisten*. Rede zur Gedächtnisfeier des Stifters der Berliner Universität, König Friedrich Wilhelm, Berlin: G. Schade, 1903.

GIERKE, OTTO VON, *Johannes Althusius und die Entwicklung der naturrechtlichen Staatstheorien* [1880], 3rd ed., Breslau: M. & H. Marcus, 1913 [*The Development of Political Theory*, transl. Bernard Freyd, London: Allen & Unwin, 1939].

HALLER, KARL LUDWIG VON, *Restauration der Staatswissenschaft oder Theorie des natürlich-geselligen Zustands; der Chimäre des künstlich-bürgerlichen entgegengesetzt*, 6 vols [1816–1825], 2nd enl. and rev. ed., vols 2–4, Winterthur: Steiner, 1820.

HATZIG, OTTO, *Justus Möser als Staatmann und Publizist*. Quellen und Darstellung zur Geschichte Niedersachsens, vol. 27, Hannover-Leipzig: O. Wigand, 1909.

HEGEL, GEORG W. FR., *Grundlinien der Philosophie des Rechts* [1821], newly ed. by G. Lasson, Leipzig: F. Meiner, 1911 [*Hegel's Philosophy of Right*, transl. T. M. Knox, London, Oxford, New York: Oxford University Press, 1967].

HEINE, HEINRICH, 'Die romantische Schule' [1833], *Gesammelte Werke*, vol. 5, Leipzig and Vienna: Bibliographisches Institut, 1898.

HELLER, HERMANN, *Hegel und der nationale Machtstaatsgedanke in Deutschland*. Ein Beitrag zur politischen Geistesgeschichte, Leipzig-Berliner: B. G. Teubner, 1921.

HINTZE, OTTO, 'Das monarchische Prinzip und die konstitutionelle Verfassung', *Preussische Jahrbücher* (1911) 144: 381–412.

HERRE, PAUL, ed., *Politisches Handwörterbuch*, Leipzig: K. F. Köhler, 1923.

HUGO, GUSTAV, *Lehrbuch des Naturrechts als einer Philosophie des positiven Rechts, besonders des Privatrechts* [1798], 4th ed., Berlin: August Mylius, 1819.

JEDELE, E., *Die kirchenpolitischen Anschauungen des Ernst Ludwig von*

Gerlach, Ph.D. Dissertion, Tübingen, 1910.

JELLINEK, GEORG, *Die Erklärung der Menschen- und Bürgerrechte. Ein Beitrag zur modernen Verfassungsgeschichte* [1895], 3rd ed., Berlin: Duncker & Humblot, 1919. [*The Declaration of the Rights of Man and of Citizens: A Contribution to Modern Constitutional History*, transl. Max Farrand, New York: Holt & Co., 1901.]

JORDON, ERICH, *Die Entstehung der konservativen Partei und die preussischen Agrarverhältnisse von 1848*, Munich-Leipzig: Duncker & Humblot, 1914.

KANTOROWICZ, HERMANN U., 'Volksgeist und historische Rechtsschule', *Historische Zeitschrift* (1912) 108: 295–325.

KAUFMANN, ERICH, *Über den Begriff des Organismus in der Staatslehre des 19. Jahrhunderts*, Heidelberg: C. Winter, 1908.

KAUFMANN, GEORG, *Geschichte Deutschlands im 19. Jahrhundert*, Berlin: G. Bondi, 1912.

KLUCKHOHN, PAUL, *Persönlichkeit und Gemeinschaft*, Halle: M. Neimeyer, 1925.

LAMPRECHT, KARL G., *Deutsche Geschichte*, Freiburg: H. Heyfelder, 1904.

LANDSBERG, ERNST, ed., *Roderich von Stintzing 1825–1883. Geschichte der deutschen Rechtswissenschaft*, 3rd part, second half-volume, vol. 37 ('Geschichte der Wissenschaften in Deutschland. Neuere Zeit', vol. 18, 3rd part, second half-volume), Munich-Leipzig: R. Oldenbourg, 1910.

LEDERER, EMIL, 'Das ökonomische Element und die politische Idee im modernen Parteiwesen', *Zeitschrift für Politik* (1911) 5: 535 ff.

LEHMANN, LUGWIG EDUARD, *Freiherr vom Stein*, 5 vols., Leipzig: S. Hirzel, 1902–1905.

LENIN, VLADIMIR I., *Sämtliche Werke*, Vienna: Verlag für Literatur und Politik, 1925.

LENNOX, RICHMOND, *Edmund Burke und sein politisches Arbeitsfeld in den Jahren 1760–1790*, Munich-Berlin: R. Oldenbourg, 1923.

LENZ, FRIEDRICH, *Agrarlehre und Agrarpolitik der deutschen Romantik*, Berlin: P. Parey, 1912.

LENZ, MAX, *Geschichte der Kgl. Friedrich-Wilhelms-Universität zu Berlin*, 3 vols, Halle: Buchhandlung des Waisenhauses, 1910.

LESSING, KURT, *Rehberg und die französische Revolution. Ein Beitrag zur Geschichte des literarischen Kampfes gegen die revolutionären Ideen in Deutschland*, Freiburg: C. A. Wagner, 1910.

LÖNING, E., 'Philosophische Ausgangspunkte der rechtshistorischen Schule', *Internationale Wochenschrift für Wissenschaft, Kunst und Technik*, 1910.

LUBLINSKI, SAMUEL, *Literatur und Gesellschaft im neunzehnten Jahrhundert*, vol. 1, Berlin: S. Cronbach, 1899–1900.

LUKÁCS, GEORG, *Geschichte und Klassenbewusstsein. Studien über marxistische Dialektik*, Berlin: Malik Verlag, 1923. [*History and Class Consciousness: Studies in Marxist Dialectics*, transl. Rodney Livingstone, London: Merlin, 1971.]

MAISTRE, JOSEPH MARIE DE, 'Considérations sur la France' [1796], in *Oeuvres*, Paris 1819. [German ed., 'Betrachtungen über Frankreich,' in R. Rohden, ed., *Klassiker der Politik*, vol. 2., Berlin: R. Hobbing, 1924.

English ed., 'Reflections on the Revolution in France', in Jack Lively, ed. and transl., *The Works of Joseph de Maistre*, London: Collier-Macmillan, 1965].

MANNHEIM, KARL, 'Historismus', *Archiv für Sozialwissenschaft und Sozialpolitik* (1924) 52: 1–60 ['Historicism', *Essays on the Sociology of Knowledge*, ed. and transl. Paul Kecskemeti, London: Routledge & Kegan Paul, 1952, pp. 84–133].

MANNHEIM, KARL, 'Das Problem einer Soziologie des Wissens', *Archiv für Sozialwissenschaft und Sozialpolitik* (1925) 53: 577–652 ['The Problem of a Sociology of Knowledge', *Essays on the Sociology of Knowledge*, ed. and transl. Paul Kecskemeti, London: Routledge & Kegan Paul, 1952, pp. 134–190].

MANNHEIM, KARL, 'Ideologische und soziologische Interpretation der geistigen Gebilde', *Jahrbuch für Soziologie* (1926) 2: 424–440 ['The Ideological and the Sociological Interpretation of Intellectual Phenomena', transl. Kurt H. Wolff, *Studies on the Left* 3, 3 (Summer 1963): 54–66].

MANNHEIM, KARL, 'Beiträge zur Theorie der Weltanschauungs-Interpretation, *Jahrbuch für Kunstgeschichte* (1921–22) 1: 236–274 [On the Interpretation of "Weltanschauung"', *Essays on the Sociology of Knowledge*, ed. and transl. Paul Kecskemeti, London: Routledge & Kegan Paul, 1952, pp. 33–83].

MARTIN, ALFRED W.D. VON, 'Weltanschauliche Motive im altkonservativen Denken', in Paul Wentzke, ed., *Deutscher Staat und deutsche Parteien*. Beiträge zur deutschen Partei- und Ideengeschichte (Festschrift for F. Meinecke), Munich-Berlin: R. Oldenbourg, 1922.

MARX, KARL, *Das Kapital*, 3 vols., [1867–1894] 9th ed., Hamburg: O. Meissner, 1921 [*Capital*, transl. Ben Fowkes (vol. 1) and David Fernbach (vols. 2 and 3), New York: Random House, 1977–81].

MARX, KARL, 'Zur Kritik der Hegelschen Rechtsphilosophie' [1844], in Franz Mehring, ed., *Aus dem literarischen Nachlass von Karl Marx und Friedrich Engels 1841 bis 1850*, vol. 1, Berlin-Stuttgart: J. H. W. Dietz, 1923 ['A Contribution to the Critique of Hegel's "Philosophy of Right"', in Joseph O'Malley, ed., *Critique of Hegel's 'Philosophy of Right'*, transl. Annette Jolin and Joseph O'Malley, Cambridge: Cambridge University Press, 1970].

MARX, KARL, 'Das philosophische Manifest der historischen Rechtsschule' [1842], in Franz Mehring, ed., *Aus dem literarischen Nachlass von Karl Marx und Friedrich Engels, 1841 bis 1850*, vol. 1, Berlin-Stuttgart: J. H. W. Dietz, 1923 ['The Philosophical Manifesto of the Historical School of Law', in Marx/Engels, *Collected Works*, vol. 1, New York: International Publishers, 1975].

MARWITZ, FRIEDRICH V.D., *Ein märkischer Edelmann im Zeitalter der Befreiungskriege*, 2nd vol. in four half-vols., ed. Fr. Meusel, Berlin: E. S. Mittler, 1908–1913.

MEHRING, FRANZ, *Geschichte der deutschen Sozialdemokratie*, Berlin-Stuttgart: J. H. W. Dietz, 1922.

MEIER, ERNST VON, *Französische Einflüsse auf die Staats- und Rechtsentwicklung Preussens im 19. Jahrhundert*, vol. 1 (*Prolegomena*), vol. 2

(*Preussen und die französische Revolution*), Leipzig: Duncker & Humblot, 1907–1908.

MEINECKE, FRIEDRICH, *Weltbürgertum und Nationalstaat. Studien zur Genesis des deutschen Nationalstaates*, 6th ed., Munich-Berlin: R. Oldenbourg, 1922 [*Cosmopolitanism and the National State*, transl. Robert B. Kimber, Princeton, N.J.: Princeton University Press, 1970].

MEISSNER, HEINRICH OTTO, *Die Lehre vom monarchischen Prinzip im Zeitalter der Restauration und des deutschen Bundes*. Untersuchungen zur deutschen Staats- und Rechtsgeschichte, ed. Otto v. Gierke, issue 122, Breslau, 1913.

MERKEL, ALFRED, *Fragmente zur Sozialwissenschaft*, Strasbourg: K. J. Trübner, 1898.

METTERNICH-WINNEBURG, CLEMENS L. W. VON, *Denkwürdigkeiten*, vol. 2, ed. Otto H. Brandt, Munich: G. Müller, 1921.

METZGER, WILHELM, *Gesellschaft, Recht und Staat in der Ethik des deutschen Idealismus*, posthumously published in an ed. by Ernst Bergmann, Heidelberg: C. Winter, 1917.

MEUSEL, FRITZ, *Edmund Burke und die französische Revolution. Zur Entstehung historisch-politischen Denkens zumal in England*, Berlin: Weidmann, 1913.

MOELLER, E. VON, 'Die Entstehung des Dogmas von dem Ursprung des Rechts aus dem Volksgeist', *Mitteilungen des Instituts für österreichische Geschichtsforschung* (1909) 30: 1–50.

MÖSER, JUSTUS, *Gesellschaft und Staat*. Eine Auswahl aus seinen Schriften, ed. K. Brandi, Munich: Drei Masken, 1921.

MÖSER, JUSTUS, *Sämtliche Werke*, ed. B. R. Abeken, vol. 1, Berlin: Nicolai, 1842/43.

MORLEY, JOHN, *Burke*, London: Macmillan & Co., 1923.

MÜLLER, ADAM HEINRICH, *Die Elemente der Staatskunst* [1809] , ed. Jakob Baxa, Vienna-Leipzig: Wiener Literarische Anstalt, 1922.

MÜLLER, ADAM HEINRICH, 'Die Lehre vom Gegensatz' [1804], in *Ausgewählte Abhandlungen*, ed. J. Baxa, Jena: G. Fischer, 1921.

MÜLLER, ADAM HEINRICH, *Über König Friedrich II und die Natur, Würde und Bestimmung der preussischen Monarchie*, Berlin: J. D. Sander, 1810.

MÜLLER, ADAM HEINRICH, 'Vom Wesen der Definition' [1808], *Phoebus. Ein Journal für die Kunst*, vol. 1, ed. H. v. Kleist and A. H. Müller. Reprinted as *Neudrucke romantischer Seltenheiten* 2, Munich: Meyer & Jessen, 1924.

NOVALIS, *Schriften*, ed. J. Minor, Jena: Diederichs, 1907.

NOVALIS, 'Die Christenheit oder Europe', *Schriften*, ed. Paul Kluckhohn and Richard Samuel, vol. 2, Stuttgart: Kohlhammer, 1960, pp. 507–524 [*Christianity or Europe*, transl. John Dalton, London: Chapman, 1844].

NOVALIS, 'Logologische Fragmente II' [1798], *Schriften*, ed. Paul Kluckhohn and Richard Samuel, Stuttgart: Kohlhammer, 1960.

OPPENHEIMER, FRANZ, *System der Soziologie*, vol. 1 (Allgemeine Soziologie), Jena: G. Fischer, 1922.

POETZSCH, ALBERT, 'Studien zur frühromantischen Politik-und Geschichtsauffassung', in Karl Lamprecht, ed., *Beiträge zur Kultur- und Universalgeschichte* 3, Leipzig: Voigtländer, 1907.

PRZYWARA, P.E.S.J., 'Introduction', to Adam Heinrich Müller, *Schriften zur Staatsphilosophie*, ed. Rudolf Kohler, Munich: Theatiner Verlag, 1923.

RACKPFAHL, 'Konservativ', in Paul Herre, ed., *Politisches Handwörterbuch*, Leipzig: K. F. Köhler, 1923.

RADBRUCH, GUSTAV, *Grundzüge der Rechtsphilosophie*, Leipzig: Quelle & Meyer, 1914.

RANKE, LEOPOLD VON, *Das politische Gespräch und andere Schriften zur Wissenschaftslehre*, Halle: N. Niemeyer, 1925.

RANKE, LEOPOLD VON, ed., *Historisch-politische Zeitschrift*, Berlin: Duncker & Humblot, 1832.

REHBERG, AUGUST WILHELM, *Untersuchungen über die französische Revolution nebst kritischen Nachrichten von dem merkwürdigsten Schriften welche darüber in Frankreich erschienen sind*, two vols., Hanover: C. Ritscher, 1793.

REXIUS, GUNNAR, 'Studien zur Staatslehre der historischen Schule', *Historische Zeitschrift* (1911) 107: 496–538.

RICKERT, HEINRICH, *Die Grenzen der naturwissenschaftlichen Begriffsbildung* [1902], 3rd and 4th rev. and enl. ed., Tübingen: J. C. B. Mohr, 1921.

ROHDEN, PETER R., 'Deutscher und französischer Konservatismus', *Dioskuren. Jahrbuch für Geisteswissenschaften* (1924) 3: 90–138.

ROTHACKER, ERICH, *Einleitung in die Geisteswissenschaften*, Tübingen: J. C. B. Mohr, 1920.

ROTHACKER, ERICH, 'Savigny, Grimm, Ranke. Ein Beitrag zur Frage nach dem Zusammenhang der Historischen Schule', *Historische Zeitschrift* (1923) 128: 415–45.

ROSENZWEIG, FRANZ, *Hegel und der Staat*, Munich-Berlin: R. Oldenbourg, 1920.

SALOMON, FELIX, *Englische Geschichte von den Anfängen bis zur Gegenwart*, Leipzig: K. F. Köhler, 1923.

SALOMON, FELIX, *Die deutschen Parteiprogramme* (Quellensammlung zur deutschen Geschichte, vol. 2) [1907], 2nd ed., Leipzig: B. G. Teubner, 1912.

SALOMON-DELATOUR, GOTTFRIED, *Das Mittelalter als Ideal der Romantik*, Munich: Drei Masken Verlag, 1922.

SAVIGNY, FRIEDRICH CARL VON, *System des heutigen römischen Rechts*, vol. 1, Berlin: Veit & Co., 1840 [*System of Modern Roman Law*, vol. 1, transl. William Holloway, Madras: J. Higginbotham, 1867].

SAVIGNY, FRIEDRICH C. VON, *Vermischte Schriften*, vols. 1–5, Berlin: Veit & Co., 1850.

SAVIGNY, FRIEDREICH C. VON, *Vom Beruf unserer Zeit für Gesetzgebung und Rechtswissenschaft* [1814], reprint of the 3rd. ed. of 1840, Freiburg: Mohr, 1892 [*Of the Vocation of Our Age for Legislation and Jurisprudence*, transl. Abraham Hayward, London: Littlewood & Co., 1831].

SCHELER, MAX, 'Probleme einer Soziologie des Wissens', in Max Scheler, ed., *Versuche zu einer Soziologie des Wissens*, Munich-Leipzig:

Duncker & Humblot, 1924 [*Problems of a Sociology of Knowledge*, transl. Manfred S. Frings, ed. Kenneth W. Stikkers, London, Boston and Henley: Routledge & Kegan Paul, 1980].

SCHELER, MAX, *Vom Umsturz der Werte*, Leipzig: Der Neue Geist Verlag, 1919. [Includes 'Das Ressentiment im Aufbau der Moralen' and 'Die Idole der Selbsterkenntnis', translated as *Ressentiment*, ed. Lewis Coser, transl. W. W. Holdheim, New York: Free Press, 1961; and 'The Idols of Self-Knowledge', in M. Scheler, *Selected Philosophical Essays*, transl. David R. Lachtermann, Evanston: Northwestern University Press, 1973.]

SCHELLING, FRIEDRICH WILHELM JOSEPH, 'System des transzendentalen Idealismus (1800)', *Sämtliche Werke*, vol. 3, Hamburg: Felix Meiner, 1856–61 [*System of Transcendental Idealism (1800)*, transl. Peter Heath, Charlottesville: University of Virginia Press, 1978.

SCHLEGEL, FRIEDRICH VON, 'Signatur des Zeitalters', published in article-form in *Concordia* between 1820–23.

SCHMITT, CARL, *Die geistesgeschichtliche Lage des heutigen Parlamentarismus*, Munich-Leipzig: Duncker & Humblot, 1923.

SCHMITT-DOROTIĆ, CARL, *Politische Romantik*, Munich-Leipzig: Duncker & Humblot, 1919.

SCHMOLLER, GUSTAV F., 'Der deutsche Beamtenstaat vom 16.–18. Jahrhundert', *Jahrbuch für Gesetzgebung, Verwaltung und Volkswirtschaft* (1894) 18: 695–714.

SCHOFFLER, HERBERT, *Protestantismus und Literatur. Neue Wege zur englischen Literatur des 18. Jahrhunderts*, Leipzig: B. Tauchnitz, 1922.

SIMMEL, GEORG, *Philosophie des Geldes*, Leipzig: Duncker & Humblot, 1900 [*The Philosophy of Money*, transl. of 2nd. rev. ed. of 1907 by Tom Bottomore and David Frisby, Boston, London, Melbourne and Henley: Routledge & Kegan Paul, 1978].

SINGER, H., 'Zur Erinnerung an Gustav Hugo', *Zeitschrift für das Privat- und öffentliche Recht der Gegenwart* (1889) 16: 275–319.

SOMBART, WERNER, *Der Bourgeois. Zur Geistesgeschichte des modernen Wirtschaftsmenschen* [1913], Berlin: Duncker & Humblot, 1920 [*The Quintessence of Capitalism: A Study of the History and Psychology of the Modern Business Man*, transl. M. Epstein, London: T. F. Unwin, 1915].

SOMBART, WERNER, *Die deutsche Volkswirtschaft im 19. Jahrhundert und im Anfang des 20. Jahrhundert* [1903], 5th ed., Berlin: G. Bondi, 1921.

SOMBART, WERNER, *Der moderne Kapitalismus*, 3 vols [1902], 2nd rev. ed., Berlin: Duncker & Humblot, 1916.

SRBIK, HEINRICH VON, *Metternich der Staatsmann und der Mensch*, Munich: F. Bruckmann, 1925.

STAHL, FRIEDRICH JULIUS, *Die gegenwärtigen Parteien in Staat und Kirche*, Berlin: W. Hertz, 1863.

STAHL, FRIEDRICH JULIUS, *Die Philosophie des Rechts*, 2 vols. [1830–1837], 5th ed., Tübingen: J. C. B. Mohr, 1878.

STEFFENS, WILHELM, *Hardenberg und die ständische Opposition 1810/11.* Veröffentlichungen des Vereins für die Geschichte der Mark Brandenburg, Leipzig: Duncker & Humblot, 1907.

241

STEIG, REINHOLD, *Heinrich von Kleists Berliner Kämpfe*, Berlin-Stuttgart: W. Spemann, 1901.

STILLICH, OSKAR, 'Die Konservativen', in Stillich, ed., *Die politischen Parteien in Deutschland*, vol. 1, Leipzig: W. Klinkhardt, 1908.

STOLL, ADOLF, ed., *Friedrich Karl von Savignys sächsische Studienreisen 1799 und 1800*, Leipzig: 1891.

TOCQUEVILLE, ALEXIS DE, *L'ancien régime et la révolution*, Paris: C. Lévy, 1877 [*The Old Régime and the French Revolution*, transl. Stuart Gilbert, Garden City, N.Y.: Doubleday Anchor, 1955].

TREITSCHKE, HEINRICH G. VON, *Deutsche Geschichte im 19. Jahrhundert*, vol. 3, Leipzig: S. Hirzel, 1886.

TROELTSCH, ERNST, 'Die kulturgeschichtliche Methode in der Dogmengeschichte: Die Bedeutung der *lex naturae* für Katholizismus und Reformation' [1901], a review of E. Seeberg's *Lehrbuch der Dogmengeschichte*, in Troeltsch, *Gesammelte Schriften*, vol. 4, Tübingen: J. C. B. Mohr, 1922.

TROELTSCH, ERNST, 'Das stoisch-christliche Naturrecht und das moderne profane Naturrecht', *Verhandlungen des ersten deutschen Soziologentages vom 19.–22. Oktober 1910*, Tübingen: J. C. B. Mohr, 1911.

TROELTSCH, ERNST, 'Der Historismus und seine Probleme', in Troeltsch, *Gesammelte Schriften*, vol. 3, Tübingen: J. C. B. Mohr, 1922.

TROELTSCH, ERNST, 'Die Soziallehren der christlichen Kirchen und Gruppen', in Troeltsch, *Gesammelte Schriften*, vol. 1, Tübingen: J. C. B. Mohr, 1912 [*The Social Teachings of the Christian Churches*, transl. Olive Wyon, New York: Macmillan, 1931].

TROELTSCH, ERNST, *Naturrecht und Humanität in der Weltpolitik*. Vortrag bei der zweiten Jahresfeier der deutschen Hochschule für Politik, Berlin: Verlag für Politik und Wirtschaft, 1923 [*Natural Law and the Theory of Society, 1500–1800, with a Lecture on 'The Ideas of Natural Law and Humanity'*, transl. Ernest Barker, Cambridge: Cambridge University Press, 1934].

VAN TIEGHEM, PAUL, *Le préromantisme. Études d'histoire littéraire européenne*, Paris: F. Rieder, 1924.

VARRENTRAPP, C., 'Rankes *Historisch-politische Zeitschrift* und das Berliner *Politische Wochenblatt*', *Historische Zeitschrift* (1907) 99: 35–119.

VENEDEY, JAKOB, *Die deutschen republikaner unter der französischen Republik*, Leipzig: F. A. Brockhaus, 1870.

WAHL, ADALBERT, "Beiträge zur deutschen Parteigeschichte im 19. Jahrhundert", *Historische Zeitschrift* (1910) 104: 537–94.

WAHL, ADALBERT, 'Montesquieu als Vorläufer von Aktion und Reaktion', *Historische Zeitschrift* (1912) 109: 129–48.

WEBER, ALFRED, 'Prinzipielles zur Kultursoziologie', *Archiv für Sozialwissenschaft und Sozialpolitik* (1921) 47: 1–49.

WEBER, MAX, *Gesammelte Aufsätze zur Religionssoziologie*, vol. 3, Tübingen: J. C. B. Mohr, 1920.

WEBER, MAX, *Wirtschaft und Gesellschaft*, Tübingen: J. C. B. Mohr, 1922 [*Economy and Society*, ed. Guenther Roth and Claus Wittich, Berkeley, Los Angeles, London: University of California Press, 1978].

WEISE, ALFRED, *Die Entwicklung des Fühlens und Denkens der Romantik auf Grund der romantischen Zeitschriften*, Ph.D. Dissertation, Leipzig: R. Voigtländer, 1912.

WIEGAND, FR., 'Der Verein der Maikäfer in Berlin', *Deutsche Rundschau* (1914): 279–91.

WINDELBAND, WILHELM, *Lehrbuch der Geschichte der Philosophie* [1892], 5th rev. ed., Tübingen: J. C. B. Mohr, 1910.

WINDELBAND, WILHELM, *Präludien* [1884], 4th rev. ed., Tübingen: J. C. B. Mohr, 1911.

A note on the text and translation

The present edition of Karl Mannheim's *Habilitationsschrift* on Conservatism reproduces, with relatively minor editorial adjustments, the actual text of a work entitled *Altkonservatismus: Ein Beitrag zur Soziologie des Wissens*, which Mannheim submitted in December 1925 to Professors Carl Brinkmann, Emil Lederer and Alfred Weber, who were acting on behalf of the Faculty of Philosophy at the *Ruprecht-Karls-Universität* in Heidelberg. It is on the basis of this work that his three examiners recommended to the Senate of the University that the *venia legendi* be awarded to Mannheim. After a delay due to the controversy concerning Mannheim's lack of German nationality, which is recounted in the 'Introduction', it was finally granted on June 12, 1926. Mannheim's inaugural lecture on that same day was entitled 'Zur gegenwärtigen Lage der Soziologie in Deutschland' (The Present State of Sociology in Germany).[1]

Nearly a year later, on May 5, 1927, Mannheim deposited in the University archives six copies of an article entitled 'Das konservative Denken', which had been published in the *Archiv für Sozialwissenschaft und Sozialpolitik* (vol. 57, 1927). It is this text which has since then often been mistaken for Mannheim's *Habilitationsschrift*, an error doubtlessly grounded on the erroneous catalogue entry in the University Library in Heidelberg.[2] In fact, however, the published essay omits two major sections of the original work altogether, including important methodological reflections by Mannheim, and contains, in all, less than half of the entire manuscript. Nothing in the seemingly complete archival record suggests that the essay was ever examined by the Faculty.

When Mannheim, shortly before his death in 1947, came to prepare an English version of this essay, he went back to the original and incorporated more of the text in the translated edition, which was eventually published posthumously by Dr Paul Kecskemti, himself a distinguished social scientist and Mannheim's brother-in-law. It is not known whether Mannheim ever saw and approved of the English translation as it finally appeared under the title 'Conservative Thought'. As with other works by Mannheim, the translation involves some shifts from the original text, as well as other problems.[3] More important, significant omissions remain even in the more complete English edition, including omissions of the reflections on 'imputation' and the materials on Gustav Hugo and Friedrich Carl von Savigny, which Emil Lederer had singled out for special praise.[4]

The full original typescript available to the present editors[5] is an uncompleted work, ending abruptly (and tantalisingly) with the introduction to a new section on Hegel. Mannheim apologises for this incomplete state in a note, but he and his assessors clearly considered the work before us as an important achievement. Although Mannheim's correspondence during the succeeding years with the influential editor, Paul Siebeck, has in part been preserved, there is no evidence to suggest that Mannheim ever undertook to complete the full project announced on p. 188 of the extant text.

For the parts of his *Habilitationsschrift* which were published, Mannheim and his editors chose, in German as well as in English, an essay title which no longer refers only to 'early conservatism' (*Altkonservatismus*), as the original title does, but to conservative thought as such. In view of the actual design of the work, this is indeed a more appropriate conception and we have consequently allowed the precedent to permit us to revise the single word of the original title to *Conservatism*.

Our editorial changes in the German text[6] are largely limited to minor improvements in Mannheim's syntax and grammar, which occasionally are reminiscent of his native Hungarian. To make sure that this process had not inadvertently introduced significant departures from the original, the English translation was checked everywhere against Mannheim's own German typescript. Mannheim's original manuscript contains marginal summary headings. These have been removed, but the table of contents includes many of these headings, making for a sort of analytical outline.

One problem regarding our source document should be noted. Pages 31 to 80 of the note section are missing in the only extant copy of the manuscript. Since the missing pages of notes correspond to the notes contained in the essay published in the *Archiv für Sozialwissenschaft und Sozialpolitik*, it seems extremely likely that Mannheim himself removed the missing pages while preparing that essay for publication. We have accordingly reconstructed the missing references by way of the published German text. Mannheim's quotations are not always wholly accurate and his bibliographical references are often woefully incomplete. These shortcomings have been everywhere corrected without express comment, and English translations of the texts cited have been indicated wherever possible, even if we decided not to quote from them. In keeping with German academic practice, Mannheim included several important excursuses in his footnote section. Where these offer immediate and valuable supplements to the principal text, they have been brought into the main body of the work, indented in the manner of quotes and enclosed by asterisks.

As the article based on the text appears in the *Archiv*, it contains some editorial emendations and a few elaborations on the original materials. Since there can be no doubt about the authorship of the latter and since their composition coincides so closely with the original work, we have integrated all of these extended passages into the text, except for the two where the elaborations represent a change in the analysis. The integrated passages are enclosed in square brackets, and the alternatives are reproduced in the notes, similiarly marked. The *Archiv*-essay, furthermore, contains a number of footnotes which are not contained in the original. These have been incorporated into the notes, and, where they can be distinguished on the basis of the materials available to us, also identified by square brackets. More new references are to be found in the published English version as well, but there is no way of knowing whether Mannheim himself or his editor was responsible for them. Moreover, the object of this edition is to give as clear and complete a presentation as possible of Mannheim's work on conservatism during his years at Heidelberg. Accordingly, the additions in the posthumous edition are not included here.

The work of editing and translating is complicated as well as helped by Mannheim's own re-editing of the text, first for publication in the *Archiv*, and then, presumably together with Paul Kecskemeti, for the English translation. For reasons discussed in the Introduction and elsewhere, this re-editing was at times influenced by considerations other than straightforward editorial ones, and the resulting text occasionally gains an emphasis different from the original; or it suffers a loss in clarity. In the important discussion of the relationship between 'socially un-attached intellectuals' and romanticism, for example, Mannheim's original text speaks of the intellectuals' turn from the rationalism of the Enlightenment as a purely immanent 'ideological' development, a swing of the pendulum from the intellectualistic extreme. The *Archiv* version, in contrast, stresses the social characteristics which distinguish romantic intellectuals, citing their origins in Protestant pastoral families.[7] A comparison between the two versions of the passage closing the whole discussion provides a clue to the reasons for the difference in emphasis. Both say that intellectuals are the bearers of 'ideals' as well as of 'ideologies'. But the original goes on to state that 'it is hard to decide which of these predominates' – and expressly cites Alfred Weber, one of the faculty referees, as source for the reflection. The published version, completed after the *Habilitation* was awarded, omits the statement of uncertainty as well as the citation.[8] The problem is not that the author changed his mind, since improvements are always possible and our interest cannot be simply an archaeological one. The problem is that the shift is only partial and renders the passage somewhat obscure. Some difficulties in the available English text will be noted below. It is the accumulation of these effects in the published versions which has hampered close reading of Mannheim's argument. The attempt to overcome these problems led to the present decision to reconsider all of the texts in combination, using the re-edited versions (and indeed the existing authorised partial translation) as an important source but ultimately relying, so far as possible, on the original typescript.

It would have been pedantic to deny the contemporary public all of the clarifications and elaborations to be found in those versions, but it would have been misleading to treat the editorial work there done or the translation available as definitive. And a scholarly variorum edition could not be justified, given the desire to make Mannheim's thinking more rather than less accessible. As a result, however, the editors and translators have had to assume somewhat more responsibility than usual for the actual state of the final text. At a few critical points, decisions on the version to include had to depend on as good an interpretation of Mannheim's overall design as we could muster. The passages are marked and the reasons indicated. In one way or another, all have to do with Mannheim's difficulty of choosing between immanent and extrinsic interpretations of the intellectual productions of intellectuals. Improved insight into that difficulty is a major objective of the project of reconsideration and republication of which this book is a part.[9]

In a curious way, Mannheim's ambivalences about intellectuals, so evident in his excursus on romantic intellectuals, have been reflected in an indecisiveness among translators and commentators about the English translation of Mannheim's most famous epithet for intellectuals. In German, Mannheim usually speaks of *sozial freischwebende Intelligenz* or *sozial freischwebende Intellektuelle*. Rendered more or less literally in English as 'socially free-floating intellectuals', the expression seems faintly ludicrous, especially in

247

view of its reminiscences of hot-air balloons and the Socrates of Aristophanes' *The Clouds*. (That such an association is not missing from the German term either is suggested by the fact that Mannheim's most brilliant students in Heidelberg cast their farewell tribute to him, on the occasion of his departure for Frankfurt to take up a professorship there, in the form of a parody of Aristophanes' comedy, with much play upon Socrates in the air.) But the translation into the more technical and neutral 'socially unattached intelligentsia' also offers a marginally poorer concept because it does not convey the full sense of the original, that the condition is exceptional and perhaps provisional, since effectiveness requires coming down somewhere to the social ground. For these reasons, the present editors, despite some misgivings, have no principled objections to the former translation. But in the present text, where all the complicating issues are expressly treated by Mannheim rather than being implicit in his epithet, we opted for the less colourful terminology, mostly because our work, without being in the least an apologia, is meant to encourage English-speaking audiences to reconsider dismissive stereotyped notions about Mannheim which pervade much professional conventional wisdom and which are fed by the odd effects of some turns in translation. The complexity of Mannheim's thinking, which he could effectively convey by the use of slightly ironic expressions in the German literary language he came to use quite well, has not been well conveyed in English translations. We now hope to improve that situation, although we must rely on analytical devices to open the text rather than on literary *esprit*.

No further general explanation is needed for the decision to reconsider the entire text as a whole, rather than simply relying on the partial translation already available. A few specific points, however, will help to avoid misunderstandings about differences in the rendering of familiar passages. Despite the awkwardness, long bemoaned by translators of Max Weber and other historical sociologists, '*ständisch*' has everywhere had to be rendered by an adjectival phrase referring to 'estates' or even by an inelegant adjectiving of the word itself. The earlier translation as 'feudal' is simply incorrect.[10]

Another term to receive such treatment is the German '*naturrechtlich*', which refers to the whole range of approaches grounded upon a conception of a universally rational order comprehensible through law-like statements about the 'nature' of things. Theories of natural law are the most common form of such an approach, but not the only one. In any case, it will not do to substitute 'liberal' or 'bourgeois-liberal' for an awkward adjectiving of this term, since that prejudices what Mannheim is at considerable pains to show. A similar lack of clarity about historical concepts was introduced in the earlier translation, 'Conservative Thought', through failure to distinguish consistently between 'liberty' and 'freedom', with the former term chosen all too often where the latter is required. That this is an important terminological issue when dealing with conservative writers can be neatly confirmed by a passage from Burke which Mannheim himself quotes: 'By this means our liberty becomes a noble freedom.'[11] The standard nineteenth-century German translation employs the German term for 'independence' (*Unabhängigkeit*) to convey 'liberty'.

More important than such specific questions about historical terminology and more symptomatic of the general fate of Mannheim's work, as it was turned into English, are translation practices regarding Mannheim's analytical concepts. Kecskemeti is rather loose, for example, in his use of 'ideological', tending towards the English usage of the time, where it often means little more than the adjectival form of 'ideas', while Mannheim always distinguishes clearly in the present text between 'ideological' developments and developments in thinking or in other dimensions of the spirit, and these distinctions have been restored in the present translation.

Every effort has also been made to restore Mannheim's rich repertory of concepts for characterising different modes of apprehending the actual and the changes that transpire in the world. In the Kecskemeti translation, the rendering of terms arising in the phenomenological and existentialist literatures which interested Mannheim at the time of *Konservatismus* often suggest the revisionist programme which is also evident in the translation of *Ideologie und Utopie*. We are offered a fairly homogenised conception of a historically developing, formed social world, which can be characterised more or less accurately and whose constituent elements can be shown to be causally interrelated. This conception contrasts, sometimes sharply, with Mannheim's much more self-reflective German language, where 'existence' and 'reality' may be distinct, for example, and the way in which things come to be as they are may be conceived in ways not comprehended by the concept of 'development', while history may be understood in ways other than the specification of the causal play of real factors which intrigues him here. With the full range of Mannheim's interests in this work made clearer by the recovery of the entire text, it becomes both possible and necessary to render into English the ways in which his own conceptualisations reflect the distinctions among different ways of conceiving the relationship between thinking and actuality, which are an important part of the subject-matter of the work.

In this effort, we have largely followed the policies explained in our 'Note on the Translation' in *Structures of Thinking*. Because most of the present text is not as remorselessly theoretical as the text translated in that volume, we have not felt as bound to adhere to Mannheim's sentence structure or to be quite as literal in dealing with certain eccentric terms, which play an important theoretical part there – with benefit to the non-specialist reader and no loss to others, we trust. '*Geist*' nevertheless almost always remains 'spirit', and cognates for terms like '*Intention*' are still avoided, where the English equivalents would be misleadingly psychological in connotation. Mannheim's key term for the central motif in the thinking of a given social tendency, *Grundintention*, is accordingly rendered as 'fundamental design', so as to take advantage of the fact that 'design' in English can refer to an objective pattern as well as to a subjective undertaking, as is also the case with the German expression in Mannheim's usage. Our basic assumption throughout is that Mannheim has deep respect for the different ways of thinking which he is studying, that he does not treat them as 'mere' ideology when he is considering them in sociological perspective. This is so much the case that his own analytical terminology reflects the different approaches he is characterising, at least to the extent of formulating his own framework in manifest recognition of the contrasts between the others and himself. The use of the historical materials as reference point for critical and constructive self-reflection is an integral part of the work, and the translation attempts to make this use evident in the language.

The Editors and Translators

Notes

1 'Einladung zur öffentlichen Antritts-Vorlesung', in Mannheim's *Habilitationsakten*, University of Heidelberg Archives. Single printed sheet.

2 Paul Kecskemeti, in his 'Introduction' to Mannheim's *Essays on the Sociology of Knowledge*, London: Routledge & Kegan Paul, 1952, does point out, however, that the *Habilitationsschrift* as such was not published, and that the previously published English text "is an abridged version based upon both the *Habilitationsschrift* and the *Archiv* text, prepared by Mannheim himself for publication in English" (p. 20, n. 1).

3 Cf. David Kettler, Volker Meja, and Nico Stehr, *Karl Mannheim*,

Chichester: Ellis Horwood, 1984; London: Tavistock, 1984, pp. 107–18.

4 See Lederer's assessment (pp. 10 ff.) of Mannheim's *Habilitationsschrift*, in *Habilitationsakten*, University of Heidelberg Archives. Typescript.

5 The typescript, *Altkonservatismus. Ein Beitrag zur Soziologie des Wissens* (1925) is now among the papers of Paul Kecskemeti at the Brandeis University Library (Waltham, Mass., USA).

6 Karl Mannheim, *Konservatismus*, ed. David Kettler, Volker Meja and Nico Stehr, Frankfurt: Suhrkamp, 1984.

7 Cf. *Konservatismus*, pp. 143 ff. [pp. 116 ff. above] and pp. 249 ff., no. 140 [p. 212, n. 143 above].

8 P. 120 above. Cf. *Konservatismus*, p. 147, where the present editors followed Mannheim's *Archiv*-version in this instance too, thereby omitting the statement of uncertainty and the reference to Alfred Weber. The significance of the contrast did not become clear to us until we began to study in detail the problem of minor shifts, moved by the larger problem of deciding what to do about the published English version. The part of the sentence omitted from *Konservatismus* is: "und es ist schwer zu entscheiden, was überwiegt (A. Weber)." *Altkonservatismus* (Typescript), p. 184.

9 Cf. Karl Mannheim, *Strukturen des Denkens*, ed. David Kettler, Volker Meja, and Nico Stehr, Frankfurt: Suhrkamp (1980) [*Structures of Thinking*, ed. David Kettler, Volker Meja, and Nico Stehr, transl. Jeremy Shapiro and Shierry Weber Nicholsen, London: Routledge & Kegan Paul, 1982. Among the recent interpretive literature see A. P. Simonds, *Karl Mannheim's Sociology of Knowledge*, Oxford: Clarendon Press, 1978; Colin Loader, *Culture, Politics, and Planning: The Intellectual Development of Karl Mannheim*, London: Cambridge University Press, 1985; David Kettler, Volker Meja, and Nico Stehr, *Karl Mannheim*.

10 For a clear introduction to the historical distinctions between feudalism and the 'polity of estates' (*Ständesstaats*), see Gianfranco Poggi, *The Development of the Modern State*, London: Hutchinson, 1978.

11 Cf. *Konservatismus*, p. 155 [p. 127 above].

Index

Routledge Social Science Series

Routledge & Kegan Paul
London, Boston, Melbourne and Henley

Contents

Authors wishing to submit manuscripts for any series
in this catalogue should send them to the Social Science Editor, ·,
Routledge & Kegan Paul plc, 14 Leicester Square,
London, WC2H 7PH.
● *Books so marked are available in paperback also.*
○ *Books so marked are available in paperback only.*
All books are in metric Demy 8vo format (216 × 138mm approx.)
unless otherwise stated.

International Library of Sociology
General Editor John Rex

GENERAL SOCIOLOGY

Alexander, J. Theoretical Logic in Sociology.
  Volume 1: Positivism, Presuppositions and Current Controversies. *234 pp.*
  Volume 2: The Antinomies of Classical Thought: *Marx and Durkheim.*
  Volume 3: The Classical Attempt at Theoretical Synthesis: *Max Weber.*
  Volume 4: The Modern Reconstruction of Classical Thought: *Talcott Parsons.*
Barnsley, J. H. The Social Reality of Ethics. *464 pp.*
Brown, Robert. Explanation in Social Science. *208 pp.*
● Rules and Laws in Sociology. *192 pp.*
Bruford, W. H. Chekhov and His Russia. *A Sociological Study. 244 pp.*
Burton, F. and **Carlen, P.** Official Discourse. *On Discourse Analysis, Government Publications, Ideology. 160 pp.*
Cain, Maureen E. Society and the Policeman's Role. *326 pp.*
● **Fletcher, Colin.** Beneath the Surface. *An Account of Three Styles of Sociological Research. 221 pp.*
Gibson, Quentin. The Logic of Social Enquiry. *240 pp.*
Glassner, B. Essential Interactionism. *208 pp.*
Glucksmann, M. Structuralist Analysis in Contemporary Social Thought. *212 pp.*
Gurvitch, Georges. Sociology of Law. *Foreword by Roscoe Pound. 264 pp.*
Hinkle, R. Founding Theory of American Sociology 1881–1913. *376 pp.*
Homans, George C. Sentiments and Activities. *336 pp.*
Johnson, Harry M. Sociology: *A Systematic Introduction. Foreword by Robert K. Merton. 710 pp.*
● **Keat, Russell** and **Urry, John.** Social Theory as Science. *Second Edition. 278 pp.*
Mannheim, Karl. Essays on Sociology and Social Psychology. *Edited by Paul Keckskemeti. With Editorial Note by Adolph Lowe. 344 pp.*
Martindale, Don. The Nature and Types of Sociological Theory. *292 pp.*
● **Maus, Heinz.** A Short History of Sociology. *234 pp.*
Merquior, J. G. Rousseau and Weber. *A Study in the Theory of Legitimacy. 240 pp.*
Myrdal, Gunnar. Value in Social Theory: *A Collection of Essays on Methodology. Edited by Paul Streeten. 332 pp.*
Ogburn, William F. and **Nimkoff, Meyer F.** A Handbook of Sociology. *Preface by Karl Mannheim. 656 pp. 46 figures. 35 tables.*
Parsons, Talcott and **Smelser, Neil J.** Economy and Society: *A Study in the Integration of Economic and Social Theory. 362 pp.*
Payne, G., Dingwall, R., Payne, J. and **Carter, M.** Sociology and Social Research. *336 pp.*
Podgórecki, A. Practical Social Sciences. *144 pp.*
Podgórecki, A. and **Łos, M.** Multidimensional Sociology. *268 pp.*
Raffel, S. Matters of Fact. *A Sociological Inquiry. 152 pp.*
● **Rex, John.** Key Problems of Sociological Theory. *220 pp.*
  Sociology and the Demystification of the Modern World. *282 pp.*
● **Rex, John.** (Ed.) Approaches to Sociology. *Contributions by Peter Abell, Frank Bechhofer, Basil Bernstein, Ronald Fletcher, David Frisby, Miriam Glucksmann, Peter Lassman, Herminio Martins, John Rex, Roland Robertson, John Westergaard and Jock Young. 302 pp.*
Rigby, A. Alternative Realities. *352 pp.*
Roche, M. Phenomenology, Language and the Social Sciences. *374 pp.*
Sahay, A. Sociological Analysis. *220 pp.*
Strasser, Hermann. The Normative Structure of Sociology. *Conservative and Emancipatory Themes in Social Thought. 286 pp.*

Strong, P. Ceremonial Order of the Clinic. *267 pp.*
Urry, J. Reference Groups and the Theory of Revolution. *244 pp.*
Weinberg, E. Development of Sociology in the Soviet Union. *173 pp.*

FOREIGN CLASSICS OF SOCIOLOGY

● Gerth, H. H. and Mills, C. Wright. From Max Weber: *Essays in Sociology.*
  502 pp.
● Tönnies, Ferdinand. Community and Association (*Gemeinschaft und Gesellschaft*). *Translated and Supplemented by Charles P. Loomis. Foreword by
  Pitirim A. Sorokin. 334 pp.*

SOCIAL STRUCTURE

Andreski, Stanislav. Military Organization and Society. *Foreword by Professor
  A. R. Radcliffe-Brown. 226 pp. 1 folder.*
Bozzoli, B. The Political Nature of a Ruling Class. *Capital and Ideology in
  South Africa 1890–1939. 396 pp.*
Bauman, Z. Memories of Class. *The Prehistory and After life of Class. 240 pp.*
Broom, L., Lancaster Jones, F., McDonnell, P. and Williams, T. The
  Inheritance of Inequality. *208 pp.*
Carlton, Eric. Ideology and Social Order. *Foreword by Professor Philip
  Abrahams. 326 pp.*
Clegg, S. and Dunkerley, D. Organization, Class and Control. *614 pp.*
Coontz, Sydney H. Population Theories and the Economic Interpretation. *202 pp.*
Coser, Lewis. The Functions of Social Conflict. *204 pp.*
Crook, I. and D. The First Years of the Yangyi Commune. *304 pp., illustrated.*
Dickie-Clark, H. F. Marginal Situation: *A Sociological Study of a Coloured
  Group. 240 pp. 11 tables.*
Fidler, J. The British Business Elite. *Its Attitudes to Class, Status and Power.
  332 pp.*
Giner, S. and Archer, M. S. (Eds) Contemporary Europe: *Social Structures and
  Cultural Patterns. 336 pp.*
● Glaser, Barney and Strauss, Anselm L. Status Passage: *A Formal Theory.
  212 pp.*
Glass, D. V. (Ed.) Social Mobility in Britain. *Contributions by J. Berent,
  T. Bottomore, R. C. Chambers, J. Floud, D. V. Glass, J. R. Hall, H. T.
  Himmelweit, R. K. Kelsall, F. M. Martin, C. A. Moser, R. Mukherjee and
  W. Ziegel. 420 pp.*
Kelsall, R. K. Higher Civil Servants in Britain: *From 1870 to the Present Day.
  268 pp. 31 tables.*
● Lawton, Denis. Social Class, Language and Education. *192 pp.*
McLeish, John. The Theory of Social Change. *Four Views Considered. 128 pp.*
● Marsh, David C. The Changing Social Structure of England and Wales,
  1871–1961. *Revised edition. 288 pp.*
Menzies, Ken. Talcott Parsons and the Social Image of Man. *206 pp.*
● Mouzelis, Nicos. Organization and Bureaucracy. *An Analysis of Modern
  Theories. 240 pp.*
● Ossowski, Stanislaw. Class Structure in the Social Consciousness. *210 pp.*
● Podgórecki, Adam. Law and Society. *302 pp.*
Ratcliffe, P. Racism and Reaction. *A Profile of Handsworth. 388 pp.*
Renner, Karl. Institutions of Private Law and Their Social Functions. *Edited,
  with an Introduction and Notes, by O. Kahn-Freud. Translated by Agnes
  Schwarzschild. 316 pp.*
Rex, J. and Tomlinson, S. Colonial Immigrants in a British City. *A Class
  Analysis. 368 pp.*
Smooha, S. Israel. *Pluralism and Conflict. 472 pp.*
Strasser, H. and Randall, S. C. An Introduction to Theories of Social Change.
  300 pp.

Wesolowski, W. Class, Strata and Power. *Trans. and with Introduction by G. Kolankiewicz. 160 pp.*

Zureik, E. Palestinians in Israel. *A Study in Internal Colonialism. 264 pp.*

SOCIOLOGY AND POLITICS

Acton, T. A. Gypsy Politics and Social Change. *316 pp.*

Burton, F. Politics of Legitimacy. *Struggles in a Belfast Community. 250 pp.*

Crook, I. and D. Revolution in a Chinese Village. *Ten Mile Inn. 216 pp., illustrated.*

de Silva, S. B. D. The Political Economy of Underdevelopment. *640 pp.*

Etzioni-Halevy, E. Political Manipulation and Administrative Power. *A Comparative Study. 228 pp.*

Fielding, N. The National Front. *260 pp.*

● Hechter, Michael. Internal Colonialism. *The Celtic Fringe in British National Development, 1536–1966. 380 pp.*

Levy, N. The Foundations of the South African Cheap Labour System. *367 pp.*

Kornhauser, William. The Politics of Mass Society. *272 pp. 20 tables.*

● Korpi, W. The Working Class in Welfare Capitalism. *Work, Unions and Politics in Sweden. 472 pp.*

Kroes, R. Soldiers and Students. *A Study of Right- and Left-wing Students. 174 pp.*

Martin, Roderick. Sociology of Power. *214 pp.*

Merquior, J. G. Rousseau and Weber. *A Study in the Theory of Legitimacy. 286 pp.*

Myrdal, Gunnar. The Political Element in the Development of Economic Theory. *Translated from the German by Paul Streeten. 282 pp.*

Preston, P. W. Theories of Development. *296 pp.*

Varma, B. N. The Sociology and Politics of Development. *A Theoretical Study. 236 pp.*

Wong, S.-L. Sociology and Socialism in Contemporary China. *160 pp.*

Wootton, Graham. Workers, Unions and the State. *188 pp.*

CRIMINOLOGY

Ancel, Marc. Social Defence: *A Modern Approach to Criminal Problems. Foreword by Leon Radzinowicz. 240 pp.*

Athens, L. Violent Criminal Acts and Actors. *104 pp.*

Cain, Maureen E. Society and the Policeman's Role. *326 pp.*

Cloward, Richard A. and Ohlin, Lloyd E. Delinquency and Opportunity: *A Theory of Delinquent Gangs. 248 pp.*

Downes, David M. The Delinquent Solution. *A Study in Subcultural Theory. 296 pp.*

Friedlander, Kate. The Psycho-Analytical Approach to Juvenile Delinquency: *Theory, Case Studies, Treatment. 320 pp.*

Gleuck, Sheldon and Eleanor. Family Environment and Delinquency. *With the statistical assistance of Rose W. Kneznek. 340 pp.*

Lopez-Rey, Manuel. Crime. *An Analytical Appraisal. 288 pp.*

Mannheim, Hermann. Comparative Criminology: *A Text Book. Two volumes. 442 pp. and 380 pp.*

Morris, Terence. The Criminal Area: *A Study in Social Ecology. Foreword by Hermann Mannheim. 232 pp. 25 tables. 4 maps.*

Rock, Paul. Making People Pay. *338 pp.*

● Taylor, Ian, Walton, Paul and Young, Jock. The New Criminology. *For a Social Theory of Deviance. 325 pp.*

● Taylor, Ian, Walton, Paul and Young, Jock. (Eds) Critical Criminology. *268 pp.*

SOCIAL PSYCHOLOGY

Bagley, Christopher. The Social Psychology of the Epileptic Child. *320 pp.*
Brittan, Arthur. Meanings and Situations. *224 pp.*
Carroll, J. Break-Out from the Crystal Palace. *200 pp.*
● **Fleming, C. M.** Adolescence: Its Social Psychology. *With an Introduction to recent findings from the fields of Anthropology, Physiology, Medicine, Psychometrics and Sociometry. 288 pp.*
● The Social Psychology of Education: *An Introduction and Guide to Its Study. 136 pp.*
Linton, Ralph. The Cultural Background of Personality. *132 pp.*
● **Mayo, Elton.** The Social Problems of an Industrial Civilization. *With an Appendix on the Political Problem. 180 pp.*
Ottaway, A. K. C. Learning Through Group Experience. *176 pp.*
Plummer, Ken. Sexual Stigma. *An Interactionist Account. 254 pp.*
● **Rose, Arnold M.** (Ed.) Human Behaviour and Social Processes: *an Interactionist Approach. Contributions by Arnold M. Rose, Ralph H. Turner, Anselm Strauss, Everett C. Hughes, E. Franklin Frazier, Howard S. Becker et al. 696 pp.*
Smelser, Neil J. Theory of Collective Behaviour. *448 pp.*
Stephenson, Geoffrey M. The Development of Conscience. *128 pp.*
Young, Kimball. Handbook of Social Psychology. *658 pp. 16 figures. 10 tables.*

SOCIOLOGY OF THE FAMILY

Bell, Colin R. Middle Class Families: *Social and Geographical Mobility. 224 pp.*
Burton, Lindy. Vulnerable Children. *272 pp.*
Gavron, Hannah. The Captive Wife: *Conflicts of Household Mothers. 190 pp.*
George, Victor and **Wilding, Paul.** Motherless Families. *248 pp.*
Klein, Josephine. Samples from English Cultures.
    1. Three Preliminary Studies and Aspects of Adult Life in England. *447 pp.*
    2. Child-Rearing Practices and Index. *247 pp.*
Klein, Viola. The Feminine Character. *History of an Ideology. 244 pp.*
McWhinnie, Alexina M. Adopted Children. *How They Grow Up. 304 pp.*
● **Morgan, D. H. J.** Social Theory and the Family. *188 pp.*
● **Myrdal, Alva** and **Klein, Viola.** Women's Two Roles: *Home and Work. 238 pp. 27 tables.*
Parsons, Talcott and **Bales, Robert F.** Family: Socialization and Interaction Process. *In collaboration with James Olds, Morris Zelditch and Philip E. Slater. 456 pp. 50 figures and tables.*

SOCIAL SERVICES

Bastide, Roger. The Sociology of Mental Disorder. *Translated from the French by Jean McNeil. 260 pp.*
Carlebach, Julius. Caring for Children in Trouble. *266 pp.*
George, Victor. Foster Care. *Theory and Practice. 234 pp.*
    Social Security: *Beveridge and After. 258 pp.*
George, V. and **Wilding, P.** Motherless Families. *248 pp.*
● **Goetschius, George W.** Working with Community Groups. *256 pp.*
Goetschius, George W. and **Tash, Joan.** Working with Unattached Youth. *416 pp.*
Heywood, Jean S. Children in Care. *The Development of the Service for the Deprived Child. Third revised edition. 284 pp.*
King, Roy D., Ranes, Norma V. and **Tizard, Jack.** Patterns of Residential Care. *356 pp.*
Leigh, John. Young People and Leisure. *256 pp.*
● **Mays, John.** (Ed.) Penelope Hall's Social Services of England and Wales. *368 pp.*

Morris Mary. Voluntary Work and the Welfare State. *300 pp.*
Nokes. P. L. The Professional Task in Welfare Practice. *152 pp.*
Timms, Noel. Psychiatric Social Work in Great Britain (1939–1962). *280 pp.*
● Social Casework: *Principles and Practice. 256 pp.*

SOCIOLOGY OF EDUCATION

Banks, Olive. Parity and Prestige in English Secondary Education: a Study in Educational Sociology. *272 pp.*
● Blyth, W. A. L. English Primary Education. *A Sociological Description.*
   2. Background. *168 pp.*
Collier, K. G. The Social Purposes of Education: *Personal and Social Values in Education. 268 pp.*
Evans, K. M. Sociometry and Education. *158 pp.*
● Ford, Julienne. Social Class and the Comprehensive School. *192 pp.*
Foster, P. J. Education and Social Change in Ghana. *336 pp. 3 maps.*
Fraser, W. R. Education and Society in Modern France. *150 pp.*
Grace, Gerald R. Role Conflict and the Teacher. *150 pp.*
Hans, Nicholas. New Trends in Education in the Eighteenth Century. *278 pp.*
   19 tables.
● Comparative Education: *A Study of Educational Factors and Traditions. 360 pp.*
● Hargreaves, David. Interpersonal Relations and Education. *432 pp.*
● Social Relations in a Secondary School. *240 pp.*
School Organization and Pupil Involvement. *A Study of Secondary Schools.*
● Mannheim, Karl and Stewart, W. A. C. An Introduction to the Sociology of Education. *206 pp.*
● Musgrove, F. Youth and the Social Order. *176 pp.*
● Ottaway, A. K. C. Education and Society: An Introduction to the Sociology of Education. *With an Introduction by W. O. Lester Smith. 212 pp.*
Peers, Robert. Adult Education: *A Comparative Study. Revised edition. 398 pp.*
Stratta, Erica. The Education of Borstal Boys. *A Study of their Educational Experiences prior to, and during, Borstal Training. 256 pp.*
● Taylor, P. H., Reid, W. A. and Holley, B. J. The English Sixth Form. *A Case Study in Curriculum Research. 198 pp.*

SOCIOLOGY OF CULTURE

● Eppel, E. M. and M. Adolescents and Morality: *A Study of some Moral Values and Dilemmas of Working Adolescents in the Context of a changing Climate of Opinion. Foreword by W. J. H. Sprott. 268 pp. 39 tables.*
● Fromm, Erich. The Fear of Freedom. *286 pp.*
● The Sane Society. *400 pp.*
Johnson, L. The Cultural Critics. *From Matthew Arnold to Raymond Williams. 233 pp.*
Mannheim, Karl. Essays on the Sociology of Culture. *Edited by Ernst Mannheim in co-operation with Paul Kecskemeti. Editorial Note by Adolph Lowe. 280 pp.*
Structures of Thinking. *Edited by David Kettler, Volker Meja and Nico Stehr. 304 pp.*
Merquior, J. G. The Veil and the Mask. *Essays on Culture and Ideology. Foreword by Ernest Gellner. 140 pp.*
Zijderfeld, A. C. On Clichés. *The Supersedure of Meaning by Function in Modernity. 150 pp.*
Reality in a Looking Glass. *Rationality through an Analysis of Traditional Folly. 208 pp.*

SOCIOLOGY OF RELIGION

Argyle, Michael and **Beit-Hallahmi, Benjamin.** The Social Psychology of Religion. *256 pp.*

Glasner, Peter E. The Sociology of Secularisation. *A Critique of a Concept. 146 pp.*

Hall, J. R. The Ways Out. *Utopian Communal Groups in an Age of Babylon. 280 pp.*

Ranson, S., Hinings, B. and **Bryman, A.** Clergy, Ministers and Priests. *216 pp.*

Stark, Werner. The Sociology of Religion. *A Study of Christendom.*
   Volume II. *Sectarian Religion. 368 pp.*
   Volume III. *The Universal Church. 464 pp.*
   Volume IV. *Types of Religious Man. 352 pp.*
   Volume V. *Types of Religious Culture. 464 pp.*

Turner, B. S. Weber and Islam. *216 pp.*

Watt, W. Montgomery. Islam and the Integration of Society. 230 pp.

Pomian-Srzednicki, M. Religious Change in Contemporary Poland. *Sociology and Secularization. 280 pp.*

SOCIOLOGY OF ART AND LITERATURE

Jarvie, Ian C. Towards a Sociology of the Cinema. *A Comparative Essay on the Structure and Functioning of a Major Entertainment Industry. 405 pp.*

Rust, Frances S. Dance in Society. *An Analysis of the Relationships between the Social Dance and Society in England from the Middle Ages to the Present Day. 256 pp. 8 pp. of plates.*

Schücking, L. L. The Sociology of Literary Taste. *112 pp.*

Wolff, Janet. Hermeneutic Philosophy and the Sociology of Art. *150 pp.*

SOCIOLOGY OF KNOWLEDGE

Diesing, P. Patterns of Discovery in the Social Sciences. *262 pp.*

● **Douglas, J. D.** (Ed.) Understanding Everyday Life. *270 pp.*

● **Hamilton, P.** Knowledge and Social Structure. *174 pp.*

Jarvie, I. C. Concepts and Society. *232 pp.*

Mannheim, Karl. Essays on the Sociology of Knowledge. *Edited by Paul Kecskemeti. Editorial Note by Adolph Lowe. 353 pp.*

Remmling, Gunter W. The Sociology of Karl Mannheim. *With a Bibliographical Guide to the Sociology of Knowledge, Ideological Analysis, and Social Planning. 255 pp.*

Remmling, Gunter W. (Ed.) Towards the Sociology of Knowledge. *Origin and Development of a Sociological Thought Style. 463 pp.*

Scheler, M. Problems of a Sociology of Knowledge. *Trans. by M. S. Frings. Edited and with an Introduction by K. Stikkers. 232 pp.*

URBAN SOCIOLOGY

Aldridge, M. The British New Towns. *A Programme Without a Policy. 232 pp.*

Ashworth, William. The Genesis of Modern British Town Planning: *A Study in Economic and Social History of the Nineteenth and Twentieth Centuries. 288 pp.*

Brittan, A. The Privatised World. *196 pp.*

Cullingworth, J. B. Housing Needs and Planning Policy: *a Restatement of the Problems of Housing Need and 'Overspill' in England and Wales. 232 pp. 44 tables. 8 maps.*

Dickinson, Robert E. City and Region: *A Geographical Interpretation. 608 pp. 125 figures.*

   The West European City: *A Geographical Interpretation. 600 pp. 129 maps. 29 plates.*

Humphreys, Alexander J. New Dubliners: *Urbanization and the Irish Family.* *Foreword by George C. Homans. 304 pp.*

Jackson, Brian. Working Class Community: *Some General Notions raised by a Series of Studies in Northern England. 192 pp.*

● **Mann, P. H.** An Approach to Urban Sociology. *240 pp.*

Mellor, J. R. Urban Sociology in an Urbanized Society. *326 pp.*

Morris, R. N. and **Mogey, J.** The Sociology of Housing. *Studies at Berinsfield. 232 pp. 4 pp. plates.*

Mullan, R. Stevenage Ltd. *438 pp.*

Rex, J. and **Tomlinson, S.** Colonial Immigrants in a British City. *A Class Analysis. 368 pp.*

Rosser, C. and **Harris, C.** The Family and Social Change. *A Study of Family and Kinship in a South Wales Town. 352 pp. 8 maps.*

● **Stacey, Margaret, Batsone, Eric, Bell, Colin** and **Thurcott, Anne.** Power, Persistence and Change. *A Second Study of Banbury. 196 pp.*

RURAL SOCIOLOGY

● **Mayer, Adrian C.** Peasants in the Pacific. *A Study of Fiji Indian Rural Society. 248 pp. 20 plates.*

Williams, W. M. The Sociology of an English Village: *Gosforth. 272 pp. 12 figures. 13 tables.*

SOCIOLOGY OF INDUSTRY AND DISTRIBUTION

Dunkerley, David. The Foreman. *Aspects of Task and Structure. 192 pp.*

Eldridge, J. E. T. Industrial Disputes. *Essays in the Sociology of Industrial Relations. 288 pp.*

Hollowell, Peter G. The Lorry Driver. *272 pp.*

● **Oxaal, I., Barnett, T.** and **Booth, D.** (Eds) Beyond the Sociology of Development. *Economy and Society in Latin America and Africa. 295 pp.*

Smelser, Neil J. Social Change in the Industrial Revolution: *An Application of Theory to the Lancashire Cotton Industry, 1770–1840. 468 pp. 12 figures. 14 tables.*

Watson, T. J. The Personnel Managers. *A Study in the Sociology of Work and Employment, 262 pp.*

ANTHROPOLOGY

Brandel-Syrier, Mia. Reeftown Elite. *A Study of Social Mobility in a Modern African Community on the Reef. 376 pp.*

Dickie-Clark, H. F. The Marginal Situation. *A Sociological Study of a Coloured Group. 236 pp.*

Dube, S. C. Indian Village. *Foreword by Morris Edward Opler. 276 pp. 4 plates.*

India's Changing Villages: *Human Factors in Community Development. 260 pp. 8 plates. 1 map.*

Fei, H.-T. Peasant Life in China. *A Field Study of Country Life in the Yangtze Valley. With a foreword by Bronislaw Malinowski. 328 pp. 16 pp. plates.*

Firth, Raymond. Malay Fishermen. *Their Peasant Economy. 420 pp. 17 pp. plates.*

Gulliver, P H. Social Control in an African Society: a Study of the Arusha, Agricultural Masai of Northern Tanganykia. *320 pp. 8 plates. 10 figures.*

Family Herds. *288 pp.*

Jarvie, Ian C. The Revolution in Anthropology. *268 pp.*

Little, Kenneth L. Mende of Sierra Leone. *308 pp. and folder.*

Negroes in Britain. *With a New Introduction and Contemporary Study by Leonard Bloom. 320 pp.*

Tambs-Lyche, H. London Patidars. *168 pp.*

Madan, G. R. Western Sociologists on Indian Society. *Marx, Spencer, Weber, Durkheim, Pareto. 384 pp.*

Mayer, A. C. Peasants in the Pacific. *A Study of Fiji Indian Rural Society. 248 pp.*

Meer, Fatima. Race and Suicide in South Africa. *325 pp.*

Smith, Raymond T. The Negro Family in British Guiana: *Family Structure and Social Status in the Villages. With a Foreword by Meyer Fortes. 314 pp. 8 plates. 1 figure. 4 maps.*

SOCIOLOGY AND PHILOSOPHY

● Adriaansens, H. Talcott Parsons and the Conceptual Dilemma. *200 pp.*

Barnsley, John H. The Social Reality of Ethics. *A Comparative Analysis of Moral Codes. 448 pp.*

Diesing, Paul. Patterns of Discovery in the Social Sciences. *362 pp.*

● Douglas, Jack D. (Ed.) Understanding Everyday Life. *Toward the Reconstruction of Sociological Knowledge. Contributions by Alan F. Blum, Aaron W. Cicourel, Norman K. Denzin, Jack D. Douglas, John Heeren, Peter McHugh, Peter K. Manning, Melvin Power, Matthew Speier, Roy Turner, D. Lawrence Wieder, Thomas P. Wilson and Don H. Zimmerman. 370 pp.*

Gorman, Robert A. The Dual Vision. *Alfred Schutz and the Myth of Phenomenological Social Science. 240 pp.*

Jarvie, Ian C. Concepts and Society. *216 pp.*

Kilminster, R. Praxis and Method. *A Sociological Dialogue with Lukács, Gramsci and the Early Frankfurt School. 334 pp.*

Outhwaite, W. Concept Formation in Social Science. *255 pp.*

● Pelz, Werner. The Scope of Understanding in Sociology. *Towards a More Radical Reorientation in the Social Humanistic Sciences. 283 pp.*

Roch., Maurice, Phenomenology, Language and the Social Sciences. *371 pp.*

Sahay, Arun. Sociological Analysis. *212 pp.*

● Slater, P. Origin and Significance of the Frankfurt School. *A Marxist Perspective. 185 pp.*

Spurling, L. Phenomenology and the Social World. *The Philosophy of Merleau-Ponty and its Relation to the Social Sciences. 222 pp.*

Wilson, H. T. The American Ideology. *Science, Technology and Organization as Modes of Rationality. 368 pp.*

International Library of Anthropology
General Editor Adam Kuper

● Ahmed, A. S. Millennium and Charisma Among Pathans. *A Critical Essay in Social Anthropology. 192 pp.*
Pukhtun Economy and Society. *Traditional Structure and Economic Development. 422 pp.*

Barth, F. Selected Essays. *Volume I. 256 pp.* Selected Essays. *Volume II. 200 pp.*

Brown, Paula. The Chimbu. *A Study of Change in the New Guinea Highlands. 151 pp.*

Duller, H. J. Development Technology. *192 pp.*

Foner, N. Jamaica Farewell. *200 pp.*

Gudeman, Stephen. Relationships, Residence and the Individual. *A Rural Panamanian Community. 288 pp. 11 plates, 5 figures, 2 maps, 10 tables.*
The Demise of a Rural Economy. *From Subsistence to Capitalism in a Latin American Village. 160 pp.*

Hamnett, Ian. Chieftainship and Legitimacy. *An Anthropological Study of Executive Law in Lesotho. 163 pp.*

Hanson, F. Allan. Meaning in Culture. *127 pp.*

Hazan, H. The Limbo People. *A Study of the Constitution of the Time Universe Among the Aged. 208 pp.*

Humphreys, S. C. Anthropology and the Greeks. *288 pp.*

Karp, I. Fields of Change Among the Iteso of Kenya. *140 pp.*

Kuper, A. Wives for Cattle. *Bridewealth in Southern Africa. 224 pp.*

Lloyd, P. C. Power and Independence. *Urban Africans' Perception of Social Inequality. 264 pp.*

Malinowski, B. and **de la Fuente, J.** Malinowski in Mexico. *The Economics of a Mexican Market System. Edited and Introduced by Susan Drucker-Brown. About 240 pp.*

Parry, J. P. Caste and Kinship in Kangra. *352 pp. Illustrated.*

Pettigrew, Joyce. Robber Noblemen. *A Study of the Political System of the Sikh Jats. 284 pp.*

Street, Brian V. The Savage in Literature. *Representations of 'Primitive' Society in English Fiction, 1858–1920. 207 pp.*

Van Den Berghe, Pierre L. Power and Privilege at an African University. *278 pp.*

International Library of Phenomenology and Moral Sciences
General Editor John O'Neill

Adorno, T. W. Aesthetic Theory. Translated by C. Lenhardt.

Apel, K.-O. Towards a Transformation of Philosophy. *308 pp.*

Bologh, R. W. Dialectical Phenomenology. *Marx's Method. 287 pp.*

Fekete, J. The Critical Twilight. *Explorations in the Ideology of Anglo-American Literary Theory from Eliot to McLuhan. 300 pp.*

Green, B. S. Knowing the Poor. *A Case Study in Textual Reality Construction. 200 pp.*

McHoul, A. W. How Texts Talk. *Essays on Reading and Ethnomethodology. 163 pp.*

Medina, A. Reflection, Time and the Novel. *Towards a Communicative Theory of Literature. 143 pp.*

O'Neill, J. Essaying Montaigne. *A Study of the Renaissance Institution of Writing and Reading. 244 pp.*

Schutz. A. Life Forms and Meaning Structure. *Translated, Introduced and Annotated by Helmut Wagner. 207 pp.*

International Library of Social Policy
General Editor Kathleen Jones

Bayley, M. Mental Handicap and Community Care. *426 pp.*

Bottoms, A. E. and **McClean, J. D.** Defendants in the Criminal Process. *284 pp.*

Bradshaw, J. The Family Fund. *An Initiative in Social Policy. 248 pp.*

Butler, J. R. Family Doctors and Public Policy. *208 pp.*

Davies, Martin. Prisoners of Society. *Attitudes and Aftercare. 204 pp.*

Gittus, Elizabeth. Flats, Families and the Under-Fives. *285 pp.*

Holman, Robert. Trading in Children. *A Study of Private Fostering. 355 pp.*

Jeffs, A. Young People and the Youth Service. *160 pp.*

Jones, Howard and **Cornes, Paul.** Open Prisons. *288 pp.*

Jones, Kathleen. History of the Mental Health Service. *428 pp.*

Jones, Kathleen with **Brown, John, Cunningham, W. J., Roberts, Julian** and **Williams, Peter.** Opening the Door. *A Study of New Policies for the Mentally Handicapped. 278 pp.*

Karn, Valerie. Retiring to the Seaside. *400 pp. 2 maps. Numerous tables.*

King, R. D. and **Elliot, K. W.** Albany: Birth of a Prison—End of an Era. *294 pp.*

Thomas, J. E. The English Prison Officer since 1850. *258 pp.*

Walton, R. G. Women in Social Work. *303 pp.*

● **Woodward, J.** To Do the Sick No Harm. *A Study of the British Voluntary Hospital System to 1875. 234 pp.*

International Library of Welfare and Philosophy
General Editors Noel Timms and David Watson

○ **Campbell, J.** The Left and Rights. *A Conceptual Analysis of the Idea of Socialist Rights. About 296 pp.*

● **McDermott, F. E.** (Ed.) Self-Determination in Social Work. *A Collection of Essays on Self-determination and Related Concepts by Philosophers and Social Work Theorists. Contributors: F. P. Biestek, S. Bernstein, A. Keith-Lucas, D. Sayer, H. H. Perelman, C. Whittington, R. F. Stalley, F. E. McDermott, I. Berlin, H. J. McCloskey, H. L. A. Hart, J. Wilson, A. I. Melden, S. I. Benn. 254 pp.*

● **Plant, Raymond.** Community and Ideology. *104 pp.*

● **Plant, Raymond, Lesser. Harry** and **Taylor-Gooby, Peter.** Political Philosophy and Social Welfare. *Essays on the Normative Basis of Welfare Provision. 276 pp.*

Ragg, N. M. People Not Cases. *A Philosophical Approach to Social Work. 168 pp.*

Timms, Noel (Ed.) Social Welfare. *Why and How? 316 pp. 7 figures.*

● **Timms, Noel** and **Watson, David** (Eds) Talking About Welfare. *Readings in Philosophy and Social Policy. Contributors: T. H. Marshall, R. B. Brandt, G. H. von Wright, K. Nielsen, M. Cranston, R. M. Titmuss, R. S. Downie, E. Telfer, D. Donnison, J. Benson, P. Leonard. A. Keith-Lucas, D. Walsh, I. T. Ramsey. 230 pp.*

● Philosophy in Social Work. *250 pp.*

● **Weale, A.** Equality and Social Policy. *164 pp.*

Library of Social Work
General Editor Noel Timms

● **Baldock, Peter.** Community Work and Social Work. *140 pp.*

○ **Beedell, Christopher.** Residential Life with Children. *210 pp. Crown 8vo.*

● **Berry, Juliet.** Daily Experience in Residential Life. *A Study of Children and their Care-givers. 202 pp.*

○ Social Work with Children. *190 pp. Crown 8vo.*

● **Brearley, C. Paul.** Residential Work with the Elderly. *116 pp.*

● Social Work, Ageing and Society. *126 pp.*

● **Cheetham, Juliet.** Social Work with Immigrants. *240 pp. Crown 8vo.*

● **Cross, Crispin P.** (Ed.) Interviewing and Communication in Social Work. *Contributions by C. P. Cross, D. Laurenson, B. Strutt, S. Raven. 192 pp. Crown 8vo.*

● **Curnock, Kathleen** and **Hardiker, Pauline.** Towards Practice Theory. *Skills and Methods in Social Assessments. 208 pp.*

● **Davies, Bernard.** The Use of Groups in Social Work Practice. *158 pp.*

Davies, Bleddyn and **Knapp, M.** Old People's Homes and the Production of Welfare. *264 pp.*

● **Davies, Martin**. Support Systems in Social Work. *144 pp.*

Ellis, June. (Ed.) West African Families in Britain. *A Meeting of Two Cultures. Contributions by Pat Stapleton, Vivien Biggs. 150 pp. 1 map.*

○ **Ford, J.** Human Behaviour. *Towards a Practical Understanding. About 160 pp.*

● **Hart, John**. Social Work and Sexual Conduct. *230 pp.*

Heraud, Brian. Training for Uncertainty. *A Sociological Approach to Social Work Education. 138 pp.*

Holder, D. and **Wardle, M.** Teamwork and the Development of a Unitary Approach. *212 pp.*

● **Hutten, Joan M.** Short-Term Contracts in Social Work. *Contributions by Stella M. Hall, Elsie Osborne, Mannie Sher, Eva Sternberg, Elizabeth Tuters. 134 pp.*

Jackson, Michael P. and **Valencia, B. Michael.** Financial Aid Through Social Work. *140 pp.*

● **Jones, Howard.** The Residential Community. *A Setting for Social Work. 150 pp.*

● (Ed.) Towards a New Social Work. *Contributions by Howard Jones, D. A. Fowler, J. R. Cypher, R. G. Walton, Geoffrey Mungham, Philip Priestley, Ian Shaw, M. Bartley, R. Deacon, Irwin Epstein, Geoffrey Pearson. 184 pp.*

Jones, Ray and **Pritchard, Colin.** (Eds) Social Work With Adolescents. *Contributions by Ray Jones, Colin Pritchard, Jack Dunham, Florence Rossetti, Andrew Kerslake, John Burns, William Gregory, Graham Templeman, Kenneth E. Reid, Audrey Taylor.*

○ **Jordon, William.** The Social Worker in Family Situations. *160 pp. Crown 8vo.*

● **Laycock, A. L.** Adolescents and Social Work. *128 pp. Crown 8vo.*

● **Lees, Ray.** Politics and Social Work. *128 pp. Crown 8vo.*

● Research Strategies for Social Welfare. *112 pp. Tables.*

○ **McCullough, M. K.** and **Ely, Peter J.** Social Work with Groups. *127 pp. Crown 8vo.*

● **Moffett, Jonathan.** Concepts in Casework Treatment. *128 pp. Crown 8vo.*

Parsloe, Phyllida. Juvenile Justice in Britain and the United States. *The Balance of Needs and Rights. 336 pp.*

● **Plant, Raymond.** Social and Moral Theory in Casework. *112 pp. Crown 8vo.*

Priestley, Philip, Fears, Denise and **Fuller, Roger.** Justice for Juveniles. *The 1969 Children and Young Persons Act: A Case for Reform? 128 pp.*

● **Pritchard, Colin** and **Taylor, Richard.** Social Work: Reform or Revolution? *170 pp.*

○ **Pugh, Elisabeth.** Social Work in Child Care. *128 pp. Crown 8vo.*

● **Robinson, Margaret.** Schools and Social Work. *282 pp.*

○ **Ruddock, Ralph.** Roles and Relationships. *128 pp. Crown 8vo.*

● **Sainsbury, Eric.** Social Diagnosis in Casework. *118 pp. Crown 8vo.*

● **Sainsbury, Eric, Phillips, David** and **Nixon, Stephen.** Social Work in Focus. *Clients' and Social Workers' Perceptions in Long-Term Social Work. 220 pp.*

● Social Work with Families. *Perceptions of Social Casework among Clients of a Family Service. 188pp.*

Seed, Philip. The Expansion of Social Work in Britain. *128 pp. Crown 8vo.*

● **Shaw, John.** The Self in Social Work. *124 pp.*

Smale, Gerald G. Prophecy, Behaviour and Change. *An Examination of Self-fulfilling Prophecies in Helping Relationships. 116 pp. Crown 8vo.*

Smith, Gilbert. Social Need. *Policy, Practice and Research. 155 pp.*

● Social Work and the Sociology of Organisations. *124 pp. Revised edition.*

● **Sutton, Carole.** Psychology for Social Workers and Counsellors. *An Introduction. 248 pp.*

● **Timms, Noel.** Language of Social Casework. *122 pp. Crown 8vo.*

- Recording in Social Work. *124 pp. Crown 8vo.*
- **Todd, F. Joan.** Social Work with the Mentally Subnormal. *96 pp. Crown 8vo.*
- **Walrond-Skinner, Sue.** Family Therapy. *The Treatment of Natural Systems. 172 pp.*
- **Warham, Joyce.** An Introduction to Administration for Social Workers. *Revised edition. 112 pp.*
- An Open Case. *The Organisational Context of Social Work. 172 pp.*
- ○ **Wittenberg, Isca Salzberger.** Psycho-Analytic Insight and Relationships. *A Kleinian Approach. 196 pp. Crown 8vo.*

Primary Socialization, Language and Education
General Editor   Basil Bernstein

Adlam, Diana S., *with the assistance of Geoffrey Turner and Lesley Lineker.* Code in Context. *272 pp.*
Bernstein, Basil. Class, Codes and Control. *3 volumes.*
- 1. *Theoretical Studies Towards a Sociology of Language. 254 pp.*
  2. *Applied Studies Towards a Sociology of Language. 377 pp.*
- 3. *Towards a Theory of Educational Transmission. 167 pp.*
Brandis, Walter and **Henderson, Dorothy.** Social Class, Language and Communication. *288 pp.*
Cook-Gumperz, Jenny. Social Control and Socialization. *A Study of Class Differences in the Language of Maternal Control. 290 pp.*
- **Gahagan, D. M.** and **G. A.** Talk Reform. *Exploration in Language for Infant School Children. 160 pp.*
Hawkins, P. R. Social Class, the Nominal Group and Verbal Strategies. *About 220 pp.*
Robinson, W. P. and **Rakstraw, Susan D. A.** A Question of Answers. *2 volumes. 192 pp. and 180 pp.*
Turner, Geoffrey J. and **Mohan, Bernard A.** A Linguistic Description and Computer Programme for Children's Speech. *208 pp.*

Reports of the Institute of Community Studies

Baker, J. The Neighbourhood Advice Centre. A Community Project in Camden. *320 pp.*
- **Cartwright, Ann.** Patients and their Doctors. *A Study of General Practice. 304 pp.*
Dench, Geoff. Maltese in London. *A Case-study in the Erosion of Ethnic Consciousness. 302 pp.*
Jackson, Brian and **Marsden, Dennis.** Education and the Working Class: *Some General Themes Raised by a Study of 88 Working-class Children in a Northern Industrial City. 268 pp. 2 folders.*
Madge, C. and **Willmott, P.** Inner City Poverty in Paris and London. *144 pp.*
Marris, Peter. The Experience of Higher Education. *232 pp. 27 tables.*
- Loss and Change. *192 pp.*
Marris, Peter and **Rein, Martin.** Dilemmas of Social Reform. *Poverty and Community Action in the United States. 256 pp.*
Marris, Peter and **Somerset, Anthony.** African Businessmen. *A Study of Entrepreneurship and Development in Kenya. 256 pp.*
Mills, Richard. Young Outsiders: *a Study in Alternative Communities. 216 pp.*
Runciman, W. G. Relative Deprivation and Social Justice. *A Study of Attitudes to Social Inequality in Twentieth-Century England. 352 pp.*

Willmott, Peter. Adolescent Boys in East London. *230 pp.*

Willmott, Peter and **Young, Michael.** Family and Class in a London Suburb. *202 pp. 47 tables.*

Young, Michael and **McGeeney, Patrick.** Learning Begins at Home. *A Study of a Junior School and its Parents. 128 pp.*

Young, Michael and **Willmott, Peter.** Family and Kinship in East London. *Foreword by Richard M. Titmuss. 252 pp. 39 tables.*
The Symmetrical Family. *410 pp.*

Reports of the Institute for Social Studies in Medical Care

Cartwright, Ann, Hockey, Lisbeth and **Anderson, John J.** Life Before Death. *310 pp.*

Dunnell, Karen and **Cartwright, Ann.** Medicine Takers, Prescribers and Hoarders. *190 pp.*

Farrell, C. My Mother Said. . . *A Study of the Way Young People Learned About Sex and Birth Control. 288 pp.*

Medicine, Illness and Society
General Editor W. M. Williams

Hall, David J. Social Relations & Innovation. *Changing the State of Play in Hospitals. 232 pp.*

Hall, David J. and **Stacey M.** (Eds) Beyond Separation. *234 pp.*

Robinson, David. The Process of Becoming Ill. *142 pp.*

Stacey, Margaret *et al.* Hospitals, Children and Their Families. *The Report of a Pilot Study. 202 pp.*

Stimson, G. V. and **Webb, B.** Going to See the Doctor. *The Consultation Process in General Practice. 155 pp.*

Monographs in Social Theory
General Editor Arthur Brittan

● **Barnes, B.** Scientific Knowledge and Sociological Theory. *192 pp.*

Bauman, Zygmunt. Culture as Praxis. *204 pp.*

● **Dixon, Keith.** Sociological Theory. *Pretence and Possibility. 142 pp.*
The Sociology of Belief. *Fallacy and Foundation. 144 pp.*

Goff, T. W. Marx and Mead. *Contributions to a Sociology of Knowledge. 176 pp.*

Meltzer, B. N., Petras, J. W. and **Reynolds, L. T.** Symbolic Interactionism. *Genesis, Varieties and Criticisms. 144 pp.*

● **Smith, Anthony D.** The Concept of Social Change. *A Critique of the Functionalist Theory of Social Change. 208 pp.*

● **Tudor, Andrew.** Beyond Empiricism. *Philosophy of Science in Sociology. 224 pp.*

Routledge Social Science Journals

The British Journal of Sociology. *Editor – Angus Stewart; Associate Editor – Leslie Sklair. Vol. 1, No. 1 – March 1950 and Quarterly. Roy. 8vo. All back issues available. An international journal publishing original papers in the field of sociology and related areas.*

Community Work. *Edited by David Jones and Majorie Mayo. 1973. Published annually.*

Economy and Society. *Vol. 1, No. 1. February 1972 and Quarterly. Metric Roy. 8vo. A journal for all social scientists covering sociology, philosophy, anthropology, economics and history. All back numbers available.*

Ethnic and Racial Studies. *Editor – John Stone. Vol. 1 – 1978. Published quarterly.*

Religion. Journal of Religion and Religions. *Chairman of Editorial Board, Ninian Smart. Vol. 1, No. 1, Spring 1971. A journal with an inter-disciplinary approach to the study of the phenomena of religion. All back numbers available.*

Sociological Review. *Chairman of Editorial Board, S. J. Eggleston. New Series. August 1982, Vol. 30, No. 1. Published quarterly.*

Sociology of Health and Illness. *A Journal of Medical Sociology. Editor – Alan Davies; Associate Editor – Ray Jobling. Vol. 1, Spring 1979. Published 3 times per annum.*

Year Book of Social Policy in Britain. *Edited by Kathleen Jones. 1971. Published annually.*

Social and Psychological Aspects of Medical Practice
Editor   Trevor Silverstone

Lader, Malcolm. Psychophysiology of Mental Illness. *280 pp.*

● **Silverstone, Trevor** and **Turner, Paul.** Drug Treatment in Psychiatry. *Third edition. 256 pp.*

Whiteley, J. S. and **Gordon, J.** Group Approaches in Psychiatry. *240 pp.*